Separatism

Separatism

Democracy and Disintegration

Edited by Metta Spencer

ROWMAN & LITTLEFIELD PUBLISHERS, INC.
Lanham • Boulder • New York • Oxford

ROWMAN & LITTLEFIELD PUBLISHERS, INC.

Published in the United States of America
by Rowman & Littlefield Publishers, Inc.
4720 Boston Way, Lanham, Maryland 20706

12 Hid's Copse Road
Cumnor Hill, Oxford OX2 9JJ, England

British Library Cataloguing in Publication Information Available

Library of Congress Cataloging-in-Publication Data

Separatism : democracy and disintegration / edited by Metta Spencer.
    p.   cm.
    Includes bibliographical references and index.
    ISBN 0-8476-8584-5 (alk. paper) — ISBN 0-8476-8585-3 (pbk. :
alk. paper)
    1. Autonomy and independence movements—History—20th century
—Case studies.   2. World politics—20th century—Case studies.
3. Nationalism—History—20th century—Case studies. I. Spencer,
Metta, 1931– .
  D445.S49   1998
  909.82'5—dc21   98-7757
                                                  CIP

Printed in the United States of America

☉™ The paper used in this publication meets the minimum requirements of American
National Standard for Information Sciences—Permanence of Paper for Printed Library
Materials, ANSI Z39.48–1984.

Contents

Preface

It is the function of social movements to clarify public consciousness about problematic social issues by generating widespread discourse. There is an overdue need for a social movement concerning separatism, which is a highly problematic process about which public opinion remains divided or even confused. In the 1990s, up to half of the wars going on at any one time were wars of secession, yet even within the peace movement (which surges and wanes, but never disappears altogether) activists and researchers lack any consensus. All the authors of this book share a deep hope that our project may help build a public discourse and thereby prevent the human suffering that accompanies separatist movements — both those that do and those that do not succeed in dividing a state.

Strangely, opinions about separatism remain virtually uncorrelated with opinions on other great historical processes. Test this for yourself. Make a list of twenty people whose politics you respect most deeply and twenty others whose politics you despise. Then ask each of them whether they believe that ethnic groups should be have the right to secede from existing states and create homelands of their own. Because pollsters hardly ever ask such a question, comparative international data are unavailable to prove the point, but you will find wide diversity of views about separatism within each political group. Among right wingers and leftists, among democrats and communists, among peaceniks, militarists, and revolutionaries, support can be found for the partition of states; there is also an easy confidence (apparently unaffected by familiarity with current events) that it can be accomplished painlessly.

The contributors to this book share a fervent desire that secession, whenever it must occur, be effected peaceably, justly, and humanely. Nevertheless, all our research indicates that smooth and benign separations are so rare that they must not be expected. Of course, some partitions are easier than others, and various procedures can be established to improve them all. For example, international law could be used regularly to determine the legitimacy of separatists' claims; the United Nations could then oversee those breakups that are judged appropriate, protecting the rights of minorities and others who are at risk. Much could be gained, also, by making the international response more predictable — more based on a rule of law and less on the vagaries influencing global financiers. Nevertheless, even at best, institutions that embody exclusion and divisiveness will impose losses on those with inclusive identities and shared interests. Thus peace researchers almost always prefer that separatism give way to reconciliation and the enhancement of justice and cooperation within a shared polity.

In completing this project, the contributors and editor are filled with gratitude toward the many colleagues and assistants who have improved the results by their critiques or by offering their skills in translating, editing, and technical support. These good people include Norman Dyson, Dietrich Fischer, Andre Gunder Frank, Janet Hyer, Julia Kalinina, Guillaume Legros, Madeleine Weiler, Jane Ormrod, Joanna Santa Barbara, Jean-Guy Vaillancourt, and Jaroslav Veis. I owe a particular debt to Slobodan Drakulic and Ken Simons for their remarkable expertise and insights. We also appreciate the unfailingly excellent cooperation of the Rowman & Littlefield staff: Rebecca Hoog, Serena Leigh, and especially an editor of exemplary patience, Dean Birkenkamp.

Introduction

The late 1980s and 1990s have been marked by two mutually contradictory trends. The first is an increasing cultural, economic, environmental, and political integration transnationally through "globalization" and the formation of international political structures, such as the European Union. The second is the upsurge in separatist movements that aspire, sometimes with success, to partition states. There are far more such movements attempting separation than seem likely ever to be accomplished. Nevertheless, even the aspiration to divide states seems puzzling, when juxtaposed to the opposing trend toward unification.

Few of the contributors to this book have met or discussed their views of separatism. However, most of us share misgivings about the trend toward the splintering of states. Most of us believe that the most urgent emerging political issues must be handled at the transnational level and that local issues will continue to diminish in relative importance. We also believe that states are losing much of their sovereignty and that ethnic communities therefore are pursuing false dreams in demanding statehood.

Even as a myth, national sovereignty fails to inspire these whose political values are inclusive and who regard ethnicity as an accident of birth instead of a basis for pride. However, the purpose of this book is not to polemicize against separatism but to analyze its causes and consequences.

Most chapters are case studies of separatist movements. The countries that we shall examine include some historic cases (Ottoman and Austro-Hungarian Empires), as well as some recent ones (Czechoslovakia, Yugoslavia, the Soviet Union) and four that, at this writing, have not accomplished their desired secession (Sri Lanka, Canada, Tatarstan, and Chechnya).

Every contemporary separatist movement is based on a sense of grievance on the part of an ethnic group (whose members may refer to it as "a nation" or "a people"). Numerous studies have sought to explain nationalism or "identity politics." It may be useful for a reader to approach this collection of cases with a checklist that identifies some of the possible causes and consequences of nationalistic separatism.

Sources of Nationalist Separatism

The following list, which is by no means exhaustive, consists of causal factors that have been proposed in various accounts of nationalism and separatism. They are not necessarily mutually exclusive.

• *Emotional resentment.* Some analysts depict the social psychology of nationalism as rooted in an emotional sentiment — including the envy of a rival community, even when the feeling is irrational and baseless.

• *The justified resistance of victims.* Other writers portray the nationalists as victims finally rebelling after suffering prolonged violations of their human rights and the denigration of their language, culture, or religion.

• *Propaganda orchestrated for political gain.* Still other writers blame conniving political leaders for deliberately whipping up intergroup hatred by propaganda campaigns for their own purposes. Thus some analysts say that it makes logical sense that nationalism became resurgent just when Communism declined; they show that former Communist leaders schemed to retain their dominance by promoting nationalism to replace the newly rejected ideology.

• *The power of a dominant ethnic group.* Some analysts attribute nationalistic hatreds to the primacy of an ethnic group in a multicultural state that refuses to share power or privilege on a more egalitarian basis.

• *Economic motivations.* Often the separatist group is portrayed as economically deprived and exploited by the richer part of the population. This is "the worm finally turns" thesis, but it does not stand up as a generalization, since the separatists often are not the poorer but the richer part of the population, as in the case of Slovenians desiring to secede from Yugoslavia.

An alternative economic theory portrays the contested territory as possessing some valuable resource that both the local group and the national government wish to control. (Examples: an oil pipeline and probable oil reserves desired both by the Chechens and the Russians.) There are several variants of the economic explanation. For instance, separatists in the Baltic states and Ukraine believed that only their regions' ties to Russia kept them below the economic level of Western Europe. Again, the weakness of this theory is that usually there is more to be gained financially from remaining unified than from secession.

• *Preservation of a threatened culture.* Sometimes the separatists believe, rightly or mistakenly, that they must win independence in order to preserve their religion, language, or other traditions. (Quebec is an example.)

• *Commitment to modernization.* Sometimes the breakup of a state can be attributed to the revolutionaries' desire to establish a universalistic regime that would bring all ethnic or religious communities under the same unified rule of law. The breakup of the Ottoman and Austro-Hungarian Empires can be seen as instances of this tendency. In the post-cold war period modernization has come to mean democracy, and many analysts see the breakup of Yugoslavia and Czechoslovakia as resulting from the introduction of decision-making by majority vote.

Structural Contributing Factors

The above list includes most of the theorized proximate causes of separatist movements. However, we can also identify a list of contributing factors that have been said to affect the probability that separatism will emerge. Among them are the following:

• *Deep cleavages between segments of the population.* Ethnicity is the most common basis for secession in the post-cold war period. (Previously, ideologically based partitions took place, as in the case of communist and non-communist Korea, both parts of which shared a common ethnicity.)

More generally, when two or more communities in a population see themselves as permanently divided and as having different interests, then relations between them cannot easily be resolved through regular democratic means, since even in democratic governments one of the groups may be permanently outvoted. However, in particular cases the cleavage between the various communities may not be as long-standing or irreconcilable as the separatists claim.

• *Centralization or decentralization of government.* Policy makers who seek to hold their federal state together sometimes propose devolutionary reforms, transferring decisions to the provincial or local levels and reducing the power of the central government to a bare minimum. By meeting the weak demands of separatists by adopting a confederation or commonwealth structure, it is hoped that the ultimate breakup can be avoided. Other analysts assert the contrary: that decentralization jeopardizes federal states, since the progressive devolution of power brings secession even closer and allows the eventual breakup to be carried out with minimal disruption.

One can adduce cases as evidence of both. Canada and Russia have devolved much decision making to provinces or republics in the hope that this will save the federal government. In his chapter, Edward Walker predicts that this adaptation will contain the separatism of Tatarstan. Within the next decade, he may be proved either correct or incorrect, but the case studies presented in this book probably cannot definitively answer this important question.

• *The size of the prospective new states.* Presumably, states benefit materially from economies of scale. Even the cost of maintaining embassies around the world can prove daunting for a small state, not to mention the cost of maintaining an army. However, there are small states (Liechtenstein, Monaco, etc.) that have survived for a long time. Therefore the crucial factor may not be the size of the breakaway state, but rather the process of breaking up any ongoing economic and political system, regardless of its size.

   • *A history of political annexation or demographic manipulation.* In some cases, states have been annexed against the wishes of their populations, who remain resentful thereafter and seize the first opportunity to proclaim their independence. (Example: The Baltic republics in the Soviet Union, whose arguments for secession had more merit than the claims of republics that had not previously been independent.)

   Sometimes the indigenous population of a region (e.g., the Tatars and Chechens) had been deported from their homeland. Moreover, a government may try to dilute the political impact of a minority population by moving large numbers of the majority group into their area. Naturally, this action intensifies the resentment of the original population, especially if it had originally had a distinctive culture or language. (Examples: Such demographic dilution was carried out in the formerly Tamil parts of Sri Lanka, in the Baltic states, and in Tibet.)

   • *The newly democratic nature of the federal state.* Separatist movements seem to occur in waves, with one such wave taking place now, in the aftermath of the collapse of Communism. One plausible partial explanation is that communism repressed nationalism by punishing anyone who promoted it; a new commitment to democracy meant allowing people to express particularistic values that were previously suppressed.

   • *Ambiguities of international law.* Many separatists believe that international law assures each ethnic group the right to "self- determination" — i.e., to secede at will. However, a new group claiming sovereign status may or may not be recognized abroad. That unpredictability encourages separatists to assert their independence as a way of finding out the results. (Examples: Germany, Austria, and Hungary were quick to recognize Slovenia and Croatia when they declared themselves no longer republics of Yugoslavia. Many observers blame this premature recognition for the warfare that immediately followed.)

Political Consequences of Partitioning States

   Among the commonly observed consequences of secession are the following:

   • *Declining status of minorities.* Secessions never leave the newly divided countries ethnically homogeneous. Minorities are often pressed to emigrate or are deported against their will. Those who remain anyway are usually subjected to worse treatment than in the previous, more inclusive state. (Examples: Israel's Palestinian minorities are second-class citizens, as are the Croatians, Serbs, and Bosniacs who remain as minority populations in the divided parts of the former Yugoslavia.)

• *Destabilization.* The assertion of political autonomy brings a breakaway region into considerable upheaval until its new institutions have been established. Civil war is a regular consequence of separating a state in two. (Rare exceptions are the breakup of Czechoslovakia in 1993 and of Norway/Sweden in 1905.)

• *Geopolitical power vacuum.* When states break up, the new states, being smaller and divided, ordinarily are regarded less as an obstacle by neighboring states with aggressive intentions. The breakup may even seem to invite invasion. (Examples: The breakup of the Austro-Hungarian and Ottoman Empires created a power vacuum in Europe; indeed, World War II can be interpreted largely as a contest between the Soviet Union and Germany to gain control of the fragments of those empires.)

• *Continuing fragmentation.* One secession typically seems to invite other groups within the same larger federal society to arrange for their own departure as well. (Examples: When the Soviet Union broke up, several regions inside Georgia, Azerbaijan, and Russia tried to secede in their turn. Likewise, Yugoslavia and Czechoslovakia (which were created from the fragments of the Austro-Hungarian and Ottoman Empires) continued the fragmentation process at a later date.

Proposed Solutions for States Facing Separatist Movements

When a unitary or federal government finds itself challenged by a separatist organization, there are various ways of responding, some of which may minimize either the risk of secession or of the negative consequences that typically accompany secession. The following list is not exhaustive, and some of the items are incompatible with the others.

• *Give up immediately and accede to the separatists' demands.* For the sake of preventing bloodshed, some analysts recommend that, when challenged by separatists, the officials of a union should quickly divide their state up in an amicable and orderly fashion. This recommendation assumes that separatists are entitled to an ethnically homogeneous state of their own or to a state in which they can constitute the majority. (Examples: Malaysia acceded quickly to Singapore's demand for independence, and Sweden permitted the secession of Norway without bloodshed.)

• *Improve the circumstances of disadvantaged minorities.* This approach, if it is to succeed, must be implemented as soon as the minority population begins to protest. Legislation can correct their disadvantages and guarantee their right to use their own language and practice their own faith. This move may reduce the sense of grievance, but it is not certain to do so. (Example: Canada authorized a "bilingualism and biculturalism" commission during the "Quiet Revolution" of Quebec. Its recommendations improved the opportunities for francophone Canadians without, however, preventing the rise of Quebec separatism.) A court system that protects the human rights of all citizens should, in principle, reduce the alienation of all subgroups.

• *Adopt asymmetric federalism.* Some writers who seek to preserve the union of a particular state recommend a special constitutional arrangement with the region in which separatism is growing. This would mean that different provinces or republics might each have a unique relationship with the center — hence the term "asymmetric." (Examples: Russia has given Tatarstan more autonomy than other provinces of Russia; Quebec has sought an asymmetric relationship with the rest of Canada reflecting its unique nature as a "distinct society.")

• *Let minorities win under certain circumstances.* When a community regards itself as a permanently distinct entity within a society, and when it is nevertheless a minority in political terms, it will be outvoted regularly. Even so, certain unusual constitutional arrangements are possible that do allow such a minority to win a political contest about which it feels especially strongly. One such arrangement would be to provide a simple veto for elected minority group leaders. Other alternatives include non-territorially based constituencies (as practiced in Malta and the Irish senate) and referendums in which voters are able to distribute their voting power according to the strength of their feelings about particular issues. The type of democracy that assures minorities a share of the power in governance (as contrasted to the simple principle of majority-rule) is sometimes called "consensus democracy" or "consociational democracy."

• *Settle for a confederation or commonwealth relationship.* When a rupture seems likely, total separation may be prevented by acceptance of a half-way measure (e.g., a confederation or a commonwealth) for the republics or provinces that would like to break away. (Examples: Russia and Puerto Rico.) However, there are many debates as to whether such a plan is a promising solution. The pages ahead will provide some evidence for evaluating these factors.

One

When States Divide

Metta Spencer

The twentieth century has been called the "post-imperial epoch," for it saw the collapse of the Habsburg, Ottoman, Hohenzollern, Ch'ing, British, and Russian Empires. But this title is too limited, for these imperial splinterings have not been the end of the matter; afterward the nationalistic spirit moved on to divide other countries that had not been empires. Today almost half the wars going on in the world are struggles for secession. Our daily newspapers refer to "peoples" and ethnically defined "nations" that claim entitlement to "self-determination" in a sovereign "homeland" of their own. In the heat of struggle for such exclusive possession, some claimants perpetrate "ethnic cleansing" — the expulsion of other groups or even genocide.

Such horrors are being carried out as these words are written, and others must be expected in the future. Yet it is with the hope of preventing or mitigating the violent consequences of nationalistic movements that the authors offer this book. The present chapter and the following one will sketch certain historical trends and attempt to discern a pattern in them. Here, and again in the concluding chapter, I shall describe, compare, and identify some potential *correctives* to the most dangerous trends.

Nationalism has been defined as "a theory of political legitimacy which requires that ethnic boundaries should not cut across political ones, and, in particular, that ethnic boundaries within a given state should not separate the power-holders from the rest."[1] Ideally, according to nationalists, the population of each state should consist of a single ethnic community, and all members of that ethnic community should live within the borders of that state. The ideal is only a dream — no "nation-state" remains wholly monocultural today, and if one did, it would be culturally stagnant. Centers of civilization have always been multicultural regions where people from diverse backgrounds meet and stimulate each other through example and dialogue.

Many nationalist movements seek to gain control of the entire existing state where they live, as in the case of colonial subjects who take over an intact state from a colonial power. Other nationalists seek to split the existing state and take control of their share of territory. This book will deal with the latter objective — separatism. We shall compare the histories of separatism and seek to identify its causes and consequences. We shall assess its contemporary trends and certain constitutional innovations that may serve to reduce its likelihood.

Waves of Secession and Democracy

Far more separatist movements arise than ever come to fruition. Such movements in the late 1990s cannot be counted, for the most marginal of such groups probably amount to nothing more than fantasy. Among the less plausible contemporary examples are the movements for the independence of Hawaii and Alaska, though even these separatists may surprise us in the future.

Secessions take place in waves. After both world wars, it was the great powers that broke up states and shifted borders around, for separatist movements were far too weak to achieve these results by their own actions. During the wave following World War II, European colonization was reversed, and several states, such as India, Korea, and Palestine, were divided to accommodate the incompatible demands of ethnic or ideological groups. During the troughs that followed those waves, maps remained fairly stable until about 1990, when a third wave of secessions began. The Soviet Union broke apart, and separatist aspirations spread to other states, both socialist and nonsocialist. It is not clear whether this wave of secessions has yet crested.

These secessionist waves correlate with another pattern: the democratization of states, of which Samuel Huntington has identified three such waves or cycles.[2] The first long wave took place between 1820 and 1920, spreading from the United States to some European states and a few British dominions and Latin American countries. This cycle was reversed to some extent between 1920 and 1945. Then, after World War II, a new wave of democratization took place because democratic societies, as the victors, were able to bring reforms to the vanquished states. That was also the period of decolonization, and most of the new states created in those days emulated the advanced democracies. This surge then waned between 1960 and 1975, as democratic states collapsed or were overthrown in several countries. Finally, since 1975, a new wave of democracy has been taking place, and in 1989, with the breakdown of Communism, it overturned almost the entire socialist world. There were 44 democracies in 1972, 56 in 1980, and 91 in 1992, when the Soviet empire was breaking apart.[3]

The temporal coincidence between surges of democracy and surges of secessionist movements will require explanation. One reason must be that secession is regarded as a manifestation of "self-determination," which conceptually would seem associated with democracy, the principle that citizens must be governed only with their own consent. To its great proponent, Woodrow Wilson, self-determination meant both (a) freedom from external coercion or alien domination and (b) the right to meaningful participation in the political process — or "internal self-determination."[4] The former meaning is the basis for separatists' demands, while the latter refers to democracy.

Democracy and self-determination are linked in other ways. A democratic referendum is often one phase of the move toward secession. In recent times, virtually all such moves toward independence have been accompanied by promises of democracy, even when there are reasons to doubt the nationalists' sincerity.

Both the left and the right portray both processes as interdependent aspects of a single progressive development, the trend toward giving human beings more control over the conditions of their own lives. Yet, despite these similarities, democracy and self-determination are two distinct projects with sometimes contradictory objectives. Before considering such an interpretation we should explore both the causes and consequences of secessionist movements.

The Nationalist Roots of Separatism

A precondition for the emergence of secessionist movements is nationalism, which has changed in character over the years. The early nationalist movements, continuing the centralizing trends begun under previous monarchies, more often sought to weld political units together than to divide them, as today. Here I shall review four roots of nationalist movements: (a) structural, (b) historical, (c) ideological, and (d) motivational factors.

Structural Conditions

One of the essential preconditions for nationalism — the system of nation-states — is omnipresent. Without nations there can be no nationalism. A second structural feature of modern society consists of the "mobilization" of populations through education, mass media exposure, travel, and migration.

The System of Nation-States: For hundreds of years, the world has been divided into a patchwork of states with clear boundaries. Every piece of land and every human being supposedly belongs to one of these entities, which are self-contained within "hard shells." The governments of these countries ideally recognize each other as sovereign and do not try to influence the internal affairs of the others except through diplomacy when their own interests are affected.

Still, the boundaries of these states do sometimes change. Before and during the early phases of nationalism in Europe, states decreased in number as they amalgamated into larger, centralized states or great empires. In recent years, however, nationalists generally have not promoted integration but rather secession,[5] so the number of states has been increasing. In 1998, some 185 of them belonged to the United Nations, and a few did not.

Because nations constitute a system, a successful claim of sovereign statehood depends on whether other states officially recognize it as such.[6] No objective standards exist for determining whether states should accept a secession. Sovereign states ultimately retain the right to decide whether to recognize other states.[7] However, dangerous ambiguity might be resolved if the United Nations or the International Court of Justice (ICJ) were to propose *minimum criteria* for recognizing secessionist claims. The present uncertainty only encourages separatist movements to test the water by claiming sovereignty.[8]

Mobilization. Nationalism is connected with the central experience of modernization — the breakdown of a stable traditional social order when a larger communication system penetrates formerly isolated communities. Karl Deutsch, who studied nationalism during the 1950s, called these changes in traditional rural society "mobilization," the process through which traditional people become conscious of the wider society.

Before their mobilization, peasants have to worry about bugs and drought, but not about their social relationships, for the only people they meet are lifelong acquaintances of predictable habits and opinions. But let a road be built, for example, and strangers, salesmen, and politicians will travel through. There will be schools, films, radios, and magazines. One will no longer know whom to trust, or whose trinkets to buy when visiting the market.

Mobilization draws traditional persons into a broad, swiftly changing social world characterized by social insecurity. They may seek to recreate their lost sense of community, seizing upon small signs of similarity — such as common accent or cuisine or holiday customs — as grounds for solidarity. Deutsch called such a new group an "ersatz" community; its pretended familiarity is contrived to substitute for the real thing and reassure those living in a context of uncertainty.

To these aspects of mobilization must be added the frequent experience of migration. Pushed and pulled by market forces, traditional people move to cities or even to foreign countries while staying in contact with their relatives back at home. In refugee camps and major cities around the world, migrants congregate and try to reestablish new-old communities, singing familiar songs, trading recipes for Easter bread, exchanging child care, and lending their friends money until payday. Nationalism attains its maximum impact under precisely such circumstances. From abroad, the expatriate nationalist writes home, advising his relatives to assert their independence. These "long-distance nationalists" continue to participate politically in the country they left behind. However, as Benedict

Anderson has noted, their participation is "non-responsible." They do not have to pay the price of the policies that they advocate from afar.

These are the social structural conditions most conducive to nationalism, and they are increasing in the modern world. Deutsch expected the period of nationalism to be only a transitional phase in a larger process. After people became familiar with modern institutions they would create pluralistic associations in their new country and organize politically to attain their security. Their dependence on ethnic solidarity would diminish and they would forget about nationalism. Perhaps Deutsch's prediction eventually will prove correct, but today it seems that the period of nationalism may not be brief.

Historical Roots of Nationalism

European states were created as a system as early as 1648 with the Treaty of Westphalia, yet the sense of nationhood did not arise at the same time everywhere. Englishmen were English before Frenchmen were French. Often, small European principalities were forged together to create centralized states with precise borders instead of the previously ambiguous frontiers. The new "hard-shelled" sovereign states maintained standing armies and governmental bureaucracies that could tax the population and maintain local surveillance over them.

The creation of national identity involved the spread of vernacular languages and the new technology of print. Nation-builders explicitly sought to create national cultures by creating a single unified language for each nation from one of the local dialects, standardizing its spelling and grammar, and teaching it in schools throughout the new country. For the first time, all semieducated persons throughout France could communicate with one another. It was this that made them into Frenchmen.[9]

A similar process took place all over Europe and beyond, but not simultaneously. One of the founders of Italy, Massimo d'Azeglio, said, "We have made Italy. Now we have to make Italians."[10] Only later, when the Ottoman Empire broke up, did people in Anatolia come to think of themselves as Turks. Nationalities often arose around the world in colonies where all those who could read the same newspapers came to imagine themselves as constituting a single community united by one history. Much had to be rewritten to create such histories, including the intentions of the nation's ancestors. Nationalists everywhere learned to speak for the anonymous dead who had not understood what they themselves had "really meant" or "really wanted."[11]

On the whole, the nationalists' amalgamation of small principalities into sizable modern states may be considered a liberalizing influence. It allowed for greater inclusiveness, so that people identified with a wider community than before, and by standardizing a national culture and legal codes, it fostered communication and cosmopolitan knowledge. Even so, the increase of communication in the vernacular languages fostered a contradictory tendency in the larger empires. Thus when German replaced Latin as the medium of governance in the

Habsburg Empire, the Hungarian and other elites began to entertain nationalistic ideas, drawing closer toward nonelites who spoke their own languages.

In our day, nationalists are exclusionary and divisive.[12] Long before the rise of National Socialism in Germany, nationalism had ceased to be benign.

Ideological Grounds

Nationalism is not a complete ideology in the same sense as communism, say, or Islam, or freemasonry. It has few theoretical proponents among philosophers and social scientists, nor does it suggest an action plan of universal scope. Nationalists do not try to spread their doctrine around the world to save us all; they only seek to justify their own group's status vis-à-vis its particular rival.

Nevertheless, nationalism employs certain concepts, such as *sovereignty* and *self-determination,* that are durable elements of general political discourse. Oddly, nationalism may be equally popular within the right, the left, and even the liberal center. Those who oppose the breakup of existing states risk being deemed bigoted and antidemocratic by their usual political allies. It is worth analyzing some of the assumptions on which nationalism is grounded.

Sovereignty. A basic assumption is that the nation-state is the fundamental unit of human society and that it possesses *sovereignty.* Ironically, claims for such self-contained states are proliferating precisely when the reality of sovereignty is being superseded by the globalization of economies and polities. Nations may exist indefinitely, but their sovereignty seems sure to continue diminishing, under pressure from such international organizations as the European Union, the World Bank, NATO, the World Trade Organization, and even such hoary institutions as the International Postal Union.

Internationalists do not think it desirable to live in a state that is governed entirely by local voters, when the decisions that are made locally affect people who lack voting rights. Why, they ask, should only local farmers decide whether to allow an international airport to locate in their region? That decision affects millions of air passengers around the world who are denied any influence in the matter. Why should only citizens of Ukraine decide whether to continue operating the dangerous Chernobyl reactors? That decision affects millions of citizens of the countries downwind who lack any opportunity to vote on the matter. Why should only the citizens of rich countries decide whether to offer weapons to one faction or the other waging a civil war in a faraway country? That decision mainly affects the victims of those weapons, who should have something to say about the matter.[13]

A more democratic world cannot be created either by transferring more power to the international level or to the local level but only by giving people more influence over the decisions that affect their own lives. Nationalists suppose that such an objective can be attained by splitting states and giving local people more local control. This is so only with regard to those decisions that can be localized.

Some decisions (e.g., whether to build new sewers) *do* mainly affect the local citizenry; other decisions (e.g., controlling the emission of greenhouse gases) mainly affect noncitizens at remote locations. It is no general solution to either increase or decrease the size of bounded, sovereign states.

Self-determination. The principle of self-determination, as well as the principle of sovereignty, is supported as a means of guaranteeing people some control over the laws by which their lives are regulated. Consent seems to be at stake here.

It is not logically necessary for this principle to entail the option to secede. There are, in fact, occasional claims for "internal self-determination," such as the demands of the aboriginal peoples of Canada for self-determination, although they do not claim the right to secede. They simply want a vastly greater degree of self-government for their own communities, in which they will make laws for themselves, police themselves, and provide social services for themselves. Since they are dispersed geographically, such devolution of power could not be based on *federal* principles (i.e., by shifting decisionmaking to smaller territorial entities) but rather by allowing *functional* units that are not localized spatially to make decisions.

In general, however, the notion of self-determination is understood to imply the option of seceding and acquiring sovereign status over territory as a member of the international system of states. This doctrine has been promoted as a right by liberals and dictators alike, for entirely incompatible objectives.

The leftist version of self-determination was advanced by V. I. Lenin, who had assigned another Bolshevik, Joseph Stalin, the task of studying the nationality question and developing a policy for the Soviet regime. This project established Stalin's reputation.[14] Theoretically, each union republic was a willing participant in the Soviet Union and had a right to secede at any time — though in practice a nationalist surely would be punished for proposing secession. Self-determination was associated with Lenin's theory of imperialism, which recast Marxism along new lines.[15] This theory was meant to justify the possibility of action for Bolshevism, despite the fact that no substantial proletariat yet existed in the nonindustrialized countries, a condition that Marx considered prerequisite to revolution. Leninism now suggested that, just as there were oppressed and oppressor classes in the industrialized nations, the world itself could be seen as consisting of oppressed and oppressor *nations*. Lenin's plan was to work with the nationalistic bourgeoisie of the oppressed nations and encourage their aspirations of independence. The principle of self-determination was formulated to legitimize such ambitions and to place social revolution on the agenda.[16]

In reality, although the Communist International entertained this principle of imperialism, many Communists could not bring themselves to support bourgeois leaders for any cause whatever. Unable to restrain themselves, they kept founding Communist parties in various colonies around the world and referring to "class struggle," despite its theoretical incompatibility with the project of national liberation. Marxism is not interested in nations as such, for Marx and Engels saw the nation as the optimum market area of a particular bourgeoisie — a social entity that would be overcome under socialism.[17] However, Bolshevik theory always asserted that the principle of self-determination meant the "right to secede." Rosa Luxemburg and her Polish Social Democrats rejected Lenin's slogan of national secession, which he formulated only for revolutionary purposes and intended to apply only when it suited the interests of the proletariat.

Yet from liberals came the same principle of self-determination. The idea was the special enthusiasm of President Woodrow Wilson, a Southern-born Democrat, some of whose ideas may have originated in the Confederacy. Wilson justified American participation in World War I as a move to advance the cause of democracy, which to his mind required a peace settlement guaranteeing every "people" the right to choose its own political system. Though he tried earnestly to apply this principle, Wilson discovered that it was far more complicated than he had supposed.[18] His Fourteen Points made it clear that the right of self-determination would apply only to peoples living in the defeated countries. Even so, the map of Europe that emerged from the process was not primarily based on the political will of the European peoples but on that of the war's victors.

The League of Nations did adopt Wilson's most cherished doctrines, at least as a declaratory position, and so did its successor, the United Nations, which incorporated the rhetoric of self-determination in its Charter. However, the United Nations in practice almost always defends the territorial integrity of states. Secretary-General U Thant put the matter bluntly, stating that "the United Nations has never accepted and does not accept and I do not believe it will ever accept the principle of secession of a part of its Member State."[19] A successor, Secretary-General Boutros Boutros-Ghali, when asked whether everyone who wants a state should have one, replied, "Certainly not. If every ethnic, linguistic, or religious group would ask for a statehood, we would have 2,000 states at the end of the century. It is not in the interests of the international community."[20]

Thus we see ambiguous views of self-determination in Marxism-Leninism, in democratic theory, and even in the policies of the United Nations. There is abundant ideological material available to nationalists who wish to claim legitimacy for their cause, yet the international community has always viewed secession with great misgivings.

Still, if we classify the nationalist doctrines as ideological, we must acknowledge that antinationalism can also be ideological. Benedict Anderson has suggested that liberals are clinging to myths when they condemn secession for its violence and justify the status quo as nonviolent. He reminds us that the dominant rulers perpetrated violence while assembling their empires and subordinating national minorities. He also contests as ideological the assertion that small countries created by secession are less viable economically than large states or that global capitalism is a peaceable system. Nevertheless, an antinationalist proponent of democracy can accept some of his points yet conclude that secession offers no advantage over other options.

Motivational Factors

Finally, we should go beyond considering the structural and ideological grounding for nationalism by taking account also of motivation — those factors that stimulate the sense of nationhood and the assertion of its primacy over other social solidarities, such as family, social class, or gender.

National identity may be rooted in various types of solidarity or even material interests. Ernest Gellner accorded a special place to language in this process. He rightly noted that much was accomplished by stitching together a single French or Italian language, making the wider society into a unified field of communication. Even today language is often of great importance, not only as a symbol of status but virtually as a *material* interest, in that many economic resources usually must be expended to acquire proficiency in a foreign language.

The hierarchy of world languages. Gellner suggested that a key motive of nationalists is to advance the place of their language in the global hierarchy. A child who is brought up speaking English as a first language has many advantages over a youth who speaks only an uncommon African tongue, plus a smattering of Swahili. The African child may benefit significantly from a movement that successfully promotes the use of Swahili in universities, publishing houses, and bicycle assembly instruction booklets.

If nationalism were only such a set of movements to advance the status of particular languages, the motivation behind it would seem rational. However, in some cases nationalism is not based on the sharing of a common mother tongue. Yugoslavia is a case in point; the Serbs, Croats, and Bosniacs speak mutually intelligible dialects of the same language, yet their country broke apart. Since then, instead of promoting its currency in the world, they have been fiercely tearing it into separate languages. University departments that formerly taught "Serbo-Croatian" now offer only "Serbian" and "Croatian."

Antipathies between ethnic groups cannot be reduced to a single basis — language (as in Gellner's theory), religion, race, or anything else — and certainly not to one simple rational argument. What all separatist movements have in common is only a conviction that the existing political order is illegitimate and that their group has been assigned to a lower status than it deserves.

Humiliation. Resentment, envy, and wounded pride form a powerful constellation of motives that may be hard to explain rationally. For example, at a time when pollsters were giving the separatist cause a fifty-fifty chance of winning their referendum in Quebec, the anglophone newspaper columnist Jeffrey Simpson cited public opinion polls showing that Quebecers were not seriously dissatisfied with their circumstances. Thus 91 percent agreed completely or somewhat with the statement that "Canada is a country where it is good to live." Also, 81 percent agreed that "we should be proud of what francophones and anglophones have accomplished in this country. By a margin of 68 to 29 percent, Quebecers agreed that after secession a "majority of people will have to undergo fundamental changes in their lifestyles." In their responses to questions dealing with their financial situation, the well-being of future generations, the level of taxation, job security, and the security of social programs, the majority indicated that they did not expect things to get better if Quebec became a sovereign state. Nevertheless, pollsters declared that there was an even chance a majority might vote for secession.[21]

Simpson claimed that these positive poll results prove that the sovereigntists are ridiculous in claiming that the francophone Quebec people feel "humiliated" by English Canadians. He reasoned that if those Quebecers admit that they benefit objectively from their position inside Canada, they cannot be feeling "humiliated." I think he missed the point. Humiliation is a subjective state of mind not necessarily based on anything substantive. Never mind that anglophones have no intention to humiliate francophones. Never mind that they have done nothing in particular to injure them. If the francophones feel humiliated, they *are* humiliated, and they may feel a need to do something about it. Many francophones in Quebec resent what they perceive as a lack of legitimacy in the decision-making processes that affect them and feel so offended that they would accept a lower standard of living as the price of restoring legitimacy to their governance.

Resentment, humiliation, and envy need not be logically defensible in order to be powerful motives. Indeed, Liah Greenfeld has suggested that resentment is the fundamental emotion lying behind nationalism. She refers to it by the French term *ressentiment*,[22] which she defines as "a psychological state resulting from suppressed feelings of envy and hatred (existential envy) and the impossibility of satisfying these feelings."[23]

England, says Greenfeld, developed nationalism independently, largely through its proud rejection of Catholicism, and Protestant Englishmen celebrated their national identity for two hundred years before a comparable state of mind developed elsewhere. All subsequent nationalities, however, have been constructed by those who felt inferior by comparison to some other group.

Greenfeld describes two structural conditions that are necessary for the development of this attitude. The first condition is the belief on the part of the subjects that they are *fundamentally* equal to the object of their envy. The second condition is that the *actual* inequality between them is too great to be overcome easily. "The creative power of *ressentiment* — and its sociological importance — consists in that it may eventually lead to the 'transvaluation of values,'" writes Greenfeld. In other words, the person who feels envy and hatred may exalt values that are contrary to those of the group or person he resents.

This is a response that Freudians call *reaction formation*. If a person is bound to fall short when judged by the prevailing system of values, he may reject those values with a vengeance. Thus a lower-class teenager who resents the achievements of his high-status classmates may engage in malicious, spiteful activities to demonstrate to others and to himself as well that he despises their fancy ways.

Greenfeld's comparative historical research is designed to show that all nationalisms except the original English version arose because certain groups were dissatisfied with their previous identity and felt it necessary to construct a new collective self-image. The dissatisfaction always resulted from comparing one's own society to another nation. She cites vitriolic comments about England by early French intellectuals that are transparent expressions of envy. Later, Germans regarded themselves as beer-drinking yokels in comparison to the sophisticated Frenchmen they hated yet admired. Likewise, Russians, perceiving their society as even more backward, claimed to have a depth of soul far beyond the comprehension of the limited Western European mind.

Greenfeld regards this kind of defense mechanism as creative, and rightly so. Nationalists do not, in general, express their *ressentiment* in as crude a way as today's urban teenager who slashes the tires of sports cars to prove that he does not want one. Nationalists select and redefine their countrymen's traits, elevating certain features and ignoring others. The construction of a national identity is a job for a humiliated fiction writer, yet when it is done well, it may have historic consequences for his society and for its relations with other societies.

Again, the humiliation of *ressentiment* need not be based on any slights or slurs intended by the more prestigious rival, which is why it is often suppressed or camouflaged. Understandably, a high-status anglophone journalist such as Jeffrey Simpson may feel baffled when francophone Quebecers seem to take offense without reasonable cause. While they admit to having few objective grievances, they cannot be expected to acknowledge feeling simple envy.

Humiliation is likely to arise in a democracy when a group constituting a local majority holds concerns differing from the rest of the society. Here too French Quebec is an illustrative case. The francophone population is a distinct society in cultural terms, possessing a rich literature and theater as well as local economic interests that are entirely unfamiliar to anglophone Canadians. Most local decision making has devolved to the provincial level, so that Quebecers cannot blame the rest of Canada for many of their problems, and indeed they benefit in material terms from being part of Canada. However, their shared opinions differ from those of the wider Canadian electorate. If, in discussing any subject with the people in their locality, they perceive themselves all to agree, yet they are outvoted in a federal election, they may view the political process itself as illegitimate.

This sense of illegitimacy or humiliation is especially likely to be felt when the local group cares deeply about an issue that is treated as trivial by those who outvote them. For example, one can imagine the outrage of Southerners who had invested large sums in buying slaves, only to be condemned by Northerners who had nothing to lose from abolition. Everyone agrees today that the Southerners were wrong, yet we may understand their desire for some kind of weighting that would allow strongly felt opinions to count more than weakly felt ones. (Indeed, weighted voting might be a good idea — at least if the slaves' opinions were also counted and weighted according to the intensity of *their* feelings.) Sometimes people feel resentful even without any rational basis for indignation. Whenever possible, imaginary slights should be rectified, along with the real ones.

The Consequences of Secession

What must we expect to be the long-term effects of secession? Tragically, we must expect secessionist movements to bring wars, in the short term and probably also the long term. Let us consider some of the empirical evidence for this assertion.

Wars and Weaponry: The Legacy of Separatism

A few numbers will illustrate the close relationship between secession and warfare. There were 40 wars fought in 34 countries during 1996, so that in a few countries there were concurrent multiple wars.[24] Many were conflicts between ascribed communities such as clans, linguistic groups, or religions, all of which I call "ethnic groups."[25] In 29 of the 40 wars, the fighting was apparently carried out by ethnic groups[26] as "nationalist" struggles.[27]

Not all internal nationalistic fights represent efforts to secede. The majority are between ethnic groups that want to preserve the existing state apparatus but gain control of it. The ethnic groups themselves may splinter into different factions, with some demanding secession and others not. In 22 of the 40 wars fought in 1996, the rebels intended to gain control of the existing state rather than divide the country.[28] There was also a third, less common, type of war: the chaos in "failed states" (e.g., Somalia) where governments are absent.

However, 16 of the 40 wars in 1996 (40 percent) were wars of secession.[29] (This represents a decline; two years before there had been 39 wars, of which 19 [49 percent] were separatist wars.) Furthermore, all 16 of these 1996 secessionist struggles, with the possible exception of Bougainville's attempt to leave Papua New Guinea, were also ethnic conflicts.[30] Although not all ethnic wars aim for secession, virtually all secessionist wars are based on ethnicity.

Strong separatist movements seem to represent a threat to peace. Of all ongoing wars in the 1990s, between 40 percent and 50 percent involve the armed actions of members of an ethnic community to secede from the country where they live.[31]

In the 16 wars of secession in 1996, some had been going on for a whole generation, while in one or two cases, the whole thing was over within a few weeks. Researchers compiling the database sometimes express their estimates of deaths as a range, rather than a specific number. In such cases, I have used the mean figure in the range. I estimate that by the end of 1994, considerably more than 2.5 million persons had been killed in the 19 countries that were undergoing secessionist wars. Let us add these deaths to approximately 13 million deaths[32] that occurred in the states divided after the two world wars, for a total of 15.5 million deaths, not counting the deaths in secessionist wars between about 1988 and 1994, for which I lack data.

But deaths are not the only price paid for attempting to secede. We must also take account of the injuries and the flood of refugees who flee from every secessionist war. Moreover, weapons and troops are expensive and, when used, destroy costly homes, cities, and sources of income. Few separatist movements achieve the independence they desire, so these costs usually are paid just for trying and failing.

Some see these facts in a different light, claiming that it is wrong to blame separatists for the violence that they bring, since they have reacted as *victims* of injustice. Secessionists invariably claim to have been gravely wronged, and sometimes this is the case.[33] Even so, past experience does not suggest that secession will necessarily bring peace and prevent further bloodshed.

When world opinion favors secession as a solution, it is usually for the sake of preventing a civil war, though the actual results often fail to fulfill that hope. In only a few cases have states been partitioned without violence. The best examples include Norway's departure from Sweden in 1905, Singapore's departure from Malaysia in 1965, and Czechoslovakia's 1993 split. The most common outcome of dividing a state is violence — both before the event and thereafter.

Previous Waves of Partitions

In reviewing the outcomes of partitions, I will draw upon Robert K. Schaeffer's thorough comparison of the outcome of secession before the collapse of Communism. The title of his book, *Warpaths: The Politics of Partition,*[34] reveals the plot of his story, which recounts the separation of several countries that were divided after the world wars — especially Korea, China, Vietnam, India, Palestine, Cyprus, Germany, India, and Ireland. The decision to divide each of these states was made by outsiders to avoid turning the state over to one of the contending groups, such as the Hindus or Muslims in India, the Communists or non-Communists in Korea, or the Jews or Palestinians in the Middle East.[35] The great powers hoped that the rival groups would ignore each other if both had their own states.

They did not anticipate the scale of social disruption that would result from the partitions. Masses of refugees migrated (17 million across the India-Pakistan border alone), leaving businesses, families, and property behind them and encountering violence along the way and hardship upon their arrival. About one million died.

Even so, many opted to stay in their original areas. Today almost as many Muslims live in India as in Pakistan.[36] Likewise, numerous Catholics remain in

Northern Ireland, and a few Protestants remain in the Republic of Ireland.[37] In all these cases, those who opted not to migrate generally experienced greater discrimination than before the partition.[38] The Communist governments discriminated against capitalists, the Jewish government discriminated against Palestinian minorities, and so on. Minorities commonly lost the right to use their language in public affairs or were excluded from military service or government jobs. The newly dominant group, feeling no obligation to protect them, could assert that if the minorities did not like having their citizenship diminished, they should move to the other sibling state where their group, now in charge there, was carrying out discriminatory policies of its own.[39]

So the minorities who did not migrate away had even more grievances than before — but now they had sympathetic allies in power in an adjacent country who supported their violent struggle. For example, the Korean War began as a civil war, but because the Northern and Southern regions were by then sovereign states, it became an international war. The Vietnam War had a similar basis.

Neither side was satisfied with the location of the new borders, and in some cases their constitutions proclaimed their right to rule the other country. The Irish, Vietnamese, Korean, German, Chinese, and Taiwanese constitutions made overlapping territorial claims. Before the secessions there had been small conflicts involving riots or guerrillas, but when the regions became states, they acquired fully fledged armies and fought big wars.

Moreover, these sibling countries usually had superpower allies who became involved in their wars.[40] The United States became involved in Korea, Vietnam, and Taiwan and (without necessarily sending troops) in Middle Eastern wars and in the struggles between India and Pakistan. Worse yet, when superpowers get embroiled in these fights they may try to end them by making nuclear threats. The United States threatened China in the 1950s over the Korean War and the status of Taiwan. The Chinese, worrying that the Soviets might not protect them if the Americans used nuclear weapons, decided to build their own bomb. Mao expected that this action would "boost their courage and scare others." However, as Schaeffer observes,

China didn't scare the United States so much as it scared India, with whom China had a war in the early '60s. China scared India into developing nuclear weapons of its own. The trouble was that, when India developed nuclear weapons, it scared China not so much as it did Pakistan, with whom India has had several wars. The Pakistanis say they're developing nuclear weapons to boost their courage and scare India. But because they called their weapon an "Islamic bomb," they make Israel and other countries nervous. . . . The French assisted the Israelis to develop their nuclear program. Israel developed nuclear weapons to boost their courage and scare the Soviet Union. Of course, they didn't scare the Soviet Union terribly, but they did scare their neighbors, Syria and Iraq. Syria never developed nuclear weapons, but biological ones. Iraq went ahead and began to develop nuclear weapons.

So partition has led to war and to the development of nuclear weapons by countries that have frequently gone to war with one another. That is an unanticipated consequence of partition.[41]

Outcomes of Secession in the Formerly Socialist Countries

How well do Schaeffer's generalizations of 1990 apply to the wave of secessions following the breakup of the Socialist bloc? Regrettably, they seem to have been prophetic. One main difference between the earlier cases of partition and the recent breakups is that in the former instances, division was imposed by foreign powers, whereas those carrying out the later breakups claimed to be acting in response to popular demand, though plebiscites were not necessarily held.

In fact, apart from the Baltic and some of the Yugoslav republics, the popularity of secession was questionable. Had all Soviet citizens been allowed to vote on the question, almost certainly the majority would have voted for the Soviet Union to remain intact, though with looser constitutional ties than before. (In a referendum, 76 percent had supported renewed union in March of the year the Soviet Union was destroyed.[42]) The same goes for Czechoslovakia: Neither the number of Czechs nor the number of Slovaks who wanted secession constituted a majority.

The case was more complicated in Yugoslavia, where plebiscites of sometimes questionable legitimacy were held after the governments had already broken down.[43] Some communities (e.g., the Serbs in Bosnia) boycotted the referendum that turned them into unwilling citizens of a new state instead of Yugoslavia or Serbia.[44]

Nevertheless, unlike Schaeffer's cases, all these decisions to separate were made not by outsiders but by indigenous national politicians. In some cases (such as Georgia) they were forced by circumstance, not preference, to separate. More often, however, they were animated by fervent nationalism. And, though they may have exaggerated their own popularity, they did enjoy the support of an ethnic political constituency. Their democratic pretension, which lent some legitimacy to separatism, did not prevent violence.

The Baltic republics had already experienced some repression from Soviet hard-liners before the coup attempt of August 1991, but thereafter their move toward independence was unimpeded. Of all the Soviet republics, their cause had the greatest legitimacy, for Stalin had fraudulently annexed them.

Ukraine and Belarus also seceded without significant violence, though not without serious military danger. Belarus surrendered the nuclear weapons on its soil to Russia for safekeeping or disposal, as did Kazakhstan, but Ukraine dickered over the terms for giving up its bombs and drove an even harder bargain over the disposition of the Soviet Black Sea fleet. Ukraine remains torn by an internal struggle between Russians living in the Crimea, who wish to secede and rejoin Russia, and other Ukrainians, particularly those in western areas.

The other formerly Soviet republics experienced worse internal conflict. Moldova broke into civil war, as many of its citizens wanted their new state to join their ethnic kindred in Romania, while Ukrainians and Russians fought to separate from Moldova.

Before the Soviet Union collapsed, Armenia and Azerbaijan had already been at war over Nagorno-Karabakh, an enclave in Azerbaijan whose population is Armenian. This war continued until 1994, producing more than 20,000 deaths.

Georgia was wracked by three different civil wars. The first began in 1990 in South Ossetia, which tried to secede from Georgia and join North Ossetia, a part of Russia. A second war was led by the ousted president, Zviad Gamsakhurdia, and continued until his death in 1994; its course was complicated by the intrigues of several factional guerrilla movements. The third war began in 1992 when the so-called "Republic of Abkhazia" declared independence and drove the Georgian government army from its territory for a time.

All Central Asian republics except Kazakhstan and Kyrgyzstan saw organized political violence and endemic violent crime after they became autonomous. The most seriously affected was Tajikistan, where a full civil war based on ethnicity broke out in 1992, resulting in between 20,000 and 50,000 deaths.

Russia, with about half the size and population of the Soviet Union, contains twenty-one autonomous republics, inhabited mainly by non-Russians. Groups in other regions also aspire toward independence, especially those with a distinct ethnic identity and possession of some valuable natural resource. The Muslims living in an oil-rich region on the Volga, who desired an independent Tatarstan, declared economic independence and nearly attempted secession.[45] Nearby Bashkortostan, another oil-rich region, also moved toward independence. The same goes for Karelia, a Finnish-speaking republic with extensive mineral and forest properties, and Sakha-Yakutia, a huge part of eastern Siberia with almost all Soviet diamond mines, plus gold, oil, gas, and coal. Since 20 percent of Russia's population are ethnic minorities controlling over half the territory and much of its raw materials, separatism understandably appeals to them.[46]

Chechnya declared its independence in 1991. Its declaration was studiously ignored by the rest of the world's states and nothing seemed likely to come of it. However, in December 1994 Boris Yeltsin ordered his forces to occupy Chechnya, and this launched a civil war costing 80,000 to 120,000 lives.

The potential exists for another dangerous policy based on ethnic nationalism — Russian irredentism, or the attempt to reunite Slavic peoples in the independent formerly Soviet republics. Russians are numerous in Kazakhstan, parts of other republics in Central Asia and the north Caucasus, Moldova, Estonia, and Latvia. Many are nationalists who seriously contemplate reviving the Soviet Union under a fascist-type regime. Russians by no means adopted a hands-off policy toward the newly independent states. According to Helsinki Watch, Russians, in the guise of peacekeepers, provided military and financial support to breakaway groups in Georgia, Moldova, Azerbaijan, North Ossetia, and Tajikistan.[47]

These, then, are the early consequences and prospects following the Soviet breakup. To judge from the record of previous partitions in which the successor states themselves subsequently nearly split (e.g., from the breakaway Pakistan broke away Bangladesh; from the breakaway Croatia broke away Krajina; the breakaway Bosnia-Herzegovina broke into three warring states that NATO then tried to hold together by force), additional secessionist movements must be anticipated in the newly separate states. What financial and human cost will be paid for secessionist movements?

The Price of Secession

When a separatist attempt succeeds, do the benefits exceed the costs? We cannot evaluate the intangible but symbolically satisfying effects. However, if we consider only the objective results, the net payoff, even of successful partitions, must be considered negative. Partition rarely puts an end to the fighting. (Seemingly interminable struggles and terrorism are still continuing in Northern Ireland, the Middle East, Kashmir, and Korea, for example, generations after partition.) Moreover, the new states resulting from the partition are generally less democratic than the unified states they replaced.[48] Nor do the new states benefit economically after the price of the war has been paid, though sometimes one of the sibling states benefits, while the other becomes poorer, as in the Baltic republics and Russia. It is not that small countries are economically disadvantaged but rather that the process of dividing any country, regardless of its size, is economically disruptive.

The reorganization of the economy was especially painful in the breakup of the Soviet Union, where centralized planning had not provided for any competition between firms. A factory might have obtained its supplies from a single source located thousands of miles away (the cost of transportation was rarely taken into account) and shipped its products to a single buyer.[49] When the republics seceded, these trade arrangements were broken, though no alternative enterprises existed in the new countries that could become substitute suppliers. Other exchanges also began to break down. Ukraine stopped selling vegetable oil to Krasnoyarsk in Russia, for example, and so Krasnoyarsk stopped accepting Ukrainian nuclear waste.[50] Every republic suffered economically from the breakup.

Secession is sometimes described as "political divorce" and the analogy aptly describes the acrimony typical of both kinds of rupture. In secessions and divorces alike, those who have contributed to the joint assets tend to resent the breakup and to consider themselves the losers, regardless of how the common property is divided. Still, divorced spouses can move apart and avoid dealing further with each other, whereas after a secession, most members of the rival ethnic groups go on living where they are, confronting each other and having to handle their conflicts.[51] In the two new sovereign states, fewer political mechanisms exist than before for resolving grievances. An ethnic community that has seceded no longer is represented in the other state's parliament or political parties, so it must try to negotiate settlements through diplomatic channels — far weaker instruments than domestic political institutions. Secession destroys existing dispute-resolution systems while increasing the need for them.

Secession also damages interpersonal relations. In peacetime, many people regard their ethnicity as a matter of little salience. They may even change from one supposedly ascribed ethnic community to another several times during their lifetime, converting to a different religion or marrying out.[52] In mixed marriages, a common way of avoiding friction is to evade the issue by refusing to identify oneself as belonging to either group. Secessionists, however, insist that everyone's ethnicity must be permanent and salient in social situations; they make it impossible for people to preserve harmony in their homes. In such situations, interethnic marriages typically break up or the families flee. The same must be said of interethnic friendships and business partnerships. The interpersonal costs of secession are always high.

International Law and Secession

A recitation of the problems that typically follow secession rarely influences the aspirations of separatists, who typically say that international law favors their cause. *Does* international law justify secession?

We turn to a 1994 book by the British expert Rosalyn Higgins, who was appointed to the International Court of Justice only months after her book appeared in print.[53] Higgins notes that the UN Charter's call for "self-determination" actually only applied to *states, not peoples,* and merely meant that no government should be dominated by another government.

Who Is Entitled to Self-Determination?

The meaning of "self-determination" gradually changed, however, under the impetus of decolonization. By 1966, the General Assembly had passed resolutions favoring the right of "peoples" to self-determination — and not only peoples who were subject to colonial rule.[54] However, self-determination was never intended to refer *only* to independence or secession but simply meant the right to decide freely.[55] Higgins argues that there is no legal right of secession where there is representative government.[56] (Not all legal experts agree; many regard self-determination as justifiable where a representative government is present but the minority nevertheless faces severe human rights violations.) In any case, the UN has consistently indicated that the principle of self-determination must never disrupt the national unity and territorial integrity of a country.[57]

But what exactly is a "people"? Who, indeed, is the "self" that is entitled to "self-determination"? There are several views. Higgins shows that the ICJ understands "a people" to include not just a dissatisfied minority with secessionist aspirations but *all* those living within the inherited international boundaries of a given state.[58] Lest this firm statement be taken as an affront to aggrieved minorities, she reassures us that,

> Of course, all members of distinct minority groups are part of the peoples of the territory. In that sense they too, as individuals, are the holders of the right of self-determination. But minorities *as such* do not have a right of self-determination. That means, in effect, that they have no right to secession, to independence, or to join with comparable groups in other states.[59]

Individual members of minorities who consider their human rights to have been violated may bring complaints against states that are party to the Covenant on Civil and Political Rights — but they may do so only as individuals, not as a class action on behalf of a group.[60]

Despite these clear statements, Higgins leaves room for more ambiguity than she perhaps intended. While these legal principles do not *require* any state to agree to the secession of any of its member groups, she acknowledges that neither do they *prohibit* secession or the formation of new states. "And where secession has in fact occurred, and a new state has emerged with its own government, not dependent on another, and functioning effectively over the territory concerned, then recognition will follow." This point suggests that *if all parties* to the secession agree to it and turn it into an uncontested reality, then the rest of the world will not object.

Such an observation is not helpful in determining when a state *ought to* allow a subgroup of its citizens to secede, even if it is technically not obligated to do so. Taking her advice, a renegade secessionist group might reasonably try to secede and see how far it can get. If it succeeds, eventually it will be recognized — whether or not its cause was just. Since this course of action is so obviously dangerous, some additional guidance seems to be needed. Higgins limits the right of self-determination to virtually the *entire* population living within the *currently recognized* borders of a state. Such a narrow principle is a minority view within international law, for it would leave so little legal basis for separatism that only renegade groups would attempt it. We are left without clear principles of international law by which to resolve the disputes that will continue to arise over territories and borders.

Territorial Rights

For insight into the question beyond the point where Higgins leaves it, we may turn to an American specialist on international law, Lea Brilmayer, for whom territorial ownership constitutes the key problem in matters of secession. She denies that *consent* is the primary issue justifying the right to separation.[61] As democratic theorists point out, citizens are not permitted to reject the authority of their government merely by withdrawing consent from it. Nor can a dominant ethnic community repudiate its obligations by withdrawing its consent. Why, then, should it be otherwise for a minority community that claims a right to secede?

Nevertheless, people sometimes do call their governments illegitimate or repressive and say they want out. This is true of secessionists and refugees alike — two categories of people whom Brilmayer compares. Ordinarily, refugees are free to leave their country if some other country will accept them. This is not the case for secessionists, for in addition to leaving their country they insist upon *taking their land with them.* In that situation, it is not enough for them to prove that they are truly "a people," nor even to prove that they have been mistreated. They must also prove that they are entitled to the territory that they want to detach from the state. Not every oppressed group can plausibly make such a claim. For example, Turkish guest workers in Germany experience discrimination and constitute an ethnic community, but they would hardly get far if they proposed to secede from Germany. Hong Kong constitutes another example. The territory was leased by Britain from China, and when the lease expired in 1997, the territory reverted to China, whether or not the majority of the inhabitants wanted that. No separatist movement could prevent it, for the ownership of the land was legally incontestable. The Hong Kong people therefore are not entitled to self-determination.[62]

The case for separatism, then, hinges on entitlement to land. In international law, says Brilmayer, a group asserting a land claim must demonstrate that the territory in question was wrongly taken from them at some previous time and that they have a historic grievance. But this argument is a slippery slope, for if one traces history far enough back, one finds countless parcels of land that have been owned by a whole series of different groups, many of whom had wrongly taken it from their immediate predecessors. It would be unreasonable to go back centuries in reallocating land, especially if the descendants of some of the previous owners had long ago dropped their grievance. What is the appropriate cutoff principle for determining which of these claims to recognize? Brilmayer suggests that, at minimum, any claimant group should prove that its land had been wrongfully taken so recently that it had kept its claim alive ever since the violation occurred.

Moreover, the historical grievance is especially weighty in cases in which the claimants' territory was wrongfully annexed, as in most anticolonialist situations. This was also the case in the Baltic states, whose expatriates had unceasingly protested that their country had been stolen from them, until finally the Soviet authorities acknowledged that this was true.

Brilmayer's territorial approach helps resolve some of the issues for which nationalists have no answer. One such issue is the problem of individuals who have to decide for themselves whether their desire to secede is a legitimate wish. Nationalists admit that not every minority within a state is entitled to self-determination, but they claim that a "nationality" or "a people" *does* have that right, including even the right to secede. There can be no objective way of determining whether or not a group constitutes a nationality. Therefore, this theory defines a "nationality" as a group of people whose members *believe* they are a nationality. Fair enough. But if the members of a community themselves disagree as to whether they are a nationality or merely a minority, how can *they* answer that question? It is not helpful to tell individuals to consult their own consciences when the question with which they are grappling is, "What should I believe?"

Neither nationalists nor Brilmayer nor anyone else can answer their question. However, Brilmayer's approach has the advantage of *reducing the importance of the question.* Instead of evaluating the separatists' arguments about their national identity, her approach advises us to investigate their objective historical claims to land. Such a claim is not necessarily an easy matter to evaluate, since hardly "any territorial boundary anywhere in the world would survive an effort to correct all historical misdeeds."[63] Nevertheless, territorial claims can be adjudicated with considerable objectivity, and Brilmayer's approach gives us a basis for addressing the legitimacy of demands for changing borders. Since we may not expect the present world map to remain frozen for all time, and since we do not want the changes to be effected by the nonlegal actions of adventurists, we need principles for adjudicating the new secessionist claims as they arise, one by one. The treatment of separatism as a land claim issue provides such principles. This criterion would restrict the legitimacy of new secessionist claims without eliminating the basis for them, as Higgins's principles seem virtually to do.

Why Territory?

To focus on territory has an additional benefit: It illuminates some of the issues that have already been mentioned. If the acquisition of territory is the objective of secessionists, what is the main basis for that aspiration? Why do they want the land they are claiming?

Of the countless reasons for wanting land, some of the most obvious reasons are material. Land can be farmed. It can yield gold, oil, minerals, timber, and access to trade routes or to the sea. Controlling land means controlling existing cities and existing populations, as well as providing space for new cities and expanding populations. We need not extend this catalog of self-evident material grounds for wanting territory, many of which surely count among the real motives of separatists.

However, another aspect of territory — its function as a political catchment area — plays an even more significant part in the thinking of secessionists. It explains the correlation between waves of secession and of democracy.

Territorial Constituencies and the Distribution of Voters

In democracies, people vote. It is sometimes important *where* they vote, for within a nation-state, ballots are aggregated in different levels of constituencies (e.g., by province, district, or municipal borough), each of which elects its own government or delegates to government. The nation-state and its subsidiary constituencies are defined territorially.

If the members of all ethnic communities, all social classes, and all political philosophies were distributed randomly throughout the country, we could simply divide the whole territory into equally populated districts and all these interest groups would be satisfied with their representation in the decision-making structures. Instead, however, people cluster together, forming neighborhoods or regions that differ markedly in terms of language, wealth, religion, cultural traditions, education, and party preference — factors that may seem relevant to a person in the voting booth. A person living in a dictatorship does not worry about such matters because nothing significant happens in his voting booth. However, when a state becomes democratic, voting becomes important and different possible voting arrangements make enormous differences in the results.

Nevertheless, the academic study of voting systems is an arcane topic. Most people assume that if two voting systems are both democratic, there is no basis for preferring one over the other. Very few citizens ask how best to aggregate votes within a democracy.

Minority groups are sometimes disadvantaged by their spatial distribution. Some of them are too dispersed in the society to win any political representation at all, while others are too concentrated in one area to maintain any sense of unity with the rest of the society. Either of these distributional situations can cause serious difficulties. Unfortunately, if members of an ethnic community take any interest at all in such problems, they may consider only the least promising approaches to solving them — gerrymandering or secession.

Gerrymandering consists of manipulating the shape of electoral districts so as to maximize the representation of one interest group or party. This kind of operation is carried out by political insiders; ordinary citizens rarely know that it has taken place. Secession, on the other hand, usually is produced by a mass political movement whose participants well understand its objectives, without necessarily understanding its disadvantages or the alternatives to it.

In an ordinary democratic election the majority wins and the minority loses.[64] Ideally, no one is outvoted all the time. Unfortunately, however, the uneven distribution of an ethnic minority throughout the society means that some groups do regularly lose electoral battles.

Dispersed minorities. Consider a group so dispersed throughout the society that nowhere can it elect a representative. The Canadian aboriginal population faces this problem. Although they constitute about three percent of the electorate, they can only rarely elect a native person to the federal parliament.

Recently an election reform commission recommended that certain parliamentary seats be reserved for aboriginal voters, whose ballots would be aggregated in their own nationwide constituency, regardless of where they live. This reform has not taken place.

Concentrated minorities. The opposite problem occurs when an ethnic community constitutes only a minority within the entire country but a sizable majority in one locality, as, for example, the francophone Quebecers (Québécois). As a minority within the entire country but a majority in Quebec, the Québécois sometimes lose political battles in Ottawa. By seceding from the rest of the Canada, they would cease to be the consistent loser; *as a majority in their own independent state they would consistently win.*

There are other ways of addressing their problem — including the same mechanism that the reformers suggested for Indians: reserved seats for parliamentarians to be elected by francophone voters, regardless of where they live in Canada. This idea has never appealed to the Québécois, who, unlike the aboriginals, are sufficiently concentrated to constitute the great majority of one province. Some 5.5 million of Canada's francophones live in Quebec, but only one million in the rest of Canada. Although all Canadian francophones share a distinct culture, their separatists no longer try to protect the rights of those dispersed through the other provinces. On the assumption that these francophones are doomed to assimilate into anglophone society, the separatists have concentrated on demanding independence for their province on the argument that it is a "nation."

In several similar situations a local majority has adopted the same solution, sacrificing the members of its culture who live elsewhere in the society for the sake of pursuing independence locally. For example, in the Transcaucasus of Russia, as well as in India, nationalities tend to be concentrated in local areas and, accordingly, communal politics usually manifests itself as a claim for territorial independence. Likewise in Sri Lanka, the Tamil separatists opted for the independence of the predominantly Tamil northern and eastern provinces instead of promoting the rights of all members of their community, wherever they live.

Self-Determination as a Guarantee of Winning Elections?
Ethnic groups demand self-determination on many grounds, including a desire to preserve their distinct culture. To claim the right to secede, they should establish the legitimacy of their claim for a piece of land. This requires them to demonstrate a historic grievance connected with the occasion when they were dispossessed. Normally, though not always, the ethnic group making such a claim also constitutes the vast majority of the population within the territory that they seek to recover.

The few exceptions to this generalization — such as Estonia, Latvia, and Tibet — are worth noting. These had previously been independent countries at various times.[65] After the Soviet Union and China, respectively, invaded and seized control of these states, they imported millions of their own people into the country. In the two Baltic states, about 35 percent of the inhabitants today are Russian or Slavic. In Tibet the demographic realities are hard to determine. In cities and fertile valleys, Chinese outnumber Tibetans by two or three to one, while in some rural areas, almost all are Tibetan.[66] Naturally, many expatriate Tibetans, Latvians, and Estonians continued to press their territorial claims. In none of these three countries does the legitimacy of the original group's territorial claim depend on its numerical strength, since they were the victims of aggression or fraud. The ICJ cannot rule on such matters unless they have been asked to do so (which would never have happened in these cases), but if it had been asked to do so, both the Baltic and the Tibetan claimants might, on the basis of the fraud, have been granted the right to secede from the state that annexed them. Even so, they would (and in the case of Estonia, already have) run into political problems because their ethnic community in some areas does not constitute a majority of the voters, which is the minimum condition acceptable to nationalists.

The Tibetans and Estonians have taken different approaches to their problems. The Tibetan national government-in-exile is urging greater autonomy from China, but not independence. The Dalai Lama's proposals to end the Chinese occupation of his homeland depart from the usual "one-state-for-one-people" strategy of nationalists. Despite the genocide of more than one million Tibetans by the Chinese Communists, the Dalai Lama's five-point peace plan, announced in 1987, was remarkable for its Buddhist spirit of reconciliation.[67]

The Estonians, on the other hand, not only continued to demand sovereignty, but they achieved it. However, the results do not satisfy everyone. Most Estonians evidently wish they could expel Russian settlers or restrict their voting in Estonian elections. To achieve this effect, they imposed language requirements as a condition for naturalization.[68]

The main explanation for the current popularity of ethnic separatism is the hope of gaining a commanding electoral position in the promised democracy. Indeed, except in such historically exceptional cases as the Baltics,[69] an ethnic group ordinarily does not demand independence unless it can expect to hold a commanding political position in the new state and in its internal territorially defined constituencies.

This observation has implications for preventing secession. Separatists' claim for territory (so essential to legitimating their desire for secession) seems to be a quest for a political constituency in which they have an improved chance of winning elections.[70] It is customary to tabulate ballots within catchment areas that are defined geographically. But suppose ballots were aggregated in constituencies that were not defined territorially but in which the ethnic group had a fair chance to win elections. Might a reform of that kind satisfy members of an ethnic community who would otherwise demand secession?

Let us compare some alternative political arrangements that were practiced by historic multiethnic societies, as well as proposals for non-territorial constituencies in modern democracies.

Multiethnic Alternatives to Territory

All contemporary societies are multiethnic. No existing state is completely homogeneous as a single culture and breeding population; most states actually contain more than five ethnic groups.[71] Nowhere have ethnic groups mixed so completely as to fully assimilate all successive waves of immigrants.[72] Much may be learned by comparing the many possible ways in which multiethnic societies have been organized. What is conspicuous is how few of them were divided into territorial units with boundaries, as nationalists consider normal.

Not only modern states are mixed; the majority of societies throughout history also have been multicultural. William McNeill notes that until our historical epoch, high civilizations were generally polyethnic societies, while homogeneity was typical only of certain isolated barbarian societies. Only slowly, and only in Europe, did the notion arise that a territory ought to be unified as a single society.[73] We may even call most empires and states throughout history "multi*societal*," since in general, various ethnic communities have shared the same territory without significantly interacting in their political, religious, linguistic, educational, or kinship affairs. The interactions of their members were normally not social, but only economic, in nature. Can such models of interethnic relations be applied in the modern world?

Asian Societies as "Layers"

According to Wolfram Eberhard, who studied the historic settlement patterns of Asia, "the concept 'multiple society,' which usually refers to America, appears to better historic describe Asian social conditions."[74] Eberhard doubted that one could properly refer to India of A.D. 1000 or China of A.D. 1700 as a society. Whereas certain tribes inhabited large areas, they were not divided by borders, but only "frontiers" — large zones of transition — and they interacted with people on both sides. The ordinary farmer knew nothing of the language, religion, or customs of the imperial rulers and, for that matter, did not know that he was a member of the Mogul or Chinese empire. He did know that strangers regularly came to demand money, but he did not know that they were "tax collectors"; probably he thought they were just robbers. Moreover, the political boundaries of the Mogul state meant nothing to the Indian farmer, who probably kept in touch with relatives and caste-brothers outside. The Brahman priest also had ties to all the other Brahman priests in other Indian states. The urban Indian merchant had business partners throughout the Middle East, such as the tea merchant in Kabul and the carpet merchant in Baghdad, and when he traveled, he felt quite at home singing the local songs in the brothels of the big cities. He probably had some contact with a few Brahmans and some urban customers in his home area, but no contact with the farmer.

The communities of Asia constituted what Eberhard called "layers" of great geographical expanse. (If writing today he might call them "networks.") Members might have numerous and intimate contacts within their own layer across considerable distances, but little contact with the members of *other* layers in their own area. Even later, in the nineteenth century, the Chinese immigrants in California or Singapore believed that they lived in "China" — and indeed, the Chinatown where they lived was truly part of a layer that included villages in Canton and several other parts of Asia. In such cases a layer was stratified in itself and upheld its own laws. Throughout most periods of history, it was considered the duty of a ruler to ensure that members of the various layers obeyed their own sets of laws.

In Canton one would find an Arab community who might be considered a minority ethnic community of China; Eberhard did not look at them in that way. He considered them to be one section of an Arab layer that covered wide areas in the Far East, Southeast Asia, South Asia, the Near East, and even parts of Europe. They enjoyed "extra-territoriality" and were regarded as belonging to a different, non-Chinese society. The Chinese rulers recognized certain Arabs as leaders of this community and required them to control their own foreigners and exact payments from them. There may have been considerable interaction between all these layers, or there may have been very little.

In Yunan province of China of the nineteenth century, for example, the Chinese bureaucracy from Peking did rule large lowland areas, but it did not rule the society that lived on the slopes of the mountains. A third society lived at the top of the mountains, again possessing its own institutions, language, values, and religion. These were not "minorities" but truly self-contained societies whose members interacted only occasionally. Studying social change in such a setting, Eberhard traced the flow of new ideas and habits *inside specific layers.* An innovation such as the compass might be carried across whole continents without leaving any trace along the route if the merchants who carried it did not find anyone of their own social circle where they stopped in their journeys.[75]

Not only the Far East but also the Roman Empire and the medieval empires of Europe as well as the late Habsburg and Ottoman Empires were "multiple societies" of numerous distinct communities.[76]

There was no such thing as secession from this kind of empire because the layers were already politically and socially independent, even though they occupied the same territory as other layers and passed each other, tolerantly but indifferently, in the streets they shared. The Ottoman Empire was especially remarkable for the autonomy in political and social matters that it granted to its various religious communities.

The Ottoman Empire as a Multiple Society

The Ottoman Empire comprised Armenians, Greeks, Bulgars, Arabs, Kurds, and many other distinct societies who spoke their own languages and maintained their own value systems, their own religions, and their own institutions. Only in a political sense did they belong together, as subjects of the sultan.[77] These groups were allowed to organize their own social functions, except that certain rules were imposed by the "ruling class," whose task it was to defend and collect taxes from them.

Ottoman society was divided into communities along religious lines, a structure called the *millet* system. Non-Muslim subjects were left to devise their own laws and regulate the behavior of their co-religionists, while local Muslims who were not members of the ruling class also formed their own group around those leaders who were responsible for enforcing Muslim laws. Subjects normally dealt with the ruling class through their millet leaders. Each millet maintained its own systems of education, religion, justice, social security, hospitals, and hospices for the poor and aged. Many of these separate institutions remain today, long after the millet courts and legal status were supplanted by nation-states when the empire gradually broke apart.

Besides the Muslim millets, there were three other basic millets — the Orthodox, which included Slavic, Greek, and Rumanian communities with independent patriarchates; the Jews, whose grand rabbi in Istanbul enjoyed great autonomy; and the Armenian community, with its own national church, which also was given authority over all other subjects, such as the Gypsies, the Assyrians, and the Bogomils of Bosnia. In addition to the major religious organizations there were numerous other smaller religious groups, such as mystic Sufis, Catholics (governed in the previous century by a representative of the pope), and Protestants, who, though living in the empire, were not subjects of the sultan but of such Western powers as France, Holland, and England.[78] By 1910, half the population in the empire was non-Muslim. All these groups enjoyed virtual immunity from Turkish laws. Christian, Jewish, and Druze communities had to pay a tax from which Muslim citizens were exempt; in exchange, however, they were exempt from military service until Ottoman rule neared its end.[79]

Conflicts took place between the various millets, including those representing various sections of Christianity. Throughout the nineteenth century, uprisings against the Ottomans took place throughout the Balkans. In response to these problems it was largely the Young Turks who destroyed their empire, intending to "modernize" their society by making everyone within a given territory subject to the same universalistic laws of a sovereign nation-state. They were reflecting the penetration of Western influence, which by then was restructuring traditional Islamic culture. The end came after World War I by the decision of the war's victors, who dismantled the empire, though some scholars argue today that it need not have collapsed.[80]

The Modernity of Universalism

The "modernistic" principle of universalism has everywhere become the chief enemy of multiple societies. If it were not such a dominant value today, it might still be possible for francophone Canadians, say, or Chechen Russians to maintain their own laws and customs and even elect their own government without bothering to secede.

Still, the universalistic ideal is not entrenched everywhere. For example, Muslims and Hindus in India retain the right to determine many of their own laws separately, including their family laws. Even Westerners are acquainted with particularistic institutions. For example, when a Canadian registers to vote in Toronto, she must declare whether she is Catholic or some other religion. If she says Catholic (whether or not this is true), her taxes support the Catholic schools and she may vote for trustees of the Catholic school board. Otherwise, her taxes and votes belong to the public school system. This arrangement gives Catholics and Protestants control over some aspects of their own lives without requiring them to occupy separate territories. For the purpose of governing school systems, Canadians are like millets.

A Nonterritorial Future for Democracy?

Why were the principles of universalism and territorial sovereignty considered modern? The Young Turks and others who wanted to modernize Asia and the Ottoman Empire insisted on integrating their societies internally, creating a single, unified culture throughout the borders of each state. They tried hard to attain this goal, but rarely did they succeed.

Today the original ethnic communities, having refused to assimilate into a single nationality, are fighting back, demanding homelands of their own and the right to follow their own traditions and speak their own languages. Though they rejected much that the previous nationalists proposed, they evidently accepted the older nationalists' belief in territorial sovereignty. Now they too aspire to hold exclusive jurisdiction over their own territory, which may be a fragment of the state their predecessors established.

They also want democracy and freedom of choice. For this reason especially, they do not wish to revive the multi-ethnic arrangements of poly-ethnic empires whereby traditional groups shared a common territory, yet retained separate cultures. Membership in the millets, or "layers," had been ascribed — fixed involuntarily at birth — while a modern democracy must allow individuals to choose their own affiliations. Some modern people actually do change their ethnic identities and loyalties. They would hardly want to be bound by the laws of any ethnic group or religious community. Modernity seems to require that the laws of

the land apply universally to all its inhabitants and be accepted by them all —
though some conclude that this modern principle calls for the state's territory to
be "cleansed" of ethnic groups who reject the common culture and laws.

Democracy, sovereignty, and universalism form a political system that, for
all its admirable qualities, may not accommodate particularistic solidarities. As
Alexis de Tocqueville anticipated, democratic states are not necessarily characterized by liberty, tolerance, or pluralism; a populist majority can be ruthlessly
tyrannical in demanding uniformity.

But there are those among us who consider universalism and sovereignty to
be overrated values. Such "postmodern" individuals reject secession in favor of
multicultural states, where different groups share the same territory but keep particularistic habits of their own. Thus a postmodern critic, Chantal Mouffe,
blames conventional territorial democracy for repressing citizens who differ in
their race, class, gender, and ethnicity. Mouffe calls for a radical new democracy
based on direct political representation of the multiple layers of affiliations. Such
a system would accommodate the change of community identities as they rise
and fall during the life of ordinary citizens.[81]

Such a proposal is not a new idea. The compatibility of multicultural politics
with democracy was demonstrated by some regions of the Austro-Hungarian
Empire, where social democrats developed a workable formula for cultural plural
ism. Each individual citizen was guaranteed the right to voluntarily choose his or
her own ethnicity, and each ethnic community was guaranteed representation in
the provincial parliament in proportion to its share of the population, without
regard to where its members were located territorially.[82]

To be acceptable today, any proposal for cultural pluralism must be democratically representative, as was the Austrian-Hungarian scheme, and must also provide for freedom of choice. Thus every constituency must be constituted on a
voluntary basis. Membership in such a system of representation must be defined
not by lines on a map or by birth into a millet or a "layer" but by the free
choices of citizens.

Some political theorists anticipate the emergence of just such a nonterritorial
democratic system. For example, David J. Elkins's book, *Beyond Sovereignty:
Territory and Political Economy in the Twenty-First Century*,[83] suggests that no
contemporary state will be able much longer to hold exclusive jurisdiction over
its territory. Indeed, he suggests that nation-states already are on the way out.
Likewise, in his book *The End of the Nation-State*, Jean-Marie Guéhenno argues
that for political effectiveness today, "The essential is not to master a territory,
but to have access to a network."[84] He speculates about the future of politics and
economics in a world where territory has become almost irrelevant: "When there
is no longer a territorial imperative, when the place of residence and the
investment are no longer a given but a choice, when added value is generated in
too abstract a fashion for its creation to be assigned to a precise location, [even]
taxation is no longer a sovereign decision."

With globalization, transnational corporations are replacing domestic manufacturing and trade and in turn are regulated by transnational governing institutions such as the World Trade Organization and the International Monetary Fund. State sovereignty is everywhere dwindling. The United Nations sometimes intervenes in the affairs of a member state against its rulers' wishes, as when it identified "no-fly zones" in Iraq to protect the Kurds.[85]

If today we were deciding whether to dismantle the Mogul, Habsburg, and Ottoman Empires, some of us would vote no. We might choose instead to democratize the layers and millets, making their membership voluntary, accountable to elected leaders, and not restricted to ethnicity as a basis for solidarity. In the twenty-first century this kind of political society may be the most advanced system of governance.

Still, this book is not about one particular version of utopia. The work ahead of us is mainly a somber project: the description and comparison of a variety of separatist movements. Only briefly at the end shall we return to a speculative approach, reflecting on several proposals for reforms that the contributors of this book propose as alternatives to secession.

Notes

1. Ernest Gellner, *Nations and Nationalism* (Ithaca, N.Y.: Cornell University Press, 1983), 1.
2. Samuel Huntington, "Democracy's Third Wave," *Journal of Democracy,* 2 (Spring 1991).
3. Yves Beigbeder, *International Monitoring of Plebiscites, Referenda and National Elections* (Dordrecht, the Netherlands: Martinus Nijhoff, 1994), 2. I will not speculate here on the *quality* of democracy, but Freedom House makes graduated ratings and, according to its list in January 1998, there were 79 independent "free" countries, plus 59 that were "partially free" where freedom is defined by criteria that depict democracies (see http://www. freedomhouse.org/).
4. Morton H. Halperin and David J. Scheffer with Patricia L. Small, *Self-Determination in the New World Order* (Washington, D.C.: Carnegie Endowment for International Peace, 1992), 16-17.
5. Nationalistic movements in Western Europe are an exception to this pattern, for they do accept the integration of the European Union.
6. Another interpretation of international law denies that countries are created by the recognition of other countries. According to the positivist view, the international community merely responds to reality and recognizes new states only when they have already gained uncontested control over their territory, are accepted by the population, and are actually functioning as independent states. Nations eventually do extend diplomatic recognition to other new states whose existence they may not welcome. However, they sometimes delay such recognition for decades in the hope that the regime may fail. Because such recognition is so fateful, if it is extended with undue haste or without regard for the rights of minorities, the action incurs blame. Germany and Austria have been blamed for

the former Yugoslavia's breakup, since they recognized Slovenia and Croatia without ascertaining that minorities were protected. The European Community established the Badinter Commission to design conditions for the recognition of the breakaway states. Croatia fulfilled the criteria formally, though not in realistic terms, and Slovenia and Macedonia did so in a fuller sense. Legally, none of these states gained independence through secession but rather because Yugoslavia ceased to exist.

7. Sir Hersch Lauterpacht, *Recognition in International Law* (Cambridge: Cambridge University Press, 1947).

8. Lawrence S. Eastwood, Jr., "Secession: State Practice and International Law after the Dissolution of the Soviet Union and Yugoslavia," *Duke Journal of Comparative and International Law* Vol. 3, No. 2 (Spring 1993): 349.

9. The mutual intelligibility of French dialects was largely attained by the seventeenth century, according to Lucien Febvre and Henri-Jean Martin in *The Coming of the Book. The Impact of Printing, 1450-1800* (London: New Left Books, 1976), 319.

10. The popularity of the *Lega Nord* in calling for the secession of northern Italy allows one to ask again whether its members "are" Italian.

11. Benedict Anderson, *Imagined Communities: Reflections on the Origin and Spread of Nationalism*, rev. ed. (London: Verso, 1983), esp. 198.

12. This divisiveness extends to irredentist movements, which seek union with a neighboring state of similar ethnic composition rather than independence.

13. David Held mentioned these examples in "Democracy, the Nation-State and the Global System," in his *Political Theory Today* (Cambridge, England: Polity, 1991), 202.

14. Joseph Stalin, *Marxism and the National and Colonial Question* (London: Martin Lawrence Ltd., n.d.). Stalin's and Lenin's policies toward nationalities did not remain identical. Initial rhetoric aside, Stalin's actions were more assimilationist than Lenin's.

15. V.I. Lenin, *Imperialism, the Highest Stage of Capitalism* (New York: International Publishers, 1939).

16. Hilferding noted, "Capitalism itself gradually provides the conquered with the means and ways for their liberation." Rudolf Hilferding, *Das Finanzkapital* (Berlin: J.H.W. Dietz, 1947), 406.

17. John Hans Paasche, *The Colonial Question in Bolshevik Revolutionary Strategy: Soviet Russia's International Congresses, 1919 to 1929* (San Francisco: Paasche, 1951, 1990), 13.

18. Derek Heater, *National Self-Determination: Woodrow Wilson and His Legacy* (New York: St. Martin's Press, 1994), 75-76.

19. U Thant's Press Conference at Dakar, Senegal, January 4, 1970. Reprinted in *UN Monthly Chronicle*, vol. 7 (Feb. 1970), 36.

20. Garry Davis, "'The U.N. Can Do Nothing!' Admits Secretary-General Boutros-Ghali," *World Citizen News,* Vol. IX, No. 4 (August/September 1995): 1.

21. Jeffrey Simpson, "Quebec's Secessionists Are Dramatically at Odds with Public Opinion," *The Globe and Mail,* August 26, 1995. He referred to a CROP

poll of March, 1995 and to a poll conducted in August 1995 for *Le Soleil* and the *Montreal Gazette*.

22. Friedrich Nietzsche, "Genealogy of Morals," in *The Philosophy of Nietzsche* (New York: The Modern Library, 1927), 627-809; and Max Scheler, *Ressentiment* (Glencoe, Ill.: The Free Press, 1961).

23. Liah Greenfeld, *Nationalism: Five Roads to Modernity* (Cambridge, Mass.: Harvard University Press, 1992), 15.

24. Here "war" is defined by the compilers of the database as a political conflict in which armed fighting between state military forces — or between one state and its opponents or inhabitants — has led to at least 1,000 deaths during the course of that conflict. See "Introduction," Project Ploughshares, *Armed Conflicts Report 1997* (Waterloo, Ontario: Institute of Peace and Conflict Studies, 1997), or see http://watserv1.uwaterloo.ca/~plough/.

25. This term must be used with caution. For example, it may not always be appropriate to call the conflicts in Algeria and Afghanistan "ethnic." I do so here because one side consisted of traditional Muslims, though their adversaries were not another ascribed community but rather a secular political group.

26. These were Afghanistan, Algeria, Azerbaijan, Bosnia-Herzegovina, Burma, Burundi, Congo, Croatia, Georgia, Ghana, India, Indonesia (East Timor), Iran, Iraq, Israel, Kenya, Lebanon, Northern Ireland, the Philippines, Russia (Chechnya), Rwanda, Somalia, South Africa, Sri Lanka, Sudan, Tajikistan, Turkey, Yemen, and Zaire.

27. By "nationalism" I mean the claim of an ascribed community for independent statehood or for hegemony over rival ascribed communities.

28. These were Afghanistan, Algeria, Angola, Burma, Burundi, Cambodia, Chad, Colombia, Congo, Georgia (at least with respect to Gamsakhurdia's faction), Ghana, Guatemala, Haiti, India, Indonesia, Iran (the Mujahideen rebels), Iraq (the Shia group in the South), Lebanon, Liberia, Peru, the Philippines, Russia (the Russian-sponsored opponents to Dudayev in Chechnya), Rwanda, Sierra Leone, Somalia, South Africa, Tajikistan, and Zaire.

29. These were Azerbaijan (by Armenians in Nagorno-Karabakh); Bosnia-Herzegovina (by Serbs and — at least until the spring of 1994 — Croats); Burma (by tribal groups); Croatia (by Serbs in Krajina); Georgia (by Ossetians and Abkhazians); India (in Kashmir mainly by Muslims, in Assam, Manipur, and Nagaland by tribal groups, in the Punjab by Sikh militants, and in Uttar Pradesh between rioting Hindus and Muslims); Indonesia (to reverse the annexation of East Timor); Iran (by Kurds); Iraq (by Kurds in the North); Israel (by Palestinians); in Northern Ireland (by Catholics seeking a united Ireland); in Papua New Guinea (by Bougainvilleans); the Philippines (by Muslim secessionists); Russia (by Chechens); Somalia (by secessionists demanding a separate Somaliland); Sri Lanka (by Tamils); Sudan (by separatists in the South fighting each other as well as the government); Turkey (by Kurds); and Yemen (by those seeking to reverse a merger).

30. Bougainville's valuable copper mine brings material considerations into the independence movement. The so-called racial factors in Bougainville's secessionist movement do exist but are perhaps less important than labor and class-related disputes.

31. A better question would be: Of all secessionist movements, what percentage result in warfare? Unfortunately, such an inquiry requires that we list all secessionist movements that are active within a specified period. This effort is fraught with too many methodological difficulties for purposes such as ours. In any case, the majority of secessionist movements eventually dissipate without accomplishing their goals or gaining much attention.

32. This is Robert K. Schaeffer's estimate.

33. The Tibetans and the East Timorese evidently are especially justified in demanding independence, for each group was forcibly annexed by another country. The Tibetans barely resisted the Chinese invaders, and up to one-third of the East Timorese population died of combat, disease, and starvation after Indonesian troops invaded in 1975.

34. Robert K. Schaeffer, *Warpaths: The Politics of Partition* (New York: Hill and Wang, 1990).

35. The British generally believed in the policy of devolution in their colonies, and the world wars stepped up the pace of that process. See Schaeffer, *Warpaths,* 97.

36. David Crystal, ed., *The Cambridge Factfinder* (Cambridge: Cambridge University Press, 1993). By my calculations (data from pp. 256 and 296) India's estimated Muslim population in 1992 was nearly 98 million and Pakistan's Muslims numbered about 114 million.

37. Crystal, *The Cambridge Factfinder,* 260, 337. About 28 percent of the Northern Ireland population is Catholic, while about 5 percent of the citizens of the Irish Republic are Protestant.

38. See interview with Schaeffer, "Secession and Its Outcomes: A Conversation with Robert Schaeffer That Quebecers Should Read," in *Peace Magazine,* May/June 1995, 12-15.

39. Schaeffer, *Warpaths,* 172-78.

40. Aspiring regional superpowers can be drawn into such conflicts, as India did by intervening in Sri Lanka's secessionist civil war, arguing that Sri Lanka should not undermine India's security. See S. W. R. de A. Samarasinghe, "The Dynamics of Separatism: The Case of Sri Lanka," in Ralph R. Premdas, S. W. R. de A. Samarasinghe, and Alan B. Anderson, *Secessionist Movements in Comparative Perspective* (London: Pinter, 1990), 57.

41. Schaeffer, interview in *Peace Magazine,* 13-14.

42. Raymond L. Garthoff, *The Great Transition: American Soviet Relations and the End of the Cold War* (Washington, D.C.: The Brookings Institution, 1994), 455.

43. Croatian, Slovenian and Croatian Serb referenda were held before 1991, in fact, *contributing* to the breakup of the federal order.

44. Regarding the questionable legitimacy of these plebiscites, see Misha Glenny, *The Fall of Yugoslavia: The Third Balkan War* (London: Penguin, 1992), 162-64.

45. See Edward Walker's analysis of the Tatarstan compromise in this volume.

46. Fred Weir, *Covert Action Quarterly,* Summer 1993.

47. Suzanne Crow, Radio Free Europe/Radio Liberty, Inc., *Daily Report,* No. 210, 2 November 1993.

48. Exceptions from the rule here are Czechoslovakia and Sweden-Norway.

49. Olga Medvedkov, *Soviet Urbanization* (London: Routledge, 1990).

50. Weir, *Covert Action Quarterly.*

51. This was Abraham Lincoln's observation in his first inaugural address.

52. Mary Waters, *Ethnic Options* (Berkeley: University of California Press, 1990).

53. Rosalyn Higgins, *Problems and Process: International Law and How We Use It* (Oxford: Clarendon Press, 1994), esp. 111- 128.

54. F. A. Cassese, *Self-Determination of Peoples: A Legal Reappraisal* (1993), 34-42.

55. The Greek population of dependent Cyprus considered integration with Greece as a possibility; the peoples of Gibraltar have decided to retain their stable arrangement with the United Kingdom; and the peoples of Puerto Rico have chosen a form of association with the United States that lies between statehood and independence.

56. Higgins, *Problems and Process*, 117.

57. Higgins, *Problems and Process*, 121, cites General Assembly Resolution 1514 (XV) and the Declaration of Principles on Friendly Relations.

58. Higgins, *Problems and Process*, 123.

59. Higgins, *Problems and Process*, 124.

60. Higgins, *Problems and Process*, 126-27. This seems to be the majority view.

61. Lea Brilmayer, "Secession and Self-Determination: A Territorial Interpretation," *Yale Journal of International Law* Vol. 16 (1991): 177-200.

62. Of course, *all* the citizens of China should have the right of self-determination — representative government and the opportunity to determine their own future.

63. Brilmayer, "Secession and Self-Determination," 198-99.

64. This generalization does not describe multiparty elections in which no party receives a majority but one party wins a "plurality" of votes. Our point is only that some groups may always find themselves losing.

65. Before that, Latvia and Estonia had belonged to Imperial Russia — and "legally" so, in that possession of territory gained by conquest was not then considered a violation of international law.

66. 1995 International Campaign for Tibet. Only a small fraction of the Chinese migrants to Tibet are registered or counted in official records.

67. See Petra Kelly, Gert Bastian, and Pat Aiello, eds., *The Anguish of Tibet* (Berkeley, Calif.: Parallax Press, 1991). The first three points of this proposal call for Tibet to be a zone of peace, for China to end its population transfer policy, and for the Tibetan people's rights and freedoms to be respected. A fourth point advocates the "restoration and protection of Tibet's natural environment and the abandonment of China's use of Tibet for the production of nuclear weapons and the dumping of nuclear waste." The fifth point, rather than advocating independence, urges the commencement of "earnest negotiations on the future status of Tibet and of relations between the Tibetan and Chinese people." The Dalai Lama's proposal differs from conventional full-sovereign status,

which would seem threatening to China, in that Tibet would be able to form its own army. The five-point peace plan, on the other hand, urges that Tibet be a democratic enclave within China. Its borders would be demilitarized to "satisfy China's legitimate security needs and build trust among the Tibetan, Indian, Chinese, and other people of the region."

68. Estonian citizenship laws are in flux, largely because of complaints from the West that the restrictive first laws violate human rights.

69. Estonians and Latvians still constitute a strong majority in their new states, though in patchy areas they are a minority.

70. Separatists claim to oppose "ethnic nationalism" while favoring instead "civic nationalism." Still, nonfrancophone immigrants to Quebec generally regard this "civic nationalism" as antagonistic to those who prefer English or oppose secession.

71. Robert O. Matthews, Arthur G. Rubinoff, and Janice Gross Stein, eds. *International Conflict and Conflict Management*, 2d ed. (Scarborough, Ontario: Prentice-Hall, 1989), 91.

72. William Pfaff, *The Wrath of Nations: Civilization and the Furies of Nationalism* (New York: Simon and Schuster, 1993), 85.

73. William H. McNeill, *Polyethnicity and National Unity in World History* (Toronto: University of Toronto Press, 1985).

74. Wolfram Eberhard, "Concerns of Historical Sociology," in *Sociologus* (Berlin) Vol. 14, No. 1, 1964, 3. Reprinted in Reinhard Bendix, ed., *State and Society: A Reader in Comparative Political Sociology* (Boston: Little, Brown, 1968).

75. Eberhard, "Concerns of Historical Sociology," 6-10.

76. Stanford Shaw, *History of the Ottoman Empire and Modern Turkey*, Vol. 1 (Cambridge: Cambridge University Press, 1976), 151; Pfaff, 99-103.

77. Eberhard, "Concerns of Historical Sociology", 9.

78. Shaw, *History of the Ottoman Empire*, 151-53; Arnold Toynbee and Kenneth Kirkwood, *Turkey* (London: Ernest Benn Ltd., 1926), 29.

79. Pfaff, *The Wrath of Nations*, 92-93.

80. Pfaff, *The Wrath of Nations*, 103.

81. Chantal Mouffe, ed., *Dimensions of Radical Democracy: Pluralism, Citizenship, Community* (London: Verso, 1992).

82. Karl Renner was the author of this plan. See John Bacher's chapter on Austria-Hungary in this volume.

83. David J. Elkins, *Beyond Sovereignty: Territory and Political Economy in the Twenty-First Century* (Toronto: University of Toronto Press, 1995).

84. Jean-Marie Guéhenno, *The End of the Nation-State*, trans. Victoria Elliott (Minneapolis: University of Minnesota Press, 1995), 8.

85. Elkins, *Beyond Sovereignty*, 25.

Two

Separatism: Rationality and Irony

Robert K. Schaeffer

After decades of failure, separatist movements in 1991-1992 achieved remarkable success, creating nearly two dozen new states, "republics" all, in just over a year. This stunning development revived long-dormant movements and triggered the formation of new ones around the world, in peripheral and metropolitan countries alike.

The simultaneous emergence of so many separatist movements indicates that it is not the coincidental expression of movements with separate origins, but a collective response to systemic problems and opportunities.

It is difficult to determine just how widespread separatist movements have become. In *Minorities at Risk,* Ted Robert Gurr reports that there are 233 "politically active communal groups," which number "some 900 million people, about one-sixth of the world's population."[1]

The universe for potential separatist movements is larger still. Gunnar Nielsson and Ralph Jones identify 575 ethnic groups as actual or potential nations, while "the geographer Bernard Nietschmann estimates that there are between three and five thousand 'nations' in the world, defined as ethnic communities whose shared identity is based on a common ancestry, institutions, beliefs, language and territory."[2] Separatist movements share the same "entelechy" or goal: They demand power in independent states.[3]

The people and lands of the world already having been assigned to existing states, such a movement can reach its objective only if an existing state is partitioned and part of its territory assigned to separatists. A social movement's pursuit of state power by the partition of nation-states is a modern, legitimate, and rational goal. Nevertheless, such an objective has serious consequences for divided states and for the interstate system as a whole.

Separatism: Modern, Legitimate, and Rational

Although separatism has a problematic character, the demand for power in an independent state is a modern, legitimate, and rational goal.[4] It is "modern" because social movements have identified state power as a goal only since the late nineteenth century. It is "legitimate" because the United States and Soviet Union, the superpower states that assembled the contemporary interstate system after World War II, promoted "self-determination" as a "right." It is "rational" because the interstate system provides real rewards to movements that obtain state power, whether they acquire power peacefully or violently.

State Power: A Modern Goal for Modern Movements

In 1876, the socialist movement based in Europe split into two factions, one led by the anarchist Mikhail Bakunin and the other led by the communist Karl Marx. The movement was known as the "First International" because its dissolution in 1876 led to the creation of a "Second" Socialist International a few years later and to a "Third" Communist International during World War I. The movement split initially because its members could not agree on a common political objective. Bakunin argued that the movement should destroy the institutions of state authority, while Marx maintained that state institutions should be seized by workers, not destroyed. In the years that followed, the socialist movement adopted Marx's position and adopted as its goal the seizure of state power.

This was a novel idea for the nineteenth century. Working-class movements generally pursued different goals: the right to vote, a shorter working day, union recognition, higher wages. The socialists' goal of winning state power influenced other movements in overseas colonies and in Europe among the nationalist movements, both republican and fascist. Movements in Asia, Africa, and the Middle East soon aspired to seize state power and win their "independence" from colonial empires. During the twentieth century this idea spread but did not become ubiquitous; other social movements emerged with other goals, such as securing civil rights for minority populations, providing economic and political opportunity for women, and conserving the environment.

Contemporary separatists argue, as did their socialist predecessors, that the state is the only institution that can effect real change. One may question this position, in view of the difficulties that socialist movements have encountered in using state power to revolutionize social and economic relations. Still, it is a "modern" assumption, a product of nineteenth century political debates.

Moreover, such a struggle was waged by modern methods, using political parties, electoral candidates, and soldiers. Delegates came together at party "congresses" to debate political issues and develop strategies. These democratic forms of behavior set separatist campaigns apart from spontaneous insurrectionary movements or secret societies. Their institutional coherence and durability allowed them to continue seeking power long after their founders had died. The development of permanent political organizations was a modern innovation, born of the need to accumulate enough money, experience, and legitimacy to contest for power against obdurate opponents. Moreover, as we shall see, separatists acquired considerable legitimacy from the contemporary interstate system, which was created after World War II by the United States and Soviet Union. Both superpowers promoted self-determination and designed an interstate system based on nation-state republics.

The Interstate System: The Legitimacy of Self-Determination

The interstate system consisting of multiple "states" has existed since the treaty of Westphalia in 1648. However, until 1945 it was politically heterogeneous, with states assuming very different political forms; some were ruled by absolutist or constitutional monarchies, with overseas colonies forming complex empires. Other states were ruled by military dictators, warlords, or tribal authorities. Certain "republics" were governed by democratically elected representatives functioning as parliaments and presidents. European empires dominated this system, which was fraught with conflict, both between European empires and colonial independence movements and between empires and republican states. In the twentieth century the "imperialist" interstate system waged two world wars. The problems associated with global conflicts led, in 1945, to the creation of a more homogeneous "republican" interstate system.

During the first of these world wars, both American and Soviet leaders began to push for a new interstate system that would consist of nation-state republics. Woodrow Wilson and Vladimir Lenin, each for his own reasons, argued that people in colonies should have the right of self-determination: the ability to choose the form that their own government should take. Both Wilson and Lenin assumed that, if given a chance, people would choose republican forms of government and that these governments would secede from empire. Strong U.S. and Soviet attempts to promote self-determination and create a new republican interstate system foundered after World War I. However, during World War II, independence movements emerged everywhere, old empires collapsed, and the two new superpowers were able create a new interstate system based on nation-state republics.

At a series of summit meetings in Tehran, Cairo, Yalta, and Potsdam, the United States and Soviet Union promised to extend self-determination, republican government, and democracy to people around the world. To consolidate this, they insisted on the breakup of empires, "decolonization," and the creation of independent nation-states. These developments lent legitimacy to demands for "self-determination," but the promise was never fully realized.

Decolonization homogenized the interstate system and increased the number of nation-states from about 50 in 1945, to 100 by 1960, and to 150 by 1990. Significantly, almost all the new states created by the decolonization process identified themselves as "republics," though communist governments qualified this term with adjectives like "Democratic" or "People's," capitalist governments used the phrase "Republic of...", and Muslim governments used the modifier "Islamic" to distinguish their "republic" from other republics.

The newly homogeneous system of republics was not created without problems. Some people were allowed to choose or create states of their own, but others were assigned to states by decolonization, partition, annexation, invasion, or treaty, often without their consent. The new republican institutions in Africa, for example, were not always appropriate because they did not incorporate "traditional" authorities that possessed greater legitimacy. Korea, China, Vietnam, and Germany were divided by the United States and Soviet Union, India by Great Britain, and Palestine by the United Nations — all with long-lasting problematic consequences. In these countries, great power partition produced social dislocations, contributed to the derogation of citizenship for minority populations, and infringed the sovereignty of neighboring, sibling states, which led to domestic conflict and interstate war. Other countries were annexed during and after the war: the Baltics by the Soviet Union, Tibet by China, Irian Jaya and later East Timor by Indonesia, and Kashmir by India. Thus new republics sought to "build" their nations by annexing or invading neighboring territories, frequently compelling subject populations to adopt the social, religious, and linguistic norms of dominant majorities. Under these circumstances, many people fled from or revolted against states they did not meaningfully choose. Finally, certain states were assigned to superpower spheres of influence by summit treaties — Greece, for example, to the U.S. sphere and Poland to the Soviet sphere.

Although the United States and Soviet Union together established the new interstate system, they disagreed about some of its particulars, such as the political and economic character of the new republics, the role of foreign investment and markets, and the form that ownership should take in their economies, particularly in Germany and Korea. These disputes constituted the "Cold War."

Though the United States and Soviet Union continued to talk about self-determination as a right, they were reluctant to let people or movements around the world exercise that right. Wilson and Lenin had used self-determination as a way to attack colonial empires, and their successors in the United States and Soviet Union understood self-determination as the right of colonies to *secede from empire*. Once decolonization had established independent nation-states, the right of self-determination was presumed no longer to apply. Moreover, having created independent republics and incorporated or enlisted them into Cold War spheres of influence, they did not want to see the legitimacy of these allied states challenged by internal social movements demanding states of their own.

Yet separatist movements refused to limit their aspirations, as the superpowers expected. This is hardly surprising, for separatism is a rational endeavor; groups that manage to acquire state power can reap real political and economic rewards.

State Power: Real Rewards

Once a group acquires state power, it may be disappointed to discover how greatly states are constrained by the interstate system and the world economy. Though they may print their own currency, for example, they will find that macroeconomic forces set its rate of exchange. Still, they enjoy rights that movements without power lack. Since the seventeenth century, even weak states have been able to levy taxes and raise armies. They have powerful tools to distribute and defend economic wealth and political power. They can participate in global political, economic, and cultural forums. They can vote in the United Nations, borrow money from the World Bank, and field athletes in the Olympic games. They can join global organizations to defend themselves from external aggression, promote economic development, and extend their own political legitimacy with domestic populations.

Dictators and revolutionaries commonly win these benefits by using force to obtain power. The post-Westphalia system is based on the "sovereignty" of constituent states. Rulers can slaughter domestic civilian populations so long as they do not harm foreign citizens or invade their neighbors. Besides, powerful states have often used force to achieve republican ends, as in the cases of both the United States and the Soviet Union, where violent insurrections and domestic civil wars were the means of achieving state power. Both countries annexed adjacent territories, sometimes by purchase, sometimes as a result of rebellion or coup.[5] As a result, leaders in both countries have long regarded revolution and civil war as "normal" political processes.

Separatist movements also appeared in European states, a product of an indigenous process — the transition from imperial to republican states after the war, a relatively neglected process that might be called "de-imperialization" — and a product of exogenous developments in the colonies. Separatism in the metropoles was inspired, in part, by separatists in the periphery. As Donald Horowitz has noted, "The independence of Asia and Africa was being felt in Europe and America. The grant of independence to the former Belgian territories in Africa (Zaire, Rwanda, and Burundi) helped stimulate the ethnic movement of Flemings in Belgium itself. If, they said, tiny Burundi can have an autonomous political life, why should we be deprived of the same privilege? . . . In Canada, some French-speaking Quebecers also cited African independence as a precedent for their own."[6]

Latin America was one region where separatism did not emerge in this period, perhaps because social groups in Latin America resided in republics that dated back to the mid-nineteenth century and because a common language

(Spanish or Portuguese) and religion (Catholicism) was widely shared by different ethnic groups of American, African, and European descent.

Historically there have been two generations of separatist movements. First-generation movements were stimulated after World War II by the wave of decolonization. Second-generation movements emerged in response to processes associated with democratization in the 1980s. We shall consider them separately for, though they share common goals, they differ in important ways.

Two Generations of Separatism

Decolonization and First-Generation Separatists

Postwar decolonization created new, independent republics in Asia, Africa, Europe, and the Middle East. However, the people in former colonies were often assigned to states not of their own making and deprived of power and economic opportunity. These disadvantages stimulated separatist movements throughout the decolonizing world, particularly in states that had been in the British empire.

In British South Asia, Karens emerged in Burma, Tamils in Sri Lanka, Kashmiris and Sikhs in India, and Bengalis in Pakistan. In the Middle East, where the British obtained Ottoman territories after World War I, Kurds emerged in Iraq, Iran, Syria, and Turkey; and Jews and Arabs emerged in Palestine. In the Horn of Africa, where Britain controlled the Sudan and obtained parts of Ethiopia and Somalia from the Italian empire in World War II, animist Sudanese emerged in Sudan and Muslim Eritreans in Ethiopia. In West Africa, Biafrans emerged in Nigeria. In North America, French-speaking Québécois emerged in Canada.

Outside the British zones, Katangans emerged in the (Belgian) Congo; Moros in the (U.S.) Philippines; Irianese in (Dutch) Indonesia; Bouganvillians in (Australian) Papua New Guinea; Kanaks in (French) New Caledonia; and Formosans in (Japanese) Taiwan. However, the proliferation of movements in former British colonies and territories can be attributed to several British practices: its divide-and-rule-ethnic policies, which arranged ethnic groups in complex social and administrative hierarchies within the empire; its hasty and often ill-conceived "deadline" decolonization process; and the insecurity of independence movements that assumed power in its postcolonial states.[7]

Decolonization brought a spate of first-generation separatist movements that organized along ethnic-religious lines. They created inter-class alliances that could contest for political power. In historical, legal, and moral terms, separatist demands for states of their own often had considerable merit. Kurdish claims to a separate state, based on promises made in the Treaty of Sèvres in 1920, had as much historical-legal merit as Jewish claims for a state in Palestine based on the "second" Balfour declaration in 1917 (Balfour "first" promised self-government to Indians in August 1917, and then promised a "national homeland for the Jewish people" in November of that year).[8] Despite the merit of their historical claims, first-generation separatists were defeated or marginalized by the rulers of the new republics. Katangans and Biafrans were crushed, while Karens, Eritreans, Moros, and Kurds fought on in obscurity and isolation.

First-generation separatists received little sympathy or assistance from postimperial European states or the superpowers, which saw them as threats to the stability of states then being enlisted in Cold War blocs. This is why, for example, U.S. officials turned a blind eye toward Indonesia's annexation of Irian Jaya and later East Timor. Second, they believed that once decolonization had occurred, self-determination, which recognized the right of colonial nations to secede from empire, no longer applied. They worried that separatism would enhance the credibility of separatist demands within their own multiethnic states.[9]

For all these reasons, first-generation separatists failed to achieve their goals prior to 1990 — with one exception. After a bloody civil war in 1971, the Awami League managed to separate Bengal from Pakistan and create Bangladesh. Several unusual developments contributed to Bengali success. Most separatists are based in minority ethnic communities, but the Awami League represented a majority of the population, not just in Bengal but in the country as a whole. Prior to the civil war it had won a majority in Pakistan-wide parliamentary elections. And after civil war broke out, the Bengalis received crucial military assistance from India and diplomatic support from the Soviet Union, at a time when the United States (which opposed Bengali separatism) was preoccupied with the Vietnam War. Such favorable circumstances, which made it possible for separatism to succeed, were not reproduced elsewhere. Despite the failure of most first-generation separatists, they did not disappear. After 1990, their persistence would pay off. Democratization and the ending of the Cold War would create new political opportunities.

Although some first-generation movements labored in obscurity for decades, they survived on the financial and political support from émigré communities and neighboring states, which often provided refuge for movement cadre. Émigré communities lobbied foreign governments for support and sometimes supplied arms or supplies to movements "back home." Neighboring states often saw in the separatists a possibility of territorial gain. Thus Pakistan has assisted Kashmiri separatists on the hope that, if Kashmir were detached from India, it might well unite with Pakistan. Sometimes the motive is only to discomfit the unfriendly neighbor. For example, Turkey, Iraq, Syria, and Iran have all used Kurds to make trouble for nearby states. Finally, some states help neighboring separatists to protect certain ethnic populations. For example, India, with a large Tamil population, first intervened in Sri Lanka on behalf of Tamils, though Indian troops later tried to destroy the separatist movement.

After the Cold War there were new opportunities for some separatists, such as the Eritreans, who had been fighting monarchist and then communist governments in Ethiopia since 1962. In the changed conditions of 1991, Eritreans defeated Ethiopia's army and captured its capital, Addis Ababa. Although its achievement was overshadowed by simultaneous events in the Baltics, the Eritrean victory was only the second real success for first-generation separatists.

Democratization and Second-Generation Separatists

Problems associated with decolonization had contributed to the emergence of first-generation separatists in the 1950s and 1960s. In the 1980s and 1990s, democratization produced a second generation of separatists. Both generations achieved success simultaneously, with the victories of Eritrean and Baltic movements in 1991, as a result of the same historical conjuncture: democratization in the Soviet Union and the end of the Cold War.[10] First-generation movements revived and second-generation movements around the world proliferated.

Democratization put an end to many of the dictatorships and one-party states that had kept separatist movements marginalized. Democratization in the Soviet Union under Mikhail Gorbachev allowed separatist movements to form in the Baltics. In the crisis following the attempted 1991 coup, the Baltics, and then other republics, were able to break away from moribund Soviet power. Soviet stopped supporting Third World countries such as Ethiopia, which gave a victory to Eritrean separatist armies.

The simultaneous success of first-generation (Eritrean) and second-generation (Baltic) separatists encouraged wide emulation because it demonstrated that the separatist project was not just modern, legitimate, and rational but also "realistic." Separatist movements have since proliferated so rapidly that recent books classifying them and charting their progress are already dated.[11]

Despite sharing a common objective, contemporary separatists have different social origins, reflecting the milieu in which they emerged. First-generation separatists, as products of decolonization, typically adopted "socialist" orientations, organizing themselves into "national liberation movements" and describing themselves as fighting the "imperialism" of a particular nation-state, an approach consistent with the anticolonial movements of the era.

By contrast, most second-generation movements eschew socialism and adopt free-market capitalist ideologies. This reflects the orientation of other movements that emerged as a result of democratization in Latin America, East Asia, the Soviet Union and Eastern Europe, and South Africa. Second generation separatists, like civilian democrats elsewhere, privatize their economies and open them to foreign investment and trade.[12]

Four Ironies

Many separatist movements around the world share common ideas and identities. I want to explore four important aspects of those contemporary identities, which seem to be somewhat self-contradictory or ironical. First, separatist movements are part of a global movement that is organizationally disconnected, resulting in an ostensible contradiction that I shall call *autonomous internation-*

alism. Second, separatist movements organize local constituencies in their "homeland" but also in diaspora and émigré communities in "foreign" countries — a pattern that I have elsewhere described as a *cosmopolitan parochial* orientation. Third, movements represent ethnic minorities who seek to rule as political majorities while nevertheless retaining their identity as ethnic minorities — a contradiction that I call a *majoritarian minority* identity. And fourth, movements seek states in which they can exercise sovereign power — yet they concede sovereignty on economic issues to other states and the world economy, resulting in what I describe as *dependent sovereignty.*

The contradictory ideas and identities of separatist movements represent their responses to the problems and promises of the postwar interstate system. As we have seen, the separatist project is both rational and legitimate. Yet these contradictions create problems for separatist movements, proximate social groups, individual states, and the interstate system, and so they should be also regarded as "antinomies" — paradoxes between equally defensible principles.

Because each facet of their political and social character is contradictory, being both understandable and problematic, it is perhaps useful to think of these movements much as Tom Nairn did when he referred to nationalism as "Janus-faced." Separatist movements have several social and political "faces," each with two sides, and they all express historically rooted antinomies.

Autonomous Internationalism

Contemporary separatist movements emerged in response to problems and promises of the republican interstate system and its constituent states. They share common experiences — involuntary incorporation and discriminatory government policies — and adopt a common goal: securing states where they can exercise power on behalf of their ethnic constituencies. But while movements around the world have adopted the separatist aspiration, some acquiring states of their own in recent years, separatist movements are organizationally disconnected. Although some Western European movements met together in a series of conferences in the mid-1970s, they made no alliances with separatist movements in postcolonial or communist states and failed to leave any institutional legacy.[13]

The absence of a collective, international separatist organization, an "international" like those developed by socialist movements and communist parties or by women's, human rights, and environmental movements in recent years, is curious and striking. Instead, separatist movements eschew political relations or tactical cooperation with other separatist movements. The development of what I would call the "autonomous internationalism" of separatist movements, movements that belong to a global social movement but that operate independently of one another, is the product of several developments in the postwar world.

First, movements that have much in common have not developed a "separatist international" because the United States and other great powers have long been hostile to the collective internationalisms of peripheral peoples and oppositional movements. U.S. leaders, for example, demanded that the Soviet Union dissolve the Communist International, which they regarded as inconsistent with the principle of nonintervention and the sovereignty of states that belonged to the new interstate system, before it would be admitted to the United Nations.[14]

Although the great powers themselves created economic and military alliances or "internationals" — the Common Market, NATO, Warsaw Pact — in the postwar period, they viewed the development of peripheral "internationals" — the movement of nonaligned nations that first met in Bandung, Indonesia, in 1956, pan-African and pan-Arabic movements, OPEC and the coffee cartel, and more recently pan-Islamic movements — with hostility, and they worked to undermine their power and appeal.

Because separatist movements need great powers to recognize their independence and admit them to the United Nations, if and when they manage to obtain state power, they are reluctant to antagonize metropolitan states by confronting them with an "international" organization that threatens to unite separatist movements determined to divide republics around the world, a development that might dissolve the interstate system itself. Instead, separatists argue that their demand for a separate state is a special case that need not apply elsewhere. Successful movements, like the Estonians', refuse to assist other movements and deny that they have anything in common with them.

Separatist movements also act autonomously because they are attempting to claim the right of self-determination, an ideological cornerstone of the republican interstate system. Although its application to ethnic minorities within nation-state republics is the subject of dispute, movements attempting to exercise self-determination may do so only for themselves. They cannot legitimately do so on behalf of others. This means, for example, that while representatives of the independence movement in Lithuania may ask the United Nations to recognize its demand for self-determination, a claim based on international law and UN convention, they may not do so on behalf of people in Eritrea or Quebec. To do so would be to interfere with either the self-determination of other peoples or the sovereignty of other states. Because they want to be accepted as members of the interstate system, they are compelled to comply with its rules, which mitigate against "collective" self-determination or peripheral internationalism.

As a result, separatist movements work assiduously to differentiate themselves from other social groups so that they may legitimately claim states for their "nation." They do this by tracing separate histories, reviving cultural traditions, defending their language and observing religions that distinguish them from "co-residential" groups, groups with whom they share the same political space. Although the social identities that emerge from this differentiation process are "invented," to use Hobsbawm's term, or "imagined," to use Anderson's, they need not be "new," but only different.[15]

And the more pronounced the observable historical, social, and political differences, the greater the social distance between separatist minority and co-residential majority, the stronger the separatist claim for self-determination. Distinctive social identity and social distance from proximate social groups will not alone suffice, but it is a necessary component of any compelling claim.

Of course, the fact remains that separatist movements are part of a global collectivity. And they can act collectively even without developing organizational ties or common institutions. They development of global media, which effectively conveys the identities and ideas of separatist movements around the world, makes it possible for separatist movements to emulate others or even to act in concert without ever meeting face to face. When Robert Van Tonder, a white South African who believed that the "sacrificial partition" of that country was necessary to create an all-Boer state, argued that his movement's quest "corresponds exactly" with the demand of Baltic separatists, or when Puerto Rico's governor Raphael Hernandez Colón criticized the Bush administration's handling of a referendum on the country's political status, likening it to "the way President Gorbachev is handling the Baltic crisis," it was apparent that the media's dissemination of information about separatist movements in one country enabled movements in distant countries to link their movements and join in common purpose with others, even if only for rhetorical purposes.[16]

The media itself encourages the development of a collective, global separatist identity. In an article on the efforts of Staten Island residents to secede from New York City, *New York Times* reporter Chip Brown linked distant and even incongruous separatisms (Staten Islanders do not want to secede from the United States), writing, "The fires of secession burn among proud, resentful Staten Islanders, just as they do among Azerbaijanis, Kurds, Québécois — and Californians."[17]

To some extent, borrowing from Benedict Anderson, the media enables movements to imagine themselves collectively as a community of oppressed minorities, even though they will never meet face to face.

In this context, the development of autonomous internationalism is a reasonable response by separatist movements to both the constraints of the interstate system's ideology and practices and to political opportunities provided by a global media. But it can also lead to problems with members of the interstate system and with proximate social groups.

Although separatist movements deny any association with other movements, separatism is a global phenomenon with widespread appeal that is readily copied by minority groups in different settings. As a result, states that are members of the interstate system, even former separatists that successfully acquired states of their own, view separatist demands with some hostility.

The republican interstate system was designed to accommodate changes that would increase the number of constituent states.[18] But governments recognize that this process has been a difficult, often violent process — the product of two world wars, decolonization, partition and annexation — and they regard the prospect of greatly increasing the number of states as destabilizing. And because "fewer than 20 [of the system's constituent states] are themselves ethnically homogeneous, in the sense that minorities account for less than five percent of the population," governments fear that the spread of separatist ideas among indigenous minorities could undermine their own legitimacy.[19]

This view was recently expressed by Spain's Prime Minister Filipe Gonzalez, who asked, "How far does self-determination go? Is self-determination up to the Lithuanians only, or is it also up to the Russians who live in Lithuania? Or the Poles who live in Lithuania? Where do we draw the line?" He went on to say that separatism raised issues not just for individual states but for the interstate system as a whole: "I believe self-determination as a principle ought to be a matter that is only agreed to and regulated internationally. Otherwise it will be an extremely dangerous situation for Europe, because there will be no end to splintering. Prudently [we should] not look at Europe as if it were a jigsaw puzzle where the pieces can be shuffled at will."[20]

Separatist movements differentiate themselves from proximate social groups so that they can sharpen their national identity and strengthen their case for self-determination. But this differentiation process may create hostility among proximate social groups who view this process as invidious. Although the separatist attempt to differentiate themselves is typically a response to involuntary incorporations and discriminatory government practices on behalf of ethnic majorities, it may create hostility among groups that did not previously exist in an organized form.

In Canada, for example, the rise of a separatist movement in Quebec was viewed with hostility by government officials but with equanimity by most Canadians for many years. But during the last decade, as Quebec separatists assumed power in the provincial assembly, adopted language and education laws designed to differentiate French-speaking Québécois from the rest of Canada, and pressed for constitutional recognition of Quebec's "distinct society" through the Meech Lake Accord, a variety of proximate social groups emerged to protest a differentiation process they regarded as invidious: English-speaking Canadians in other provinces announced their opposition to further "concessions" to Québécois separatists; the English-speaking Jewish minority in Montreal organized the "Equality Party" in 1988 as an expression of their opposition to Québécois language and education laws; English-speaking residents of Quebec in the early 1990s organized "Option Canada," a group demanding the secession of English-speaking areas of the province if Quebec secedes from Canada; recent French-speaking immigrants from other countries (Haiti, Vietnam, francophone Africa) asked that their children be sent to English-speaking schools in the province (they cannot unless the parents speak English); and Cree and Mohawk Indian tribes, some of whom live in territories that were not part of the "original" province of Quebec but which were subsequently added by the

Canadian government, opposed the demands of Québécois separatists as those of a "privileged" white group that would disadvantage them. The emergence of organized opposition to Québécois separatists by a variety of proximate social groups is a recent phenomenon, a product of the differentiation process initiated by Québécois separatists. "I feel uncomfortable with a nationalism that is anti-individual right, anti-minority. The Québécois want their own nation, fine, but don't put me down at the same time," argued Tony Kondaks, chief of staff of the Equality Party.[21]

Cosmopolitan Parochialism

Like the independence movements that emerged in European colonies at the beginning of this century (movements that did organize formal and informal "internationals"), separatist movements demand self-determination and power in sovereign states, which are cosmopolitan ideas that originated in Europe, but do so on behalf of an exclusive group defined in ethnic, religious, and linguistic terms, an orientation that is consciously parochial. The simultaneously cosmopolitan and parochial orientation of separatist movements particularly, and nationalist movements generally, stems from their recognition of two organizational necessities. First, they understand that they can secure power in states of their own only if members of the interstate system recognize the sovereignty of states that movements have acquired. In this context, movements learn the language of power in the interstate system, a language in which cosmopolitan ideas like self-determination and sovereignty are central words in the vocabulary.[22]

In practical terms, separatist movements have to lobby for state power in the capitals of great power states. In Washington, D.C., for example, many separatist movements staff offices, "embassies-in-waiting," along K Street so they can lobby for and negotiate on behalf of distant movements. Gurmit Singh Aulakh, president of the Council of Kalistan, is one such separatist lobbyist. Using a cosmopolitan language, he argues that "India is a ruthless empire, like the Soviet Union," and should be undone so that "the Sikh nation can exercise its self-determination" and achieve its independence. "The time has come to impose sanctions on India. If the U.S. can send troops to free Kuwaitis, why not do so to free the Sikhs of the Punjab?" he asks.[23]

Second, movements understand that they can contest for power only if they organize a large, cohesive, and interclass collectivity into an identifiable "nation" in their "homeland." This is not easily done with appeals to abstract, cosmopolitan ideas like self-determination and sovereignty. Instead they use a vernacular political language that can appeal across class lines to members of ethnic minority communities. In New Zealand, for example, a Maori political party that calls itself *Mana Motuhake* (self-determination) argues that independence will provide Maori with *turangawaewae,* "a place for the feet to stand upon."[24]

In many settings, separatist movements use the language of family or home to make their political appeal. In San Juan, Puerto Rico, a cab driver who supported the separatist *independistas* explained, "You don't come into my house and tell me what to do."[25]

Or as Claude Bernard, director of the secretariat for the Parti Québécois, said, "We just want independence to pursue our own destiny — to be master in our own house."[26]

In Slovakia, when demonstrators jostled Czechoslovakia's President Václav Havel in 1990, they shouted, "This is our house! We want a free Slovakia!"[27]

Or, again, as many separatists told the reporter Michael Ignatieff, "We just want to be at home with ourselves . . . a majority in our own place."[28]

Family is also part of the separatist vernacular. In Puerto Rico, Maria Cecilia Benitez, a representative of the Independence Party, likened independence to adulthood: "It's not right for an individual who is twenty-five or thirty to be dependent on his parents [the United States] and to ask permission for everything."[29]

This discussion of Puerto Rico's political future as a family matter is widely used. Senator Marco Rigau criticized pro-statehood party members by saying, "They are like a woman who allows herself to get pregnant from a rich man because she knows he'll have to support her."[30]

And in a debate over whether Puerto Rico should remain a commonwealth, its present status, or become a U.S. state, Roberto Plats Palerm, a governor's aide, argued that commonwealth status was "like a relation between a man and a woman who neither marry nor divorce, they just date." His pro-statehood opponent then argued that statehood was like "a couple who did the right thing and married," to which Palerm replied, "this union would be a marriage without love."[31]

All these analogies are the vernacular expressions of cosmopolitan ideas, designed to organize parochial constituencies. The success of separatist movements depends in part on their ability to translate cosmopolitan ideas into indigenous vernaculars. As Tom Nairn observed, "The middle-class intelligentsia of nationalism had to invite the masses into history, and the invitation card had to be written in a language they understood."[32]

Just as separatists converse in both cosmopolitan and parochial political languages, they organize in "foreign" lands among émigré and diaspora communities and among minority communities in their "homelands." Émigré and diaspora communities play important roles for separatist movements, providing financial support and sometimes arms, safe haven for movement cadre, and political pressure on host countries. Indeed, émigré communities are often more emphatic about separatism than people back "home."

Among Puerto Ricans living in New York, for example, support for the independence movement is stronger than it is on the island. And separatist movements sometimes come to rely wholly on populations outside their homeland, as was the case for Baltic separatists in the years after 1952 — when their guerrilla war with the Soviet Union ended — and before reform in the late 1980s made it possible for the exogenous movement to contact the new indigenous one. A similar situation existed for the Palestinian movement, which was largely displaced from Israel and the occupied territories and chased from one country to the next. The foreign-based movement was finally "reunited" in peace talks with an indigenous movement in the occupied territories that had emerged largely on its own initiative. The part of the movement based "abroad" has significant differences with the movement based "at home."[33] Without émigré and diaspora communities to rely upon, separatist movements would have a difficult time surviving government efforts to eradicate them.

But while the cosmopolitan-parochial orientation and organizational efforts of separatist movements is useful and functional, it can nonetheless create problems that grow out of the relation between "foreign" and "domestic" populations.

When separatist movements in the Baltics obtained power in 1991, they immediately extended citizenship to ethnic Lithuanians, Latvians, and Estonians living in diaspora and émigré communities in other countries, "foreigners" really, because most of them possessed citizenship in other countries and resided there on a permanent basis. Some did return to claim their citizenship, recover property seized by the Soviet government, or serve as government officials (one U.S. army officer took a post as head of the fledgling Estonian army, a move that threatened his army pension and U.S. citizenship).[34] These generous policies were the legacy of movements' cosmopolitan orientation and their affinity with émigré populations.

But at the same time, Baltic movements that assumed power restricted the meaning of citizenship for domestic populations, particularly for Russian residents. They typically refused citizenship to Russian residents as an automatic right, arguing that they were "immigrants" who, as in other countries, cannot automatically claim citizenship in their country of destination, even though many of them had immigrated decades earlier or had been born in the country. The new governments insisted that ethnic Russians pass rigorous language tests or meet stringent residency requirements before they would be granted citizenship. These policies were the legacy of the movement's parochial orientation. The problem, of course, was that this greatly antagonized resident populations, not only of Russians but of Poles and Germans, who organized opposition to these policies in "Russian-dominated city councils, trade unions in Russian-populated areas, and newspapers and Russian-language mass media."[35]

They argued that the provision of citizenship for foreigners but not residents was inconsistent and unfair, and they were able to find support for this position from the Russian government but also from international human-rights groups like Helsinki Watch, which wrote, "No one denies that the [Baltic] governments have the right to adopt citizenship laws, yet special considerations should be given to Russians and others who moved to the Baltic states at a time when the Soviet republics were all one country," and that Russian residents "should be presumptively eligible for citizenship whether [or not] one views the Soviet presence . . . as an illegal occupation."[36]

This kind of problem emerges wherever movements adopt cosmopolitan and parochial views of citizenship. One of the most difficult issues in peace negotiations between Israelis and Palestinians is the definition of citizenship, not only for residents of these territories, but also for diaspora and empire populations living outside them. The simultaneous insistence, by both Israelis and Palestinians, that citizenship be both widely available to diaspora populations but also rigorously restricted to members of nonethnic residents (Arab Palestinians in Israel, Jewish settlers in the occupied territories), an insistence born of paired cosmopolitan-parochial orientations, creates enormous difficulties for each and presents a major obstacle to any permanent resolution of their differences.

Majoritarian Minorities

Except for Bengali separatists, who won a parliamentary majority in all-Pakistan elections prior to the civil war and partition of that country in 1972, separatist movements typically consist of ethnic minorities who hope to secure a state so that they can rule as a majority on their own terms. Most separatist movements aspire to become a political majority that retains its ethnic minority identity.

Separatists become "majoritarian minorities" in response to problems they experience in states where governments effectively prevent minorities from obtaining power through available political channels. Whether they reside in dictatorships or democracies, separatist movements emerge where the relative political power associated with majority and minority positions has become closely related to ethnic identity and where it is extremely difficult for people with a given ethnic identity to change political positions, a situation that prevents members of ethnic-identified minorities from become part of the political majority. As Lani Guinier has written, "Where a fixed majority refuses to cooperate with the minority," where people in ethnically defined majority and minority positions cannot easily change political places, a "tyranny of the majority" may emerge.[37]

Of course the relation between political position and ethnic identity may also be fixed or hardened by movement efforts to differentiate themselves from proximate social groups, as has happened in Canada, where the separatist movement has encouraged the creation of an ethnically identified bloc of voters and members of Parliament. Under either of these circumstances, where political positions and ethnic identities become fixed, separatists can argue that ethnic minorities should try to obtain states of their own where they can become a political majority and retain their minority ethnic identity.

Where separatist movements have acquired states of their own, governments in many have adopted policies aimed at solidifying the association between majority political power and their own ethnic identity.

The Eritreans are unusual in this regard. They seem determined to create a secular state in which different ethnic groups may participate. This is a product of their successful strategy of developing a multiethnic separatist movement (consisting of Muslims and Christian Eritreans) and allying with non-Eritrean rebel movements who also opposed the Ethiopian regime. But this may be a difficult project for them to sustain, as Muhammad Ali Jinnah, the leader of the Muslim League in India and founder of Pakistan, discovered. Although he argued that Muslims in British India should acquire a state of their own, a claim based on their separate ethnic identities as Muslims, Jinnah tried to create a secular state where power would not be closely with ethnic identity. "You may belong to any religion or caste or creed — that has nothing to do with the business of the state," he argued.[38]

But this view did not long survive. Arguing that it was inconsistent to demand state power on the basis of ethnic identity and then not exercise it in ethnic terms, movements in Pakistan demanded that the state cement the association between political power and ethnic identity, and they eventually declared Pakistan an "Islamic Republic."[39]

Although the attempt to become a political majority defined in ethnic minority terms is a logical response to problems many ethnic minorities experience, it can create difficult problems once separatist movements come to power. It is a problem because when ethnic minorities become political majorities in new states, they assume power in states where other "minority" social groups reside.

When separatists acquired states as a result of partition in Ethiopia, Yugoslavia, the Soviet Union, and Czechoslovakia, many people migrated across newly created borders. In Yugoslavia, partition "uprooted an estimated three million people, 600,000 of whom have fled the Balkans altogether."[40] Some people migrated voluntarily, while others were forced from their homes by "ethnic cleansing" campaigns, a process common to many partitioned states.[41]

But while one might expect these migrations to result in the creation of states inhabited by homogeneous ethnic populations, they do not. There are always some people excluded from the majority: members of previously "majority" ethnic groups (Russians in the Baltics); sub-minority groups (Germans and Poles in the Baltics); and "Romeo-and-Juliet" minorities (people who have "intermarried"). And efforts by newly empowered majoritarian minorities to cement the relation between state power and ethnic identity not only antagonizes these "new" minorities but also ethnic groups and relatives living in neighboring countries. In Croatia, the Serbian minority boycotted the separatist-sponsored referendum for independence, took up arms as soon as Croatia declared its independence, demanded a state of their own, and received considerable military support from the Serbian-dominated government in Belgrade. They did so largely because Croatian separatists insisted that political power be coterminous with ethnic identity.

The problem is that demographic realities intrude on the separatist attempt to rule as majoritarian minorities and fix the association between political power and ethnic identity.

Dependent Sovereignty

Separatist movements seek states so that they can obtain political "sovereignty" or independence and self-government. But they concede that their ability to exercise sovereignty in economic matters will be constrained or limited in important respects. When I asked representatives of separatist movement what image they would put on the new state's currency, many replied that they would use the currency of another state. "We'll keep the Loonie [the Canadian dollar coin, which is engraved with a loon]," replied Claude Bernard of the Parti Québécois.[42]

Maria Cecilia Benitez, a representative for Puerto Rico's independence party, said much the same thing: "[After independence] we'd have to make a treaty [with the United States] to keep the dollar as our currency, just like Panama."[43] And Slovak separatists announced that they would keep the Czech crown after partition.

This is an ironic development because currencies have long been emblematic of state sovereignty. For years, British residents referred to the country's gold coins as "sovereigns." It is also extremely significant because control of a country's currency enables governments to adopt economic policies that affect the rate of exchange with other countries, which affects trade, and the rate of interest, which affects levels of investment and growth, rates of inflation, and employment. In Panama's case, government officials helplessly watched the value of "their" currency (the U.S. dollar) plunge after the United States devalued the dollar as a result of the 1985 Plaza Accords.

Although it is odd that separatist movements should seek political sovereignty while acknowledging their economic dependence on other states, they do this because they recognize implicitly the relation between the character of the interstate political system and the world-economy.

The interstate system consists of multiple and increasingly numerous political units or states, which take a fairly homogeneous political form (the nation-state republic) but which have different degrees of political power (what I have elsewhere described as an "egalitarian hierarchy," since states possess nominal political equality but are also arranged in a hierarchy with superpower(s) at the top).[44]

Immanuel Wallerstein has argued that the creation and maintenance of multiple political units, a feature of both the old imperial and new republican interstate systems, acted as a hedge against the creation of a world empire and made it difficult for strong states to do more than establish brief periods of "hegemony."[45]

But while there are multiple political units in the interstate system, the world economy is a singular entity. And because it is singular, none of the states in the system have ever really possessed the kind of economic sovereignty that they might have expected. Even the United States has recognized that its economic sovereignty is limited by political and market forces beyond its control. What's more, the emergence of global economic institutions — transnational corporations, global and regional trade agreements, monetary and economic organizations such as the World Bank and G-7 — have made states even less sovereign than they once were.[46]

In this context it should not be surprising that aspirants for power in weaker states would recognize that the interstate system and world economy constrain and limit their economic sovereignty, making them dependent on other states and global economic institutions and market forces.

The problem for separatist movements is that their ethnic constituencies expect state power to provide both political and economic benefits. One economic feature of many contemporary separatist movements is that they represent "not-so-badly-off" ethnic groups. Per capita income in the Baltics was higher than in Russia and two or three times higher than in many other Soviet republics.[47]

And separatist movements in Slovenia and Croatia, Eritrea, Punjab and Kashmir, Quebec, and Lombardy represent groups that are at the upper economic echelons of people in the region.[48]

Indeed, many movements argue that they need separate states so they can slough off the indolent, ethnic masses living elsewhere in the country, masses that act as a drag on their economic development. "We're tired of paying all the taxes to support lazy southerners and corrupt officials in Rome," explained Roberto Ronchi, a representative of the Lega Nord (League of the North).[49]

And the separatist movement demanding the creation of a "Republic of the Pampas" in southern Brazil, which draws support among European descendants, makes the same case, arguing that their taxes go to support the lazy poor in the Amazon.[50]

Separatist movements do not always represent well-off minorities. Separatists in Slovakia, which was the poorer region of Czechoslovakia, argued that they needed independence from a state dominated by Czechs so they could protect themselves from free-market policies that contributed to high levels of unemployment in Slovakia.[51]

Because economic issues are important considerations for supporters of both rich and poor separatist movements, their constituents expect government officials in newly created states to promote economic development on their behalf. But this is difficult for governments to do if they cannot adopt economic policies that control rates of exchange, interest, investment, growth, inflation, or employment. And where separatist movements have been unable to control economic developments, in Slovakia, Lithuania, and Ukraine, separatist movements that came to power have been defeated in recent elections and replaced by residual "communist" parties, which were antiseparatist before independence and now argue that separatist economic policies be rescinded or modified.[52]

The antinomies of separatist movement ideas and identities are the understandable responses to a variety of historical developments in the interstate system since 1945. But the contradictory, ironic, or inconsistent character of these identities creates problems, dilemmas, and issues for separatist movements and others. Because they are a response to fairly recent developments, these ideas and identities are not immutable, and the problems they create are not insoluble. But they must first be recognized and understood as problems.

Problematic Outcomes

For several reasons, separatism almost inevitably becomes problematic. It demands the partition of existing states, but such an attempt often leads to violent conflict. Moreover, successful separatist movements typically construct "conditional democracies" that derogate the citizenship of resident minorities. Contemporary economic difficulties undermine the ability of states to promote growth and hampers their ability to sustain even conditional democracy.

In *Warpaths*, a study of the causes and consequences of partition in Korea, China, Vietnam, India, Pakistan, Palestine, Cyprus, Germany, and Ireland, I found that the division of these countries by the great powers led to several problems. First, partition created social dislocations as people were forced or persuaded to move to their "assigned" states. After the partition of India, there was the largest, fastest migration in human history, as millions migrated across the new borders. Other divided states experienced similar, socially disruptive migrations. And when migrations ended, usually after states reasserted their control over borders, substantial residual populations remained behind.

After the division of states, the movements that have assumed power typically have disenfranchised or derogated the citizenship of residual minority populations. This practice has exacerbated friction with domestic minorities and with their communities in neighboring states. Indeed, many of these communities formed movements to challenge newly created governments. They point out that they had little say in the partition process or that partition unfairly assigned territory and people to sibling states. Challenging their neighboring state, they keep it from becoming a full-fledged member of the interstate system. Contests over territory and sovereignty frequently lead to war between divided states and to superpower military intervention — including sometimes the threat of limited nuclear war. Countries threatened with nuclear destruction by either superpower several times have opted to develop nuclear weapons of their own.

One might expect subsequent partitions in other states to create similar problems. Of course, the projection of outcomes requires us to pay attention to important differences between the partitions effected by "great powers," where indigenous movements played minor roles, and contemporary "do-it-yourself" partitions, in which indigenous movements play major roles and the great powers are relegated to the sidelines.

When disputes between divided states arise, it is more difficult for great powers to intervene because they played only a minor role, if any, in the process of partition. Thus the 1992 decision by representatives of Czech and Slovak parties to divide their country, which was reached by mutual agreement, attracted only passing attention from neighbors and great powers. And the unilateral decisions by parties in Yugoslav republics to divide that country, which led to open conflict and war, did not immediately trigger great power intervention.

But there are also similarities between postwar great-power partitions and contemporary do-it-yourself partitions. Both kinds have led to socially disruptive migrations, to the derogation of minority citizenship and contests over the sovereignty of sibling states. And these problems have often led to internecine conflict and sometimes war. In the former Soviet Union and in Yugoslavia, conflict has erupted within and between many, though not all, of the former republics. And new fissures within and between successor states have fractured community and political life. In countries where separatist movements are active but have not yet achieved their goals, irregular and civil war have become permanent features of the political landscape. In South Asia, separatist movements in Burma, Bangladesh, Sri Lanka, and India have prompted ruling governments to establish martial law in some regions and deploy troops to wage war with separatist combatants. In the subcontinent, Eastern Europe, and the former Soviet Union, these conflicts have not triggered intervention by great powers, which regard them with relative indifference.

Of course, partition has not led to conflict everywhere. Separatist movements argue that the "Velvet Divorce" of the Czechs and Slovaks and the peaceful withdrawal of Baltic republics and then other republics from the Soviet Union demonstrates that partition is not inherently problematic and need not lead to conflict. Just so. But they have not identified how peaceful outcomes can be achieved and conflict routinely avoided. The difficulty stems in part from the fact that separatists insist on the unique features of their own experience, which makes it difficult to generalize from this experience or develop a general theory based on idiosyncratic history.

And while open conflict has so far been avoided in some recently divided states, separatists have not dispensed with problems related to migration, citizenship, and sovereignty. Where partition has been peacefully achieved, and, of course, where it has been violently contested, governments have uniformly derogated the citizenship of resident minorities. In their attempt to create ethnically homogeneous states, government officials have placed ethnic-religious-linguistic "conditions" on the ability of residents to participate as citizens. Of course, western democracies have historically used property, gender, age, and place of birth as conditions for citizenship, though many of these conditions have been eliminated (property and gender) or eased (age) over time. But to this list of rou-

tine conditions, movements in divided states have added a host of additional conditions — residency and language requirements, religious and ethnic criteria —
that effectively diminish the ability of residual minority populations to participate fully as citizens.

Movements that have assumed power do not anticipate or fully appreciate the
cumulative social consequences of these measures. In a sense, separatist movements are utopian, not realistic. They seek to create a state composed of a compact, ethnically homogeneous nation. This seems realistic because they assume
the interstate system uses the nation-state as its constituent unit. But this is a
utopian assumption because the nation is constantly being transformed by global
developments and internal forces. Global migrations effectively change the ethnic
"face" of nations located in individual states. And the people living in particular
states change the meaning of the nation because they change their own identities
over time, continually redefining who they are in relation to their predecessors
and their contemporaries. What it means to be "French" today does not correspond to what it meant to be "French" in the 1930s, much less in the seventeenth century. As a result of external and internal developments, the effort by
governments to capture, distill, and institutionalize national identities and make
this identity congruent with territorial boundaries is a utopian project, doomed to
fail.

Finally, while the end of the Cold War has provided real political opportunities for first- and second-generation separatists, it has not created commensurate
economic opportunities. And economic difficulties may undermine the ability of
states to sustain even conditional democracy.

Democratization, the devolution of power from dictators and one-party states
to civilian democrats and sometimes separatists, was the product of economic
crisis in different regions: indebtedness in Latin America, rapid growth in East
Asia, stagnation in the Soviet Union and Eastern Europe, embargo in South
Africa.[53] To address separate economic crises, democrats and separatists uniformly adopted similar economic policies, privatizing state assets, opening their
economies to foreign investment and trade, and demilitarizing their economies.
But policies designed to address longstanding economic problems and promote
real growth, which would consolidate democracy, have encountered several difficulties.

First, democrats and separatists are trying to promote rapid economic development during a global downturn. Sluggish demand and intense competition
have made it difficult for rich and poor countries to record substantial growth.
Second, by simultaneously adopting identical economic policies, democrats and
separatists have glutted capital markets with up-for-sale state assets. Attempts to
lure foreign investment has led to cutthroat competition among capital-hungry
states, leading them to provide tax relief and subsidies to investors that largely
negate the domestic benefits of foreign investment. And open trade policies have
encouraged middle-class consumers to import high-priced, first-world goods long

unavailable to them, and this has led to trade deficits and currency depreciations. Some democrats have achieved some savings by demilitarizing their economies, but converting defense industries has been difficult. And where domestic or inter-state conflicts threaten, governments have been unable to demilitarize.

And third, first-world states have adopted strategies that either promote com-petition among newly democratizing states or reduce first-world dependence on third-world suppliers. First-world investors have established multiple suppliers for many products, which tends to push down prices. First-world firms have also deployed technologies that replace third-world products with goods made in first-world countries. So new technologies allow first-world producers to replace cane sugar from the Philippines with high-fructose corn sweeteners from Iowa or sub-stitute fiber-optic cable made by Corning Glass for copper wire once made in Chile. And energy conservation in Japan and new drilling technologies that sup-ply North Sea oil to Europe have reduced their dependence on OPEC suppliers and lowered oil prices in real terms to preembargo levels. First-world "import substitution" has reduced the demand for and prices of products supplied by third-world countries. This has made it difficult for them to use export strategies to promote economic growth.

If democrats and separatists are unable to use state power to provide economic wealth to class-based or ethnic constituencies, they may be unable to retain power. And failure to address economic problems may invite the revival of dictatorship, though probably in some new political configuration, as has already occurred in Peru and in some of the former Soviet republics.

For these reasons, the separatist goal should be regarded as problematic. Although it emerged as one possible solution to problems associated first with decolonization and then with democratization, it is a solution that itself creates problems. As such, alternatives to separatism and partition should be explored. If partition has any value, it is as "an expedient of the tired statesman," the phrase Conor Cruise O'Brien, Ireland's ambassador to the United Nations, used to describe the partition of Cyprus. This phrase also describes the partition of Bosnia, where statesmen have tried and, finally, despaired of finding a just or permanent solution to the problems afflicting former Yugoslav republics. If one is serious about extending democracy and deepening its meaning, one should look elsewhere for solutions.

Notes

Research for this paper was funded with the assistance of research and travel grants from the California State University and the San Jose State University Foundation. A version of this paper was presented to the panel on "The Partition of Nation States" at the American Sociological Association meetings in Miami, August 1993.

1. Ted R. Gurr, *Minorities at Risk: A Global View of Ethnopolitical Conflicts* (Washington, D.C.: United States Institute of Peace Press, 1993), 4, 5.

2. Gurr, *Minorities at Risk,* 5.

3. See Robert Schaeffer, "The Entelechies of Mercantilism," in *Scandinavian Economic History Review,* Vol. XXIX, No. 2, 1981.

4. Schaeffer, "The Entelechies of Mercantilism."

5. Gérard Chaliand and Jean-Pierre Rageau, *Strategic Atlas: A Comparative Geopolitics of the World's Powers.* (New York: Harper and Row, 1985), 77-79, 86-87.

6. Donald L. Horowitz, "Ethnic and Nationalist Conflicts," in *World Security: Trends and Challenges at Century's End,* ed. Michael T. Klare and Daniel C. Thomas (New York: St. Martin's Press, 1991), 229.

7. Robert Schaeffer, *Warpaths: The Politics of Partition* (New York: Hill and Wang, 1990).

8. Schaeffer, *Warpaths,* 62.

9. Schaeffer, *Warpaths,* 248.

10. Robert Schaeffer, "Democratic Devolutions: East Asian Democratization in Comparative Perspective," in *Pacific-Asia and the World-Economy,* ed. Ravi Palat (Westport, CT: Greenwood Press, 1993).

11. Gurr, *Minorities at Risk.*

12. Schaeffer, "Democratic Devolutions."

13. Walker Connor, "Ethnonationalism in the First World," in Milton Esman, *Ethnic Conflict in the Western World* (Ithaca: Cornell University Press), 23. Linnart Mall, a professor at Tartu University in Tartu, Estonia, reports that there is now an "Organization of Unrepresented Nations," but it has not, as yet, evolved into a substantial institution that in fact represents "nations" that have yet acquired states of their own.

14. See *Warpaths,* e.g., 76-77.

15. Eric Hobsbawm and Terence Ranger, *The Invention of Tradition* (Cambridge: Cambridge University Press, 1983); Benedict Anderson, *Imagined Communities* (London: Verso, 1983).

16. *Washington Post,* July 22, 1990; *New York Times,* May 17, 1990.

17. Chip Brown, "Separatism Surging," *New York Times Magazine,* January 30, 1994.

18. Gunnar Nielsson, "States and 'Nation-Groups': A Global Taxonomy," in *New Nationalisms of the Developed West: Toward Explanation,* ed. Edward A. Tiryakian and Ronald Rogowski (Boston: Allen and Unwin, 1985), 30.

19. Michael E. Brown, "Causes and Implications of Ethnic Conflict," in *Ethnic Conflict and International Security,* ed. Michael E. Brown (Princeton: Princeton University Press, 1993), 6; Anthony D. Smith, *The Ethnic Revival* (Cambridge: Cambridge University Press, 1981), 9-10.

20. Nathan Gardels, "Dangers of Self-Determination: Interview with Prime Minister Felipe Gonzalez," *San Francisco Chronicle,* October 28, 1991.

21. Personal interview, January 6, 1992.

22. See *Warpaths,* 24-5.

23. Personal interview, January 8, 1992.

24. David B. Knight, "Geographical Perspectives on Self-Determination," in Peter Taylor and John House, *Political Geography: Recent Advances and Future Directions* (London: Croom Helm, 1984), 180.

25. Personal interview, January 14, 1992.

26. Personal interview, January 7, 1992.

27. *New York Times,* March 15, 1991; June 5, 1991.

28. Tony Judt, "The New Old Nationalism," *The New York Review of Books,* May 26, 1994, 50.

29. Personal interview, January 14, 1992.

30. Personal interview, January 14, 1992.

31. Personal interview, January 13, 1992.

32. Tom Nairn, *The Breakup of Britain* (London: New Left Books, 1977), 240.

33. See Claudia Dreifus, "Hanan Ashrawi's Separate Peace: How a Palestinian Feminist Rebuffed Arafat to Pursue Her Own Agenda of Nationalism and Civil Rights," *New York Times Magazine,* June 26, 1994, 22-25.

34. Andrus Park, "Ethnicity and Post-Soviet Transition: The Case of Estonia in Comparative Perspective," *Global Forum Series* (Durham, NC: Center for International Studies, Duke University, 1993) 7-9.

35. Park, "Ethnicity and Post-Soviet Transition," 25.

36. Park, "Ethnicity and Post-Soviet Transition," 29-30.

37. Lani Guinier, *The Tyranny of the Majority: Fundamental Fairness in Representative Democracy* (New York: The Free Press, 1994), 5.

38. Tariq Ali, *Can Pakistan Survive?* (London: New Left Books, 1983), 42.

39. M. J. Akbar, *India: The Siege Within* (New York: Penguin, 1985), 44.

40. Brown, "Causes and Implications," 17.

41. See *Warpaths,* 154-55.

42. Personal interview, January 7, 1992.

43. Personal interview, January 14, 1992. Panama uses the U.S. dollar as its official currency.

44. See *Warpaths,* 81-82.

45. Immanuel Wallerstein, *Historical Capitalism* (London: Verso, 1983), 57.

46. Robert K. Schaeffer, "State and Devolution: Economic Crises and the Devolution of U.S. Superstate Power," in *The International Journal of Sociology of Agriculture and Food,* Vol. 4, 1994.

47. *World Paper,* May 1991, 8-9; *New York Times,* August 6, 1989.

48. Milica Zarkovic Bookman, *The Economics of Secession* (St. Martin's Press, 1993), 57.

49. Personal interview, June 10, 1992.

50. James Brooke, "White Flight in Brazil? Secession Caldron Boils," *New York Times*, May 12, 1993, A6.

51. Czech Prime Minister Václav Klaus was such an ardent conservative free-marketeer that his supporters describe British economist John Maynard Keynes as "the father of Western Socialism," a derogatory epithet in post-Communist Czechoslovakia. It should be noted that Richard Nixon described himself as an adherent of Keynes, saying, "We are all Keynesian now."

52. "In Ukraine, Worries Grow about Reform," *New York Times,* June 17, 1994, A3.
53. Schaeffer, "Democratic Devolutions."

Three

The Economics of Secession

Milica Z. Bookman

After the late 1980s, there was an increase in the number and intensity of secessionist movements across the globe. It might seem that this was due to the
loosening of central control associated with the collapse of Communism, yet
Eastern Europe and the Soviet Union have not been alone in experiencing drives
for regional autonomy. Early signs of the unraveling of national unions can be
encountered at various levels of development and under diverse economic and political systems: India, Papua New Guinea, Canada, Sri Lanka, and the Sudan
have all been contending with significant secessionist drives. These movements
exist despite odds against their success. Indeed, over the past century, successful
secessionist efforts were few (including those in Belgium, Norway, Ireland and
Bangladesh),[1] yet today, the recent success of the Soviet republics, Slovenia, and
Eritrea fuels the fires in numerous regions that struggle with their unions.

Despite this increase in successful secessions and the concomitant need to set
up independent political and economic systems, the focus of study has remained
the religious, ethnic, cultural and nationalistic elements of secession. Few questions are asked pertaining to the economic factors that are associated with secession,[2] despite clear cases of their importance in determining the nature of regional demands (such as those in Lombardy, Punjab, and Russia) and the use of
economic policy as a tool for the appeasement of subnational regions with active
secessionist movements (Bougainville, Slovakia, and Quebec).

Economic issues are relevant in the study of secession in explaining events in
various phases of the movements. First, before secession: How do economic is-

sues contribute to the desire to secede? What economic concessions might be made by the union in order to prevent secession or accommodate to the reality of secession? What is the nature of the cost/benefit analysis of secession both for the seceding region as well as the center? Second, once secession is in process, how do the new economic entities disentangle their economic ties? How does the new region go about setting up an independent economy, including the establishment of new currency, a new banking system, international monetary relations, and the adjustment to the loss of old markets? Third, what economic factors contribute to the success of a region's efforts to secede? Which of these also contributes to the economic viability of the region as an independent entity?

This chapter consists of two parts: The first includes a study of the three phases of the secessionist process, the periods of reevaluation, redefinition, and re-equilibration, roughly corresponding to the before, the during, and the after periods.[3] Understanding the role of economics in all phases of the secessionist process may shed light on both how to avoid secession in the future and how to minimize the disruptive effect on the economies of both the departing and the remaining regions. The second part of the chapter argues against secession and state fragmentation and in favor of integration and reintegration, and points out some recent events in that direction. Descriptions of secessionist movements at various stages — including those in Ukraine and Slovakia, where secession has been completed — are included.

The Phases of Secession

Phase I: Reevaluation

During this first phase, the seeds of secession are planted and anticenter sentiment percolates. This phase may last a few months or a few centuries. At some point in this phase, demands are formulated by a segment of the population. These greatly vary in scope and tenacity. Indeed, they may simply be demands for increased favoritism by the center toward a region or a targeted segment of the population, or they may be demands for a dramatic change in the participation of a region in the central and state affairs, or the demands may be such that nothing short of severance of preexisting economic and political ties with the center is acceptable. The latter demand is referred to by Peter Leslie as the "we want out" demand, while Ian Bremmer called it the "exit option."[4]

The relative importance of economic factors in secessionist aspirations varies widely among the cases. Sometimes, economic perceptions of injustice have been among the most important, if not the single most important issue, that has given secessionist movements substance, such as in Slovenia, Slovakia, Punjab, Singapore, Bougainville, and Lombardy, among others. Those regions in which economics is secondary, but nevertheless important in the secessionist motivations, include Kashmir, Assam, Catalonia, Basque Provinces, Transylvania, and

North and East Sri Lanka. In all of these regions, several issues in region/center economic relations have consistently emerged as imperative in forming secessionist aspirations. These are (a) the share of central budget and capital investment allocated to the regions, (b) the proportion of input in the form of taxes that the region contributes to the center, (c) the degree of autonomy in decision making pertaining to economic issues, (d) central bias favoring a sector that is underrepresented in the region in question, such as pricing policies biased against agriculture and in favor of industry, and in some cases, (e) the share of foreign exchange and external funding.

Regional perceptions pertaining to these issues are dependent upon the region's relative economic position within the state. Indeed, the regions that had relatively lower incomes (such as Slovakia) tended to believe that their region received an insufficient share of capital investment; enjoyed insufficient autonomy in the decision making over their resources or in their representation at the center; was subject to biases in pricing policies and allocation of foreign exchange regulation; and received a small share of foreign investment, aid, and other forms of foreign intervention. The perception by the population in the relatively high income regions tends to be that they receive insufficient capital and budget allocations while making high contributions to the central budget (such as was the case in Slovenia). In addition, the population deems itself to have too small a role in decision making relative to its economic importance and too little power over its own resources. These regions (such as Croatia) also tend to demand an increase in their share of foreign exchange and foreign funding on the grounds that they are often most responsible for the accumulation of foreign currency and that given their environment is conducive to growth, investment on their territory is most likely to result in growth. Numerous countries in the world contain both high- and low-income regions that have made these respective claims: Yugoslavia (Slovenia and Kosovo), India (Punjab and Kashmir), the Soviet Union (Ukraine and Tajikistan), and Italy (Lombardy and the Mezzogiorno).

These economic concerns thrive even in cases in which other factors, such as culture, politics, religion, and language, dominate secessionist aspirations. For example, the civil war in Northern Ireland has been partly based on the economic advantages that Protestants have and Catholics do not share equally. Linguistic issues seem to dominate the Catalan efforts at increased autonomy; however, the economic strength of the region is often underscored by the leaders of the nationalist movement.

Phase II: Redefinition

During the period of redefinition, a region breaks its existing ties with the center and formulates new ties to both its former union and to the international economy. These include a settlement pertaining to the division of national and international debts, the division of federal or central budget, foreign currency holdings, and other financial holdings and property. The obligations of each side must be calculated with respect to social security, armed forces, etc. While these ties are being severed, the new economy must introduce a new currency, a new monetary policy, a new tax system, a new army, new border crossings and regulations, etc. In the international sphere, trade agreements, joint ventures, and investments must be renegotiated.

The nature of the negotiations, as well as their outcome, will largely depend upon agreement (at least in principle), between the region and the center, pertaining to the breakup. If there is a general acceptance of the idea that the region will secede, then negotiations about the division of assets, although turbulent and controversial, can proceed in an atmosphere of peace. This was the experience in most parts of the former Soviet Union: For example, while there were clearly topics within the negotiations that were explosive (such as the Black Sea fleet and the status of Crimea), there was no question about Ukraine leaving the union. If war precedes the distribution of assets, as in Bangladesh, then negotiations are more difficult to conduct since there is basic disagreement on the issue of secession. The example of the velvet divorce in Czechoslovakia, with its intricate sixteen-point program of economic divorce, is the exception with respect to negotiated secession rather than the rule.

Internal Issues to Be Resolved

The outcome of all internal economic disputes arising during secession are dependent upon the relative strength of the seceding region and the remaining state. An indicator of such strength is the region's wealth, its international support, the nature of its popular support, and, in the case of war, its military capacity.[5]

1. Public and foreign debt. Many of the countries currently experiencing secessionist drives have significant national debts: in Canada, it is estimated to be C\$350 billion, while in Yugoslavia, it was on the order of \$20 billion. Secession entails the apportioning of the debt by region. However, the grounds on which this division should take place are not clear, since regional proposals vary to reflect regional self-interest: The seceding region tends to favor the leaving behind of the debt, as part of the negative baggage that it chooses to forget, while the center tends to try to make the seceding region pay for its secession by forcing it to shoulder as large a share as possible. Within these extremes, on what principle does one base the division of the debt? It is possible to use a per capita calculation, or to base responsibility on the basis of territory; that is, a secessionist region that contains 20 percent of the population or territory then receives 20 percent of the debt burden. However, both the per capita and the territorial principles are bound to raise numerous accusations of injustice as populations begin to demand justification for the expenses incurred by the debt. For example, did the population of Quebec really benefit from the union sufficiently to justify accepting over approximately \$90 billion of debt, which is arrived at on a per capita basis?

Alternatively, the basis for the division of the debt might be the relative bene-fit derived from it. In other words, a link might be made between debt and assets, so that the same percentage share in the payment of debt and in the receipt of central assets is used. This is a path that Estonia had proposed, agreeing to pay the same percentage of debt as it receives in gold and currency reserves from the Soviet Union. However, the calculation of the benefit from the public debt, as well as its precise division, is a laborious task with insurmountable hurdles since it is bound to elicit facts and fiction from both sides of the negotiating table. For example, upon the first inklings that Slovenia was contemplating se-cession, studies were published in both Serbia and Slovenia claiming that each side had benefited unjustly from the public debt.[6] Similar attempts were made in the former Soviet Baltic republics: despite possible benefits from the allocation of funds from the central public debt, economist Larry Summers claimed that the Soviet center should pay the Lithuanians for having caused a decrease in their level of living, which before the war was comparable to the Finnish and lagged behind by 50 percent by the time of partition.[7]

Another aspect of the question of who benefited from the public debt is the question of what the debt was used for. If the use, in one region, had positive or negative externalities, or by-products, how should those be accounted for in the division of the share of the debt? If those externalities extended beyond the con-fines of the seceding region, how does the spillover effect enter the calculations? An example of these questions emerged in the discussions preceding the breakup of Czechoslovakia: The Slovaks claimed that, despite the investment from the central budget that was injected into their industry, they should carry a less-than-per capita share of the public debt since that investment proved to be at a great expense to the environment, and the Slovaks alone will be responsible for the expenses of cleaning up.

It is clear that the scope for debate and disagreement in the division of the debt is great. To enforce its decisions pertaining to the division of the debt (as well as other assets), the center has power to freeze all assets of the seceding region that are under its jurisdiction. Meanwhile, the seceding region has the power to con-fiscate all federal assets on its territory. A simple solution, such as the canceling of all preexisting contracts, including the debt, and calling a moratorium on the discussion of debt division, might serve to start off new relations from a clear slate; however, it still leaves someone holding the bill and the concomitant re-sentment. The difficulty in reaching an agreement on the principle to apply in the division of the debt is underscored by the sixteen point program between the Czech Republic and Slovakia that outlined all economic matters *except* the divi-sion of the federal debt and assets.[8]

The division of the foreign debt is even more complicated and sensitive than the public debt. First, it entails the use of foreign currency, which in most se-cessionist regions tends to be in scarce supply. The seceding region, as well as the remaining region, need to maximize their foreign reserves to tide them over the initial, disruptive period associated with secession. Second, foreign debt includes foreign countries and institutions with whom commitments must be honored. Indeed, failure to shoulder one's responsibilities has a long-term effect on future access to funds and generally on financial ties to the global economy.

The experience of the former Soviet Union in servicing its external debt of over $89 billion and dividing the principal has received much attention. It showed how the newly independent regions favored leaving as much debt as possible with the center, which became equated with Russia, and it also showed how international pressure was put to ensure a unified approach to debt repayment. Initially, Ukraine had promised to serve and pay off its share of the foreign debt, which it estimated to be 16 percent. Prior to March 1992, it insisted first on receiving its "fair" share of Soviet assets of gold and hard currency income. However, after that date, it agreed to shoulder a greater share of the debt because some regions, such as Moldova, simply could not pay their share. This change in attitude occurred as a result of pressure from the Group of Seven, which refused to grant Ukraine credits until it signed the debt-repayment deal that it had worked out with the former Soviet Union in 1991.[9] Clearly, the loss, in terms of forgone credits, to Ukraine of refusing to sign this agreement was greater than the cost of signing. In the former Yugoslavia, the sharing of the foreign debt has been linked to the division of hard currency holdings. Yugoslavia's hard currency reserves were estimated to be between $4 and $7 billion, of which one-third was claimed by Slovenia. This claim was not made on the basis of population, nor territory, but rather on a subjective estimation of the region's contribution to the economy. The international community intervened in the squabbling among the former Yugoslav republics by assigning the following responsibilities with respect to the share of foreign debt: The IMF quota of 918.3 million Special Drawing Rights (SDRs) is divided such that 335.4 goes to the new Yugoslavia, 261.6 to Croatia, 121.2 to Bosnia-Herzegovina, 150.4 to Slovenia, and 49.6 to Macedonia. The US $217 million debt to the IMF is to be split among them in the same proportion.[10]

With respect to a division of the foreign debt of the former Czechoslovakia, decisions were again made by the IMF: the Czech Republic will be assigned 69.61% of assets, liabilities and quotas, while Slovakia will get 30.39%. The US $1.54 billion debt will be split in the same proportions.[11]

2. Public assets. How are state-owned companies and buildings, national airlines, museum contents, and other public assets to be divided among the seceding region and the remaining state? Two principal questions arise: what items are negotiable, and how is their price to be determined? One possible method of division merely entails the taking over, by the seceding region, of the public assets on its territory. This is the principle of "finders keepers," according to which legal possession of an asset is determined by its physical location. Such a unilateral decision on the part of the seceding region would almost certainly provoke retaliation by the ex-union, in the form of confiscation of its assets held on the remaining state territory. This in fact occurred when the secessionist government in Biafra declared its independence and took over Nigerian federal assets on its territory. Sometimes, the value of assets within the region is roughly equal to those outside the region, making a simple exchange possible. This arrangement has the advantage of simplicity and expediency. Such expediency was proposed by Estonia in the dispute over public assets: Estonia was willing to drop its claims on property in other regions of the former Soviet Union if it was to be allowed, through a simple legislative act, to keep Soviet property in Estonia.

Short of this simple policy of "tit for tat," another possibility is to evaluate the value of assets and then make an exchange. But how does one determine the price of assets? The simple neoclassical approach of determining price by supply and demand is inappropriate under conditions (e.g., in the formerly socialist countries) in which the market has not functioned as a pricing device and public goods are involved. How does one calculate the price of a museum containing the historical and cultural heritage of a people? Surely not by how much somebody is willing to pay for it, as in a simple real estate evaluation. The process of price determination is no simpler in the case of a factory. After summing the value of the real estate, the building, and the infrastructure — no easy feat in states without a functioning market or with high inflation rates — there inevitably arise questions of justice arising from past decisions, such as the opportunity cost of placing assets on a given territory and the interest rate that was charged.[12] In the course of 1991, the central government of the Soviet Union devised a pricing scheme according to which it set prices for its state companies at which the departing regions could buy central assets on its territories. The prices were deemed too high in the seceding regions. Indeed, the Estonian government went so far as to refuse to pay for companies on its territory at all, on the grounds that part of its budget was used to invest in public projects throughout the country, including government buildings in Moscow, and none of those assets could be recouped.

In some cases, postsecessionist ownership may be determined by what was brought into the union. This type of accounting is possible only when the union is relatively young and when there has been little economic growth and proliferation of assets during union. In the case of a recent union, the seceding economy might not have been fully integrated, and investments and allocations for it might still be treated separately than for the rest of the state. For example, valuations of economic interregional flows between North and South Yemen might have been possible given that the union was only two years old when the south declared its intention to leave. Moreover, valuations of property in East Timor may also be feasible, given that it has been part of Indonesia for less than two decades and has a special status in government bookkeeping. However, this type of calculation is extremely difficult in the case of, for example, Kazakhstan, which has been intricately tied to the Russian economy for centuries. The question of public assets that were brought into the union is presently discussed in the breakup of Yugoslavia: Serbia, victorious after the First World War, brought into the Kingdom of Serbs, Croats, and Slovenes more physical, cultural, and territorial assets than Slovenia and Croatia. How is that to be weighed relative to the economic contribution of Slovenia in the postwar years?

In the case of assets that are not physically located in a seceding region, power, boosted by international support, seems to be the basis for ownership. The region that has subsidized the assets tends to inherit the right to them in the absence of international opposition. A clear example of this is the unilateral decision taken by the Russian government with respect to Soviet assets in November 1991 that entailed the taking over of the foreign ministry and embassies abroad. Ostensibly, this was done because the central government did not have the funds to keep it going. However, international outrage was not forthcoming, and Russia was accepted as the inheritor of these assets. International opposition prevented inheritance of Yugoslav assets abroad by Serbia and Montenegro (the post-1992 Federal Republic of Yugoslavia). Alternatively, the question of size (territory and population) may be brought to bear in the division of central assets. The division of assets of Czechoslovakia was divided partly according to territory and partly by population.

The recent experience of successful secessions indicates that the center takes a big risk in placing its assets on the territory of a region that has joined the union involuntarily. Allen Buchanan aptly draws an analogy with the following: "If you force your way onto my land, take over my house, and then proceed to make improvements in it, I owe you no compensation for your investment when I finally succeed in expelling you."[13] This argument is not limited to regions that have joined unions involuntarily, since there are counterexamples (such as Slovenia and Croatia) of regions that have joined voluntarily and later changed their minds. Indeed, the question of the location of assets is bound to become an issue as states begin to evaluate potential secessionist regions. Surely, new investments entailing central assets in, for example, Catalonia, Scotland, Wales, Corsica, and Alto Adige will be carefully evaluated in the future.

3. Tax payments. One of the first signs of the economic disruption of relations is the cessation of tax payments by the seceding region. With the disruption of revenue flows to the center, the seceding region withdraws its contribution to the central budget. This action provokes the cessation of central budget allocations to the regions. The timing of the playing of this "tax card" may depend on the goals of the secessionist region: sometimes it may merely want to make a statement, such as in the case of Slovenia and the cessation of its contribution to the Central Federal Fund long before its declaration of independence. Alternatively, a region may be well into the secessionist process by the time it alters its tax status, such as was the case in Biafra, when the regional government ordered all tax revenues paid in its territory to go directly to its budget.[14]

4. Currency and banking. As in the case of divorce, after the initial euphoria of "freedom" wears off, monetary issues arising from secession are the first to demand attention. These include the disentanglement of two economies intricately tied by a series of economic relationships and the setting up of new institutions to take over where the old ones left off. The first step in the creation of a new monetary system is the creation of a new currency, which also requires a central bank and the setting up of foreign bank accounts to eliminate the role of the central bank in the former state. A new currency has the effect of providing a psychological boost to the population insofar as it has tremendous symbolic value. But more important is the need of the secessionist region to extricate itself from the monetary problems of its former union. The clearest economic advantage is the isolation of the currency of that region from that of the remaining state so that monetary oscillations, such as changes in the money supply, interest rates, and inflation, are not transmitted to the new region. In the absence of an independent banking system dependence on the center remains for capital inflows such as consumer and business credit, interest rates are not controllable, and inflation rates are transmitted intraregionally. Indeed, the creation of a new currency in Slovenia shielded it from sharing in the inflation in other parts of Yugoslavia, which at the time of secession was peaking at 35,000 percent annually. Another reason why it is important for the seceding region to have its own currency is to avoid being blackmailed or suffocated economically by the center. The case of Biafra provides an example of this blackmail by the center: In 1968, the Central Bank of Nigeria announced the introduction of new currency notes, thus invalidating the currency in use in Biafra. If Biafra had its own currency in place before, it would have been impervious to such a move by the central bank. Lastly, after a separate currency and its corresponding banking system, have been established, then an independent monetary policy can be pursued, giving economic independence to the seceding region.

However, the introduction of a new currency is not an easy task. Among the minor problems to be solved are, for example, the choice of the currency. Slovenia first introduced the lipa in 1990, and then, in 1991, it introduced the toler; Croatia first introduced the Croatian dinar, and only in 1994 renamed it the kuna.[15] Another minor problem is the determination of the location for the printing of the currency, an issue that is especially poignant as long as the region is still part of the state. Indeed, Estonia printed its kroons abroad, while Ukraine chose Canada for the printing of its coupons. But these are minor considerations in comparison with some long-term problems raised by introducing a new currency. Among these, the biggest is that the seceding region has the disadvantage of minimal backing for its currency, it has inexperience in dealing with monetary matters (except in the case of presecession decentralization, such as in Slovenia), and it is faced with the lack of acceptance of that currency in the global economy. The introduction of a new currency entails the establishment of the value of the new currency, the pegging of it usually to another (or the choice that it will freely fluctuate), and the determination of convertibility. In addition, there is the problem of the macroeconomic effects of withdrawing of the old currency from circulation. The negative effects of this spillover into the ex-state were evident when for example, Slovenia dumped its dinar holdings and thereby further aggravated inflation in dinar regions.

There is wide variation in the monetary efforts of the secessionist region of the former Soviet Union. While Ukraine's parliament voted in March 1992 to completely replace the ruble with the local currency (coupon) on April 1, regions such as Kazakhstan had chosen to remain within the ruble zone. The leader of the new state, Nursultan Nazarbaev, opted not to create a separate currency and therefore to continue the old pattern of trade while introducing local monetary institutions that were not available through the Commonwealth. The critical problem faced by the former Soviet republics, including Russia, had to do with the difficulties involved in the creation of new banking systems. None of the republics had experience in handling their own spending. The central state bank, which ceased to exist as of January 1, 1992, collected the republic's revenues and then gave out funds in return. This system has been replaced by a series of banks with Western-style banking relations, in which the republican banks are required to operate their own system of debits and credits and to use balance sheets. The enormity of the problem is underscored by the fact that balance sheets were alien to the leaders of the banking world in some seceding regions, while they are studied by first-year economics students in Western countries.

5. Interrepublic investments. States with industrial policies tend to channel investment capital into regions in which the returns are greatest. They follow the principle of comparative advantage in order to maximize returns. Even the private sector is not immune to government's incentives for the development of a predetermined location. Industrial policy, coupled with regional policy aimed at aiding the less developed regions, has resulted in a set of intricate interregional investment patterns linking regions within a union. At the time of secession, how are these links to be disentangled? If the seceding region is the recipient of investment, it may simply unilaterally retain the assets on its territory and cease loan repayments. Alternatively, if it is the seceding region that has made the investments, it may try to reap its assets and call in its loans. The difficulty of finding a solution that goes beyond "finders keepers" is exemplified by the exchange of remarks between the Soviet center and Lithuania: When Gorbachev presented Lithuania with a bill for the investment over the past few decades, Lithuania responded by threatening to present a bill for decades of socialist mismanagement and inefficiency.

If interregional investments are not interrupted, but as a result of economic reasoning on both sides are deemed to continue, the fact that one is dealing with international arrangements, rather than internal domestic ones, will raise a new series of questions. Among the issues to be determined is the question of the repatriation of profits: If the seceding region is the lender, should it be allowed to take out its profits from its ex-state? Furthermore, what currency is to be used in these transactions? If the seceding region has adopted a new currency, should it be acceptable in the former state, or should the seceding region use its holdings of the old currency? The determination of a legal framework within which investments are to occur is a serious obstacle to the continuation of interregional investments. Whereas before secession a single set of laws was in effect, in the aftermath of secession not only are there two sets of legal systems, but they will both be relatively new and thus unfamiliar and untested. If secession has been particularly bloody or abrupt, there will be a legal void, similar to a legal anarchy, that is likely to negatively affect interregional investments. Finally, with secession, taxation practices will change in at least the seceding region, raising the necessity to reevaluate the economic grounds upon which the initial investment was made.

6. *Adjustment to cessation of subsidies.* Most states subsidize the production of some goods. The nature of those goods and the location of their production is determined by regional and development policy of the state. In the aftermath of secession, the newly independent region has to face the unpleasant adjustment period associated with the loss of subsidies. This often entails shortages and higher prices. In Estonia, for example, the price of heating oil, imported from the former Soviet Union, went from 83 rubles a ton to 12,000 rubles following independence.[16]

7. *Externalities.* Responsibility for positive and negative externalities that occur across regional borders must be assessed during the period of redefinition. The entanglement of economies, coupled with the continuous geographical space prior to secession, has given rise to numerous positive and negative externalities, including the benefits to Serbia from a dam in Bosnia-Herzegovina, and the costs to Belarus from the spill-out at Chernobyl in Ukraine. Presently the seceding regions tend to focus on the negative externalities that they have experienced from the center, from which they expect compensation, while the center tends to focus on the positive externalities that seceding regions have benefited from and demand compensation for those. The most prominent externality issue that has recently been debated and most negotiated is pollution.

Most regions currently undergoing secessionist drives are not subject to regulation pertaining to the protection of the environment from industrial production as this has, until recently, tended to characterize the more developed Western states. In the absence of regulations restraining pollution, significant damage to the environment occurred. This is especially acute in the Communist countries, where there was both outdated technology as well as limited exposure of the problem. In Slovakia's secessionist efforts, the Slovaks blame the Czechs for environmental damage due to industrial production, the Bougainvillains blame the Papua New Guineans for the wreckage of their natural habitat by the exploitation of the mines, the Karen blame the Burmese for the deforestation of their traditional homeland, and the Cree and Inuit blame the Québécois for the exploitation of the northern woods. The Kazakhstanis have another concern, namely, the radiation-induced illnesses that hundreds of thousands of people seem to be suffering from. This is due to the testing of nuclear weapons, as well as chemical and biological testing, whose effects, it is estimated, will take decades to clean up. Who should be responsible for the cleanup expenses? Is it just the center, or should the responsibility be shared by the newly independent regions?

To date, very little progress has been made in the allocation of prices to these externalities in order for compensation to be determined. This is because externalities are ranked low among the issues to be resolved. Indeed, it is difficult enough trying to unwind relationships that are more pressing, and divide assets that are tangible, that the division of responsibility of intangibles such as pollution is bound to wait or go unresolved.

8. Social security, pensions, and medical insurance. Secession raises questions pertaining to the ownership of all social funds and creates problems in the dismemberment of these funds. Who owns the funds: the administrations at the regional levels, or the populations that made payments? When a region secedes, what happens to unemployment or pension payments to the workers that come from the center? Should a proportion of the fund be handed over to the seceding region in order to ensure no interruption of pension payments or medical care?

Social funds tend to be centralized, even in decentralized states such as Belgium and Canada, where the devolution of the social security system, although under discussion, is perceived as the beginning of the unraveling of the state. One exception is the former Yugoslavia, where pension funds, social security, and medical insurance have been administered at the republic level for decades. Consequently, the problem of dismemberment by region does not arise. However, the lack of agreement as to the boundaries of the seceding regions of Croatia and Bosnia-Herzegovina have led to the following two problems. First, decentralization of social security, health, and pension systems is not done on a county basis; therefore, the social funds of the population of Krajina continued to be held centrally in Zagreb while that region was under Serbian control. Second, given the large interregional displacement of workers due to the civil war, it is unclear which central administration is to pay for the refugees' social benefits. For example, the Serbian refugees from Slavonia who have relocated to Serbia have ceased to receive their pensions from Zagreb. Which new state is responsible for these payments: the secessionist region of Croatia, which has absorbed their workers' contributions, or the receiving region, to which this labor force ethnically belongs?

9. Division of the army and military arsenal. An army represents a unifying force within a country. An army draws population and monetary contributions from all regions of the state and thus is truly a state service. With secession of one region, or the unraveling of the entire state, the question of dismemberment of the army, as well as ownership of military assets, gains prominence. Moreover, there is often a rush by the new states to create an army (Macedonia is a conspicuous exception). The creation of new, regional armies is perceived as a national symbol. Indeed, according to the defense minister of Ukraine, "When the talk is of creating an army, everyone applauds. But when economists speak of the problems of 'going it alone', nobody listens."[17]

When the Soviet Union broke up, the division of the army and nuclear arsenal were the most pressing aspect of the negotiations between Russia, Ukraine, and Kazakhstan during early 1992. For a limited time, it even seemed that the division of the former Soviet army might tear the new Commonwealth of Independent States apart. Among the CIS members, eight decided in February 1992 that they would retain their armed forces under one central control: Six agreed to a single command of conventional forces for a few years, while Belarus and Uzbekistan agreed but with great reservations.[18] Ukraine, Azerbaijan, and Moldova will set up their own armies. In March 1992, President Yeltsin began moves to create a Russian army. This raises the question of which military assets would go to these republics. There are several approaches to this resolution: The formula preferred by the three republics is that they will take control of everything located on their soil, with the exception of strategic weapons. This was done in the case of Moldova, when President Snegur simply announced the takeover of former Soviet military property in the republic. This type of takeover was perceived as unfair by the Russians, who claimed that a disproportionate quantity of the arsenal was located in Belarus and Ukraine since these were border republics heavily manned for defense purposes. Therefore, the formula for division should be based on territory, population, and the length of borders. Such a formula would yield very different results.[19]

External Issues to Be Resolved

1. International economic relations. In the aftermath of secession, a region will establish economic relations with the international economy and, following a lag, with its former state. Among the steps that newly independent states must take in establishing themselves in the international arena includes the taking over of their borders and customs. Associated with this is the opening of embassies and representatives abroad. Included in the representatives are often those to international economic organizations whose participation is sought. Indeed, among the regions that declared sovereignty in the course of 1990-1991, most of them have attempted entry in the European Union, the OECD, the World Bank, and NATO. Former Soviet republics were accepted into the IMF, while former Yugoslav republics became members of the Organization on Security and Cooperation in Europe. Acceptance of membership to all these international organizations is dependent upon how the existing organizations perceive themselves. The World Bank and the United Nations will most easily accept newcomers because of the nature of their mandate. However, for the EU, such a potentially wide membership raises numerous questions as to how big can the association get before diseconomies of scale start setting in.

The seceding region will need to establish ties with its former state. Pragmatic concerns such as geography and economics often dictate these ties. Unlike a husband and wife who following divorce can have no interaction, seceding regions have that option only if their territory is not contiguous, as in the case of Bougainville. Even when secession occurs under conditions of war, the healing process postpones relations somewhat, but some of the ties that bind regions in the first place prevail. Indeed, in the case of Bangladesh, political and economic ties were reestablished with Pakistan shortly after secession, and trade links were revived within one year of the conflict.

The nature of ties between a secessionist region and its former state can take numerous forms. At one end of the spectrum, the two may have no formal political ties, and the cessation of trade may have left economic relations to a mere dwindling of preexisting relations. At the other end of the spectrum, the two political entities may decide to share in numerous activities while retaining sovereignty in others. Various forms of integration, commonwealth, and confederation arrangements have been proposed and have sprung up. For example, in the former Soviet Union, the Commonwealth of Independent States was created in December 1991 to replace the political links between eleven of the former fifteen Soviet republics. In former Yugoslavia, various organizational forms have been suggested to replace the federation established by the constitution of 1974. Prior to the breakup, Croatia and Slovenia proposed a confederal agreement that gave virtually no power to the center; Bosnia proposed an asymmetrical federation; and after the war broke out, the European Community suggested a Swiss type of confederation composed of ethnically based cantons for the solution of the Bosnian and Herzegovina crisis. Still other confederal arrangements have been suggested for the future beyond the Dayton Accords.

2. Trade. Upon secession, the nature of trade undergoes a transformation. Trade in the global markets, as well as trade with the former state, is altered because of the new status of sovereignty. Although trade between the secessionist region and the former state becomes international trade, it is treated separately here since it entails a different set of concerns. With respect to trade with the global economy, a newly seceded region is likely to try to solidify and expand the preexisting ties. The benefits to it of a speedy integration into the global system include access to foreign currency, to manufacturing inputs and raw materials, and to consumer goods. These are often all essential to the regional economy if it is simultaneously adjusting to the loss of state markets or to the elevated prices that trade with the former state probably entails in the absence of central subsidies.

However, the seceding region is faced with numerous obstacles in its attempt to break into international trading networks. These often include, first, the lack of experience in trade, especially in regions where foreign trade was channeled through a central trading unit (such as the secessionist regions of Lithuania, Casamance, and Punjab). Also, the lack of hard currency with which to import is a problem for the seceding region. Second, if the region has its own currency, then the issue of convertibility of that currency must be resolved before it becomes an acceptable currency for trade. A third obstacle to be overcome in international trade has to do with the (often) low quality of goods offered for export that previously were not subject to international competition. It has been a rude awakening to many East European producers to find that some shabby goods that were successfully traded in less developed countries and other Eastern states do not fare well in hard currency markets. Fourth, another obstacle arises when the seceding region had enjoyed the advantages of subsidized central prices. The loss of these subsidies and the entry into world markets tend to produce an inflationary shock to the economy.

As a result of all these obstacles, it may be wise for the seceding region (and often also for the former state) to encourage the continuation of trade relations in the aftermath of secession. Indeed, profitable exchanges can benefit both sides: For example, independent Estonia continued to ship 90 percent of its industrial goods to the former Soviet Union, and some of its factories buy 80 percent of their inputs from there. The degree to which such trade relations occur depends on several factors. First, the relative dependency of the seceding region on the former state (or vice versa) will determine the magnitude of the loss of each other's markets. Even Slovenia, which has been highly insulated from the markets of Yugoslavia, continued to engage in trade with Serbia, despite attempts to encourage a boycott of Slovenian goods. Second, the relative prices of goods must be renegotiated. In many cases, internal trade occurred with prices set by a central price commission in order to pursue central policy. This implied biases that hurt or aided regions. With secession, new prices need to be determined, and these will reflect supply and demand in the global markets. This may prove to be a rude shock to both trading partners. Third, it must be determined what currency trade will take place in. If the seceding region has not introduced a new currency, trade can proceed with payments in the familiar currency, as happened in trade between Russia and Kazakhstan. However, if a new currency is introduced, then that currency should be made convertible as soon as possible to ensure proper and fair valuation of goods. Fourth, secession implies that the newly independent states have the right to enter into new forms of protection in their trade arrangements. This in fact is a big obstacle to the progress of trade between regions since protection may be perceived as a way of rectifying old wrongs. The higher the degree of dependency between regions, the greater the disruption to trade caused by such protective practices. This led Anders Aslund to say that, in the case of the former Soviet Union, "everything should be done to maintain the existing economic links."[20]

However, the potential for trade disruption is great in the cases of seceding regions. To minimize this, Oleh Havrylyshyn and John Williamson have made three concrete suggestions:[21] First, the regions should have a commitment to ban any restrictions to interregional trade. Second, regions should guarantee the same treatment to firms from other regions as in their own. And third, regions should agree to adopt common industrial standards, subject to either central or international authority. By adopting these guidelines, regions might avoid the recessionary pitfalls associated with abrupt decrease in trade.

3. Foreign investment and capital flows. International and interregional financial flows, as trade flows, become altered in the aftermath of secession. A secessionist region will try to maintain and enlarge financial links with the world economy while at the same time establish new links with its former state. It will try to ensure the inflow of foreign capital, investments and loans, grants and aid, technical assistance, etc. There are several simultaneous processes that warrant consideration during the period of redefinition with respect to financial flows: the disengagement from those foreign commitments that are deemed unbeneficial, the division of foreign commitments between the seceding region and the former state, and the encouragement of new financial ties.

The major problem with severing old ties arises because the seceding region is usually the recipient of international inflows by way of the center. Therefore, flows were negotiated, contracted, and executed via the former state. Upon secession, the future of those contracts is uncertain, producing confusion that is amplified by the introduction of new tax and foreign currency laws as well as new legal systems in both the seceding region and the former state. This confusion was so evident in Yugoslavia, where, at the time of Slovenia's secession, some 8,000 international agreements made with Yugoslavia had to be renegotiated or terminated.

With respect to setting up new international arrangements, the seceding region has the task of providing potential investors with the following: First, it must convince them that there is a valid reason, economic or political, for their investments. Second, the seceding region must provide an atmosphere conducive to the inflow of capital. This entails a clear taxation policy, a coherent legal framework, a commitment to the establishment of an infrastructure (where it is not already in place), and so forth. Third, the seceding region must have indisputable rights over the territory involved in the international agreements.[22]

Phase III: Reequilibration

A study of the "aftermath" of successful secession must address itself to questions pertaining to the economic life of the region as an independent economic entity. The nature of the arrangements made in the "during" period, as well as other economic factors inherent in the particular situation that characterizes the region, are relevant in determining the economic future of the region — in other words, its viability. Economic viability, as secessionist aspirations, is a concept fraught with imprecision. A recent study by the Deutsche Bank calculated the viability of Soviet Republics (the "Independence Potential") by identifying various economic criteria for success and then testing for them.[23] Wei Ding conducted a similar study of the Yugoslav republics.[24] For the purposes of this study, the economic viability of a region is defined as its ability to sustain economic growth at or above the preindependence levels, in the short-run aftermath of secession.[25]

The period of reequilibration is characterized by precarious adjustments in the political, social and economic spheres. Postsecessionist regions will vary in their ability to surmount the obstacles that will present themselves after severance of ties with the center. The secessionist regions of the world do not all have the same resource advantages, the same international support, and the same ability to manage their economies independently. There are various economic factors that determine the viability of regions. These include, among others, the method by which secession was achieved. If independence is achieved through peaceful means, then the new region is not encumbered with reconstruction costs as it might be when the economy is devastated by outbursts of violence in response to secessionist demands. Indeed, the civil war that ensued from the declarations of independence in both Biafra and Katanga so devastated their regional economies that they ceased to be viable.

Another consideration in the viability of a secessionist region is the ethnic homogeneity of the population, which tends to minimize labor force disruption in the aftermath of secession. Minorities in the seceding region might be threatened by secession, as their rights are usually reevaluated. This process of ethnic rivalries may translate into significant disruption of economic activity, as occurred when the rights of the Gagauz and the Trans-Dniesterians in Moldova were threatened by presecessionist activity, as were those of the Russians in Latvia and Estonia. Viability is also determined by the degree of price deviation from international prices, since that determines the facility with which a region can integrate itself into the global economy. Clearly, a region accustomed to subsidies will undergo a costly adjustment following independence. Indeed, it was estimated that Lithuania would pay double for the purchase of various raw materials in the absence of central subsidies.[26]

However, there are other even more important determinants of viability. For example, there is a positive relationship between viability and economic development: The higher the level of development, the higher is its capital stock, its factor productivity, and the development of its infrastructure and services. With respect to economic development, there is wide variation among secessionist regions, ranging from some of the most developed in the world (Lombardy) to some of the least developed (East Timor). The issue of economic development is also complicated by the fact that some regions have the potential for more development than they have actually achieved, usually as a result of the possession of lucrative assets, such as in the case of Bougainville, Katanga, Russia, and others. The potential of this group of secessionist regions places them in a different category from less developed secessionist regions that have few resources to count on upon independence.

There is also a positive relationship between viability and interregional flows. These flows include the allocation of funds from the central budget that flow into the regions and the outflow of tax revenue from the states to the central budget. Interregional flows affect viability insofar as the severing of ties to the state implies the curtailment of outflow from the region, which may translate into a larger pool of resources for regional use and thus enhance the chances of sustained economic growth after independence. If the region is a net recipient of interregional flows, then its viability will suffer from secession. The experience of the secessionist regions varies: In Slovenia, for example, the net value of resource flows was negative. In other words, the center sent to Slovenia less than it contributed, implying that the costs to the regions of federal demands are lower than the benefits. The fragmentary evidence on the subject seems to point to similar net flows in Lombardy, Bougainville, Biafra, and Katanga. In Lombardy, the net transfer out of the region, both with respect to capital as well as to goods and services, exceeds the inflow. The regions wealthy in resources, such as Bougainville, Biafra, and Katanga, are the principal income contributors in their countries and as such do not benefit from the center in central budgetary allocations. In these five cases, the net outflow of resources has contributed to aggravating presecession perceptions of injustice (whether it is called a tax revolt, as in Lombardy, or the "milking of the cow," as in Biafra), as well as the perception that with secession those funds will be available for local use. With respect to Punjab, Quebec, and the Baltic republics of the former Soviet Union, the evidence is inconclusive since some data support the contention that the region is a net recipient of central funds, while other data indicate it is a net loser.[27]

There is also a positive relationship between viability and decentralization of economic power insofar as decentralization fosters self-sufficiency of the region and gives it experience in dealing with its affairs. Decentralized regions enjoyed extensive regional powers with respect to economic decisions and processes and include regions such as Slovenia, Quebec, Punjab, and Bougainville. Such local powers were not realized in regions that were part of a centralized political system, such as Lombardy, Katanga, Biafra, and the former Soviet republics.

There is a negative relationship between viability and trade dependency of the secessionist region on the union. Trade dependency on the union is likely to decrease viability because secession will affect the economy, while trade dependency on international markets is positive since it indicates an already established link that is an advantage in the aftermath of secession. In Bougainville, Katanga, and Biafra, the extraction of copper, petroleum, and other natural resources occurred principally for the international markets. In these cases, the technology, the know-how, and supportive materials for the production process were provided from foreign companies with little input from the national level. Prior to the breakup of Yugoslavia, the national trading system had increasingly become so fragmented that Slovenia was more integrated into the international markets than those of Yugoslavia. Punjab also has a low trade dependency on the nation since it was remarkably successful in creating an economic self-sufficiency with respect to the principal inputs for its production. Although it does depend on national markets for the sale of its output, this can be attributed to the national food policy that prohibited Punjab from trading its primary products in the international markets. Lombardy also has a low trade dependency: It no longer depends on southern Italy for cheap labor, it has been purchasing other resources from the more expensive international markets, and it has harbored extensive trade ties with northern European nations such that a large proportion of its output is exported. The evidence with respect to regional dependency in Quebec is inconclusive. There the Québécois are increasingly taking on positions that previously were in the hands of "outsiders" (namely, the Anglos). Further, reports indicating that the loss of the Ontario markets would not significantly impact on the region (as long as the U.S. markets remained open) imply that regional dependency is low. In the former Soviet republics, trade dependency seems high in all regions except Russia.

On the basis of the above, it seems that Lombardy, Slovenia, Quebec, and Catalonia are all viable entities that could, with little adjustment, sustain their preindependence economic status. First, they are all developed regions, and development is positively related to viability. Second, the net flows (to the extent that it is possible to determine) seem to be positive in Lombardy, Catalonia, and Slovenia. The greater the net outflows, the greater the viability when those outflows are stopped. Third, with respect to trade dependency, Quebec, Lombardy, and Slovenia have extensive trade ties with the international economy. The lower the trade dependency, the greater the viability. Finally, decentralization has been most prevalent in the case of Slovenia, followed by Quebec and Catalonia (Lombardy belongs to a highly centralized economic and political union).

There are numerous secessionist regions that have failed to achieve high levels of development but do have development potential (e.g., Bougainville, Punjab, and Katanga). Their viability is questionable but probable. Indeed, Bougainville is responsible for a large share of the world's copper production, and it produces 45 percent of the Papua New Guinean revenues. For decades, Punjab has been the highest-income region within the Indian union, surpassing the industrial states of Maharashtra and West Bengal. Of all the states of India, Punjab has the most viability as an independent region. Not only has it achieved the highest rates of growth, but it is also self-sufficient in agriculture, and it is a net exporter of foodstuffs. Moreover, its economic growth has diffused into nonagricultural sectors so that its industrialization is geared to increasing the capacity of its own economy. Katanga was the wealthiest region of the Belgian Congo, and by some estimates one of the wealthiest in Africa. Although landlocked with inadequate transportation systems and infrastructure, the region was viable as an independent entity because its economic potential was so vast and because it had foreign interests that would have continued to invest in the region.[28]

Secessionist regions that have achieved low levels of development and have a low potential for development seem un-viable as independent entities (e.g., Kosovo, Tajikistan, Western Sahara, and East Timor). However, it is with reservation that one dismisses them as such because regions with even fewer apparent possibilities have sustained their independence over long periods of time. All four regions share characteristics that contribute to making them less developed in the first place: Their natural characteristics are infertile soil (Western Sahara, Tajikistan), lack of access to water (Kosovo, Tajikistan), lack of big cities as centers of commerce and trade, poor transportation systems, etc. The labor force is characterized by below-average education and skill levels, and the regions are not self-sufficient in foodstuffs. Only Kosovo is rich in mineral deposits, many of which are not properly mined for lack of investment and infrastructure. Furthermore, only Kosovo has the potential to be self-sufficient in foodstuffs. However, Kosovo has interethnic population problems that greatly imperil the functioning of its labor markets, as well as the training of its future labor force. Tajikistan is likely to have similar interethnic problems. Indeed, with respect to the Deutsche Bank assessment of viability, Tajikistan ranks the lowest of the former Soviet republics, with a total score of 18 out of a possible 100.[29]

Against Fragmentation and Reintegration

The above description of the economic aspects of the "before," the "during," and the "after" of secession indicates that economics plays a role in all phases of the secessionist process. However, absent from the description was any assessment of the desirability of secession, nor an evaluation of the benefits and costs of secession to both the seceding and the remaining regions. Yet, such an assessment is imperative in the mid-1990s as a result of the wave of secession, partitions, and breakups that are not only a cartographer's nightmare, but also have enormous economic implications.

Let us for a moment explore the trend towards state fragmentation that is occurring in some parts of the world. The example of the Balkans is useful insofar as it incorporates both secessionist and irredentist drives towards fragmentation. What if Yugoslavia's fragmentation were to ripple through the entire Balkans and pressures for secession mounted in places like North Epirus, Transylvania, and Greek Macedonia?[30] In addition, what if pressure for other forms of irredentist ethno-territorial adjustments increased, such as the incorporation of parts of Vojvodina into Hungary or parts of Moldova into Romania? Over twenty new states would dot the Balkan map. The Balkans are not alone in this fragmentation trend: The new states of the former Soviet Union are challenged by separatists demanding the creation of dozens of small entities, such as Yakutia and Chechnya in Russia, Crimea in Ukraine, Trans-Dniestria in Moldova, and Abkhazia in Georgia. In Africa, the interethnic intolerance that rages in Rwanda, Sudan, and Angola underscores the pressure to redraw state boundaries. And in

Asia, the movements for secession in India, Sri Lanka, and Papua New Guinea pale against the possibilities that arise if China begins to break up. In North America, might a secessionist Quebec have to contend with a secessionist north to accommodate the territorial demands of the Cree?

If the international community were to rush to recognize the legitimacy of all the secessionist demands enumerated above, as it did with the former Soviet republics and (selectively) in Yugoslavia, the result would be a proliferation of numerous nation-states of varying sizes and resources, and thus of varying potential and viability. While some writers have identified positive aspects to the creation of microstates, such as the increased ability to sustain peace (notably Hans Kohr[31]), the increased tendency for cultural revival (notably Dean Keith Simonton[32]), or the justice entailed in national self-determination (Michael Lind),[33] there would be numerous problems in their proliferation under the present conditions. Clearly, microstates exist and have thrived throughout the world; for example, Andorra, San Marino, Bhutan, and Liechtenstein. However, they are usually single microstates existing within the context of larger states with which they have a patron relationship, rather than within a sea of similar microstates.

In addition to political, ethnic, and strategic concerns of fragmentation, the economic potential of small nation-states warrants discussion. Fragmentation implies the creation of regional units that must deal with the loss of benefits associated with size, such as economies of scale and a varied resource base. The resulting loss of markets increases dependency on the outside world and costs because of duplication of services and inefficiency. Moreover, the mere threat of fragmentation that permeates multiethnic states today is a severe restraint on central investment. Indeed, it is unlikely that allocations from the central budget will be made for investment into regions that are contemplating secession (Kosovo is unlikely to get many funds from the Yugoslav federal budget), severely restricting the prospects for economic development. In addition, the new states incur costs embodied in the creation process, as they face the daunting prospect of setting up independent institutions (such as currencies, central banks, legal and tax systems, etc.) to enable independent functioning of their economies (the remaining state also faces enormous costs of adjustment, as clearly indicated by Ethiopia and Serbia-Montenegro in the 1990s). Then, if fragmentation occurs in a previously communist state that is undergoing a simultaneous transition to a market economy, then this structural change also imposes its short-term costs on the new economy. Moreover, if fragmentation occurs under conditions of war, then the costs are compounded as economies convert to war economies and incur the cost of warfare. All three of these changes — adjustment to sovereignty, transition to capitalism, and conversion to war economics — are simultaneously convulsing the successor states of Yugoslavia, obscuring a clear assessment of viability of the newly emerging states. Under the best of circumstances, economic obstacles embodied in any one of these three processes may be hard to surmount.

Instead of the creation of small enclaves, let us explore what would happen if that trend were reversed and states were encouraged to expand to include more territories and ethnic groups. Such an integrative trend is evident among both formerly divided regions (such as Germany), formerly united regions (such as the Commonwealth of Independent States), and among formerly unrelated states (such as the European Union).

The economic advantages of larger heterogeneous units are many, including economies of scale, extended markets, and consequently enhanced viability. These benefits are best exploited when states have economic links that transcend mere trade. Indeed, trade between many small states represents an expensive duplication of services and institutions. It also implies likely protection policies that hurt consumers and ultimately producers. There is no reason to assume that cooperation among these trading partners would take place without some other level of cooperation, such as common economic policies. Moreover, reintegrated units would convey to the international community of investors that there is a commitment to stability in the region, thus increasing the chances of foreign investment and aid. Also, given that fragmentation and secession have often been associated with the creation of ethnically pure states (the nation-state), large heterogeneous states have the advantage of incorporating numerous ethnic groups into a political superstructure, thus institutionalizing heterogeneity and deriving strength from size and diversity. From the point of view of economics, tolerance of heterogeneity is important because, in the short run, it avoids the disruptive effects on the labor force associated with the migration and ethnic cleansing that underlie the creation of ethnically pure states. Such population movements result in imbalances in supply and demand of labor and may take up to a generation to adjust fully to the loss of skills.[34]

In only a few years after the wave of successful secessions began in 1990, the world is already witnessing some form of reintegration of past breakups. To a large extent, this is due to the realization that sovereignty is not necessarily accompanied by material benefits. Shattered hopes, impatience, and unrealistic expectations may manifest themselves in a nostalgic attempt to re-create past economic securities, such as in Hungary, Poland, Ukraine, Lithuania, and sections of East Germany, all of which voted to reinstate former Communists within a few years after their demise. Indeed, a few years ago, independence was more important a focus than economic reality: According to *The Economist,* "They [Ukrainian leaders] were more interested in flags and army uniforms, the symbols of independence, than in economic strength."[35] Alternatively, those shattered hopes may also impose a more pragmatic review of economic relations with one's ex-state. This is most evident in the former Soviet Union, where some newly independent states soon "volunteered to transfer sovereignty to Russia in the hope of reviving their economies through reintegration with it."[36] While the member states of the CIS have the satisfaction of knowing they are in a voluntary association, in reality many of the interregional links have changed little since 1991. Belarus and Tajikistan returned to the Russian monetary system, relinquishing their right to issue currency and conduct monetary policy.[37] Trade concessions are also being made by Russia to various new states: For example, Ukraine has been the beneficiary of guaranteed gas deliveries from Russia. Also, after refusing to join the CIS, several smaller states changed their position. Both Moldova and Georgia joined in response to secessionist activity within their borders (Trans-Dniestrian separatists and Romanian irredentists and Abkhaz separatists, respectively), hoping that Russian support and peacekeeping forces might prevent fragmentation.

The willingness of some former Soviet republics to renew ties with Russia has to do with the realities of economics. Ukraine, which had the best chances for viability as an independent economy, experienced severe economic difficulties and the voters became increasingly open to reintegration with Russia, where the standard of living became several times higher than in Ukraine.[38] Such steps towards some form of reintegration with Russia have been met with restrained support within Russia, where a poll showed that almost one-third said it would be worth some hardship to renew political union with both Ukraine and Belarus.[39] The former Russian Finance Minister Boris Fedorov had said that a monetary agreement with Belarus would indeed pose much hardship for Russia unless accompanied by political unification, and Belarus has in fact moved close to that outcome.[40]

Even in the former Yugoslavia, time may bring a new rapprochement of the former Yugoslav peoples and republics. Before the Yugoslav war was over, some Croats expressed a desire for renewed economic ties: In May 1993, a poll in Croatia showed almost 60 percent favoring some kind of "loose customs and economic links between Croatia and rump Yugoslavia."[41]

A form of economic reintegration of former Yugoslav lands has been called for and predicted by many individuals: Yugoslav businessmen like Boris Vukobrat,[42] former politicians like Milan Panić,[43] historians like Christopher Cviic,[44] and economists like Branko Horvat.[45] Indeed, the last claimed that in the absence of some form of economic integration in the Balkans, the population of his native Croatia is bound to be like that of the Caribbean states — "waiters on the outside, peasants on the inside." Even the president of Montenegro, Momir Bulatović, said that the future must consist of the normalization of economic relations between former Yugoslav republics.[46]

With time, some newly seceded regions face economic hardships that were not part of the independence dream. Reality has forced them to consider new economic relations with their former states. Was independence necessary, in order to redefine new (but similar) economic relationships? President Rahman of Singapore believed so: At the time of the break between Singapore and the Malaysian Federation, he claimed that there may be prospects for reunification in the future, after a taste of sovereignty, since "absence makes the heart grow fonder."[47] This view was also voiced by the Ukrainian minister of defense: "What we need today is a chance to breathe some freedom, to really feel some sovereignty. Then maybe in five years or so we will start talking of uniting or some association."[48]

Is secession necessary to bring about a reestablishment of economic ties? The question may be unresolved in the minds of nationalists, ethnic leaders, and international leaders. Economists, on the other hand, focus on the waste associated with the violence, the wars, and the economic hardships of struggling for the redrawing of state boundaries. To them it is necessary to explore other ways of addressing nationalist concerns without incurring the huge costs of secession.

Notes

1. Belgium seceded from the Netherlands (1830), Norway from Sweden (1905), Ireland from Britain (1919), and Bangladesh from Pakistan (1971).

2. The rare studies of economics in secession include the following: Miroslav Hroch, *Social Preconditions of National Revival in Europe* (Cambridge: Cambridge University Press, 1985); Beth Michneck, "Regional Autonomy, Territoriality, and the Economy" (paper presented to the American Association for the Advancement of Slavic Studies, Washington, D.C., October 1990); Anthony Birch, *Nationalism and National Integration* (London: Unwin Hyman, 1989); and *Ethnicity and Resource Competition in Plural Societies,* ed. Leo Despres (The Hague: Mouton, 1975).

3. While scholars have studied secession from the point of view of stages, none have focused on the economic components they have considered neither the after stage nor the possibility of peaceful successful secessions. See John Wood, "Secession: A Comparative Analytic Framework," *Canadian Journal of Political Science,* Vol. 14, No. 1, March 1981; and Anthony Smith, "Introduction: The Formation of Nationalist Movements," in *Nationalist Movements,* ed. A. D. Smith (New York: Macmillan, 1976).

4. Peter Leslie, "Ethnonationalism in a Federal State: The Case of Canada," in *Ethnoterritorial Politics, Policy and the Western World,* ed. Joseph Rudolph and Robert Thompson (Boulder: Lynne Rienner Publishers, 1989), 47; Ian Bremmer, "Fraternal Illusions: Nations and Politics in the USSR" (paper presented to the American Association for the Advancement of Slavic Studies, Miami, 1991), 47.

5. Military capacity is not necessarily a determining factor, as the war in the former Yugoslavia shows: While Serbia was unequivocally the strongest military power, it was unable to harness that power to complete the war because of international support extended to its enemies.

6. *International Herald Tribune,* March 23, 1990

7. Bookman, *The Economics of Secession,* 79-80.

8. On October 29, 1992, Czech Prime Minister Václav Klaus and Slovak Prime Minister Vladimir Mečiar signed sixteen comprehensive agreements defining interstate relations after breakup. The economic components include the creation of

a customs union, as well as a treaty on monetary arrangements, social security, and intraregional employment. The noneconomic aspects of the agreement include treaties on border regulations; legal matters concerning personal documents, car registration, and weapons registration; a border treaty; the establishment of a common approach to residency requirements for third-country nationals; visa requirements; joint use of archives belonging to the federal ministry of internal affairs; cooperation in communications, health care services, and environmental protection; legal assistance; cooperation in education; and mutual recognition of legal documents issued by each republic.

9. According to the agreement, the following principles were to be applied in the division of the debt: the regional share of national income, the share of federal exports, and the share of the Soviet population. See Valerii Semenov, "Republics Agree to Divide Federal Cake," in *Commersant,* July 29, 1991, 2.

10. *Transition,* vol. 3, no. 11, December 1992-January 1993: 12-13.

11. *Transition,* vol 3, no. 11, December 1992-January 1993: 12-13

12. Indeed, after Slovenia's bid for secession, the central government began questioning its past industrial location policies as well as biased monetary policy that favored credits for industrialization.

13. Allen Buchanan, *Secession* (Boulder: Westview Press, 1991), 107.

14. This unilateral decision caused the central bank in Lagos to retaliate by blocking the transfer of all foreign currency to the region.

15. This renaming was a very sensitive issue, since the kuna was used as the Croatian currency only during its fascist period in World War II.

16. *New York Times,* January 24, 1992.

17. *New York Times,* October 30, 1991.

18. The Ukrainian government halted the transfer of tactical nuclear weapons to Russia for a time because, according to President Kravchuk, there was no guarantee that Russia was destroying them, as previously agreed.

19. *The Economist,* February 22, 1992.

20. Anders Aslund, "Should the Soviet Union Get Western Assistance after the Coup?" (Stockholm: Stockholm Institute of Soviet and East European Studies, 1991), quoted in Oleh Havrylyshyn and John Williamson, *From Soviet Disunion to Eastern Economic Community* (Washington, D.C.: Institute for International Economics Policy Analyses in International Economics, #35, 1991), 17.

21. Oleh Havrylyshyn and John Williamson, *From Soviet Disunion to Eastern Economic Community.*

22. Sakhalin in Russia has been an example of the role played by unclear territorial rights on foreign investment: There has been dispute between the regional level administration and Moscow as to who holds the power to make decisions pertaining to oil exploration in this potentially lucrative region.

23. The Independence Criteria include the following: degree of industrialization, degree of self-sufficiency, mineral resources, agricultural hard currency earning potential, raw materials hard currency earning potential, and business mindedness. Deutsche Bank, *The Soviet Union at the Crossroads: Facts and Figures on the Soviet Republics* (Frankfurt: Deutsche Bank, 1991).

24. Wei Ding, "Yugoslavia: Costs and Benefits of Union and Interdependence of Regional Economies," *Comparative Economic Studies,* Vol. 33, No. 4, 1991.

25. The distinction between the long run and the short run is relevant since most regions are able to survive in the long run after reconstruction and the formation of new economic relationships with the international economy and its former union.

26. *The Wall Street Journal,* February 14, 1990.

27. Milica Z. Bookman, *The Economics of Secession.* (New York: St. Martin's Press, 1993) pp. 79-80.

28. In the period immediately before attempted secession, 1950-1957, its real rate of growth averaged 6.7 percent. See *Revolt in the Congo 1960-64,* ed. Howard Epstein (New York: Facts on File, 1965).

29. The highest scores were achieved for the location of mineral resources and the hard currency earning capacity of these raw materials. However, even this should be taken with a grain of salt since almost one-half of the territory houses the Gorno-Badakhshan Autonomous Region. This separate administrative unit is mostly inhabited by the Ismaili Muslims, who differ from the Sunni Muslims who are Tajiks, and therefore the two groups are likely to experience an increase in problems rather than a harmonious alliance (Deutsche Bank, *The Soviet Union at the Crossroads,* 38-39).

30. The movements for independence that preceded or accompanied the wars occurred at both the republic and the subrepublic level. Slovenia and Croatia declared independence in June 1991, and were followed by Bosnia-Herzegovina and Macedonia. In April 1992, Serbia and Montenegro declared a new federation under the name of Federal Republic of Yugoslavia. The Serbian population of Croatia declared an independent Republic of Serbian Krajina (December 1991), the Albanians of Kosovo declared independence (September 1991) while the Serbs of Bosnia-Herzegovina proclaimed the Sprska Republic (March 1992), the Croats in Bosnia-Herzegovina proclaimed the Croatian Community of Herceg-Bosna (July 1992), and Muslims in the Bihac pocket, under the leadership of Fikret Abdić, declared secession from Bosnia and called themselves the Autonomous Province of Western Bosnia.

31. Hans Kohr, "Disunion Now: A Plea for a Society Based upon Small Autonomous Units," *Commonwealth,* September 26, 1941.

32. Dean Keith Simonton claims that Eastern Europe presently shows the greatest promise because there, as in the city-states of Italy that produced the Renaissance and the small German states that produced Goethe, Hegel and Mozart, there is no cultural homogeneity (*New York Times,* March 22, 1992).

33. Michael Lind, "In Defense of Liberal Nationalism," *Foreign Affairs,* May-June 1994.

34. In addition, large multiethnic units would, first, lend protection to the smaller ethnic groups currently disadvantaged by nationalist constitutions. Numerous ethnic groups, as a result of their histories of conquests and repression, live in fear of the moment their ethnic groups become a minority, because as Uri Ra'anan pointed out, "when minorities become majorities, their political morals change." See *State and Nation in Multi-Ethnic Societies,* ed. Uri Ra'anan et al. (Manchester: Manchester University Press, 1991). Second, they would control the mutually exclusive aspirations for the restoration of former territorial

glory, such as in the Balkans, Greater Bulgaria, Greater Serbia, Greater Albania, Greater Croatia, etc.

35. *The Economist,* May 7, 1994, Survey, 3.

36. *The Economist,* September 18, 1993, 51.

37. With respect to Belarus, only the first stage of the monetary union has occurred at the time of writing (namely, the lifting of trade and customs restrictions between the two countries). The second stage, the exchange of the two currencies on a one-to-one basis, has yet to pass Parliament.

38. *The Economist,* May 7, 1994, Survey, 5.

39. This poll was taken in April 1994 (*RFE/RL Daily Report,* April 13, 1994: 5).

40. *RFE/RL Daily Report,* April 13, 1994, 4.

41. *RFE/RL Daily Report,* May 12, 1993.

42. *Nin,* August 6, 1993, 17.

43. Milan Panić, former prime minister of Yugoslavia, promotes a Balkan economic union, without which all Balkan countries are "doomed to inviability." *RFE/RL Daily Report,* June 21, 1993, 6.

44. The Balkan federation that is proposed by Cviic excludes Slovenia, Croatia, and Bosnia in their Titoist administrative borders (these states, according to Cviic, are to be a part of a union with Austria and other former imperial states). Yet such an exclusion divides religions and ethnic groups across borders (namely, Serbs and Muslims) and is thus a constant provocation to war. Christopher Cviic, *Remaking the Balkans* (New York: Council on Foreign Relations Press, 1991), 105.

45. Horvat claimed that this integration is necessary because the EU is unable to absorb the multitude of small, underdeveloped states. *RFE/RL Daily Report,* September 7, 1993, 7.

46. *Borba,* July 1, 1993.

47. C. M. Turnbull, *A History of Singapore 1819-1988,* 2nd ed. (Singapore: Oxford University Press, 1989), 288.

48. *New York Times,* October 30, 1991.

Four

The Collapse of the Austro-Hungarian Empire

John Bacher

The collapse of empires, and even the breakup of smaller states, regularly lead to serious geopolitical instability. Here I shall examine the ramifications of the dissolution of Austria-Hungary at the end of World War I, an event that contributed to the conditions for the subsequent disasters of the twentieth century.

Austria had been a minor player in European politics from the Middle Ages until 1683, when the invading Ottoman armies reached the gates of Vienna then were rolled back and forced to cede territories. Austria, acquiring them, became a major power, especially because the European Christian rulers recognized the need for a strong power in the region to confront the Turks. In 1867, Austria was divided into a dual empire, Austria-Hungary, which began a steady evolution toward democracy and pluralism.

When at last Ottoman power in the Balkans was removed by the beginning of this century, a powder keg of nationalism exploded among the diverse people of the region,[1] destroying Austria-Hungary as well. After partition in 1918 most of its lands became continuously stained by dictatorship, war, and more or less violent ethnic conflict. The critical architect of the destruction of the Austrian-Hungarian Empire, Tomáš Garrigue Masaryk, had hoped in 1918 to create on its ruins a Slav federation comprising a democratic Russia, Yugoslavia, and Czechoslovakia. By 1938, the entire former Habsburg region was under the rule of fascist or monarchist dictatorships. Pan-Slavism of a sort would be achieved briefly, but only in the form of Stalin's dictatorship, which imposed unity on Eastern Europe after World War II.

During the Cold War all lands of the former Empire, with the exception of Austria and the areas annexed by Italy, came under the rule of Communist tyrannies. In the post-Communist period since the end of the Cold War, much of the region has been dealing with nationalism and religious extremism that the pro-empire reformers had been trying to defuse back in 1914.

Masaryk, who would become first president of the Republic of Czechoslovakia, was the key figure in breaking up the Austro-Hungarian empire by leading a separatist movement in its industrial heartland of Bohemia. Though he was a reformist while serving in the Austrian parliament before World War I, he took a revolutionary course after the war had begun. Going into exile in order to organize international support for his separatist crusade, he mobilized American émigré Slavs to influence President Woodrow Wilson. This liberal man, like the more authoritarian Lenin, would launch a crusade for "self-determination of nations," which would prove so destructive to the world's peace in the twentieth century.[2]

Tragically, it was easier to create a democratic, multinational Czechoslovak state on paper, in the glittering Versailles Palace, than to sustain it through the difficulties of governing by compromise and moderation. Czechoslovak politicians would be especially challenged during periods of economic hardship such as the great depression of the 1930s, when German politicians veered to extremism, and at the end of World War II, when the Czech political elite went through a similar period of vindictiveness.

In his book, *The New Europe: The Slav Standpoint,* which in 1918 became a bible for those bent on the destruction of Austria-Hungary, Masaryk displayed naiveté regarding the dark nationalist powers he was setting in motion. This is most evident in his optimism regarding future border disputes between Germany and Czechoslovakia.

In that book, the cornerstone of the new republic, Masaryk set the dynamite that Hitler would use to blow it up. He wrote that the parts of "Bohemia where there are only a few Czechs might be ceded to German Austria." The military problems of defending Czechoslovakia seem never to have entered his mind. He believed that the dissolution of Austria-Hungary would instantly result in "a democratic, non-militaristic Europe, where all nations will be good neighbors."[3]

By suggesting that the Sudetenland area of Czechoslovakia could be annexed to a German state, Masaryk made an error common to the overly optimistic separatist founders of many new states. He ignored the fact that changes to the border would make Czechoslovakia militarily indefensible. His country would lose three million citizens, most of its heavy industry, and its arms manufacturing capacities. The border inherited from Austria was easily defensible, being ringed with fortifications in mountainous areas difficult to invade. By ceding this defensible terrain to Germany, Czechoslovakia would leave itself vulnerable to invasion from troops attacking across a flat plain.

In 1938 Hitler, using the rhetoric of national self-determination as a convenient pretext, wrested German control of the Sudetenland area through the infamous Munich pact with Great Britain and France, signed over Czechoslovakia's objections. Had he been familiar with Masaryk's text, Hitler could have cited it as justification for seizing this strategic border area, for in it Masaryk laid the basis for the state that Nazi Germany intended to destroy. Also, Hitler's arguments for self-determination, although cunning and insincere, were difficult for Great Britain and France to refute, since they had used the same arguments in 1918 to carve Czechoslovakia out of Austria-Hungary. Since this annexation left Czechoslovakia largely defenseless, Hitler's subsequent invasion of the rest of the country went largely unopposed.

After occupying Prague, the Führer harnessed the racial hatreds of the dictatorships surrounding Czechoslovakia to finish off the last surviving democracy in Central Europe. Hitler parceled out sections of Czechoslovakia to neighboring Poland and Hungary. He created Slovakia as a German satellite that engaged in its own anti-Semitic and racist actions against Czechs, Jews, and Gypsies. Many fascist Slovaks later went to North America to escape prosecution for war crimes, where in the company of other "Cold Warriors," they dreamed of creating Slovakia anew — a dream that has since been achieved.[4]

Embittered by the Sudeten Germans' aid to Nazi Germany, Czechoslovakia became a pioneer in ethnic cleansing after the war, when its borders were restored. The three million Germans expelled from Czechoslovakia far exceed the one million persons later expelled, if more brutally, from the former Yugoslavia. Although Masaryk had predicted that the German minority would be treated well in Czechoslovakia, he was proved wrong in 1946.[5] Surprisingly, the Germans were expelled in an authoritarian fashion at that time, well before Communist dictatorship was imposed in 1948.

This expulsion became sort of an original sin for the restored Czechoslovakia, tying it more closely to the Soviet bloc. Discussion of the German exile question became a rigid taboo, for such talk terrified the surrounding Communist states in Eastern Europe, who had their own German expulsion skeletons in the closet. Consequently, they were troubled when discussion of the issue was opened up during the Prague Spring in 1968. The Poles in particular feared it would result in challenges to the legitimacy of their own national borders. Embittered Slovak exiles in North America made common cause with expelled Germans during the cold war and helped divide the country quickly after the Velvet Revolution restored democracy.

The tragic quality of Masaryk's predictions shows what dangers this liberal humanist intellectual had been playing with when he abandoned his support for Austria-Hungary and took up the separatist cause during World War I. He and other like-minded liberal Czech intellectuals, such as Edward Beneš, who succeeded him as president, made the best effort in Central Europe to establish a stable democracy that respected the rights of ethnic minorities. They were relative moderates who were converted to the separatist cause of more extreme Czechs only after concluding that Austria-Hungary was being annexed into Germany by the pressures of the war. With the support of the victorious allies at the end of World War I, they were able to see Czechoslovakia created. However, the democratic country they had envisioned would be destroyed by the authoritarian nationalist forces they had unwittingly unleashed.

The "father" of both Czechoslovakia and Yugoslavia, Masaryk was ultimately to see his nation-building efforts lamented by his own biological son, Jan Masaryk. The younger man later regretted his father's creations and observed that the Czechs were never happier than when they had been in the Austro-Hungarian empire.[6] After seeing the ill effects of his father's handiwork, Jan would die (according to investigative journalists during the 1968 Prague Spring) by falling or (as many believe) by being pushed out a window. He was the chief obstacle to the imposition of a Communist dictatorship in 1948 as the only cabinet minister not under its party discipline.

The Demise of the Empire and the Rise of Absolutisms, Right and Left

Jan Masaryk's death, whether murder or suicide, was an eloquent sign of courage or protest against the dictatorships that had swept over Central Europe since 1918. This repression was all the more tragic for reversing the general trend toward gradual liberalization in the Austrian Empire since 1860.

No king in Europe on the eve of World War I had been as ruthless as the dictators who would control much of the continent during the decades following that war. They came to power by manipulating the hatreds of race, religion, and class. With the dissolution of Austria-Hungary, clandestine nationalist extremists, who had been previously pushed to the sidelines in the interests of imperial unity, found new opportunities. They would take up the labels of Communists and Fascists and even change their labels to suit the momentary needs of holding power. As authoritarian nationalists, they found democracy more disturbing than Communism and Fascism. The new absolutism which emerged in Europe manipulated the forces of pan-Germanism and pan-Slavism that had earlier wreaked such havoc in World War I. These movements were ultimately directed from Berlin and Moscow, by Hitler and Stalin. Despite their ritual attacks on each other, they sometimes collaborated, even openly, as witnessed by the infamous Hitler-Stalin pact.

Despite such periods of collaboration, the roots of World War II on the eastern front can be traced to quarrels between Nazi Germany and Stalinist Russia over the division of the former lands of the Austro-Hungarian Empire. The nations between these two powers, unable to unify for the common defense, often intrigued with Germany against their neighbors. Hungary allied with Germany to attempt to expand to its 1867 borders, which had been reduced by the Treaty of Versailles in 1919. Slovakia allied against its own Czech former co-citizens suffering under Nazi occupation. Poland even allied with Germany to carve up Czechoslovakia a few months before it was itself dismembered by Hitler in cooperation with Stalin.

Although postwar Soviet apologists tried to justify the Hitler-Stalin pact as a defense against future German aggression, this was not how the treaty was viewed by its supporters in the Kremlin in 1939. Instead, it was essentially a criminal conspiracy — a violation of international law as set out in the Briand-Kellogg Pact — to carve up Poland, donate the Baltic states to the Soviet Union, and give Hitler a free hand to conquer much of Western Europe. As often happens among criminals, however, the Russo-German allies broke into a quarrel over the division of spoils not foreseen in their original alliance. In this case, the disputed booty was the former lands of the Austro-Hungarian Empire, south of the former province of Galicia, which was amicably divided — along with the rest of Poland — in the pact between the two great dictators.

The conspiracy of Hitler and Stalin broke up in November 1940 during the Molotov-Hitler conversations in Berlin. After this important meeting, German Foreign Minister von Ribbentrop explained to Japanese Foreign Minister Matsuoka their failure to cement the anticipated alliance between Japan, the USSR, and Germany. The reasons for the split among the dictators had nothing to do with ideology and everything to do with quarrels over territory in southern Europe. Molotov told Matsuoka that the quarrel emerged since Germany "could not permit a penetration of the Russians into the Balkans," although "Russia kept trying to push in that direction."[7] This is exactly what the Soviet Union subsequently achieved after the Nazi invasion of 1941. In an irony appropriate to his skillful manipulation, Stalin, with the aid of democratic allies, obtained much of the Balkan lands that he had been unable to conquer while cooperating with Hitler.[8]

Moderates' Failure to Unite against Nationalist Extremists

The tragic death of Austria-Hungary resulted from the failure of moderate political forces to effectively coalesce against authoritarian, nationalist-minded groups of the far left and right. This extremism contributed to World War I, prolonged the conflict, and deepened its destructive consequences. Why did they fail so seriously?

It was not that they favored the authoritarians. Moderates who accepted liberal, constitutionally based notions of human rights had more in common with each other than the emerging totalitarianisms of right and left. Unfortunately, they did not understand this and missed important opportunities to reform Austria after universal suffrage had been introduced in that part of the empire in 1907.

Both before 1918 and after, the bastions of extremism were located in Berlin and Moscow, the respective capitals of the pan-German and pan-Slav nationalist movements. With Hitler and Stalin these nationalist ideologies would eventually triumph, albeit for a limited period. Pan-Germanism would dominate Europe for a few years during World War II, achieving the goal of uniting Germans in a single state to dominate the rest of Europe. It was immediately replaced in the East by the Communist bloc, when the Soviet Union brought all the Slav states under its rule until 1948, when Tito split from this Pan-Slav empire.

Most socialists in Europe rejected Lenin's authoritarianism. The majority of nationalists in Austria-Hungary, who were largely moderates, preferred to keep the empire together rather than to carve it up. Few conservatives wished to go back to the authoritarianism that had governed most of continental Europe through terror in the 1850s. By 1914, varied moderate political groups were supporting freedom of expression, trade union rights, and an evolving social welfare state by 1914. Despite such a broad area of consensus, moderates' political conflicts were focused on each other more than on the extremists, who seemed to be marginalized, insignificant groups. The moderate leaders of Europe's varied political parties on the eve of World War I overlooked the dangers posed by their own extremist supporters.

Vienna, as a capital of a multinational empire, was a counterweight to the extremism of the right, which proved a powerful force in Berlin and Moscow. Austria's moderating interventions helped Germany to back away from the brink of war in potentially explosive conflicts involving colonies in Asia and Africa. The destruction of Austria-Hungary was a necessary precondition for either of the Pan-Slav or Pan-German movements to triumph. Under Hitler and Stalin, these nationalistic extremists would ultimately clash over the division of the empire's former lands.

Moderates before 1914 were lulled by their own achievements in international law, human rights, and social justice. Liberals, Catholics, and Social Democrats could all see the universe as unfolding as it should but did not see a darker side of human nature represented by those who did not appreciate such democratic gains as universal suffrage, multiculturalism, a free press, trial by jury, or a social insurance safety net.

The theorist who came closest to recognizing the dangers in store for the twentieth century was the Polish Jewish socialist intellectual Rosa Luxemburg, who was then important in the leadership of the German Social Democratic Party. Luxemburg's geographic origins help explain her prophetic view of the dangers posed by separatist nationalism. She was from the Russian sector of occupied Poland, a part of Europe then affected by violent ethnic conflicts. Her life had been so endangered by anti-Jewish pogroms that this inspired socialist speaker, often remembered for applauding "spontaneous" actions of militant class struggle, suffered from a fear of crowds. Her appreciation of civil liberties would cause her to clash with the architect of socialist totalitarianism, Lenin.

Luxemburg's ethnic group, the Jews, suffered more from mob violence than any other in Europe, ominously foreshadowing the holocaust. While she advocated diverse measures to respect minority languages and cultural rights, she condemned all nationalist movements and remedies that advocated the partition of states.

While Luxemburg outshone her contemporaries intellectually, this articulate foe of nationalism could not imagine how chauvinism would combine with the extremism of right and left. Consequently she was the most influential theorist of the socialist movements in Europe to condemn cooperation with centrist, "bourgeois" political parties. Had Luxemburg anticipated the strange devil's brew of left and right nationalists, her political ideas might have been more accommodating to notions of moderation.

In the semidemocracies of Russia, Austria-Hungary, and Germany such a sectarian approach could be justified, but Luxemburg carried her opposition to "ministerialism" so far as to oppose participation in ministries in fully democratic France. This kept the talented foe of militarism and nationalist extremism, Jean Jaurès, out of government office, unable to use his abilities to defuse a number of potential crises that could lead to war.

Luxemburg and her allies argued that a general war in Europe could be prevented through a general strike. Subsequent events showed such a remedy to be totally ineffectual in the hysterical atmosphere of crisis in July 1914. A more practical course would have been to have effective leaders such as Jaurès in ministerial office. Here they could discover extremists' schemes that might provoke war and propose fair solutions to nationalist quarrels, such as the German annexation of Alsace-Lorraine.

Luxemburg's opposition to "ministerialism" also erected a barrier to cooperation with the Catholic Center Party. This might have had a limited platform aimed at curbing German militarism, winning a more liberal constitution, and ending the persecution of the French, Danish, and Polish minorities of the empire. To judge from the election returns of the period, such a platform would have been supported by two-thirds of German voters in the voting returns in the last decade before World War I.

Unfortunately, the moderates did not combine forces in the stable political climate of Europe before 1914. Had they been able to do so, they could have defused potential time bombs through accommodation, such as France's border with Germany and the complex minorities questions of the Balkans. Instead, World War I erupted and exacerbated class and ethnic hatreds and antagonisms.

Hitler and Stalin rose to power on forces that were alive in the prewar era. Fortunately for the tranquillity of this period, such extremist ideologies were confined to the fringe. The tragedy of the twentieth century was that these megalomaniacs eventually controlled most of Europe and slaughtered a great proportion of its population.

Both Hitler and Stalin were in Vienna in 1913, outside the corridors of power. Neither of their extremist doctrines could garner substantial electoral and parliamentary support anywhere in Europe at that time. Pan-Germanism was also dismissed by intellectuals except in the military-industrial complex of Germany. Extremist notions of the vanguard party were confined to Lenin's breakaway faction of the Russian Social Democratic Party. Lenin's faction did not enjoy the support of even the most radical of socialists outside of Russia.

Hitler was a minor figure in Vienna in 1913, a poor artist surviving partly through the assistance of Jewish charities. Stalin was already a more important figure, having been sent to Vienna by Lenin to study the national question. These two figures, part of declining political movements in 1913, would dominate Europe less than twenty years later.

Even the most pessimistic of prophets could not have envisaged the horrors that would be unleashed by Communism and Fascism within two decades. It is true that Rosa Luxemburg spoke of the danger of "socialism or barbarism," a prophecy based on the horrors of Western imperialism in Africa. Still, in her darkest moments, she could not imagine that the atrocities Hitler and Stalin would impose on her native Poland.

Luxemburg and her mentor, Karl Kautsky, although both critical of Lenin's authoritarian theory of the vanguard party, did not direct their fiercest polemics in his direction. Regarding Lenin affectionately as well meaning, if errant, they aimed their theoretical fire in the wrong direction, against the democratic socialist theorist Edward Bernstein.

While Lenin was preparing a Communist dictatorship, Bernstein was developing imaginative, ethically based concepts for harmonizing the often conflicting movements for peace, human rights, democracy, and social justice in Europe's Indian summer of nonviolent gradual change. Bernstein gave theoretical expression to what social democrats were actually doing in practice — winning improvements for their working class political base, such as stronger trade union rights and improved social welfare measures. Unlike many otherwise similarly moderately inclined trade union based socialists, Bernstein supported the European peace movement and opposed social imperialism. Had his ideas been embraced, social democracy would have been in a better position to counter the drift towards World War I.[9]

The Bolsheviks' adherence to the authoritarian notion of the vanguard party, an elite cadre of professional revolutionaries that would guide the working class, was not held by any other socialist party in Europe before World War I. Luxemburg dismissed it as part of an authoritarian, conspiratorial "Jacobin" tradition in socialism and attributed its emergence as due to the "backward political conditions of Russian society."[10] No socialist theorists outside Russia would attempt to remodel their parties along Lenin's authoritarian lines before the Russian Revolution. Nor would any other member party of the Socialist International break up over questions of party organization.

The Pan-German movement that Hitler admired was unable to gain significant support in Austrian elections. It was a movement subversive to the Habsburg regime, advocating the absorption of their empire by a Prussian-dominated Germany. Pan-Germanism in Austria was declining as a political movement. The empire's political elite cleverly helped bring this decline about through an alliance with Social Democracy. This gave it a stronger voice after universal suffrage was achieved in 1907, which benefited Social Democratic, Catholic, and Peasant parties, at the expense of the largely middle class Pan-Germans. The Pan-Germans' goal of annexing Austria to Germany in order to enslave its non-German minorities was combined with anti-Semitism. Although printed freely in Germany, Pan-German literature, based on the stirring up of racial hatred, was banned in Austria. Like Stalin in his journey to Vienna, it was smuggled in.

Stalin had been sent to Vienna by Lenin to investigate the national question. This mission would give him the luster of being an important socialist theorist, which would be critical to his rise to power in the Soviet Union. Lenin assigned Stalin this sensitive task despite his well-known anti-Semitic views, which continued right up to the period shortly before his death, when he was planning a widespread imprisonment of Soviet Jews.[11] Stalin rejected the Austrian Social Democrats' support of cultural pluralism, which envisaged a reformed, democratized, but united Austria. Instead of such a reformist course, Stalin endorsed the more explosive principle of the "self-determination of nations," which he and Lenin viewed as having more revolutionary potential.

Lenin's democratic-minded critic Rosa Luxemburg poured scorn on what she viewed as the Bolsheviks' bizarre fetish for self-determination. She was amazed at how they could display "cool contempt for the Constituent Assembly, universal suffrage, freedom of the press and assembly, in short, for the whole apparatus of the basic democratic liberties of the people," while treating "the right of self-determination of peoples as a jewel of democratic policy for the sake of which all practical considerations of real criticism had to be stilled." She saw Lenin as falling for "hollow, bourgeois phraseology and humbug." Luxemburg believed that "all forms of separatism" were "mere bourgeois traps," and regarded the Bolsheviks' use of the phrase "self-determination" as an implicit "slogan for the disintegration of Russia."[12] She wanted to maintain the unity of Austria-Hungary while democratizing it.

Austria before World War I: Evolving into a Multinational Federation

Austria-Hungary's tragedy was its arrested development toward a multinational, democratic federation. Since Austria's conversion to a liberal constitution in 1860, it had evolved, like other European monarchies, in the direction of a more democratic system. It had established trial by jury, universal suffrage, parliamentary representation, freedom of religion, and a broad range of civil liberties. Austria was also a European leader in the establishment of an effective social welfare state.

Most significantly, Austria had evolved toward a distinctive model of cultural pluralism. This was at variance from the norm in other European states that were democratizing in this period. Democratic France had in particular an aggressive effort to homogenize regional cultures, including distinctive nations such as the Basques and Bretons. Their national languages, which received no legal recognition by France, are as distinctive from French as Slavic tongues are from German. In semidemocratic Imperial Germany an aggressive culture war was waged against the Catholic Church. While conflicts over family law were part of this "culture war," aspects of it also involved the persecution of Germany's Polish minority, most of whom were educated in Catholic schools. Bismarck's "culture war" was also used to get Poles, many of whom were Jewish, to move out of Germany and into the Russian and Austrian parts of the former Polish kingdom. Among the supporters of this pioneering effort in ethnic cleansing was the noted sociologist and shaper of the future Weimar Republic's constitution, Max Weber.[13]

In Austria, unlike the rest of Europe, trends toward cultural pluralism tended to go hand in hand with liberalization and democratization. The cynical slogan attributed to the Habsburgs in the repressive nightmares after the 1848 revolution was "divide and rule." This reflected the regime's ability to carry on as the Czechs and Germans collided with each other and the Hungarians clashed with Croatians. In the more liberal atmosphere after 1860, the regime's survival tactics became more benevolent. Rather than division, compromise became the guiding principle. Instead of stoking ethnic passions in the fashion of authoritarian nationalists, supporters of the empire's unity sought to work out compromises between varied ethnic and religious groups. The tragedy of this pattern of arrested development toward multiculturalism is that it suddenly was reversed after 1918 with the empire's demise.

The granting of autonomy to the Hungarian half of the empire in 1867 fostered effective parliamentary constitutional development in the remaining Austrian lands. The complex arrangement, in which the two halves of the empire presented a united front to the rest of the world while having autonomy in their internal affairs, strikingly differed from the centralizing, homogenizing policy of other major European states. With its separate cabinets and parliaments, united only by a foreign minister, the Austro-Hungarian model still provides other multinational states a model of how to achieve autonomy short of a partition that would invite war.

Hungary's policy of assimilating national minorities — similar to that of France — was a source of instability for the empire. It was tempered however, on a number of grounds. Hungary's Croatians had autonomy in the sensitive areas of education and culture. National minorities in districts where they accounted for 20 percent of the population had significant education rights. All forms of legal discrimination against Jews, which had previously barred them from certain professions, were removed.

The biggest barrier to democratization and cultural pluralism in Hungary was the limited suffrage for its parliamentary elections. Even here, however, the great majority of largely disenfranchised peasant voters successfully used economic pressures to influence petty-bourgeois electors. Socialists who defied the Hungarian Social Democrats' antipeasant ideology found that they could be elected to parliament.[14]

In the Austrian half of the empire, multiculturalism was vividly expressed both in the many languages that appeared on its currency and in parliamentary debates. Laws respecting minority language rights were effectively enforced in the courts. Under the language ordinance of 1880, Czech was recognized as an official language in Bohemia, Moravia, and Silesia. Typical of the empire's penchant for compromise was that Italians were given privileged status, having higher representation in parliament than numbers warranted. A policy of multiculturalism encouraged the development of a cosmopolitan civil service, with Poles, Czechs, Italians, Germans, and Hungarians frequently working side by side and intermarrying. In this sense they were forerunners to the multicultural civil service of the European Union.[15]

The most intelligent members of the political ruling class of Austria understood that the working class and peasantry of the empire, if satisfied by social democratic state intervention geared to eliminating poverty, would provide a bulwark against nationalistic discontent arising from the middle class. This was the view of the greatest Austrian statesman, Klemens Wenzel von Metternich, who had served as chancellor of the empire from the end of the Napoleonic Wars until the revolution of 1848. He was hostile to all nationalist movements, especially Pan-Germanism, which he attempted to suppress through his controversial "Carlsbad decrees." Metternich was a fervent internationalist, and his concept of the "concert of Europe" was similar in nature to the League of Nations. He supported a federal system for the reform of the empire, which unfortunately was not adopted. Metternich also favored public works for the relief of unemployment and viewed himself as a "conservative socialist."[16]

Metternich's moderate brand of socialism is what the Social Democratic party leader Karl Renner was working out before World War I for the reform of the empire. This involved orchestrating considerable public pressure, such as strikes and demonstrations. At the same time Renner enjoyed the support of important officials of the imperial government who also desired such reforms. When the Social Democrats used a general strike in 1907 to achieve universal suffrage, the Habsburgs were happy to see it happen.[17]

War Reverses the Momentum toward a Democratic Europe

Long before the crisis of July 1914, war was being schemed by officers in the Austrian general staff, contrary to the wishes of the Habsburgs' ministers and prominent family members. The Hungarian political leadership of the empire, especially Archduke Ferdinand, who would later be assassinated, also opposed war. The origins of the war lay in extremist cliques in Moscow and Berlin who were committed to Pan-German and Pan-Slav courses, either of which would mean the destruction of the Austro-Hungarian empire.

Like Lenin's Bolsheviks, the Pan-German nationalists could not triumph through the ballot box. Even in Germany they were declining, as Social Democrats increased their power in parliament. It was difficult for a German government to overtly take a militaristic posture because of the growing strength of the Social Democrats.

In Russia no strong political party openly pursued the Pan-Slav agenda, which might have been rooted out of government policy, had the reforming Prime Minister Peter Stolypin not been assassinated by a secret police agent disguised as a revolutionary. Stolypin's support for an alliance with Germany and Austria would have eliminated the Pan-Slav agenda in its very heartland. The Pan-Slavs, the Pan-Germans, and the Bolsheviks were all committed to revolution and violence, as opposed to the ballot box. All such extremist movements would be strengthened by the outbreak of war.

Austria-Hungary was trapped into war by the maneuvers of Pan-German and Pan-Slav extremists. Serbo-Yugoslav extremists in Serbia and Pan-Slavs in Moscow plotted the Archduke Ferdinand's assassination to provoke a Slavic war of liberation. At the same time, those in power in Berlin used it to launch a war that would integrate Austria-Hungary more closely into Germany. Austria-Hungary was pressured to issue its fatal ultimatum to Serbia by Germany's threat that otherwise it would withdraw from their military alliance. The war party in Berlin saw the conflict as the last opportunity to establish a German-dominated Europe, which it believed would soon become impossible because of the quick pace of Russian industrialization.

The crisis of July 1914 highlighted the worst consequences of the semidemocratic constitutional systems of Austria-Hungary, Germany, and Russia. The bullet, perfectly aimed to break up the Austro-Hungarian Empire, was worthy of the careful research of its Pan-Slav supporters in Moscow.[18] It killed the most prominent foe of a military solution to Austria's conflict with the Serbian state. In the view of the regime's hawks, this necessitated the elimination of the Serbian state, by dividing it between Albania, Bulgaria, and Hungary. Franz Joseph was also the strongest advocate of a stronger role of Slavs in the governance of the empire and had opposed the annexation of Bosnia. Had he actually carried out these reforms, called "trilism," and achieved an equal partnership of Hungarians, Germans, and Slavs, Pan-Slav ambitions would have failed. With "trilism" there would be no issues to exploit concerning injustice and oppression against minorities in Austria-Hungary.

The bullet also provided a convenient pretext for all the militant hawks in Europe to push for war. Though they had been planning war for many years, their actual power had been declining and peaceful trends had been developing — such as the establishment of the International Court of Justice in The Hague. Because of the limitations of democracy in all these countries, the militarists had been able to evade the effective scrutiny of a free press, political parties, and parliaments. Before the war, defense and foreign policy remained a prerogative of kings, even in Britain and Scandinavia, though this would no longer be the case by 1920.

The crisis quickly undid the work of those who had been in opposition to the hawks in power for two decades. Still, there were moderate Serbian statesmen who did not approve the policy of terrorism and who suggested that the International Court mediate its dispute with Austria-Hungary after the assassination. This would have been a reasonable way to allow Austria to save face without recourse to war and establish a stable peace in the region. Moves toward the establishment of a system of world government such as the Court of Justice were strongly resisted by the most powerful military nation, Germany, which nevertheless felt to some extent compelled to compromise with other world powers, including its ally, Austria-Hungary.

As the war progressed, it increasingly fostered nationalism. Austria-Hungary, although able to send out its own peace feelers through secret diplomacy, was increasingly integrated into Germany during the course of the war. This in turn was ultimately fatal to its survival as a state, since war provoked trends to Pan-Germanism by increasingly integrating Austria-Hungary into Imperial Germany. This Germanization inspired a counterreaction among the Czech political leadership. Most significantly, this changed the outlook of former moderates such as Tomáš Masaryk, who for the first time in their careers embraced the separatist cause. These new converts had great skill in getting support from allied nations, especially Woodrow Wilson in the United States, in part through effective work with the American Slavic émigré community.[19]

Social Democracy's Role in Reforming the Austro-Hungarian Empire

Social democracy played an important role in reforming the Austro-Hungarian Empire. In the Austrian half of the empire, the Social Democratic Party benefited from the relatively heavy industrialization of the region, which increased its representation in parliament despite its neglect of peasant issues. Moreover, peasant parties throughout the Austro-Hungarian Empire worked for a similar

agenda because they tended also to foster ethnic harmony rather than confrontation. Their chief rivals for political support in urban areas tended to be nationalists, whose chauvinistic posturing countered peasant parties' demands for democratic reforms. Peasant party support was important in securing a model accord
for cultural pluralism developed by Social Democrats in Moravia. Here the party's leader, a highly educated peasant turned civil servant, Karl Renner, owned a
farm jointly with his sister.

Although Austria's Social Democrats were not always able to win over minority ethnic groups in their homelands, especially in Bohemia, they won substantial support from these groups in Vienna. Until the breakup of Austria-
Hungary in 1918 Vienna had substantial populations of ethnic minority groups.
They were working-class voters from quite diverse ethnic groups who strongly
supported cultural pluralism. They had no interest in separate national states but
favored minority rights, and so were important in cooling ethnic tensions and
keeping the multinational empire together.

The visionary prophet of nationalism's future "barbarism," Rosa Luxemburg,
praised the nationalities program of Austrian Social Democracy while attacking
what she termed the "metaphysical" formula for "self-determination" put forward
by Lenin's Bolsheviks. She approved the way the party had conceived of a federal
union for the various nationalities of the empire, combined with provision "for a
special law to protect the smaller minorities in the newly created national territories." The Social Democrats' approach, she favorably observed, did not simply
attempt to solve the nationality question by "self-determination," or allowing
each nationality to fight out its own future according to its own whims. Instead
it sought to work out these problems "by means of a well-defined plan."[20]

The author of what Luxemburg saw as a "well designed plan" for overcoming
ethnic conflict was that talented Austrian civil servant and socialist leader, Karl
Renner. Had the empire not blown up in war and revolution, Renner would
likely have emerged as the new Metternich of a federated Austria in a united
Europe. Luxemburg recognized the merits of his proposals for democratizing on
the basis of cultural pluralism.

Renner served as librarian in the imperial parliament, an influential position
that would have been inconceivable for a socialist to hold in Germany or Russia.
The regime showed its appreciation of his skill as a negotiator and consensus
builder in keeping Austria-Hungary together, since only here in the semi-demo-
cratic empires could a prominent socialist leader also serve as an important civil
servant. Renner borrowed from the visionary principles of a federation of nations, developed by a critical liberal revolutionary of 1848, the Hungarian Jewish
physician Adolf Fischof.

The Habsburgs had lacked the intelligence to collaborate with Fischof in
1848, but by the early twentieth century they had learned enough from the disasters of two major wars and the threats to their empire to work with an individual
of similar outlook. Renner borrowed Fischof's notion of personal autonomy in

ethnicity, so that each citizen could have national rights without the creation of new boundaries for independent nation-states. Had this proposal been implemented more widely, many of the disasters of the twentieth century could have been averted.

With the support of Catholic, Peasant, and Social Democratic parties, Renner was able to persuade his native Moravia to adopt his model of cultural pluralism in 1905. This reform saw seats reserved in the provincial diet for each national group, in proportion to its share of the population. For certain types of legislation the concurrence of two-thirds of the representatives was required. Local civil servants were chosen from nationalities in the same proportion as legislators. Municipalities could determine the language to be used by civil servants.[21]

After bringing ethnic concord to Moravia, Renner's winning formula was successfully applied to Burgenland, a border region between Austria and Hungary. Although most of Burgenland is now in Austria, under the empire it was entirely within Hungary. Consequently it provides a good example of how Hungarians could adopt policies of cultural pluralism, accommodating successfully the demands of minorities.

In Burgenland the Catholic Church was an important force for cultural pluralism. While in Austria the school system was secular, in Hungary Catholic control of education helped foster cultural diversity. Catholic schools encouraged the survival of Croatian villages.[22]

In Galicia the main source of ethnic conflict had been the Polish majority oppressing the Ukrainian minority. This problem began to subside after 1907, with the granting of universal suffrage. This voting power also helped the Ukrainians make major gains in education, including the establishment of their own university. On of eve of war in 1914, an agreement between Poles and Ukrainians had been reached in Galicia for power sharing on the basis of individual choice of ethnicity.[23]

Thus Catholic, Peasant, and Social Democratic parties were able to apply Renner's inspired model to three areas of the Austro-Hungarian empire. Efforts were made by moderates to have the model extended to Bohemia, but this failed because of extremists on both sides. Here the Social Democrats lost much of their Czech working-class base to an ominously titled "National Socialist" movement, which favored the creation of a Czech state within a Slavic federation.

Bohemian extremists clung to hard line Pan-German and Pan-Slav ideologies. These favored the destruction of Austria-Hungary by big new states that would inevitably have their own oppressed minorities. When Masaryk wrote his book calling for Pan-Slav solution to the nationality question of Austria-Hungary, which proved so influential on American opinion through Woodrow Wilson, he omitted any reference to the success of the Moravian constitution, so different from his own proposal.[24]

The failure of the empire to resolve ethnic conflict in such critical regions as Bohemia and Bosnia would be fatal. However, these situations did not get out of control except under the extreme conditions of a world war. After ruling Bosnia since 1878, Austria-Hungary annexed it in 1907, and by 1910 it had an elected parliament. Its incorporation in the empire was supported by its Croatian and Muslim majority, although not by most Bosnian Serbs. Ethnic rioting never took place on a large scale. The deaths of ten persons in the worst clashes were minor in comparison to those caused by the wars, revolutions, and dictatorships that swept Central Europe after 1918. Nor was Austria-Hungary the land of the pogrom. Although rioting against Orthodox Serbs by Muslims and Catholic Croatians broke out after the assassination in Sarajevo in 1914, this soon stopped after martial law was declared and troops were brought in.[25]

The Muslim majority in Bosnia preferred protective incorporation in Austria over the threat posed by the aggressive nationalism of the Orthodox Christian Serbs in neighboring Serbia and Montenegro. In 1848 the Orthodox Montenegrin Bishop Petar Petrović Njegoš composed a historical play, *The Mountain Wreath,* which is still viewed in Montenegro as the greatest piece of Serbian literature ever written. Its plot centered around the extermination of South Slavic converts to Islam, who allegedly betrayed the Serbian race. This play is still used for inspiration by Serbian nationalists, who have changed its call for "religious cleansing" to "ethnic cleansing." When Serbian troops entered Bosnia at the end of World War I, Nikola Pašić of the Serbian Radical Party gave Muslims[26] "perhaps forty-eight hours to convert to the religion of their forefathers." He promised that "those who resist we shall slay as we have done in the past." Violence by the Bosnian Serbs against Muslims was common until the more liberal Yugoslav constitution of 1921 was adopted.[27]

The empire continued its pattern of gradual reform until 1914 because internationalist movements of Peasant, Catholic, and Social Democratic parties proved stronger than the voices of ethnic nationalism. After two years of war this stable alliance began to slip. This robbed the moderate parties and their most effective leader, Karl Renner, of the inheritance of a federal and democratic Austria-Hungary, which was keeping pace with trends that brought democracy to the rest of Europe by 1919.

Extremism after the Destruction of the Austro-Hungarian Empire

After the breakup of the Austro-Hungarian Empire, extremism flourished in its former lands. The Austrian Social Democrats were cut off from their former strongholds among German workers in what became Czechoslovakia, who eventually succumbed to the manipulations of the Nazi movement. The multiethnic working class of Vienna, the bastion of the Social Democratic party's influence over the former empire, was dispersed over thousands of miles, becoming ambassadors of embittered extremism. With unemployment facing Vienna, caused largely by the disruptive end of the central European trade bloc, most members of ethnic minorities felt their chances of getting a job would be better in their native lands. Often this extremism would take on bizarre forms.

In Hungary, Communists ruled briefly for three months, coming to power after Soviet agents had bribed previously social democratic trade union leaders. Lacking any peasant base, the Communist government terrorized the countryside, attempting to impose collectivization. It was able to garner a degree of popular support, however, because it attempted to maintain Hungary's old 1867 borders. These included many ethnic minorities who wanted out of Hungary. Conflict with Romania over the mixed population area of Transylvania led to Hungary's military defeat from a Romanian invasion. The memory of the first disastrous Communist regime in Central Europe contributed to an extremist fascistic political backlash and further stoked ethnic antagonisms throughout Central Europe.[28]

In the early 1920s Austria was briefly under the leadership of Renner, who as first president of the republic steered a moderate social democratic course. From 1919 to 1921 a coalition government of Social Christian and Social Democratic parties introduced the eight-hour work day, increased paid vacations, eliminated child labor, and improved social insurance. The Social Democratic municipality of Vienna launched an impressive housing and municipal public works program. All of this was done despite a very unfavorable economic situation resulting from the end of the empire's common market in central Europe.

Despite a consensus between Social Democratic and Social Christians on major issues, relatively trivial disputes caused the coalition to break up. The Social Democrats' withdrawal was contrary to Renner's wiser, more moderate counsel. The dangers of going into opposition were compounded by the armed nature of the two political parties. The armies attached to parties were one of the worst aspects of the transition from empire to republic. A minor armed clash in 1926 later led to extensive street rioting in Vienna that caused sixty deaths. One of the consequences was a socialist declaration that party members should not attend church, thus deepening divisions in the nation. Such fundamental conflict resulted in the fatal clash between Christian Socialists and Social Democrats in Vienna in 1934. The resulting absence of civil liberties — from 1934 to 1938 — had not been seen in Austria since 1860. As a result of the dictatorship, the class-conscious workers of Vienna would not resist the invasion of Austria of 1938.[29]

A New Generation:
Austria Recovers from the Loss of Empire

The Austrian equilibrium of 1914 was not restored until the withdrawal of foreign troops in 1955 and the return to moderate politics. Unfortunately, this restored level-headedness was only accomplished by the imprisonment of Social Christians and Social Democrats in Nazi prisons after 1938. The harsh experience of dictatorship encouraged a new respect for the virtues of democratic moderation. Renner became president of the restored Austria, and his standing in his party was greatly enhanced after 1945, when his militant ultraleftist foes in the party had virtually vanished from the scene. Likewise, the Social Christians' guilt over their extremism in the interwar period was shown by their new name, the People's Party, to avoid the stigma associated with their party's earlier antidemocratic actions. Renner was able to outwit both Stalin and Tito and prevent Austria from being partitioned into eastern and western occupied zones for a long period, as in Germany.

When in 1955 a stable democracy was achieved in Austria, it would succeed brilliantly. The bewildering ways of compromise that the Habsburgs had invented to ensure social harmony were adapted to fit new circumstances. Among these were constitutional guarantees for the educational rights of the Slovene and Croat minorities, enhanced by multicultural supports such as press subsidies, road signs, and television.

After the tragic defeat of Austrian democracy, the leaders of the Social Democrats and the People's Party developed a new way to ensure consensus and promote social welfare, prosperity, and full employment. This was done by having the real decisions on economic matters made by complex commissions that would represent every conceivable interest group. Parliament simply ratifies such decisions, as parties are reluctant to clash over agreements forged by diverse stakeholders. Politicians of both major parties are frequently civil servants, on leave from their posts, adapting the old rule by Austrian bureaucrats of the imperial age to new democratic circumstances.

Although the national consensus achieved by the Social Democrats and the People's Party broke down over environmental controversies in the 1980s, which provoked the emergence of a national Green Party, even here Austria's penchant for compromise worked miracles. Although both major parties supported a Danube dam and nuclear power plant, neither project was completed. The dam was killed by court action after massive civil disobedience, while nuclear power was stopped by a national referendum. After the Chernobyl disaster, the constructed, but inactivated, reactor was dramatically dismantled. With the emergence of the Greens, however, the Austrian Social Democrats lost much of their élan and reformist drive. While the nation's reputation was stained by the election of former Nazi Kurt Waldheim as president, this figurehead position obscured the ongoing role of Social Democrats in setting Austria's priorities, although it was weakened by the emergence of the Green Party. The Social Democrats' foreign policy continued the imaginative ideas of its leader in the 1960s and 1970s, Bruno Kreisky. His nonaligned foreign policy emphasized work for peace in such difficult situations as the Middle East. Austria's border with Hungary would become the first hole in the Iron Curtain. Austria is now supporting the former Soviet bloc states in their quest for integration into the European Union — states that once had been part of its empire.[30]

Pan-Europeanism as the New Austrian Mission

With Vienna a major refugee center for war-torn former Yugoslavia, a new sense of the Austrian mission is emerging. This underscores the need for Eastern Europe to integrate into a united, prosperous European Union. The renewed close ties between Budapest and Vienna are helping to bring East and West together, instead of shunting aside the former Communist world as a backward economic colony of Western Europe.

As a strong European Union integrates the post-Communist world, the multinational Austrian ideal for the Pan-European movement becomes more important. One of its founders in the 1920s was an Austrian aristocrat, Richard Coudenhove-Kalergi, son of a diplomat who was married to a Japanese woman. Coudenhove-Kalergi viewed the destruction of World War I as resulting from the wasteful conflict between the Pan-Slav and Pan-German movements. His models for European unity were taken from proposals for the reform of Austria-Hungary. Anticipating the dominance of the Soviet Union and the United States during the Cold War, he correctly predicted that Europe would become insignificant if it did not federate. He lived long enough to see many of his ideas become reality with the establishment of the European Common Market. He advocated a mixture of socialist and capitalist ideas that resembles the type of social democracy promoted in the EU's social charter over the opposition of such conservatives as Margaret Thatcher.

The disastrous breakup of the Austro-Hungarian Empire eventually has been countered by the salutary movement for European unity. Significantly for the long-term prospects of peace and democracy in Europe, nationalists and would-be dictators are constrained by the fact that human rights violations will prevent their entry into the EU. Had such incentives been in place before World War I, it could have outshone Pan-Slavism and Pan-Germanism, the forces that destroyed both the peace of Europe and the Austro-Hungarian Empire.

In many ways the European Union resembles the semi-constitutional Austro-Hungarian Empire with its imperfect quasi-parliamentary system. As with Austria from 1907 to 1918, the EU has an elected parliament chosen on the basis of universal suffrage, but one that is viewed as more symbolic than powerful, with real power in the hands of a confusing array of bureaucracies and ministerial councils. Like the Austro-Hungarian Empire, the reform and democratization of the European Union requires peace and time to bring unity to Europe.

Notes

1. Edward Crankshaw, *The Fall of the House of Habsburg* (London: Longmans, 1963), 1-15.

2. Crankshaw, *Fall of the House of Habsburg*, 411-15.

3. Tomáš G. Masaryk, *The New Europe: The Slav Standpoint.* New edition, ed. W. Preston Warren and William B Weist (Lewisburg: Bucknell University Press, 1972, original printed in 1918).

4. Gabriel Kolko, *The Politics of War* (New York: Random House, 1968) 123-28.

5. Masaryk, *The New Europe.*

6. Arthur May, *The Passing of the Habsburg Monarchy* (Philadelphia: University of Pennsylvania Press, 1966), Vol. 2, 825.

7. Peter Viereck, *Conservatism Revisited* (New York: Collier, 1949), 17-192.

8. Viereck, *Conservatism Revisited*, 17-192.

9. Peter Gay, *The Dilemma of Democratic Socialism* (New York, 1952).

10. J. P. Nettl, *Rosa Luxemburg* (London: Oxford University Press, 1966), 287.

11. Viereck, *Conservatism Revisited*, 170-90; Frederick Morton, *Thunder at Twilight: Vienna 1913/1914* (New York: Macmillan, 1989), 19-24.

12. Rosa Luxemburg, "The Nationalities Question in the Russian Revolution," in *The National Question: Selected Writings by Rosa Luxemburg,* ed. Horace Davis (New York: Monthly Review Press, 1976), 292-99.

13. Ernest Fischer, *Germany's Aims in the First World War* (London: 1967); Roger Brubaker, *Citizenship and Nationhood in France and Germany* (Cambridge, MA: Harvard University Press, 1992).

14. Crankshaw, *Fall of the House of Habsburg,* 410-14; Rudolf Tokes, *Bela Kun and the Hungarian Soviet Republic* (New York: Praeger, 1967), 5, 8.

15. Brubaker, *Citizenship and Nationhood;* Crankshaw, *Fall of the House of Habsburg,* 274; May, *Passing of the Habsburg Monarchy*, 430-33.

16. Rudolf Tokes, *Bela Kun,* 5, 8; Viereck, *Conservatism Revisited.*

17. May, *Passing of the Habsburg Monarchy,* 400-30.

18. Henry Gilford, *The Black Hand at Sarajevo* (New York: Bobbs Merrill, 1975).

19. Crankshaw, *Fall of the House of Habsburg,* 420-30.

20. Rosa Luxemburg, "The National Question and Autonomy," in *The National Question,* 103, 104.

21. May, *Passing of the Habsburg Monarchy,* 340, 341, 427.

22. May, *Passing of the Habsburg Monarchy,* 480, 481.

23. May, *Passing of the Habsburg Monarchy,* 480, 481.

24. Masaryk, *The New Europe.*

25. May, *Passing of the Habsburg Monarchy,* 480-500.

26. Tokes, *Bela Kun.*

27. Amila Buturović, "Producing and Annihilating the Ethos of Bosnian Islam," in *Cultural Survival Quarterly,* Summer 1995, 29-33.

28. Tokes, *Bela Kun.*

29. Melanie A. Sully, *Continuity and Change in Austrian Socialism: The Eternal Quest for the Third Way (*New York: Columbia University Press, 1982).

30. Sully, *Continuity and Change in Austrian Socialism.*

Five

Citizenship and the Collapse of the State: The Ottoman Case

Yıldız Atasoy

The crisis of the nation-state in our day reveals the difficulty, within a hetero-geneous empire, of constructing equality of citizenship, unconnected with the social boundaries dividing religious or cultural communities. The history of the breakup of the Ottoman Empire provides an excellent early example of the same problems.

In proposing a solution to these problems, I shall argue in favor of dissociat-ing citizenship from national identity. The nation-state project was a manifesta-tion of the opposite principle. Its dangers, as Hannah Arendt pointed out, lay in its postulating a homogeneous public and eliminating cultural differences so as to create a unified, egalitarian political identity.

What does the Ottoman experience tell us? Does it demonstrate the impossi-bility of achieving a type of citizenship that is both egalitarian and heteroge-neous? Or does it show us that we have to redefine political group identifications and develop alternative ways living as groups, free of dogma calling for national homogeneity within states?

The problematic to be examined in this article concerns the relationship be-tween egalitarian and heterogeneous conceptions of citizenship. Let me sketch out my main argument. The Ottoman ruling elite developed various strategies to prevent the breakup of the empire. The response of the Ottoman ruling elite was a protective one, defending the empire from partition by "modernizing" the state and by creating an ideology of nationhood. Large processes were operating within the state system to prompt the breakup, whereas there were also protective Ottoman responses that involved reforms. The nation-state played out the tension between these two tendencies. By exploring this tension, we can see the roots of today's crisis of the nation-state project. Thus, my ultimate intention here is to draw contemporary lessons from the historical case of the Ottoman state in its decline.

Ideological Unity in the State and Heterogeneity in Society: The Classical Age (1300-1600)

The Ottoman Empire was a cosmopolitan, multinational, multireligious empire — a vast territory of diverse economic, cultural, and religious regions in the Balkans, Central Europe, the Middle East, and North Africa. How were the Ottoman rulers able to establish a powerful state structure over such vast territory? This is a compelling question, given the fact that the Ottoman political system was based on inequality. Religious distinctions constituted the principal barrier to a heterogeneous egalitarianism in the empire.

The Ottomans accorded partial autonomy to the Muslim, Christian, and Jewish communities and emphasized religious differences between various cultural groups. Through this model — called the *"millet* system" — the center accommodated a variety of religious and regional particularisms.[1] There were mainly two millets: Muslim and non-Muslims. Regardless of the ethnic and language differences that divided them, all Muslims constituted one single millet. Non-Muslims were divided into separate millets according to their religious affiliations: Orthodox Christian, Jewish, and Armenian. Urban and rural populations were alike divided into millet categories. The members of different religions lived in separate quarters of the city under the leadership of their own religious leaders. Imams, priests, and rabbis, in their separate wards of the city, led their own communities and performed the political function of representing their community before the government.[2]

These religious communities were internally autonomous, self-administering local units. However, they were linked to the central authority via the representation of their religious leaders in the provincial and local administrations. These leaders exercised power locally in the name of, and derived from, the center. However, the semiautonomy enjoyed by these millets did not mean equality among the subjects of the empire. The Muslim and non-Muslim millets were subject to different laws and different officials. For example, the non-Muslim millets were denied opportunity of access to the ruling positions in the central bureaucracy unless they converted to Islam. Nor were they allowed to serve in the military but had to pay an exemption tax. Within the religious and cultural mosaic of the empire, the Muslim millet was dominant. All the members of the ruling class were required to be Muslim, but not necessarily Turkish. Christian-

or Jewish-born non-Muslims had to convert to Islam if they were to be part of the ruling class. This was an important aspect of religious inequality and was clearly implicated in the *devshirme* system,[3] whereby Muslims made converts to Islam from non-Muslims.

The "collection" system was a unique recruitment strategy based on the recruitment of Christian boys into ruling positions, especially from the Balkans, converting them to Islam and training them as soldiers for the prestigious *Janissary* military corps and as administrators and officials for the central and local/provincial governments. They were considered members of the Sultan's dynastic family, while the native-born Muslims were for the most part excluded from the privileges of the ruling positions. Though they obtained high positions of power and wealth, their Muslim-born children could not inherit their position and wealth.[4]

Despite the multiplicity of cultural-religious communities in the empire, the legitimating ideology of the Ottoman state structure was Islam.[5] The devshirme system allowed religious unity among the members of the ruling class while keeping any ethnic group from becoming politically dominant. Islam justified hierarchic division between the rulers and the ruled on the basis of divine rule.[6] The religious unity in the state organization was, however, not independent of the Sultan's absolute authority![7] There were no permanent institutional arrangements for enforcing Islam against a ruler.[8] Non-Islamic laws, on the other hand, led neither to participatory politics nor to public accountability of politics. The state did not promote an ideology of nationhood through Islam. Community cultures of various subject people continued to exist independent of the state and constituted the "little" cultures of the imperial system, while the ideological unity between Islam and the state formed the imperial "great" culture of the Sultan and his ruling cadres.[9] There was no unifying ideology of nationhood between the rulers and the masses, nor was there a desire to constitute one.

All members of the ruling class were required to be Muslim. On the other hand, among the ruled masses there was no difference between Muslims and non-Muslims. From time to time the sultans sought to fulfill the provisions of the *shariat,* by issuing laws forbidding non-Muslims from wearing the same clothes, from owning slaves, and so forth, but such practices occurred only occasionally and were ineffective.[10] Non-Muslims were all subjects of the state, yet they enjoyed a partial autonomy from the state in their internal affairs. This autonomy was rooted in the simple fact that they needed to be protected as an important source of tax revenue.

The fundamental principle of the state was to protect its subjects. Ottomans applied the Islamic principles of rule through a kind of social contract about what the state was going to deliver to its subjects and, in exchange, what they were to do for the state. This was captured by the "circle of justice" practice, providing subjects with justice and protection from the state while the subject people provided obedience and fiscal resources for sustaining the fiscal requirements of the state.[11] This principle allowed millets free exercise of their own religion and the right to their own religious laws.

Despite the fact that the ruled population was classified into separate categories of religious communities, living in their own quarters of the city, no social and economic boundary lines separated these communities from each other. Muslim and non-Muslim merchants, farmers, and craftsmen enjoyed the same rights of their work position. Those who engaged in trade and agriculture, whether Christian, Jew, or Muslim, were considered the sultan's subjects and paid taxes. Only members of the ruling class (men of religion, bureaucrats, and their dependents) who were not engaged in production were exempted from taxes. The sultan's subjects *(reaya)*, regardless of their religion, were essential as producers and taxpayers. Both Muslim and non-Muslim millets were allotted state lands for farming in the form of *timars*[12] (fiefs). In the fifteenth and sixteenth centuries, as the proportion of timar-holding cavalry of Turkish-Muslim origin gradually declined, a large part of this cavalry comprised native-born Christians.[13]

These fiefs were the main unit of production. Agricultural exports, especially grain, were restricted by high export duties designed to retain sufficient food for internal consumption. Most grain was consumed on the farm.[14] The rural cavalry in their military fiefs imposed taxes in kind, which allowed them to raise cash for the army[15] while supplying the towns with food.[16]

This system of land allocation and production legally prohibited peasants from selling and subdividing land allotted to them, though they had direct access to the land.[17] Parcels of conquered lands were allocated to those rural cavalry who fulfilled military and administrative functions in the districts.[18] The rural cavalry had no claims of ownership over the land or the producing peasants. Their role, as intermediaries between the central authority and the peasants, consisted of collecting taxes in a specific area under their administration for a specific period of time. In return, they had to support and deliver during the time of war a specific number of mounted native-born Muslim soldiers.[19]

Through the timar system the Ottoman army was intimately integrated with the agricultural economy. The timar-holding cavalry formed the basis of the Ottoman army. In order to establish the timar system and to maintain a continuous and centralized state authority, private property on land was not allowed. As an indivisible and unalterable unit, the timar made active politics in society impossible and kept any sector of the economy or local community from becoming economically dominant and politically powerful.[20]

The Ottoman army was split into two separate segments: the Janissary corps and *sekban* (mercenaries). The Janissaries, who had been converted as boys from Christianity to Islam through the devshirme system, constituted the backbone of the Ottoman standing army.[21] The Sekban, on the other hand, was organized by rural cavalries among the native-born Muslim peasants, who were excluded from the privileges of the Janissaries.[22] Rural cavalry recruited mercenaries locally in times of war, to be then disbanded at the end of the war and return to work the land allocated to the rural cavalry.[23]

Despite its inequalities, this system served the Ottoman Empire well for four centuries. The heterogeneous nature of the society was maintained while unity among the ruling cadres around Islam was achieved.

Yet during the seventeenth century, the central government gradually began to lose control over its distant territories, leading ultimately to the disintegration of the empire. What went wrong then?

Intensification of Differences: Structural Causes of the Dismemberment of the Empire

The beginning of the end for the Ottoman Empire is to be found in the breakdown of the linkage between the land allocation system and the military organization. Disintegration was initiated by the internal development of capitalism under the influence of Western capitalism. Three important external economic factors led to the decline in the tımar system and the rise of private ownership of land. These were (1) the flow of silver from the Americas to the empire through Europe, (2) a shift in trade routes from Ottoman lands to new overseas territories via the Atlantic, and (3) the capitulations.

The flow of Mexican and Peruvian silver to Europe during the mid-sixteenth century caused huge price increases. Food prices increased sharply in Europe. As a result, much of Ottoman trade with Europe turned to contraband.[24] Contraband trade in cereals was common especially along the coastal areas and the Aegean Islands and was carried out mostly by Greek merchants.[25] Not only merchants, but even the state bureaucrats, who held land grants, engaged in the smuggling of agricultural produce.[26] This resulted in shortages in grain and raw materials, which were essential for internal consumption and production. It also contributed to decreasing state revenue from trade.

The other aspect of the silver circulation was its inflationary effect on the Ottoman economy. Low silver prices encouraged the import of large amounts of the metal. European silver inundated the Ottoman market, and prices doubled. Fixed income groups such as tımar-holding cavalry were suddenly impoverished[27] and abandoned their tımars. The Ottoman army began to lose its strength.

The decline of Ottoman military and economic power was also affected throughout the sixteenth and early seventeenth centuries by the overseas expansion of European states. Europeans not only dominated the social and political relations of colonial production[28] but also shifted the direction of their long distance trade.[29] After the discovery of sea routes to India, agricultural products and manufactured goods of China and India no longer had to pass through the Ottoman territories.[30] With the foundation of the East India Company in 1600, for example, the British preferred to buy directly from India, avoiding the custom duties levied in Ottoman ports. The British Levant Company brought the entire Levant into its sphere of trade control by the 1840s.[31]

Combined, the effect of both the silver flow and the changes in the European trade routes spelled a decline in Ottoman state revenue, gradually leading to the disintegration of the empire. Instead of adapting to the changed conditions of the modern world economy, the sultans kept to traditional economic principles, their main concern being to encourage imports and discourage exports in order to provide for the consumption needs of home markets. They saw no danger in granting the capitulations to the Europeans. Their failure to design a new export regime increased both the contraband trade (carried out mostly by non-Muslims of the empire) and also the economic interest differentiation between Muslims and non-Muslims. Non-Muslim traders and agriculturists of the Balkans, for example, came to dominate Ottoman trade with Europe and cash crop production.[32]

An integral part of all these changes in the empire was the granting of capitulations — namely tariff concessions — to the French and later the English, as well as other foreigners.[33] The Ottoman rulers, being concerned more with the creation of abundance of consumer goods in the home market and increased custom revenues, considered the capitulations beneficial. Capitulations were also thought of as a political/diplomatic weapon enabling the empire to play rival European powers off each other. The sultans granted France with capitulations to receive its support against the Venetians during wars over military control of the Mediterranean during the fifteenth and sixteenth centuries and against the Habsburgs during the sixteenth century. Capitulations of 1569 granted to France allowed France to displace Venice in Levant trade. Later in 1580, to counter Russian expansion in the trade route from Iran-Azerbaijan to Hormuz, the English were granted trade concessions with a low custom rate of 3 percent.[34] With the foundation of the Levant Company, the English competed fiercely against France and Venice.

These capitulations opened the Levant markets to the Europeans and enabled them to dominate regional trade. After the industrial revolution in Europe the continuing capitulations had disastrous consequences for the Ottoman economy: (1) they exposed the handicrafts to European competition and hastened its decline,[35] (2) they prevented government from protecting home manufacturing and delayed the development of industry, and (3) they facilitated the export of raw materials and foodstuffs. The Anglo-Ottoman Commercial Convention of 1838 was the most important of all economic concessions granted to the Europeans.[36]

These changes did not affect all the national communities of the empire in the same way; some groups benefited while others were disadvantaged. Under the freely competing European products, Muslim craftsmen, who were the backbone of handicraft production in the Balkans, were transformed into unskilled labor. On the other hand, non-Muslim merchants and agriculturists became dominant in cash-crop production and trade with European business that favored non-Muslims as their trading partners.[37]

The state's military and political order, taxation system, and forms of land tenure deteriorated. The tımar-holding rural cavalry was reduced in number, to the detriment of the Ottoman state's military power. In order to generate taxes for maintaining the strength of the army, some of the lands allocated as tımar*s* were brought under the state treasury, and the right to collect their revenue was farmed out (tax-farming), while some passed into individuals as private lands. Provincial administrators, urban merchants, local notables, and even the Janissaries began to operate as landowners in these plantation-like farms. The state lost its control over land and its revenues, so the linkage was broken between the land allocation system and the military organization. Ottoman rulers eventually accepted private ownership of land and recognized the peripheral status of the empire among the European economies. Thus the Ottoman Empire turned to exporting raw materials and foodstuffs, while importing manufactured goods.

During the seventeenth century the Ottoman Empire began to experience an externally imposed capitalization process, which took the form of peripheralization.[38] This economic change, combined with military and diplomatic pressures of the inter-state system, led to the dismemberment of the empire. Opening the empire for free European commerce had exaggerated the differences between its various national and religious communities and linked them in varying ways to the European economies. Greek separatist nationalism, for example, had already developed to the extent that Greek merchants were dissociated from the Ottoman economy and incorporated with the European business interests.[39] During and after the Greek War of Independence in 1821, tension between the Muslim rulers and non-Muslim subjects took the form of "ethnic" separatist movements.

The Search for an Ideology of National Unity: Equality and Homogeneity in Society

The Ottoman response to this disintegration was to "modernize" their state, both by turning it into a rational bureaucratic state[40] on the one hand, and creating an ideology of nationhood on the other.[41] The modernization of the state and the Ottoman nationhood project were directed toward the issue of equality among the Muslim, Christian, and Jewish millets of the empire. The question of equality was, in fact, forced on the empire by the increasing complaints of Christian millets, who found several great powers that would, as part of the power politics, protect their interests and impose demands on the Ottoman sultans.[42]

In the remaining portion of this chapter I will discuss the externally imposed project of Ottoman nationhood, which led to a contradiction. The economic and cultural differences between the various communities of the Muslim and non-Muslim millets intensified in opposing the creation of an Ottoman nation. This issue was affected externally by the changing relations among the great powers, who were competing to expand their sphere of military and political influence into the Ottoman territories. The following analysis centers on the economic and military/diplomatic relations of the great powers, which divided the Ottoman Empire into multiple states under their spheres of political influence.

Tanzimat Reforms and the Creation of Ottoman Nationhood

The Tanzimat Reforms of 1839 were designed to halt the empire's economic decline and disintegration. The intention behind them was to change the political structure from a patrimonial empire into a rational bureaucratic state.[43] The Tanzimat (or Charter of Regulations) was meant to make the central government more efficient and interventionist in its dealings with the provincial governors and landed gentry. One aim of the charter was to increase state revenues under the Central Treasury. Additional reforms included the security of life, honor, and property.

The most novel aspect of the Tanzimat is its official declaration of equality in status and rights to non-Muslim subjects of the Empire. This was adopted in order to prevent separatist movements and to establish a direct link between the state and the people via a secular concept of citizenship. This was to be an Ottoman nation in which citizens would benefit from identical civil rights, automatically conferred with citizenship and not dependent on religious affiliation.[44] Theoretically, this would also mean the dissolution of the millet system. Equality before the law among all Ottomans became the official policy of the Tanzimat era. This covered the areas of educational opportunity, appointment to government posts, the administration of justice, taxation, and the military.[45] The intention was to level out and depoliticize cultural-religious differences and thereby to constitute a secular principle of citizenship. This would establish a unified Ottoman nation on a purely territorial basis, unbroken by millet particularism.

The reforms of the Tanzimat era (1839-76) were used primarily as weapons of diplomacy during international crises. The reformers were trying to avoid foreign intervention by proclaiming that the empire was already reforming itself.[46] However, large parts of the Tanzimat reforms, the Hatt-i Humayun in particular, were dictated by British, French, and Austrian diplomats. The competing Great Powers favored the maintenance of a strong empire for two reasons: (1) a stable government in Istanbul would extend trade concessions,[47] and (2) the disintegration of the empire would bring about unpredictable consequences regarding the future map of Europe.[48]

The most important question here was the potential impact on the Great Powers of the territorial division of the Balkan nations. Diplomatic pressure by the British ambassador, Lord Stratford de Redcliffe, was paramount in designing the reforms.[49] The British aim was to prevent Russian influence from increasing in the Balkans.[50] Russia, as protector of Orthodox Christians in the empire, encouraged separatist movements by Orthodox Slavs in the Balkans.[51]

Tanzimat reforms were undertaken to strengthen the central authority of the Ottoman government against the background of the Greek War of Independence as well as the Serbian uprisings during this period.[52] The aim was to curb growing Russian involvement in Balkan politics.

Tanzimat reforms provided the first liberal critique of the Ottoman patrimonial system. They were, however, bound to lead to a contradiction, and the program of equality between Muslims and non-Muslims remained largely unrealized. On the one hand, the secularizing elite had no way of legitimizing these reforms.[53] On the other hand, many of the Christian subjects of the empire wanted these reforms of equality to fail. They were not interested in equality but national independence, although boundaries were not defined. For example, the 1862 Greek uprising in Crete and other parts of the empire demanded not equality but union with Greece and the extension of Greek rule to Macedonia and Thessaly. The Serbs demanded not equality but independence for Serbia and union with it. They were not even interested in a kind of federal equality with the empire.

The equality project of the reforms led to unrest and large uprisings among the non-Muslim subjects,[54] who objected to the principle of equal taxation and the abolition of all community privileges and exemptions (such as serving in the military). For the first time, non-Muslims would have to pay considerably higher taxes. In Bulgaria, for example, rich Christians, involved in cash crop production for the European markets, would be paying taxes in proportion to their financial means and business profits whereas before the Tanzimat reforms their taxes had equaled those of the poor peasants.[55]

The Tanzimat reforms did not unify the culturally and religiously diverse peoples of the empire. The major obstacle toward the realization of equality consisted of the elimination of special community privileges granted to the non-Muslim millets during the classical age. The dilemma was how to grant equal rights of citizenship, yet maintain special community privileges.[56]

The classical Ottoman state structure was undermined by the paradoxical nature of the Tanzimat reforms. The millet system had traditionally sustained the central government, allowing the sultans to dominate vast territories through local intermediaries. Once the principle of equality and unity was imposed, the central government's ability to rule through the local communities was threatened. Ironically, while the Tanzimat strengthened the central authority, it also undermined its most important feature — the millet system.

Uprisings against the reforms became commonplace in the empire among both non-Muslims and Muslims. The Islamic opposition interpreted shifts in the state structure as the penetration of alien Western influences;[57] and the material conditions of the Muslims deteriorated after the Anglo-Ottoman Commercial Convention of 1838.[58] Muslims, including the reforming elite, began to resent the fact that the reforms were dictated by foreigners. The great powers of Europe continuously interfered, in the name of protecting Christians. And despite the reforms, Christian rebellions continued, angering the Muslims and provoking opposition against the reforms.

Islamic opposition to the reforms intensified during recurring crises,[59] particularly in the 1870s, when Christians rebelled against the Ottoman state and external pressure on the government increased dramatically. That crisis was a general uprising in the Balkans, which showed the failure of the Tanzimat reforms to unify the religiously and culturally diverse peoples of the empire. What failed, in fact, was the idea of embedding "citizenship" within nationhood, unconnected from religious affiliation. A small group of intellectuals known as the Young Ottomans came up with that "solution." They believed that the Tanzimat had failed because of the special concessions given to the Christians, which had violated the very concept of nationhood. The Young Ottomans sought to resolve this contradiction by strengthening state-citizenship ties through Islamic legitimation. The ideology of nationhood was to be Islam, which they considered progressive enough to accommodate the new institutions from Europe.

The Young Ottomans: Islam as the Ideology of Nationhood

The Young Ottomans represented devotion to Ottomanism. Their intense patriotism was rooted in such concepts as liberty and the motherland — ideals meant to foster the equal cooperation of peoples of all religions to save the empire. However, they opposed special concessions for the Christians. The unifying theme among the Young Ottoman intellectuals was reform for Ottomans, by Ottomans, and along Islamic lines — though they thought of themselves as Westernizers, following the political lead of Western Europe.[60]

The Young Ottomans' aim was to develop an identity of nationhood in the form of Ottomanism that would be achieved through a synthesis of European political institutions and Islamic political theory. They hoped to restore state authority by constitutional rule and create an ideology of unity under Islam. This synthesis was expected to promote loyalty and obedience to the state, despite the fact that many non-Muslims still wanted to establish a separate national-state of their own. The Young Ottomans' goal was to turn the Islamic theory of responsible governing into a Western theory of representation through a constitutional government. This was difficult to accomplish because they lacked a workable theory of opposition and clear distinctions between the state, the individual, and the local community.

Under Sultan Abdülhamit (1878-1908) and following the abandonment of constitutional rule,[61] Islam was reintroduced to the Tanzimat ideology of Ottoman nationhood, and pan-Islamism was institutionalized.[62] As part of his pan-Islamist policy, the Naqshbandi *tariqa*[63] (among other Sufi orders) received the sultan's patronage, was reorganized by the state, and was instrumental in organizing popular Islamic-Ottomanism.[64] The Naqshbandi tariqa aimed to restore the shari'a and the sultan's authority in the name of Islamic solidarity against an aggressive Christian world. However, that Sufi order did not necessarily oppose the constitutional regime.

During and after the pan-Islamist era of the Sultan Abdulhamit, the Naqshbandi order became one of the most important of Ottoman political factions, as it underpinned the official nature of Islam.[65] The strategy was to link the Naqshbandi order to the Ulema, the state educational system, and the army.[66] Linked to the state, the Naqshbandi order was used to mobilize Muslims politically, so that pan-Islamism as a political movement was developed on its mobilization.[67] The political role played by the order reflected the success of this long-term organizational strategy.[68]

The Naqshbandi strategy was to organize small, community-based networks based on personal relations and to link them into a centrally organized structure. This plan defined how knowledge was to be acquired for the mobilization of Muslims; it was to be the pursuit of self purification, sought through absolute conformity with the teachings of the *shaykh*. There are three sources of knowledge: (1) book knowledge, (2) the use of memory, and (3) the practice of *Rabita*.[69] A link is established between the shaykh and the follower, and a chain of such linkages produces a Naqshbandi network and enables information to flow. This system of interpersonal linkages among the Naqshbandi underpins its political success. In addition to its traditional organizational strategy, the Naqshbandi tariqa was also successful in using the print media techniques of "modernity" that the reforming political elite had already introduced into the Ottoman Empire.

Abdülhamit's attempt to develop an Islamic ideology of Ottoman nationhood had implied Ottoman unity despite the multiplicity of religious and cultural groups in the empire. In the face of a strong Islamic attitude, the realization of Ottoman unity and equality within the heterogeneous empire between Muslims and non-Muslims faced enormous difficulties. The difficulty with Abdülhamit's "solution" was that the real material conflict of interest had already been intensified among these groups. The Christians of the empire continued to push toward separatism. Competing nationalisms again crowded out the concept of Ottomanism. Christians and also Muslims[70] were searching for a nationhood of their own. It was within the context of recognizing the futility of Ottomanism that a group of intellectuals, known as the Young Turks, developed a solution. Their solution was the advancement of a rival Turkish ideology of nationalism — one that accepted the futility of Ottomanism. The Young Turk solution was a "Turkist" answer to the question of nationhood.

The Young Turks: Turkism and the Creation of a Nation

The Young Turks' aim was to create a new civil-military bureaucratic elite in opposition to the more traditional faction of the ruling bureaucracy. They argued for the restoration of the constitution, in opposition to the sultan's absolutism, along with various military and administrative reforms in the central government.[71]

Since they also wanted to create Ottoman nationhood in the remaining territories of the empire,[72] one must ask why they began to advocate Turkish nationalism. The answer is that the development of a constitutional monarchy was hampered by a succession of foreign crises.

There was alarm in the Austria-Hungarian Empire when the Young Turks forced the Sultan Abdulhamit to restore constitutional parliamentarism in 1908, for this meant that the delegates from Bosnia and Herzegovina, under the protection of the Austria-Hungarian Empire since 1878, now would be represented in the Ottoman parliament. Bosnia and Herzegovina might be reintegrated into the Ottoman state, as indeed might also be the autonomous principalities of the Balkans such as Bulgaria. Thus the restoration of the constitutional regime raised questions about the limits of Ottoman rule in the Balkans. Therefore, on September 5, 1908, Bulgaria declared its independence from the Ottoman Empire. The next day Austria-Hungary announced the annexation of Bosnia and Herzegovina. On the same day, Crete announced its decision to unite with Greece. By 1911 the empire was at war in Libya against Italy, abandoning that territory to Italy when the coalition of Balkan states threatened to attack in October 1912. The Balkan wars of 1912-13 were disastrous for the empire. The Ottoman army lost virtually all of its European territories.

Seeing these territorial losses, the Young Turks concluded that Ottomanism was futile. The Naqshbandi religious order pointed out that the coming of a constitutional regime had coincided with the resumption of territorial losses, when for many years Abdulhamit had been able to resist the loss of any territory. These territorial losses spurred the Naqshbandi order into revolts, which were organized during the constitutional regime of the Young Turks (1908-18).[73] They demanded the restoration of the Sultan's absolute authority in the name of Islamic solidarity and declared a *jihad* against the aggressive Christian world.

The Naqshbandi opposition to the Young Turks was not based on their opposition to the constitutional regime, but on the abandonment of Islamic Ottomanism.[74] Since international pressures overrode any attempt at achieving Ottomanism, the Young Turks began to formulate a competing concept: Turkish nationalism.[75] They "discovered" the existence of a Turkish nation within the Ottoman Empire on the basis of race and language. This represented a radical discontinuity from the previous Ottoman nationalism of Tanzimat and Abdulhamit, which had never defined the "national" history as the Turkish-Ottoman history.[76]

During the Young Turk era, the history of the Turks was written for the purpose of creating a nationalist mythology. One such account was by the Hungarian anthropologist Vambery (1852-1913) and another by Ottoman Mustafa Celaleddin Pasha of Polish origin. They explored the origin of the Turks before Islam and claimed that the Turks, on the basis of their presumed racial characteristics, were part of the larger race of "Turan," which comprised Finns, Hungarians, and the Turks of Central Asia and the Caucasus.[77] These works were about "discovering" a Turkish nation with a claim of a homogeneity in language and race of origin.[78] The aim was to create a homogeneous Turkish state by connecting culturally unified people to the state.

This "Turkist" solution crowded out the concept of Ottomanism. In the end, the Tanzimat ideal for reaching equality while maintaining the heterogeneous structure of the empire was totally abandoned. Out of the multiplicity of cultural and ethnic communities within the empire, there emerged competing national states with a claim for cultural homogeneity within their territories. The end of World War I and the ensuing peace settlement determined the post-Ottoman map of the Balkans and the Middle East. These newly emerging states all depended on the great powers of Europe, which were expanding their sphere of strategic influence over the Ottoman territories.

Conclusion

I have argued that the classical Ottoman strategies did not aim at achieving an overarching national unity over the vast territories and diverse cultures under their rule. Despite the lack of a unifying ideology or any egalitarian vision of society, the Ottoman Empire successfully created an integrated economic, military, and administrative structure. The multiplicity of religious and cultural groups coexisted for more than three centuries without a unitary theory of society. Plurality and inequality were the defining features of the classical Ottoman state structure.

I examined the disintegration process in the second section of this chapter and found that it intensified the differences between these various communities. This fact raises a question as to whether cultural pluralism is necessarily incompatible with an egalitarian notion of society. If so, there must be an equally necessary conceptual linkage between unity and equality. I argued in the second and third sections of this chapter that this reasoning prompted the ideological search by the Ottoman reforming elite for national unity in the Ottoman Empire. The reformers tried to level out cultural differences by creating a unifying notion of Ottomanism.

The disintegration of the empire was caused by a combination of external economic and political-military factors. Great power rivalries over the Ottoman territories intensified the differences within the empire. The Ottoman reforms promoting an ideology of unity were a protective response to external challenges and took various forms such as Ottomanism, Islamism, and Turkism. The intention was to secure the territorial integrity of the empire. The Ottoman Empire failed to achieve unity, while the notion of equality remained an obscure concept.

The theoretical incompatibility between pluralism and equality seems, in the case of the Ottoman Empire, to be well founded historically. That is, the breakup of the Ottoman Empire could be taken as evidence that it is impossible to achieve equality within a culturally plural state. Seeing pluralism as the obstacle to unity, the Young Turks came up with a "solution": to impose uniformity. This involved the "discovery" of cultural homogeneity within the remaining territories of the Ottoman state, mainly the "discovery" of a Turkish nation within the empire.

The successive Ottoman reform movements culminated in the search for an ideology of unity in the empire. The Ottoman reformers tried to impose uniformity as a way of leveling out cultural differences, but they failed to achieve unity.

This should lead us to rethink the relationship between pluralism and the supposed unattainability of unity and to think again about the misconceived linkage between unity and equality. The Ottoman breakup was rooted in a theory of equality that associated citizenship with a unified concept of nationality. A contemporary lesson for us to draw from the Ottoman experience is that we need alternative conceptions of citizenship that are dissociated from nationality and linked to the plurality of communities.

Notes

1. H. A. R. Gibb and H. Bowen, *Islamic Society and the West* (London: Oxford University Press, 1962), 207; S. Mardin, "Center-periphery relations: a key to Turkish politics?" in *Daedalus* Vol.102, No.1 (1973): 171.

2. H. Inalcık, *The Ottoman Empire: The Classical Age, 1300-1600* (New York: Praeger, 1973; reprint, London: Phoenix, 1994), 150-51.

3. *Devshirme* means "collection" in Turkish, the term I will use. The "collection" system was developed from the mid-fourteenth century and lasted until the beginning of the eighteenth century. It was designed to enable sultans to eliminate Anatolian Turkish notables, who had threatened central authority since the thirteenth century. See S. J. Shaw, *History of the Ottoman Empire and Modern Turkey* (Cambridge: Cambridge University Press, 1976), 53-58. Their elimination by the fifteenth century consolidated the basis of the Sultan's power and prevented a landed aristocracy from emerging as a counterforce to the Sultan. See F. Ahmad, *The Making of Modern Turkey* (London: Routledge, 1993), 18-20.

4. Gibb and Bowen, *Islamic Society and the West,* 39-199.

5. K. Karpat, "The Transformation of the Ottoman State, 1789-1908," *International Journal of Middle Eastern Studies* 3 (1972); K. Karpat, "The Stages of Ottoman History," in *The Ottoman State and Its Place in the World History,* ed. K. Karpat (Leiden: E. J. Brill, 1974); S. Mardin, *The Genesis of Young Ottoman Thought: A Study in The Modernization of Turkey's Political Ideals* (Princeton: Princeton University Press, 1962), 97-108. From the fourteenth century, Sunni Islam was the official religion of the state; see I. Gündüz, *Osmanlılarde Devlet-Tekke Munasebetleri* (State-Tekke relations in the Ottoman Empire) (Ankara: Seha Yayınları, 1983). Religious members of the ruling cadres and Sunni religious orders constituted Sunni orthodoxy against the political expansion of Shi'a Islam (Gündüz, 3-147). Naqshbandi was among the most important Sunni orders in the empire.

6. H. Inalcık, "The Nature of Traditional Society, Turkey," in *The Political Modernization in Japan and Turkey,* ed. R. E. Ward and D. Rustow (Princeton: Princeton University Press, 1964); H. Inalcık, "The Application of Tanzimat," *Archivum Ottomanicum* 3 (1973); and S. J. Shaw, *History of the Ottoman Empire and Modern Turkey* (Cambridge: Cambridge University Press, 1976).

7. Islamic law was never strictly applied. Non-Islamic laws were also widely used. See H. Inalcık, "The Emergence of Big Farms, Ciftliks: State, Landlords and Tenants," in *Studies in Ottoman Social and Economic History* (London: Variorum Reprints, 1985); S. Mardin, *Din ve Ideoloji,* 2nd ed. (Istanbul: Iletisim Yayinlari, 1983); and N. Berkes, trans. *The Development of Secularism in Turkey* (1964; reprint, Montreal: McGill University Press, 1976). Sultan's non-Islamic laws were concerned with the state regulation of production, distribution, consumption and with taxation. The combination of Islamic and non-Islamic laws was a non-theocratic form of rule.

8. C. Findley, "The Advent of Ideology in the Islamic Middle East," *Studia Islamica* (1982), 158.

9. Community cultures were powerless against the "great" culture of the ruling circles. The tension between the high culture of the rulers and the little cultures of the subjects was the source of an unstable form of integration.

10. Inalcık, "The Application of Tanzimat," 7.

11. Ş. Mardin, *The Genesis of Young Ottoman Thought: A Study in The Modernization of Turkey's Political Ideals* (Princeton: Princeton University Press, 1962), 97-108.

12. *Tımar* refers to the allocation of state lands as military fiefs.

13. Inalcık, "The Application of Tanzimat," 114.

14. I. Sunar, "State and Economy in the Ottoman Empire," in *The Ottoman Empire and the World Economy,* ed. H. Islamoğlu-Inan (Cambridge: Cambridge University Press, 1987); C. Issawi, *The Economic History of Turkey: 1800-1914* (Chicago: University of Chicago Press, 1980).

15. Ç. Keyder and H. Islamoğlu, "Agenda for Ottoman History," *Review* 1 (Summer 1977), 39-40

16. Islamoğlu-Inan, *Ottoman Empire and the World Economy*, 123-126.

17. Inalcık, "Emergence of Big Farms," 106.

18. Inalcık, "The Application of Tanzimat," 104-108.

19. Keyder and Islamoğlu, "Agenda for Ottoman History," 38.

20. H. Inalcık, "The Nature of Traditional Society, Turkey;" K. Karpat, "Millets and Nationality: The Roots of Incongruity of Nation and State in the Post-Ottoman Era," in *Christians and Jews in the Ottoman Empire*; S. Mardin, "Center-Periphery Relations: A Key to Turkish Politics?" *Daedalus* (Winter 1973); Keyder and Islamoğlu, "Agenda for Ottoman History."

21. H. Inalcık, "Military and Fiscal Transformation of the Ottoman Empire, 1600-1700," *Archivum Ottomanicum* 6 (1980): 297.

22. Mardin, "Center-Periphery Relations," 171-172.

23. R. Kasaba, *The Ottoman Empire and the World Economy: The Nineteenth Century* (Albany: State University of New York Press, 1988), 16.

24. E. Wolf, *Europe and the People without History* (Berkeley: University of California Press, 1982), 37.

25. L. Güçer, *Asırlarda Osmanlı Imparatorlugunda Hububat Meselesi ve Hububattan Alınan Vergiler* (Grain question and the taxation of grain in the Ottoman Empire during the 15th and 16th centuries) (1964).

26. Keyder and Islamoğlu, "Agenda for Ottoman History," 44.

27. Inalcık, "The Application of Tanzimat," 49.

28. Colonization was guided by competitive growth in European manufacturing and export of finished goods. D. W. Tomich, *Slavery in the Circuit of Sugar: Martinique and the World Economy 1830-1848* (Baltimore: Johns Hopkins University Press, 1990).

29. Wolf, *Europe and the People without History.*

30. The Ottoman system had blocked direct European access to the East and thus diverted European expansion to the Americas and the sea routes around the Cape. After the conquest of Syria in 1516 and Egypt in 1517 the Ottoman Empire incorporated the separate economic, cultural, and religious regions of the Middle East into its economic space. Wolf, *Europe and the People without History*; F. Braudel, *The Perspectives of the World: Civilization and Capitalism (15th-18th Century)*, Vol. 3 (London: Fontana Press, 1979), 467-68; Inalcık, "The Application of Tanzimat," 121-39.

31. Bailey, *British Policy and the Turkish Reform Movement*; C. Emsley, *British Society and the French Wars* (London: Rowman, 1969).

32. I. Wallerstein, H. Decdeli, and R. Kasaba. "The Incorporation of the Ottoman Empire into the World Economy," in *The Ottoman Empire and the World Economy*, 92.

33. Inalcık, "The Application of Tanzimat," 136-39.

34. When the English were granted a 3 percent custom duty, the French and other foreigners were paying 5 percent. In 1673 the French succeeded in having it reduced to 3 percent (Inalcık, "The Application of Tanzimat," 138).

35. O. L. Barkan, "The Price Revolution of the Sixteenth Century," *International Journal of Middle East Studies* (1975).

36. British free trade policy triumphed in 1838. The Convention allowed British merchants to purchase goods anywhere in the empire, paying only a very small import or export duty. It imposed only a 3 percent duty on imports, 12 per cent duty on exports and 3 percent duty on transit (Issawi, *Economic History of Turkey*, 74-75). The other European states also became part of the Convention, which led to the expansion of cash-crop production in the empire. In addition to Egypt, Syria, and Western Anatolia, waste and state lands in the Balkans were converted into plantation-like farms producing cash crops such as cotton.

37. Issawi, *Economic History of Turkey*; Issawi, "The Transformation of the Economic Position of the Millets in the Nineteenth Century," in *Christians and Jews in the Ottoman Empire* Vol. 1, eds. B. Braude and B. Lewis (New York: Holmes and Meyer, 1982); T. Staianovich, "Land Tenure and Related Sectors of the Balkan Economy," *The Journal of Economic History* 13 (1953).

38. Kasaba, *Ottoman Empire and the World Economy*; S. Pamuk, *The Ottoman Empire and European Capitalism,1820-1913* (Cambridge: Cambridge University Press, 1987); C. Keyder, *The Definition of a Peripheral Economy: Turkey 1923-1929* (Cambridge: Cambridge University Press, 1981).

39. E. Kedourie, *Nationalism in Asia and Africa* (Cleveland, 1970).

40. C. Findley, "The Advent of Ideology."

41. D. Kushner, *The Rise of Turkish Nationalism* (London: Frank Cass, 1977); R. H. Davison, "Nationalism as an Ottoman Problem and the Ottoman Response," in *Nationalism in a Non-National State: The Dissolution of the Ottoman Empire*, eds. W. W. Haddad and W. Ochsenwald (Columbus: Ohio State University Press, 1977); Karpat, "Millets and Nationality."

42. A. Palmer, *The Decline and Fall of the Ottoman Empire* (London: John Murray, 1992).

43. C. Findley, *Bureaucratic Reform in the Ottoman Empire: The Sublime Porte, 1789-1922* (Princeton: Princeton University Press, 1980); R. H. Davison, *Reform in the Ottoman Empire, 1856-1876* (Princeton: Princeton University Press, 1963), 46-48.

44. Mardin, *Genesis of Young Ottoman Thought*; Findley, "The Advent of Ideology."

45. Yapp, *Making of Modern Middle East*, 111.

46. For example, the Hatt-i Humayun of 1856, which reaffirmed the 1839 Charter of Regulation by asserting the full equality of Muslims and non-Muslims in the empire, was an attempt to prevent foreign supervision of reforms.

47. E. R. J. Owen, *Cotton and Egyptian Economy, 1820-1914: A Study in Trade and Development* (Oxford: Oxford University Press, 1969).

48. D. Urquhart, *Turkey and Its Resources* (London: Saunders and Otley and Conduit Street, 1833).

49. Palmer, *Decline and Fall of the Ottoman Empire*.

50. Ottoman military power had been weakened by Russia during the Ottoman-Russian wars of 1768-74, 1787-92, 1806, 1809-12, 1828-29, and 1854-56.

51. Bailey, *British Policy and the Turkish Reform Movement*; J. A. R. Marriot, *The Eastern Question: An Historical Study in European Diplomacy* (Oxford: Clarendon Press, 1924).

52. Russian advances in the Balkans during the Ottoman-Russian war of 1828-29 intensified the Greek and Serbian demands for independence. At the Treaty of Adrianople in 1829 Russia secured concessions for Serbian autonomy. In 1830 the London Protocol set up a small sovereign Greek kingdom guaranteed by Russia, Great Britain, and France as protecting powers. Most of modern Greece was within the Ottoman territories (Palmer, *Decline and Fall of the Ottoman Empire*, 99-100). Though Greece became independent and Serbia obtained autonomy, their territories were not defined.

53. R. H. Davison, *Reform in the Ottoman Empire, 1856-1876* (Princeton: Princeton University Press, 1963), 238-250.

54. Inalcık, "The Application of Tanzimat," 98-127.

55. Inalcık, "The Application of Tanzimat."

56. Mardin, *Genesis of Young Ottoman Thought*, 14-15.

57. H. Islamoğlu-Inan, "State and Peasants in the Ottoman Empire" in *Ottoman Empire and the World Economy*.

58. Issawi, *Economic History of Turkey*; O. Koymen, "Imperialism of Free Trade," paper presented to International Congress of Economic History, Moscow, 1970.

59. The most important events of the period consisted of the dispute over privileges in the Holy Places (1850); the revolts of the Greek community in Crete (1857, 1866-8, 1879 and 1889); and the Serbian and Montenegrin war against the Ottoman state, followed by the uprisings in Bosnia, Hercegovina, and Bulgaria (1875-78). Palmer, *Decline and Fall of the Ottoman Empire*, 104-188.

60. Mardin, *Genesis of Young Ottoman Thought*; T. Z. Tunaya, *Turkiye'de Siyasi Partiler, 1859-1962* (Political parties in Turkey, 1859-1962) (Istanbul: 1952), 94.

61. Sultan Abdulhamit initiated Constitutionalism in 1877. When he abolished the constitution within its first year, however, the liberal Young Ottomans condoned this, demonstrating that they were more nationalist than liberal. Sultan Abdulhamit faced no organized opposition during his thirty years of autocratic ruling.

62. M. Türklöne, *Siyasi Ideoloji olarak Islamcılığın Doğuşu* (The Advent of Islamism as an Ideology) (Istanbul: Iletişim Yayınları, 1991).

63. The Naqshbandi order has been a constant force since the fifteenth century without "national" or regional characteristics. It was one of the most powerful transnational religious Sufi orders.

64. Gündüz, *Osmanlılarda Devlet-Tekke Munasebetleri*; H. Algar, "The Naqshbandi Order in Republican Turkey," revised version of paper presented at the History and Society in Turkey conference, Berlin, 1983; Mardin, "The Naqshbandi Order in Turkish History" in Religion, Politics and Literature in a Secular State, ed. R. Tapper (London: I. B. Tauris & Co., 1991).

65. Gündüz, *Osmanlılarda Devlet-Tekke Munasebetleri*; Mardin, "The Naqshbandi Order in Turkish History;" E. B. Sapolyo, *Tarikatlar Tarihi* (The history of Tariqas), 1964.

66. Gündüz, *Osmanlılarda Devlet-Tekke Munasebetleri.*

67. Gündüz, *Osmanlılarda Devlet-Tekke Munasebetleri*; I. Bozdag, *Abdulhamit'in Hatıra Defteri* (Memoirs of Abdulhamit) (Istanbul: Tercuman Yayınları, n.d.)

68. Y. Atasoy, "Transnationalization of Economy and the Dilemma of Political-Cultural Identity in Turkey," paper presented at a conference in honor of Charles Tilly, Toronto, Ontario, 1995.

69. *Rabıta* means absolute conformity to the thought of the leader (*shaykh*) of the order.

70. One reason for the rise of Muslim Arab nationalism was the growth in Jewish immigration to Palestine since the 1880s, which ran counter to Abdulhamit's determination to achieve Islamic unity and integrate Arab lands more closely to the Turkish Muslim lands. In Palestine the Jewish population increased from 24,000 in 1880 to 49,000 in 1903 and 90,000 by the outbreak of World War I. The cause of Jewish immigration to Palestine was anti-Semitism in Central Europe and Russia. The Ottoman government feared that the Jewish settlers could provoke chronic conflict with the Arabs. Sultan Abdulhamit rejected Theodor Herzl's demand for a legally assured home for the Jews in Palestine. Nevertheless, Germany, for example, continued to support the settlement efforts of the German Jewish organizations in Palestine. Muslim Arabs began to attack pioneer Jewish agricultural settlements as early as 1886 (Palmer, *Decline and Fall of the Ottoman Empire*, 193-195).

71. S. Akşin, *Jön Türkler ve Ittihat ve Terakki* (Young Turks and the union and progress), (Istanbul, 1980).

72. Mardin, *Din ve Ideoloji*, 219-223; Mardin, *Jön Türklerin Siyasi Fikirleri, 1895-1908* (The political thoughts of the young Turks, 1895-1908), 2nd ed. (Istanbul: Iletişim Yayınları, 1983), 96-101; Mardin, "Center-Periphery Relations," 172-174; C. Keyder, "The Political Economy of Turkish Democracy." *New Left Review*, no. 115 (1979), 4.

73. M. van Bruinessen, "Kürtler Arasında Bir Siyasi Protesto Aracı Olarak Naksibendi Tarikati" (Naqshbandi order among the Kurds as a means of political protest), in *Kürdistan Üzerine Yazılar* (Writings on Kurdistan) (Istanbul: Iletisim Yayınları, 1992), 90-97.

74. In spite of these revolts, most Naqshbandi leaders argued for Ottomanism. See the collection of Said Nursi's writings in the *Içtima-i Reçeteler* (Social Prescriptions), reprinted in 1990.

75. B. E. Behar, *Iktidar ve Tarih, Türkiye'de "Resmi Tarih" Tezinin Olusumu, 1929-1937* (Power and history, the formation of the "Official History" thesis in Turkey, 1929-1937) (Istanbul: AFA Yayıncılık, 1992), 60-85; N. Berkes, trans., *Turkish Nationalism and Turkish Civilization, Selected Essays of Ziya Gökalp* (New York: Columbia University Press, 1959).

76. M. H. Yinanc, *Milli Tarihimizin Adı* (The name of our national history) (Istanbul: Hareket Yayınları, 1969).

77. Behar, *Iktidar ve Tarih*, 64-65.

78. Among these intellectuals was sociologist Ziya Gökalp, considered the father of Turkish nationalism, which began between 1908 and 1918. Gökalp developed "Turkism"— an attempt to synthesize westernization, Islamism, and Turkism with nationalism (Y. Atasoy, "Gökalp Sosyolojisindeki Bazi Kavramlar" [Some concepts in Gökalp's sociology], Middle East Technical University, Department of Sociology, 1985). Gökalp opposed Islamic nationalism, for it included Muslims of other ethnic-linguistic categories. His aim was to "Turkify" Islam and make religion one component of a linguistic culture.

Six

Who or What Broke Up the Soviet Union?

Feodor Burlatsky

In March of 1996, the State Duma of the Russian Federation — the lower house of the Russian Parliament — on the initiative of the Communist parliament passed a sensational resolution denouncing the Belovezhsk Accords on the breakup of the Soviet Union (USSR). This agreement was undertaken in the Belovezhskaia Pushcha in Belorussia on December 12, 1991, by the leaders of three Soviet republics: Boris Yeltsin (Russia), Leonid Kravchuk (Ukraine), and Stanislav Shushkevich (Belorussia). It was confirmed by the Supreme Soviet of the Russian Soviet Federal Socialist Republic (RSFSR), which was then the parliament of Russia. This was the very act of legislation that was later denounced by the State Duma of the Russian Federation. This denunciation was undertaken with the express purpose of dealing a blow to Yeltsin and threatening his reelection as president of Russia. It impels us to review the issue of who bears responsibility for the breakup of the Soviet Union and to what degree it was unavoidable.

This chapter will review the crucial phases through which the state moved toward its dissolution, beginning in the middle years of Mikhail Gorbachev's time in office. We can discern four stages:

(a) *The period of rising nationalism.* Secessionist groups, beginning in the Baltic Republics and Azerbaijan, attempted to leave the Soviet Union.

(b) *The Novo-Ogarevo period.* The president finally decided to revise the Soviet constitution and redefine the relations between the governments of the republics and the center. The negotiations (carried out in a dacha outside Moscow called "Novo-Ogarevo") yielded a "New Union Treaty" that would have been adopted on August 20, 1991, had a coup not been attempted on the preceding day.

(c) *The postcoup negotiations toward a new Union Treaty.* After the putsch, the new Union Treaty could not be signed in its initial form, but efforts continued to be made to find a common basis for union among some of the republics.

(d) *The Belovezhsk Accords.* The final phase of the breakup occurred when the leaders of three republics, including Russia, met in Belorussia and signed this document, which announced their departure from the Soviet state and their creation of a new "Commonwealth of Independent States." As a result of this decision, the Soviet Union was officially disbanded at the end of 1991.

The Rise of Nationalism during the Gorbachev Years

At the time of the First Congress of Peoples Deputies of the USSR in 1989, in which I had the opportunity to participate, the first lightning bolts of the national movements lit up new clouds over our heads. The sky was no longer blue, sprinkled with the stars of the "friendship of the peoples." Rather, it was covered with dark clouds signaling the approaching national storms.

Nagorno-Karabakh was the first of them.[1] Not long before the congress, Gorbachev's assistant, Georgii Shakhnazarov, an ethnic Armenian, brought to him Zorii Baloian, a brilliant journalist elected from that region. He presented Gorbachev with a plan for allowing Nagorno-Karabakh to secede from Azerbaijan.

Gorbachev doubted the plan's realism and argued against it but did not move to halt its advance. He did not take a stand on the issue. Thus was tied one of the most cruel knots in international relations. During the Congress, and then tens of times in sessions of the Supreme Soviet, representatives of Armenia and Azerbaijan were at each other's throats. Gorbachev and the delegates from Russia and other republics dissociated themselves from the problem on the principle: You made your bed, and you have to lie in it. In the USSR appeared a crack, which subsequently became a gaping chasm that swallowed thousands of lives.

An even harsher blow to the Union was dealt by the representatives of the Baltic states. They demanded the recognition of the illegality of the entry of the Baltic states into the Soviet Union, and a denunciation of the Hitler-Stalin pact. The Lithuanian delegation stormed from the meeting hall in protest, leaving it in deathly silence. Gorbachev was taken unaware, not knowing what to do. I approached a microphone and proposed a break in the session so that Gorbachev could negotiate with the Lithuanians and convince them to return and continue their struggle.

There was then still a possibility of declaring the issue of the Baltic states to be a special problem, not connected to the general reconstruction of the Federation. But Gorbachev feared that any concessions to the Balts would open the door to other republics. He was mistaken. Since the Balts were then open to compromise, they could have remained a relatively autonomous part of a confederation, but the opportunity was lost.

At the Congress, there was also a remarkable explosion of Russian national consciousness. The writer Valentin Rasputin proposed that, if the national republics want to secede, then let them secede. Russia will survive without them. She is ready to leave the Union herself. A large portion of the delegates — Russian people from localities — applauded him, not realizing that they were applauding the beginning of the breakup of the Soviet Union.

However, the heaviest blow to the Soviet Union came not from the Baltic states but from the least expected source: the Supreme Soviet of the Russian Federation declared its sovereignty and independence from the USSR. The Russian Federation occupied two-thirds of the territory of the USSR and housed more than half its population and many of the key natural resources. Its secession marked the beginning of the end of what had been the Russian empire.

Gorbachev was faced with a dilemma: What should be done? Boris Yeltsin, together with other representatives of the "opposition," was stirring up the nationalist sentiments of the Russian people. Nationalist politics found a ready response, for the simplest of motives: The quality of life was declining steadily. Goods were disappearing from the store shelves. Many people had the impression that other republics were responsible. They could not understand where Russia's resources were going. The peoples of Belorussia, Ukraine, Central Asia, and other republics had the same sentiments: Free yourselves from the yoke of the center, from the demands of other republics, and life will immediately improve.

Gorbachev, as always, sought compromise and balance. He ceded to Yeltsin's pressure when the RSFSR declared its sovereignty. But, as a counterweight, Gorbachev supported the creation of a Russian Communist Party (none had existed previously). This was a losing proposition from the start. Ivan Polozkov, the leader of the new party, was no match for Yeltsin. By indirectly supporting Polozkov, Gorbachev only lost credibility with the public.

But even Yeltsin did not anticipate the consequences of his own moves. Following Russia's sovereignty came no less than twenty other declarations. Not only Union republics, but autonomous republics, districts, and regions began to bow to the new god, sovereignty.

The group of People's Deputies of the USSR to which I belonged held a session shortly before this "parade of sovereignties." We discussed the theme "Union, Federation, Confederation, or Commonwealth?" Several of my colleagues and I spoke in favor of a commonwealth of a confederative type, but then Yeltsin's close associate, Mikhail Bucharov, spoke in a different way. He repeated the words "Russia" and "Sovereignty" ten times. I asked him, "Okay, suppose we break up the Soviet Union. Then what will the Russian Federation do? What will you do if Tataria, Bashkiria, Chechnya, and Ingushetia also declare their sovereignty and leave the RSFSR?" He became confused and answered, "We'll negotiate with them."

And that was it. Since then the leaders of Russia have seen how far they had gone. The Tatars, Chechens, and other nationalities have tried to get from them what Russia tried to get from the USSR — sovereignty.

Gorbachev, on the other hand, refused to support the idea of a confederation and defended the preservation of the USSR. Still, the republican elites obviously wanted to play a new role in the Union. At the beginning of perestroika Gorbachev had an opportunity to include all the leaders of the republics in the Politburo of the party and later to form a state council where they could each have a vote. Such a body could also have included the leaders of the autonomous republics in a consultative capacity. Such suggestions were made at various times, but were never supported.

Gorbachev bears considerable responsibility for failing to prevent the farcical putsch of August 19-21, 1991, organized by his colleagues. The putsch resulted in the suspension of the signing of a treaty creating a new union. Indeed, the plotters' main political goal was precisely to prevent the signing of the Union Agreement.

On August 20, the leaders of the republics, together with the president of the USSR, were supposed to sign the new Union treaty. Many federalists, who had supported the preservation of the Federation in a new form, were ill-disposed toward the agreement. Then there were the "confederates" who believed that too many powers remained in the center — particularly that a central Union government would be preserved. Some leaders from the Central Asian republics publicly supported the Federation, although they were privately drawn toward the latter group. Toward the end of the discussions, there appeared a group that spoke out in favor of the creation of a commonwealth — at first economic, then political — resembling the model of the European Council, the European Parliament.

At the last July session of the Supreme Soviet of the USSR in 1991, Sergei Alekseev, chair of the Committee on Constitutional Direction of the USSR, outlined the aims of the federalists and argued in favor of confederation. Anatolii Lukianov[2] raised his arguments in a letter about the agreement, which was published on August 19, together with other documents of the putsch organizers.

For my part, in my speech to the Supreme Soviet, I called for support of the signing of the Union Agreement. I declared that, in any case, real interests would in the end take priority over emotions and passions. Had it not been for the putsch, the Agreement would have been signed and the state would not have fallen apart. That farcical putsch undermined the transformation of the USSR into a new federation of relatively autonomous states. However, one should not assume that the Communists as a whole were responsible for the putsch. The Communist faction of the Russian Supreme Soviet later voted to confirm the Belovezhskaia decision. Though the attempted coup of August and the subsequent Belovezhsk Accords were both putsches, they were carried out for antithetical reasons — the former for the sake of keeping the Soviet Union unified to some degree, the latter for the sake of breaking it into independent states. Yet paradoxically the former event conferred greater legitimacy on the republican leaders who later, in effect, made the second putsch.

After the August putsch, Gorbachev made heroic efforts to preserve the Union in a less centralized form. From September to December 1991, at Novo-Ogarevo, the leaders of all the Soviet republics met to discuss the issue. Gorbachev fought like a lion, was as clever as a fox, and was as nimble as a rabbit. He used all possible means of political struggle to prevent the breakup of the state.

Tens of meetings transpired with Yeltsin, Kravchuk, Nazarbaev, Shushkevich and the other leaders, all of whom bought the expansion of their personal power with the currency of the sovereign will of their peoples. The Novo-Ogarevo process before and after the putsch was the heroic struggle of a leader pressing a doomed, rear-guard battle for the preservation of the state. Gorbachev showed a flash of greatness in his struggle for the preservation of the crumbling union, which finally collapsed, relieving him of his post as president. If we criticize him for suspending the Congress of the Peoples Deputies (USSR), the Supreme Soviet of the USSR, the Party, and other bases of his power without creating alternative structures, we must also note that he accepted his removal with dignity. The Union, which he had defended to the end, had fallen apart. It was a dramatic moment of Shakespearean dimension, something that no one in history had survived — not Churchill, who lost power after the collapse of the British Empire, nor De Gaulle, who was forced from power after the loss of the French colonies. Gorbachev's weakness and defeat were so extreme that, after his resignation, he found almost no support among the population.

On December 25, 1991, he resigned as the first and last president of the USSR. Though preserving his dignity and sense of historical responsibility, he left without completing his mission, often misunderstood, and without even himself fully understanding the dramatic process that had unfolded before our eyes.

Gorbachev addressed the people of the USSR with a speech stating his motives for resigning and summarizing his time in leadership:

> My dear countrymen, fellow citizens. In keeping with the situation as it has evolved, with the formation of the Commonwealth of Independent States, I bring to an end my activity as president of the USSR. I have taken this decision on considerations of principle.
>
> I spoke out strongly in favor of the independence of peoples and sovereignty of the republics, but at the same time for the preservation of the union government and the unity of the country. Events have taken a different turn. The movement toward the dismemberment of the country and division of the state has come to dominate, and I cannot agree with this.[3]

What the president said was true, but unfortunately, only a partial truth. Another, fuller truth about the USSR concerned the consequences of perestroika, which had brought a collapse of production and the standard of living. It had transferred power to provincial, largely nationality-oriented, incompetent elites, who reversed many of the victories of perestroika. It had reduced Russia's status as a superpower by voluntarily suspending its position on the world stage. About this, the president said nothing.

Why did the destruction of the Communist dreadnought bring to its end an empire that had held together for centuries? The first blow to the dimensions of this unique state was delivered in 1917, when it lost Poland, Finland, and the Baltic States. But the Bolsheviks, who pronounced the principle of the self-determination of nations, had a sudden change of heart. They defeated Petliura's troops when he declared the independence of Ukraine. They suppressed separatist movements in Georgia, Azerbaijan, and Central Asia.

In the end, the captain who ran the Communist ship aground was a Communist leader who had worked twenty-five years in the Party apparatus, who had fed on its ideology as on mother's milk. Is this a puzzle? No! We can find many parallels, such as Christ's challenge to his own Jewish faith, the struggles of Luther with the Catholic Church, the erosion of Francoism and Peronism. History digs its own steps under our feet.

Gorbachev had the charisma necessary to destroy the system that had created him. Therefore, to Communist fundamentalists he appears a traitor. He betrayed the Party and brought it to the edge of a chasm. It remained only for Yeltsin to nudge it off the cliff. Gorbachev betrayed the ideology of Leninism, and traded it for the Western values of freedom, open society, and a presidency. Yet these were but signposts on the road to the destruction of the past.

It is strange, however, that history gave this role to Gorbachev. By nature, he is a creator, and not a destroyer. He is a talented, kind, and considerate man, incapable of thoughtless action. His main failure was his inability to use his power, even when necessary. For this reason, he lost it.

Having initiated perestroika, Gorbachev could hardly have known that it could spark a revolution. He had intended to bring gradual reform, which would lead step by step to the creation of a modern society, Western civilization. But he underestimated the underlying, national movements that would explode.

The breakup of the USSR was delivered by the leaders of the three Slavic republics: Yeltsin of Russia, Kravchuk of Ukraine, and Shushkevich of Belorussia. To this day, there are several versions of these events. Therefore, I shall let each of the main participants present his version.

Yeltsin

I will start with Yeltsin. I will examine his explanation of events as they appeared in a book issued two years after the fact, in a new period when the

Belovezhsk Accords were viewed by a majority in Russia as a national tragedy. Yeltsin does not offer a full explanation of the events that, in his opinion, made the collapse of the USSR inevitable. His thoughts and feelings on the issue are peppered throughout the text as in a fantastical kaleidoscope, mixing historical accidents with large forward movements of history and the minor psychological details of his dealings with Gorbachev. The whole issue of the destruction of the great state is viewed through the prism of the personal battle among the president of the USSR, the president of Russia, and other republican leaders. He carefully draws a picture of the Communist bosses and their new ambitions.

In Yeltsin's mind, at least as it is represented in his "notes,"[4] three main stages are delineated:

1. Prior to the putsch: the Novo-Ogarevo process of forming a basis for a federative type of union treaty.

2. Immediately following the putsch: the attempt to return to the interrupted process on new principles of confederation.

3. The Belovezhsk Accords: the formation of the Commonwealth of Independent States.

In his commentaries, Yeltsin suggests an underlying sense of regret over the dramatic collapse of the Union. Here, it seems, he inadvertently expressed a huge gap between his feelings at Belovezhskaia — the victory of Russia and his personal triumph — and what he felt two and a half years later, given the new and more complicated problems that he faced.

The Novo-Ogarevo Process prior to the Putsch

Gorbachev, it seemed, finally decided to sacrifice his conservative colleagues and find common ground with Yeltsin and Nazarbaev. In all probability, he had not yet completely overcome his hesitations about and fear of Yeltsin, his increasingly powerful competitor, although in principle he engaged Yeltsin and the other "Great Princes" in the expansion of republican sovereignty.

Yeltsin describes the circumstances of the Novo-Ogarevo process, when the leaders of the republics prepared a proposal for a union agreement:

> Gorbachev and I bore on ourselves all of the moral responsibility for working out the contentious issues. To my surprise, this never resulted in hostility or unpleasant encounters. Why? He liked the unprecedented role of being the leader of not one but several democratic states. It was an excellent base from which to project himself as a world leader.

> But there was also the psychological background. The situation dictated (and permitted) that we work together in the process of negotiations as normal people. All personal considerations were left behind. Each of our words had too high a price.

And further on, a crucial passage: "What a great opportunity we missed! Gorbachev and I suddenly felt that our interests were compatible, that our roles suited us: Gorbachev preserved his seniority and I my independence. It was an ideal solution for us both."

One can observe that personal motivations came first — and at a time when the fate of our great nation hung in the balance. On the eve of the putsch, an agreement in principle was finally reached between Yeltsin and Gorbachev on the conditions of a new union agreement. It constituted a complete change of the political regime, the end of Pavlov's government, and the confirmation of union government, which would be agreed to by Yeltsin, Nazarbaev, and, in time, the other leaders. Gorbachev appeared to accept an entirely new approach, in which all major decisions could be taken only with Yeltsin's assent. In other words, it involved a division of power when the final word belonged not to the president of the USSR but to the leadership of Russia and the other republics.

Why then did Yeltsin not uphold this agreement after triumphing over the putsch organizers, when he had the power to dictate his own conditions? His book offers no clear answer to that question. Yeltsin writes that, immediately after the putsch, Gorbachev replaced the leaders of three key ministries (defense, security, and foreign affairs) without consulting Yeltsin. Yeltsin demanded that Gorbachev retract these already announced decisions, and was forced to compromise. Yeltsin demanded the suspension of the Congress of Peoples' Deputies of the USSR. The leaders of the other republics supported him, and Gorbachev ceded even this point.

On the evening before the meeting of the Congress of Peoples' Deputies of the USSR, Yeltsin tells us, the leaders of the union republics met in the Kremlin to work out their tactics for dealing with the Congress. Long before this, the majority of them held the opinion that the Congress had to be dissolved, that this organ of state power had outlived its day. But each of them knew that it would not surrender power without a fight.

After intense work, a joint declaration of the heads of the ten republics was prepared. This declaration proposed to the Congress that it form an interrepublican structure of power for a transitional period preceding the adoption of a new USSR constitution. Then, the Congress was to cease to exist. Should the declaration be accepted, various crucial articles of the existing USSR constitution would be suspended and power would be transferred to the Councils of the heads of state, including the president of the USSR and the leaders of the union republics. During the work on this document, Gorbachev was ever ready to compromise, not mindful of the details, trying to bring the heads of the republics together. But the situation changed radically after the putsch. In declaring their sovereignty, one republic after another shifted its political foundations within the former — for this was now obvious to all — Soviet Union. In the new reality, Gorbachev was left with the role of the unifier of the now scattered republics.

The work at Novo-Ogarevo continued actively and intensely. But Gorbachev could barely keep up with events. He constantly ceded ground in a way that, before August, would have been unthinkable. He agreed that a future union should be a confederative state. A fairly strong center, however, was to be preserved, deciding issues of defense and a portion of financial questions. There remained a single president who acted as guarantor that the agreement would not be violated. He would represent the Union of Sovereign States (USS — a new variation of the abbreviation for USSR) in its relations with the rest of the world. The central government still had a post of prime minister, and Moscow was supposed to have a two-chamber parliament.

It seemed as if everything had worked out well, that a suitable foundation had been set for an agreement on a confederation of all republics, and thus the preservation, in a new form, of a single government on the territory of the USSR. What happened to upset it? Was it the unstable position of Ukraine? Yes, that was probably so. But to an equal degree it was Yeltsin, who was determined to completely eliminate the center — that is, Gorbachev. For this, a confederation, wherein there existed a post of president and other general institutions of power, was unacceptable. There had to be a break with the past, a complete dissolution so that history could begin again with a clean slate, on which would be written in large gold letters, "Russia, Democracy, Yeltsin."

> It was an excellent winter evening. A gentle frost. A light snow. A genuine crisp December. In the residence of the Chairman of the Supreme Soviet of the Republic of Belarus we gathered, the three of us: Shushkevich, Kravchuk and I. We gathered in order to decide the fate of the Union.

With these lyrical phrases, Yeltsin begins his description of the events in Belovezhskaia Pushcha.

> Instead of a gradual, calm transition from a unitary union to a looser, freer confederation, we got a complete vacuum of the political center. The center, in the person of Gorbachev, was utterly demoralized. He had lost whatever interest had remained in him regarding the national states. We had to do something.

Thus Yeltsin describes the motives of the three leaders in signing a treaty on the liquidation of the USSR and the formation of the Commonwealth of Independent States. But he does not state his own primary motive — to rid himself decisively of Gorbachev.

The "great" troika, and particularly Yeltsin, had a variety of options for the dissolution of the USSR. First, to gather the leaders of all the republics, present the declaration, and then discuss what to do. Second, to offer the resolution of the issue to the congresses and parliaments of the republics. Third, most obviously, to undertake a referendum and ask all citizens once again whether they were prepared to live under one roof or to go their own way and live in separate republican structures.

Nothing of the kind was done. On the contrary, the great troika ordered a group of Yeltsin's advisors to throw together a document on the dissolution of the USSR. In a Belovezhskaia bathhouse (literally) they hammered out a proposal which they themselves considered muddled and incomplete. But, as I have learned from a participant, the three republican leaders cheered it as it was.

Nevertheless, I would not attribute the whole affair to Yeltsin's personal motives when we are discussing an event of world-historical significance, such as the destruction of the great Russian state. A significant role was also played by the "drunkenness with democracy" that he and those around him were experiencing at the time. It seemed that they were opening a new chapter in the thousand-year history of Russia, a sharp move toward Western civilization — democracy, the market, human rights — a new, finally discovered paradise. Therefore, it was necessary to break once and for all with the past, bury it, and not deal with such petty issues as a constitution, a referendum, and the centuries-old tradition of many nationalities living together. Here is a typical Yeltsin benediction:

> I believe that the twentieth century ended on 19-21 August 1991. And if the election of the first freely elected president of Russia was an event of great significance for all Russia, then the failure of the August putsch was an event of global, planetary significance. The twentieth century was, for the most part, a century of horror. Such nightmares as totalitarianism and fascism, the nightmare of communism, concentration camps, genocide, and atomic destruction the world had not yet known.

> Within these three days, one century ended and another began. Perhaps some will consider this assertion too optimistic, but I believe it. I believe it because, in these days, the last empire collapsed. And it was imperial politics and imperial thinking in particular that, at the beginning of the century, played an evil joke on humanity, serving as a detonator of all of these processes.

Once again, ideological stereotypes were pounded into the heads of Russians. The word "empire" underscored the whole of Russian history, reducing it to a litany of violence, repression, and conquest. The word "democracy," which was naively associated with a single act — the election of the president of the RSFSR — stood as a justification for the destruction of a great power.

Thus Yeltsin understood his mission at Belovezhskaia. Now we will turn our attention to two other participants in these events: Kravchuk and Shushkevich. Then we will turn to the one who (in the words of Vysotsky)[5] did not "shoot": Nazarbaev.

Kravchuk

Kira Vladina and I conducted a series of interviews with the presidents of the independent states that grew out of the rubble of the USSR. I say "we," though she conducted the interviews and I included only a few questions regarding the fate of the Russian state and edited the text.[6] We were interested in the questions: Who was the initiator of the collapse of the USSR? Are there prospects for the formation of a Eurasian Confederation and, if so, in what form? I think that it will be interesting for the reader to hear the words of the very participants in these tragic events.

The first visits to the president of Ukraine, Leonid Kravchuk, took place in 1992 and 1993, when he was still in power. Here are some excerpts from the interviews.

Who initiated the dissolution of the Union when you met at Belovezhskaia Pushcha?

The initiator of the meetings was Ukraine.

And not Yeltsin?

No, not Yeltsin. We did not simply take the initiative, we prepared for it. We collected various opinions and views, and prepared proposals. But that they would have such consequences I did not foresee! I tell you honestly that I went there thinking that we would talk and prepare a little declaration. I insisted on it because, if we had not come up with one, the center would have taken over. I knew that well.

And you were against the center then?

I was categorically against the center, because I knew where the center would lead. But when we sat at the table and started to discuss various options, Yeltsin openly and honestly said, "I must present you with three questions, not from me but from Gorbachev. I ask you to answer them, not to me but to Gorbachev, although I too have an interest in the matter. First question: do you agree with the proposed treaty?

I indicated those articles that I wished to remove and so on. When I answered all the questions negatively, Yeltsin asked, "What conclusions should we draw from this?"

As such, Yeltsin fulfilled the mission given him by Gorbachev. In his actions, Yeltsin did not betray either the Union or Gorbachev personally?

No. He honestly said that he, Yeltsin, would decide the position of Russia conditional upon my response. If I had said that Ukraine would sign the union treaty, then Yeltsin would have signed.

In politics, such honesty is a rare thing.

Yeltsin is very consistent. You will remember his declaration when everyone was there but me. What did Yeltsin say? "I cannot see a union without Ukraine." That is consistency.

And Gorbachev said all the time, "Kravchuk will come with us. He will come. We cannot do anything without Ukraine."

That is why I say that history itself posed the issue, and Gorbachev and Yeltsin. Without Ukraine there is no Union.

But you betrayed Nazarbaev.

I do not think that we betrayed Nazarbaev. No way. It is a mistake that journalists constantly repeat. I explained everything to Nazarbaev twice and he said to me, "I believe you now."

When we went to Belovezhskaia Pushcha, I did not know what the outcome would be. It was necessary for the three of us to talk. If we had included others, then we might not have been able to get a result. Russia, Ukraine and Belarus were the basis, the foundation of the old Union. There was some kind of logic that the three of us should talk, and then approach the others. As soon as we came to an agreement, we called Nazarbaev and they told us, "He is on his way to Moscow." We sent someone out to the airport so that Nazarbaev would call as soon as he arrived. And we said, "We are sitting here. The document is in draft form. We have not held a press conference, but simply said that we had reached an agreement. Come down so that you can sign it with us." "Okay," he said, "I'm on the way." Some time later his opinion changed and then he met with Gorbachev. I understand that he was offended because we did not invite him in the beginning.

Do you think that you will go down in history as a liberator and creator of a new independent state, or as the destroyer of the great and powerful Soviet Union, which was feared throughout the world?

But the Union had already been destroyed.

Yes, but with your participation? Your role was the main one.

I do not deny my role, because everyone agreed that there could be no union or confederation without Ukraine. Therefore, I made it very clear at that time: Ukraine will never take part. And that was the decisive factor in the dissolution of the Union.

Shushkevich

The third active participant in the historic conference at Belovezhskaia Pushcha was the president of Belorussia, Stanislav Shushkevich. His answers were not as earnest or open as those of Kravchuk. But some new details characterizing the event, particularly concerning the prospects for the Commonwealth of Independent States, can be gleaned from our interview with him.

What is your attitude to the Commonwealth of Independent States? Will you fight for the Commonwealth? How do you see the Commonwealth?

You know, I have spoken about this so many times that I am afraid of getting confused. The logic here is very simple. Without very, very close contacts with Russia, we cannot survive now, in any form of economic relations. Presently, we export to Russia over 80 percent of our production. We have almost no fuel resources. They are in Russia.

For centuries, Belorussian has not been recognized as the language of the nation. Only now is it becoming the language of state, although it is unlikely to become a language of international communication. What language is most appropriate for Belorussia in this regard? Polish, French, English, Russian?

You are deeply mistaken. The Belorussian language has been the state language for a long time. The great Lithuanian princedom and the Princedom of Russia used Belorussian. The constitution of this princedom was written in Belorussian. This had no equals or analogs in Russia. This status served to a considerable degree as a basis for the creation of legislation in many European countries. But then our "Big Brother," or, rather, not his best representatives, dragged away with them the earnest, educated and dignified people and methodically drew many into confusion. As such, we speak of the restoration of a language which existed long ago.

A second position is that, in the middle of the last century, the Belorussian language was officially prohibited. The third position is that we have a generally flat landscape and were saved only by the bog, in contrast to Bulgaria, which was saved by monasteries and religion. There you have it — a powerful neighbor to the left, Poland, and a powerful neighbor to the right, Russia. I will not tell you the rest, like how our country became a passageway. Belorussia has lived through periods when every second Belorussian was killed and, in the last war, every fourth or, more likely, every third. Nevertheless, the nation and its language survives.

Belorussia has always been distinctive for its national tolerance, even in Tsarist times. Russian, Belorussian, and Jewish communities lived in peace. Belorussia was free of anti-Semitism at other times too. Should we fear that the germ of national hos-

tility, which has infected almost the entire territory of the former Soviet Union, will get to Belorussia too?

I tell it to you as it is. Among the common folk there is no nationality-based hostility. It will always be this way. But passions are lit by politicians — unelected, dirty politicians, without the support of the people. I do not foresee any problems here and I think that the state can regulate this. On a level of earnest intelligence, interethnic problems do not exist.

Nazarbaev

Particularly valuable are the opinions of Kazakhstan President Nursultan Nazarbaev as to the reasons for the collapse, and prospects for the integration, of the USSR.[7]

I will never forget how you appeared on TV after Belovezhskaia Pushcha, while journalists approached you as you descended from the plane. You always have an opinion. People believe in you. But then you were confused. To one journalist's question, you responded, "Politics is a matter of realism." Do you think that mistakes were made at Belovezhskaia Pushcha, and do you think it possible to correct these mistakes today?

We had set a meeting for noon on 9 December 1991, with Gorbachev and four presidents: Yeltsin, Kravchuk, Shushkevich, and myself. We were supposed to have decided what to do with the political aspects of the USSR. After the putsch, there was a meeting of government leaders in Alma-Ata, where we signed an economic treaty, and signed it again in Moscow. And then it was necessary to work on the terms of that treaty. But Gorbachev rushed ahead with political union — the Union of Independent States, the Commonwealth, the Union of Sovereign States.

We couldn't work it out. First, Ukraine was unsatisfied with something, then Russia. Gorbachev was not prepared to agree to a confederation on any terms. He said, why then would we need a president? A government?

On 7 December, we called Yeltsin, who had planned a trip to Belorussia. He was supposed to sign a joint treaty with Belorussia like the one we had signed with Russia. He said, "I went there and invited Kravchuk along." Before our meeting on 9 December I had to talk with Kravchuk, to be sure that he was with us on the Union. It was very good of him and very necessary. None of us wanted to move without the participation of Ukraine. We all wanted Ukraine to be with us. Our economies are closely connected. It is a big state with a large population. Therefore, I said, "If you do this and the three of you come together with some sort of agreement in hand, I will go along with you." That was the essence of our conversation.

He left on 7 December and I flew to Moscow on the eighth. There was no telephone on the plane and I knew nothing. So consequently, when I got off the plane and the journalists started asking questions, I told them that I did not yet know anything about it. But then somebody came up and told me that Yeltsin wanted to talk with me by telephone from Belorussia. I went to the telephone and he told me that they had been trying to get through to me for hours, that they had reached an agreement, and they were waiting for me in Moscow. Yeltsin said, "We have talked for many hours and not resolved anything. So if we want to stay together, keep good relations, a single economic zone. . ." Incidentally, a copy of the entire interview that they gave on TV on 9 December has probably been preserved. What eloquent phrases they used! He said, "We have worked out an agreement."

I responded, "I have not seen it. How am I supposed to sign it?"

"We think that you will go along with it. There is no way that we can do it without Kazakhstan."

I said, "Boris Nikolaevich, I cannot do it. First of all, I have never laid eyes on it. What you have come up with is very serious. What happens to the Union?"

"There will be no union. We are the founders of this affair."

"But for starters," I said, "Give me a copy of the text and I will think about it." I read the document and thought that it was a very serious matter. Then, Kebich (Chairman of the Belorussian Government) called me and, after Kebich, Shushkevich. Then I said to Kebich, if I am not mistaken, "I can't come to the meeting. First, I have to consult with my advisors at home. Then, I have to figure out the opinion of the republics of Central Asia." They had already been calling me, wanting to know what was going on. "Keep us informed of what is happening," and so forth. Consequently, I did not go. At first, when they told me that they had met and that it was necessary to discuss matters together, I had said, "Okay, I will come."

That is what the interchange was like: "We will discuss everything and then fly to Moscow tomorrow." That was not too bad. But when they told me that they already had a text and that Kazakhstan was the fourth signatory, then I thought — this is serious. So I called a press conference. Of course, there was a lot to consider and I said that every politician had to be a realist and get his hands dirty. That is, politics is the art of the possible.

Apparently, at that moment you had not made a decision. Was that why there was a look of uncertainty on your face?

At twelve o'clock, Gorbachev insisted that I come. Only two or three minutes later, in walked Yeltsin. We were there, the three of us, then Aleksandr Nikolaevich Iakovlev arrived. We sat there and Gorbachev asked us one question after another. But the document was already on the table. "Well, all right, you have made this decision. But what happens with the Army, with Foreign Affairs and things like that?" Of course, Yeltsin had no answers. In the end he was upset. "What, is this some sort of interrogation that you've set up?" He was looking rather tired.

Do you think that the decision to break up the Union was a mistake and that it is possible to rectify it?

It is already too late. All the Central Asian republics got together in Ashkhabad afterward. I recommended to Niiazov that we meet in his capital and discuss the matter. Then, Yeltsin called us every half hour. I was worried about how we were going to work it out. And there on the table lay a document about the creation of a confederation of Turkmeni states. Can you imagine what that meant? It would have meant a total confrontation. I had to work through half the night telling them all, persuading them, that they must not do it, that we have not lived so many years together for nothing. You cannot tear up relations among peoples. We must see other approaches. We wrote in our declaration that everything had to be worked out legally and legitimately, which meant convening the Supreme Soviet of the USSR or a Congress to resolve the issue. And they told us that Russia had already withdrawn its delegates, as had Ukraine and Belorussia, from the Supreme Soviet. I was told that 70 percent of the delegates had been withdrawn. Nevertheless, we wrote in the protocol that the legal basis of the Commonwealth of Independent States had to be provided.

Who, then, shut down the Congress of Peoples' Deputies of the USSR?

It shut itself down! In Gorbachev's or Lukianov's place, I would have sent the deputies invitations and called a meeting of the Congress. How they failed to do this and tried to present themselves as heroes I cannot understand.

In Moscow, they speak of a confederation of three states: Russia, Belorussia and Kazakhstan. It is said that this is your idea. Do you think that it is realistic?

They proposed a confederation at the time of the Novo-Ogarevo process. I spoke about it with Gorbachev. Incidentally, Yeltsin was in favor of it, Karimov[8] was for it, but Gorbachev was categorically opposed! "I will not permit the destruction of the Union! There would be no support within the government." And so we dropped the issue. Later, after the putsch, the "patriots" started to scream from the tribunes of their meetings that "we are the Great Russia; we will crush everyone and return to our lands." If you remember, I spoke at the session. It was a sudden turn of events. There was no way that Kazakhstan would enter a union of any kind as either a senior or a junior partner. It was over, because it was impossible to trust Russia, which was declaring its pretensions from every podium as threats to everyone. There was no further need to speak of confederation. I don't speak about it any more. Think about it. There are about ten of us in the CIS [Commonwealth of Independent States]. Of them, six or seven want closer relations, a single system of defense, a public zone, a single economic zone, a single customs system. The rest do not want it. They want to be members of the CIS but not to participate in it, not to have any coordinating organs.

I suggest to those who want to have closer contacts, use the ruble in a single economic zone, have open borders and a single defense system. Let's form a core. Let that core have coordinating organs, a single banking system, which will be responsible to all the governments. You can call it whatever you like. But there is no need to bring up terms that scare people. This is just run-of-the-mill cooperation. I mean that we need to join forces as in the European world. We have already dropped the ideas of union and of confederation: They were dreams. Maybe the next generation of leaders will rise to it and understand why it is useful, because Europe is coming together toward a single government, currency, and customs system. Unfortunately, Russia is not at all acting or speaking like a truly democratic state. Look, I will give you an example. Genscher told me that Germans, as democrats, in Europe, openly apologized before the entire world for fascism. But in Russia, it is completely the reverse. There are only pretensions to property, territory, and borders.

I don't know how Yeltsin is, but some sort of game is going on around him. We see it. From this point of view, I cannot justify Kravchuk or Shushkevich. Russia is big, and if it is thinking about future geopolitical dealings, or about the future in general, then Russia will forgo its ambitions. If it wants to be surrounded by friendly states close to Russia, then Russia will treat us as equals and draw us in that way. It can do this, but it is not doing so, and that surprises me.

Who Was Responsible for Destroying the Soviet Union?

Having compared the positions of the three leaders, what can we conclude about the Belovezhsk decisions that brought the demise of the Soviet Union?

First, the decision was emotional and not rational — more spontaneous than maturely and thoroughly considered. Not one of its participants, not Kravchuk, not Shushkevich, not even Yeltsin, was prepared for what happened. Kravchuk said it directly: "We do not want to stay in a union," though he did not hope to walk away that easily. Shushkevich did not have a position at all. He supported Yeltsin against Gorbachev while testing the direction of the prevailing winds. Yeltsin was not prepared for the outcome, even though he firmly held a course to rid himself of both the center and Gorbachev personally. Do not forget that he never totally rejected the idea of leaving Gorbachev as rightful president of the USSR elected by all of its peoples. But it would have been a long, unpleasant route for him. Instead, he took another route, one that he brought on himself. We can only guess what would have been the fate of the Great Russian state, were it not for the impatient desire of the three princes to be crowned as tsar.

Second, there never was any clear concept of the character of a new union. A Commonwealth of Independent States did not enter their minds. The new union agreement prepared at Novo-Ogarevo under Gorbachev's leadership, which was to have been signed on August 20, was subverted by mutual consent. In its place, they offered a declaration on the dissolution of the union and in all probability did not think about what would follow, what would happen to all the other former republics.

Third, Yeltsin nurtured the thought that there would be some kind of integration in the future. He was disturbed by the idea that the process of dissolution could spread within the Russian Federation itself. But he probably calmed himself with the thought that, in the name of common interest, he could still resort to the use of force. In time, he showed that this was not mere words but a matter of real policy.

As a whole, this act of world-historical significance — the dissolution of the great Eurasian state — occurred in a context typical of the meetings of the communist leaders, who were certain that they had the right to decide anything and everything without considering the will of the people or their responsibility to history.

So what were the reasons for the dissolution of the Soviet Union, after so many millions of lives had been sacrificed to preserve it? The very mechanism of dissolution was an invention of former Communists Gennadi Burbulis, Egor Gaidar, Andrei Kozyrev, Sergei Shakhrai, and other advisors.[9] They own the copyright to this model.

It seems to me that only the papers on the coronation of the first False Dmitrii were similarly prepared in such a hurry, in a context of such universal deception.[10] Deception, because it was conducted behind the back of the president of the USSR, whose fate was sealed by the previously subordinate leaders of the republics; behind the back of the as yet undissolved Supreme Soviet, as well as the Supreme Soviets of the three republics; and behind the backs of all the other republics, who were faced with a *fait accompli*. Yesterday, they were members of a Union; today, expelled without a process of consultation. The deception occurred behind the backs of all the peoples of the USSR who had voted for the preservation of the Union.

Another question defies explanation: Why did the dissolution take place so effortlessly, without resistance from the Union government or protest from the people? There was not even scandal in the media, which has subsequently showed its ability to confront the powers, particularly in the case of the war in Chechnya.

Perhaps the fruit had ripened, so that Yeltsin had only to shake the tree. A year before, the Supreme Soviet of the Russian Federation had launched its destructive struggle for republican sovereignty from the center itself by proclaiming Russia's sovereignty over union law. Not a word was spoken about limits to such sovereignty, only complete sovereignty, total independence, total power on one's own territory with the right of secession from the USSR. The slogan was picked up by other republics, the leaders of which (excluding the Baltic states) did not understand that sovereignty meant the destruction of the USSR and the formation of new states. The process proceeded from there, from the so-called White House, which subsequently took on the significance of a burning torch as a symbol of the destruction of a great state.

It may appear odd, but the main catalyst for the dissolution of the USSR was the provincial *nomenklatura* of the Russian federation. Yeltsin expressed this perspective well in his "confession," when he described his arrival in Moscow and his irritation at the privileges of the conceited officials in the capital and of pampered Muscovites in general.

As an inhabitant of the capital, I found it initially difficult to understand the nature of the provincial Russian nomenklatura. Those who came to Moscow for *kolbasa*, or the issuance of budgetary subventions, to arrange a party or state job at home in the periphery, or to obtain a prize for an exceptional work of art — they hated Moscow. They felt that it oppressed and demeaned them. It made them second-class citizens. It gave preference to Asian, Caucasian, and Baltic people. These people developed a sense of offense on behalf of the Russian Republic — the RSFSR — which they genuinely considered to be the real country. These provincials simply had no sense of the whole Soviet Union as their homeland — a state that included dozens of peoples, as had the former Russian Empire.

This sense of offense settled deeply in the consciousness of the party and literary elite of the Russian provinces: "We made the greatest sacrifices in the Revolution, in World War II, in the construction of socialism; but we live more poorly than all the other peoples of the Union." This primitive view of the complex process of the creation and defense of the great state became the psychological soil for the wave of disintegrative forces. The other republics had similar feelings: We fed Moscow; we fed Russia.

Now, when all the republics have begun to live separately, when the dismemberment of the live body of cooperation and mutual assistance of the Eurasian peoples has done colossal damage to their interests, they all see how wrong and dangerous was the Belovezhsk divorce. There was no discussion of conditions, of common economic interests, of mutual security, of cultural exchange. If you ignore historical perspective, it is impossible to see where you are going, with whom, and in the name of what.

It is impossible to understand the motivation that drove a Russian man, Boris Yeltsin, to proceed so easily to the destruction of the Soviet state at Belovezhskaia Pushcha. I accept that Kravchuk, a scion of West Ukraine, was genuinely committed to the idea of an independent Ukraine. But Yeltsin? What motivations directed him? Why was that state destroyed? Democracy? To escape the burden of feeding the borderlands? It all seemed to me to be a ludicrous mistake — absurd and nonsensical. In my eyes, the economic arguments for the breakup made no sense. Even then, it was obvious that there was no proof of the advantages of drawing a profit from raw materials, especially from oil and gas, sent to Ukraine, Belorussia, and other, former republics. It all seemed doubtful to me, because they had nothing with which to pay. On the other hand, the destruction of the old productive and economic connections counterbalanced any benefits. Most importantly, as a result of the dissolution, Russia lost completely its former role as great power and all hopes of competing with the United States. How can one make that kind of choice? It is hard to believe that Yeltsin did it solely to strengthen his personal power, to free himself from Gorbachev, and to acquire total independence. A state official of his rank, in my view, should not take this step under any circumstances.

Only three years later did the period of sobering up begin. But in that time, the process of separation had gone so far that the search for paths of integration, new models for the friendly cohabitation of the peoples, became tortuous. It will take an entire epoch for these paths to be found in the common interest.

What Lies Ahead?

The main issue of the future can, in the end, be reduced to a simple question. Will the peoples of Ukraine, Belarus, the Caucasus, and Central Asia find a better life in conditions of separation from the Russian people? This has not yet happened. As yet, there have only been new problems for all: a decline of production due to the interruption of production contracts, energy crises, and military and economic conflicts. In relations between Russia and Ukraine, the problem of the division of the Black Sea Fleet and the division of Crimea continues to be an issue. All of these sacrifices could have been justified had they given rise to a flourishing of the new states and Russia. Otherwise, all that Belovezhskaia Pushcha accomplished will be denounced as the most monstrous mistake in the whole history of the Russian state.

Yeltsin bears personal responsibility for the decisions taken at Belovezhskaia Pushcha, but he shares the responsibility for the dissolution of the Soviet Union with Kravchuk and Shushkevich and also with the participants of the August 1991 putsch, the RSFSR Supreme Soviet, and the historical totalitarian state which subverted the Russian Empire.

As he sought reelection, Yeltsin reworked his views on the reintegration of the former Soviet republics, cleverly capturing the mood of the people and of the Duma, and his political fortunes revived. Yeltsin replaced several leaders of the power ministries responsible for the war in Chechnya. He gradually formed a coalition, centrist government. What will become of the reforms — first, the economic reforms, which led to a chaotic, bureaucratized market, and second, the political reforms, which led to unchecked presidential power — begun under his governance?

The "Belovezhskaia Peace" was viewed by its creators as a breakthrough to a new democracy in Russia and other republics through national separation and division. Since then, two of the three participants on the agreement have been cast aside by their electorates. It is unrealistic to hope that Russia, Ukraine, Belarus, and Kazakhstan will live again under one roof. But there are several possible resolutions of the problem — confederation, economic union, a common market, or a Eurasian parliament with minimal powers, as in Europe.

With the rapid dissolution of the USSR and the creation of the CIS, key military, political, economic, territorial, organizational, and ethnic issues were never resolved. Russia has yet to defend its national interests within the former Soviet Union against the pressure of Ukraine, the Baltic States, and several other republics who are determined to destroy the hated "center." Only a year after the dissolution of the USSR, Russia issued a declaration that the geographic area of the former Soviet Union was a zone of Russia's special interest. Then began the difficult process of regulating a huge mass of issues — nuclear weapons, the army, navy, currency, payments for resources, regional conflicts, and the mutual defense of the borders of the former Soviet republics.

There is also the plight of the Russians who, in the course of one night, became citizens of foreign states. At first, the democratic leadership of Russia ignored the problem. Twenty-five million Russians — equal to the population of a large European state — were left to their own fates and lost their homeland without gaining a new one. They are often labeled as colonizers, occupiers, and undesirables. The time has come to define clearly the relations between the peoples of the former Soviet Union and the Russian diaspora.

The guiding principle should be the protection of the Russian population living in Russia, in the "near abroad," and in other regions of the world. This entirely corresponds to international law and practice. It is appropriate to distinguish between political citizenship and ethnic identity. A Russian with Lithuanian citizenship, for example, is a Lithuanian; but in an ethnic sense, he remains a Russian who had a right to some ethnocultural and religious relationship with the citizens of Russia. By the same token Russia, as a state, has an understandable concern for the well-being of ethnic Russian people abroad — including their experience of discrimination on national or religious grounds.

Finally, the Russian population is entitled to a degree of cultural autonomy in the states of the "near abroad." It is disturbing that precisely after Russia allowed minority nations to freely determine their status, the countries of the CIS refused to recognize the cultural rights of densely populated Russian areas.

In the preparation of agreements and decisions of the CIS, it is necessary to reinforce a system of principles that would equally affect the situation of

Russians in other countries and Ukrainians, Caucasians, and Central Asians on Russian territories.

There is pressing need to review the issues of cultural autonomy, dual citizenship, travel without visas, schools, universities, print and television media, special conditions for currency exchange for those traveling to their historical homelands, the creation of sociocultural organizations, and other humanitarian issues. Obviously, these rights should be offered to the native peoples of other republics. In cases where dual citizenship is rejected, Russia might consider issuing a special identification card for expatriate Russians who have regular business and family connections in the Russian Federation.

It is appropriate to prepare a long-term program for the resettlement of Russians and Russian speakers who wish to immigrate from the near abroad. These should be state programs, based on considerations of geography, professional orientation, and financial assistance and should be confirmed with the states from which these people are to emigrate.

Mutual agreements are necessary to allow civil rights organizations to defend the human rights of ethnic populations equally in Russia and other countries. It would also be desirable to have in the structure of the CIS an international court, which would review especially dangerous cases of ethnic discrimination or genocide. One could discuss the issue of Russians serving in the Russian Army, while offering similar rights to Ukrainians, Belorussians, and other nationalities living in Russia. It is also appropriate to regulate the question of issuing pensions to those who had received that right before the collapse of the USSR.

The CIS has passed through two stages since the collapse of the USSR. The first, from 1992 to 1993, was the stage of discussion. The second, beginning in mid-1993, has marked a turn toward rapprochement and the beginning of reintegration in several spheres. The initiative for reintegration in the second stage came not from the "center" — Russia — but from the other republics, particularly Belarus, Kazakhstan and Kirgizia. This group of states, together with Russia, began to form a new entity within the CIS. A crucial factor was that the countries of the commonwealth owed Russia $3 billion for exports of oil and gas and that they had no prospect of paying off these debts or paying for future supplies. However, economic interests were not the only issues. For Kazakhstan, a larger role was played by the demographic factor: a considerable part of its population is Russian speaking. For Kirgizia, geopolitical interests played a role as it suffered the incursion of Islam from Iran. Furthermore, one should not forget cultural proximity: The elites in former republics were raised not only within their native, but also Russian, culture.

Since 1993, the aforementioned states have made agreements on a single economic zone; a customs union; an inter-parliamentary assembly (taken by all members of the CIS, excluding Ukraine, Moldova and Turkmenistan); the coordination of pricing policy (between Russia and Belarus); the mutual regulation of external economic activity (between Russia and Kirgizia); and other issues. With

Tajikistan, an agreement was signed protecting existing borders. Such agreements are being realized for the borders with the Transcaucasian republics.[11]

On April 2, 1996, a treaty of union between Belarus and Russia was signed. This significant agreement marks a new turn toward integration. At the same time, it shows that three or more levels of rapprochement may emerge: close union, as with Belarus; confederation, as with Kazakhstan and Kirgizia; and cooperation on the former norms of the CIS, as with Ukraine. While any attempt to restore the Soviet Union is bound to fail, integration in contemporary European forms is realistic.

Foremost in economics, culture, and education is the free movement of ideas and capital throughout the CIS. A confederation of several states — Russia, Belarus, Kazakhstan, and perhaps others, excluding Ukraine — is also possible. But the intensity of this process will depend on the internal development of Russia itself, whether it successfully follows on the path of contemporary civilization and democracy.

Conclusion

In the twentieth century, Russia has exemplified horrific barbarity — the destructive civil war and the monstrous specter of Stalinism, which grew out of perverted extremist theories borrowed from the West. But Russia has also shown examples of greatness and courage in the struggle against fascism and in the accomplishments in education and culture. The greatness of Russia brought it the position of second superpower in the world. However, an internal erosion of spirit and social institutions brought the destruction of the Soviet Empire.

A hundred years may pass before Russia integrates fully with Europe. It will be a peculiarly Russian path: as painful as the torture chambers of Ivan the Terrible; as grandiose as the transformations of Peter the Great; as unpredictable as the reforms of Nikita the Brave, Mikhail the Blessed, and Boris the Fierce. But it will be a path to contemporary civilization. The barbarity handed down to Russia from its past will cede to civility — to culture, science, and technology.

Notes

1. Although there had been few open demonstrations of nationalism during the Soviet period, the potential for it had always existed, as can be seen from an appeal that some Armenians had directed to Khrushchev as early as 1963.
2. Lukianov was then the chairman of the Supreme Soviet of the USSR and had long been a close ally of Gorbachev. He would soon join the putschists. [Editor's note.]
3. Mikhail Gorbachev and Boris Yeltsin, *1500 dnei, politicheskogo protivostoianiia,* comp. L. Dobrokhotov (Moscow: Terra, 1992).
4. Boris Yeltsin, *Zapiski presidenta* (Moscow: Ogonek, 1994).

5. Vladimir Vysotsky was a beloved ballad-singer who openly criticized the Soviet regime in the 1970s. One of his songs celebrates the heroism of refusing to follow an order to shoot. [Editor's note.]

6. The interviews were published in *Nezavisimaia gazeta*. Extracts from the original interviews are included here with Vladina's permission.

7. Feodor Burlatsky, *Russkie gosudari* (Moscow: Shark, 1996).

8. Islam A. Karimov was the president of the Soviet Republic of Uzbekistan.

9. These men were all close advisers to Yeltsin who served as his ministers in the Russian government.

10. The first False Dmitrii was Russian Tsar in 1605-6, claiming (apparently falsely) to be the son of Ivan the Terrible. His ascension to the throne was a result of a conspiracy by a group of Russian nobles supported by the Polish king and the Jesuits. He was overthrown in a rebellion by some of the boyars who had put him in power.

11. *Nezavisimaia gazeta*, February 17, 1996.

Seven

The Breakup of Yugoslavia

Metta Spencer

If separatism is usually a misguided project, Yugoslavia's breakup is worse: it is a disaster that is still ongoing. And as in many other cases of partition that have led to war, the negative consequences may continue to unfold for generations yet to come.

Yugoslavia had been the most successful of all the socialist countries. In the 1970s and early 1980s, the Western tourists who vacationed in its Renaissance stone cities on the Dalmatian coast or its ski resorts returned home full of admiration for that country's novel attempt to combine egalitarian socialism with grassroots worker-management, some features of a market economy, and a modicum of liberty. Compared to other communist societies, it seemed pleasant, civilized, and almost prosperous.

Why, then, did it fail? This question deserves to be addressed. By identifying the mistakes that led to Yugoslavia's tragedy and learning its hard lessons, we may anticipate and perhaps even avert similar disasters elsewhere.

The Cultural Diversity of the Former Yugoslavia

"Yug" means "south" in Serbo-Croatian, the main language of the "South Slavs," the diverse but closely related cultural groups for whom Yugoslavia was named.[1] Throughout history the frontier between Western and Eastern civilizations had run through the region, originally dividing Western Christendom from Byzantium. Later, the Danube and Sava rivers had divided the Ottoman Empire from the Habsburg Empire. About half the Yugoslav population (especially the Serbs in the Ottoman region) had practiced Orthodox Christianity and had used the Cyrillic script, while about one-quarter (especially the Croats and Slovenes) had been Catholic and had used the Latin script.

When the Ottoman Turkish conquerors had come in the fifteenth century, they had imported Islam, which was adopted in Bosnia by a heretical Christian sect, the Bogomils. In the last years of Yugoslavia, this Muslim community constituted about one-fifth of the population; however, I shall designate them not in the usual way as Muslim (for in many cases they no longer practiced Islam), but as Bosniacs.

When the former Yugoslavia began to dissolve at the beginning of the 1990s, its population numbered some 23 million. Nationality was an inordinately salient factor in the structuring of social and political life. Officially, the country comprised five "nations" and — unlike the case in the West — the essential reality of "nationhood" was hardly ever questioned. In fact, the state was supposedly formed voluntarily by its "constituent nations" — Serbs, Croats, Macedonians, Slovenes, and Montenegrins — though this last group was disputed by some who claimed that Montenegrins are actually Serbs.

Three other communities — the Albanians of Kosovo, the Hungarians of Vojvodina, and the Bosniacs — claimed that they should be recognized as "constituent nations." The Albanians belong ethnically to the people of the adjacent state, Albania, but since the days of the Ottoman Empire there have been Albanian populations in Montenegro, Macedonia, and southern Serbia. The largest Albanian presence is in the Serbian autonomous province of Kosovo, where they form 90 percent of the population. Some of their leaders demanded that Kosovo become a republic, while others even wanted to secede from Yugoslavia and join Albania instead. The Bosniacs were recognized as a "nation" by a constitutional change in 1963, which designated them as "Muslim."[2] There were also smaller religious or ethnic communities, such as Jews, that were considered as minority groups.[3]

About 5 percent of the population declined to identify themselves as members of any particular nation, but rather called themselves simply "Yugoslavs." Others described themselves in the census as "undecided." In some cases an identification with the federal state instead of with a nation reflected a political commitment, while in others it simply meant that the person was a partner in, or the offspring of, a mixed marriage.

Yugoslavia in the World

Yugoslavia had been created at the end of World War I from the fragments of two old, disintegrating, multicultural empires: the Ottoman and the Habsburg (which had become the Austro-Hungarian) Empires. Initially called the "Kingdom of Serbs, Croats and Slovenes," the new country was created by a merger of victors and vanquished in 1918, when the Serbian Prince Alexander, having been on the winning side of the war, agreed to unite his territory with the former Habsburg lands. It was not to be an easy matter. Many Croatians had long promoted Yugoslavism, the unification of all South Slavs, on the assumption that their city Zagreb would be the capital of such a state, for it was especially advanced culturally and economically. They were disappointed when a highly centralized state was formed with Belgrade as its capital.[4] The Habsburg institutions were all replaced by the Serbian bureaucracy and army, and the former Habsburg subjects were forced to transfer huge funds to Serbia.[5]

Three frameworks for integration would be attempted successively — all with poor results. The first was a "Greater Serbia" model, the second involved the creation of a synthetic "Yugoslav" identity, and the last was intended to be a compromise between the dominant Serbs and the Croats, though this model had no time to succeed because of the approach of World War II.

Since no nationality held a majority of the parliament, government had to be by coalition, though this proved impossible. A political stalemate between Serbs and the former Habsburg subjects lasted until 1928, when five Croatian deputies were shot in parliament and King Alexander took control of the country as a dictator and renamed the country Yugoslavia.[6]

A movement in favor of creating an independent Croatia was led by Ante Pavelić, who founded the Ustasha-Croat Revolutionary Organization. This group, which was trained and funded by Mussolini, assassinated King Alexander in 1934. The murder had been intended to destroy Yugoslavia, but paradoxically it united public opinion against the perpetrators. Alexander was succeeded by his young son's regent, Prince Paul, who tried to reconcile Croats to Yugoslavia by setting up an autonomous province of Croatia within the country. The arrangement was never fully implemented and in any case would not have offered much relief to other nationalities, such as Hungarians, Albanians, Macedonians, and Bosniacs, whose status was even lower than that of Croats and who were also disenchanted.[7] In the 1920s the Albanians of Kosovo had carried out an unsuccessful guerrilla war against the federal Yugoslav state.

During the 1930s Prince Paul was forced by French and British appeasement policies to enter into agreements with Hitler, but he negotiated to keep German troops out of his country. Some outraged Yugoslav officers seized power and tried unsuccessfully to wrest more concessions from Germany. Instead, this prompted Hitler to invade Yugoslavia and ensure an open route for his troops and equipment on their way to his campaign in Greece. He divided Yugoslavia up and gave portions of it to Germany, Italy, Hungary, Bulgaria, and Albania. Then he set up the Croatian Pavelić and his prewar terrorist force, the Ustasha, as a quisling regime to rule the remainder of the country, which included some of Serbia, Croatia, and Bosnia-Herzegovina. These fascists intended to kill a third of the Serbs, expel another third, and convert the others to Catholicism.[8] They killed an estimated 85,000 people of all nationalities in a single death camp,

Jasenovac.[9] Approximately 6.4 percent of Yugoslavia's population died during or immediately after World War II, with the highest percentage losses taking place in Bosnia-Herzegovina and Montenegro.[10]

In 1941 two military leaders, Josip Broz Tito and Draža Mihailović, began separate campaigns against the German rulers of Serbia. Tito, a communist who was born in Croatia, found supporters among all Yugoslav peoples; Mihailović, a royalist, had only Serbian followers but claimed to be the leader of guerrilla fighters called Chetniks. In fact, he had little control over the Chetniks, who engaged in atrocities comparable to those of their enemies, the Ustashas. Mihailović had counted on British support, but Winston Churchill decided in 1943 to support Tito instead. For Yugoslavia, World War II actually consisted of several civil wars that had little to do with the larger war being fought elsewhere.[11] By the end, Mihailović chose to fight against Tito's partisans instead of against the Germans, who were not numerous in Yugoslavia. Nevertheless, thanks to the strength of his forces and his willingness to include terrorism among his tactics against his enemies, Tito won.

Immediately after the war, his partisans, who had increased to 700,000,[12] imposed retribution on their former enemies, including Mihailović, who was executed after a show trial. By January 1946 a communist constitution was approved for the country, which had six republics, plus two autonomous entities within Serbia — Vojvodina and Kosovo. Borders between republics could be changed only with the consent of all sides. Each republic (but not Vojvodina or Kosovo) was given a right to self-determination and to secession, though this outcome was not expected, nor were any conditions for it specified.[13]

There is no reason to regard Yugoslav Communists or Tito himself in those first years as different from communists of the day in other countries. A new international organization, Cominform, was created to replace the Comintern and was based in Belgrade. Tito accepted Stalin's leadership without question and until 1948 had no plan to leave the international communist movement. It was Stalin who precipitated the break, forcing Yugoslavia's expulsion from the Cominform, evidently as a purge arising from Stalin's own paranoia.

Tito rose to the occasion, purging his own Communist party of potential dissenters and mobilizing against an expected invasion of Soviet forces. When no invasion took place, Tito found ways of manipulating both sides of the Cold War to his advantage. Western countries were delighted to see a split within the socialist camp, and the United States in particular was glad to fund the spunky Yugoslavs, who could provide a defensive bulwark against Soviet military access to the West. Billions of dollars of nonrepayable aid arrived over the years, in addition to loans, allowing the Yugoslavs to live far above the level of their own economic productivity. Deciding that Stalin had misunderstood Marx and Lenin, Tito planned for the state to "wither away" and be replaced by "workers' councils," which did not prove to be a particularly competitive economic system.

In foreign relations, Tito had mixed results in his effort to play each bloc against the other. Yugoslavia was not given Marshall Plan money or membership in the Council for Mutual Economic Assistance, but did hold observer or associate status in both alliances after 1955. Tito turned instead to creating and leading a neutral bloc. He helped found the Nonaligned Movement and the Group of 77, which stood apart from either superpower bloc.[14] In this way, Yugoslavia occupied a much more prominent place in the international arena than could be accounted for by its own size and power. When the Cold War came to an end, its leveraged influence would suddenly plummet, a fact that many Yugoslav politicians would refuse to acknowledge.

Nationhood and Governance

Scholars who specialize in studying Yugoslavia are united in arguing against a simple ethnic explanation of the 1990s wars in that former country. Nationalism played its part, to be sure, but it did not emerge and run rampart as the spontaneous revival of old hatreds. It may be more accurate to call nationalism a *consequence* than a *cause* of the disintegration of Yugoslavia. The tragedy of that country was the deterioration of a government that had been relatively successful for several decades.[15] To understand that breakdown, one must understand the national problem, which its constitution had been designed to manage. The chief difficulty was that of reconciling two alternative understandings of "nationhood" — the first being the sovereignty of a state or republic occupying a particular territory, the second being the right of a group sharing a common culture to make its own collective decisions. What constitutes a "nation" that is supposedly entitled to self-determination — the people or the territory?

This very problem had bedeviled the multicultural Habsburg Empire, though the leaders of the Austrian Social Democrats had proposed a solution to it. Karl Renner and Otto Bauer meant to preserve the territory of the empire intact by allowing each *individual* to choose and express his or her own nationality without regard to where he or she lived in the state. Having eliminated the dispute over sovereignty, the only problem remaining would have been to devise ways of granting cultural autonomy and political representation to these self-declared social groupings. Such an approach separated the cultural dimension from national sovereignty and statehood.[16] Although this system was adopted successfully in a few places elsewhere,[17] it was unacceptable to the Yugoslav national movements, which invariably considered their nationhood to entail their right to statehood and independence, not merely their expressions of distinctive cultures.

The irreconcilable nature of the problem arises from this: Sovereign ownership of land means exclusive ownership. By that definition, then, it cannot be shared by two or more claimant nations — even if in practice those nations actually could cooperatively inhabit the same territory by controlling their own separate institutions. (Such a political system had, in fact, been practiced during the Ottoman period when the religious communities of a single territory had constituted semiautonomous *millets,* each one governed by its own authorities.)[18]

The pursuit of the mutually exclusive, territorially sovereign version of nationhood has culminated in "ethnic cleansing" in our day. Still, this outcome was averted for decades by a system of balances artfully designed by Tito. It involved a notion of ethnic equality that differs from the prevailing one in the West, where *individuals'* rights are protected, but not those of their groups. Each major Yugoslav ethnic community was a "constituent nation" entitled to its own republic, within which other minority nationalities might also live, enjoying certain collective protections such as linguistic rights. In this highly decentralized system, the federal government had to be scrupulously egalitarian. Cultural rights of national expression were encouraged — even funded — but any political expression of national*ism* was prosecuted. There was an elaborate effort to maintain equality among the so-called constituent nations by making sure they were represented proportionally in all public events. Indeed, when one person was charged with an offense, the authorities would attempt to balance this by prosecuting an appropriate number of individuals from the other ethnic communities of the area![19]

The Constitution of 1974

The "second" Yugoslavia — the post-World War II one — changed its constitution rather frequently. The 1946 version imitated Stalin's constitution of 1936. It was amended in 1953, when self-management was introduced. A new constitution was created in 1963, then amended in 1968, 1970, and 1971.[20]

The 1974 constitution (amended in 1981 and 1988) was a long, poorly written document of 406 articles that profoundly decentralized governance. It defined republics as nation-states and gave them almost all the attributes of statehood, including the right to be regulated by their own constitutions, subject only to the condition that these not contradict the federal constitution.[21]

Further, the 1974 constitution prescribed a system in which parliamentary deputies were elected, not by the citizens, but by lower-level "delegations" that were themselves elected by ordinary voters. The deputies were obliged to follow the instructions of those delegations and could be dismissed and replaced for failing to do so.[22] Many of the legislative functions of parliaments were meant to be given instead to the newly emphasized self-managing bodies that would not create law but "compacts."

Probably the most important change in the 1974 constitution was its recognition of additional nations that had not previously been considered "titular" or "constituent nations." The Bosniacs had been recognized three years before as a constituent Yugoslav people; now the Albanians and Hungarians were elevated in their status as nationalities, though it was ambiguous whether they had the right to secede or create a separate republic, (e.g., in Kosovo). Since each of the two latter nations had homelands outside the boundaries of Yugoslavia, there was theoretically no call for one inside these boundaries.

The most serious aspect of the 1974 constitution, however, was that it enabled any decision to be blocked by the veto of a single federal entity — even one of the autonomous provinces of Serbia. Federal parliamentarians could not make a decision until they had all been instructed by the assemblies of the republics and autonomous provinces. As a result of this rule, there was little deliberation in the federal legislative bodies. The delegates spent much of their time waiting in the corridors for instructions from the delegations to which they were accountable.[23] The constitution did provide a means of breaking an impasse caused by lack of consensus among the republics, but only for urgent measures, and only for the period of one year.[24]

Tito, who was given by the constitution a lifelong role as virtual dictator of the country (a degree of power that no successor was supposed to inherit), had his reasons for dividing power in this way. There was a real danger that one of the constituent nations — most likely Serbia — would get too much power and use it to dominate the others. Tito went to great lengths in order to guarantee the equality of these "titular nations" and their respective sovereign republics. For example, the presidency itself was to consist of a group, not an individual, in which all the republics and autonomous provinces (Kosovo and Vojvodina) would be represented, and the role of presiding over this group presidency would rotate in alphabetical order, for a one-year term, among the republics. This consensual model could be considered undemocratic, for the majority did not necessarily win, nor did the minority lose. The preferred method of reaching a decision was one of "harmonizing interests" — negotiating a compromise that would keep any nationality from feeling excluded. Tito set this system up with the sensible intention of keeping any nationalist group from gaining too much power. In this he succeeded, but at a terrible price: He kept his successors from being able to function effectively at all.

Post-Tito Politics

Tito died in 1980 at the age of 88. He had been masterful in persuading ethnic leaders to be flexible, but none of his successors had his skill or personal power. In the late 1980s and 1990 the League of Communists of Yugoslavia (LCY) dissolved amid new demands for democracy. It was clear that the federal constitution would have to be amended, but it could be changed only with the consensus of all federal units. The widening disagreements among the republics, especially on the question of centralization versus decentralization, made it impossible for them to reach significant agreements on such amendments.

In Yugoslavia, as in the other socialist states, people associated liberal democracy with decentralization or even separatism. In the first phases of democratization the reformers typically suppose that to attain political self-expression, each republic needs to be liberated from the centralized state, either by acquiring more autonomy within a confederal system or by breaking away and becoming independent. Ordinarily it is the communists who want to preserve the centralized state. Only later (too late) do the aspiring democrats recognize the inherently harmful effects of breaking up a union.

But not all socialist states are alike. Yugoslavia especially differed from the Soviet Union, where most important decisions were indeed made in Moscow, not in the regions. Tito had already decentralized Yugoslavia by the 1974 constitution to the point that the center no longer had the power to make necessary decisions, and there seemed to be no way to reconstitute the broken federation. Politicians already put their own republics' interests ahead of Yugoslavia's interests. The tragedy of Yugoslavia resulted not from heavy-handed control by a totalitarian center, but rather from the *weakness* of the federal government — its inability to devise and administer reforms, protect citizens' rights, and maintain stability. The party appointed commissions — one in 1981 to amend the constitution, and one in 1983 to develop an economic reform program — but in the end, nothing could be implemented unless adopted by parliament and the cabinet, which were paralyzed by rules requiring the consensus of republics, which represented "titular nations."

Nevertheless, the imagination of reformers in the more affluent, liberal republics ran in the direction of demanding not less but *even more* autonomy. Slovenia was particularly insistent on this point. Croatia and Serbia, of course, had long clashed on the same issue, with Croatians often wanting more autonomy and Serbians generally wanting more control by the center. Now Slovenia and Croatia jointly insisted on further decentralizing the Yugoslav government by a new constitution defining a loose confederation of sovereign states; Serbia and Montenegro, on the other hand, wanted instead to strengthen the existing federal state. It was all too easy to interpret this conflict as a simple reenactment of the old Serb-versus-Croat struggles, which had been ethnic in nature. The fight over constitutional reform was played out by Croatia, Serbia, and Slovenia, and by the Yugoslav People's Army (*Jugoslovenska narodna armija*; JNA), which had a voting role in the presidency along with the republics. In the alliance between Slovenia and Croatia, Slovenia probably acted as a brake to restrain the Croatians who wanted autonomy and who might otherwise have dealt more aggressively with the Serbian centralizers.[25]

The Economic Crisis

Economic factors also played a part in polarizing the positions of these three republics on the centralization-versus-decentralization issue. The whole country had slipped seriously into debt, partly because the Western countries had been especially lenient to Yugoslavia as an incentive in the cold war, and partly because Yugoslavia experienced a serious trade deficit during the OPEC-created oil crisis of the early 1970s.

However, the republics faced very dissimilar situations. Slovenia was the most prosperous — the only region with nearly full employment. It and Croatia, with its scenic Dalmatian coast, attracted Western tourists who spent freely during their vacations. Serbia lacked this extra income, and indeed some of its poor regions, such as Kosovo (where unemployment levels were at 50 percent in the 1970s), depended on receiving substantial subsidies from the federal state.

The oil crisis of the 1970s caused a worldwide recession in the 1980s. It began at about the time of Tito's death. Numerous Yugoslav guest workers lost their jobs in Western Europe and their remittances declined. About 80 percent of all households soon found their savings vanishing.[26] Interest rates on loans soared, driving Yugoslavia's debt up. (It would reach $14.3 billion by 1988.)[27] Only in 1982 was the true scale of the debt discovered, for the republics and autonomous provinces had been spending money recklessly, without even informing the federal government, and their spree accounted for fully 65 percent of the country's debt. They could do this only because the 1974 constitution had removed their accountability to the federal authorities.[28]

The International Monetary Fund required the federal government to introduce an anti-inflationary stabilization program of austerity, with trade and price liberalization. The IMF also demanded that Yugoslavia's central government develop workable procedures for making and enforcing economic decisions, especially by means of majority voting. This violated Tito's system of consensual voting, which gave a veto to every republic, including their various governors of the central bank.

Not surprisingly, the international financial community's demand for responsible federal control over the budget was opposed by those who had benefited from the extraordinary decentralization. The strongest opponents were republican politicians from the richer northwestern areas, who favored democracy in principle but actually had privileges to protect. They proved to be the most nationalistic and resistant to reform, defending the "national interests" of their respective republics.[29] As Susan Woodward has pointed out,

> The two loudest opponents of the institutional aspects of reform were Slovenia and Croatia. . . . As the main proponents of consensual decision-making and a republican veto (as a protection for smaller nations within Yugoslavia), they were particularly antagonistic toward pressure from foreign creditors to end the stalemate in federal decisionmaking by introducing majority rule.[30]

Most republics stopped paying their share of the federal budget, and by late 1986 they agreed that the center should subsist entirely on federal revenues, without any contributions from the republics. This gave the republics fiscal sovereignty. The Serbian government was still the locus of support for liberal economic policies and a stronger federal government, but its autonomous provinces, Kosovo and Vojvodina, were able to block even its internal economic reforms. Kosovo was considerably poorer than Serbia as a whole and Vojvodina somewhat richer. Each province had its own special reason for opposing fiscal reform. Affluent Slovenia, at the other extreme, opposed economic reforms because it was faring well, even if Yugoslavia was not, and would survive nicely if the central government should collapse.

Tito's system of guaranteeing equality among the constituent nations had worked well in restraining conflict, but those guarantees were being eroded from two sides. On the one side, republican politicians (especially in Slovenia and Croatia) were undermining the effectiveness of the central government and its institutions. On the other side, the international financial institutions were promoting recentralization of governance, but with decision-making procedures based on majority rule instead of rotating leadership and consensus; this prospect raised the fears of some constituent nations that they would soon be under Serbian domination.[31]

For a time there was a real opportunity for the impasse to be resolved. Ante Marković, the country's last prime minister, took office in March 1989 in a period of crisis. Kosovo, which had lost its autonomy in 1988, was the scene of Serbian nationalist revival and organized violence against the province's majority Albanians; unemployment approached 20 percent, inflation soared, and workers were striking all across Yugoslavia. Even in such a situation, Marković was prepared to accept the IMF's demands by increasing painful austerity measures. Soon the LCY broke up, leaving him in a strengthened role as the leading federal politician with responsibility for holding the country together. After trying unsuccessfully to mediate between Serbia and Slovenia, he decided to promote his own strategy. He believed that the crisis was largely economic in nature and that if the economy could be turned around, the political struggle — centralization versus decentralization — would more or less take care of itself. Given the urgency of the IMF's pressure at his back, Marković had, for the moment, sufficient power to win a financial package from the IMF in exchange for implementing economic reforms.[32] He devalued the dinar, froze wages, and liberalized prices, immediately achieving great success: Inflation dropped and the country's currency reserves increased. He became the most popular politician in Yugoslavia since Tito.

Translating this popularity into political support, however, was quite another matter. Marković realized that it would be necessary to hold federal elections very soon — before the communist-governed republics held their own elections. His doing so might confer legitimacy on the federal government. He asked the Slovenian government, therefore, to delay its elections, which were scheduled for April 1990. Had Slovenia's Prime Minister Kučan complied, Marković might have succeeded, but he was unwilling to do so. The Slovenian communists left the LCY, renamed themselves the "Party of Democratic Reform," and went to the voters on schedule. Croatia did likewise two weeks later. These developments reduced Marković's domestic authority and virtually eliminated the prospect of Yugoslavia's survival as a federal state. The elections were understood to be the equivalent of a plebiscite on separatism and, except in Serbia, the separatists won.[33]

Ideology after Marxism

Credit for ending the Cold War must go, above all, to Mikhail Gorbachev. After he had been in power for even one year, it was clear that the arms race would be reversed. It also became clear that there would be no more Soviet support for communist revolutions around the world and no more invasions by Soviet troops to suppress change in other socialist countries. In fact, Gorbachev said of his own country, "We need democracy, just as we need air to breathe."

The statement did not escape the attention of Marxists in other countries, where the positive aspects of democracy had not, in fact, gone wholly unnoticed. Yugoslavia was not one of the countries where communist regimes fell during that astonishing contagious movement of 1989; its break from the Soviet Union had already occurred forty-one years before. Nevertheless, the legitimacy of its government's ideology was shaken by the crisis of Marxism, and the LCY dissolved during that period.

Two changes should be mentioned in connection with the ending of the cold war: (1) the impact of Yugoslavia's stature on the global scene, and (2) the evident need of former ideologues for a new doctrine that resembles, yet differs from, communism.

Throughout most of their lives, the politicians of Yugoslavia had enjoyed the privileges inadvertently created by Tito's row with Stalin. The superpowers had maintained an ambiguous relationship with Tito thereafter — neither of them fully accepting him, yet each valuing his separateness from the other bloc and offering financial and other concessions such as military aid and cheap Soviet oil to keep him in that position. And as long as the neutral and nonaligned countries occupied a comparable status, Tito was at the head of that list too, enjoying the limelight. By the end of his life, his international role interested him far more than domestic politics, which he was generally delegating to others.

No one inherited Tito's mantle, and within a few years all the benefits of being a buffer between the superpowers diminished. No longer did other countries regard Yugoslavia's affairs as vital to their own interests, and no longer would Yugoslavs win financial concessions by flirting with the "other side." Some politicians failed to comprehend this diminution of their bargaining power and delayed when Europeans and Americans warned that they must put their financial house in order.

Yugoslav politicians also manifested another tendency that is more typical of formerly socialist countries during the transition from communism: their turn toward nationalism. The regularity with which this switch has occurred throughout Europe must cause some puzzlement until one considers that every communist was indoctrinated with a collectivist outlook stressing solidarity with one's own side and "struggle" against a clearly defined enemy. Without having some "other" to oppose, such a person may feel simply bewildered and unable to act politically and socially. The elimination of class struggle from political discourse therefore left a void that required the development of a new enmity in which one could identify members of the group almost automatically. "Such group identification was most readily found in ethnicity, which can be demonstrated simply through language (or dialect) or even by name (or family name) in such a way that it cannot be easily stopped or controlled," notes Žarko Puhovski.[34]

The earliest manifestation of this shift in Yugoslavia occurred in Serbia, where a group of nationalist intellectuals of the Serbian Academy of Arts and Sciences developed a memorandum in 1985 that criticized Tito's multinational policies for being anti-Serb. They claimed that not only did Serbs encounter discrimination throughout Yugoslavia but in Kosovo they were being subjected to genocide by the Albanians![35] (In fact, the Albanian resistance movement was committed to nonviolent methods learned from Mahatma Gandhi.)

Kosovo had been the seat of the medieval Serbian Empire until 1389, when the Turks arrived there and established Ottoman rule by winning a great battle that is remembered every year by every Serb. (The symbolic importance of Kosovo to Serbs is perhaps best compared to the importance of Jerusalem to Jews.)

Yet for a long time the majority of people living in Kosovo have been some of the most disadvantaged people in Europe: Albanians. Owing to their high birthrate, their proportion in the population of Kosovo grew to 77 percent in 1981, while Serbs have emigrated in such numbers that their percentage of the total population fell to 13 percent by then.[36] With that trend came more intergroup conflict too. Tito's decision to confer greater autonomy on Kosovo was seen as an insult by the Serbs, who never accepted his decision.[37] From a practical political point of view, probably he did grant an excessive degree of autonomy to both of the provinces within Serbia.[38] With the intention of reversing this autonomy, a Serbian politician devised a plan in 1988 to topple the leaders of Vojvodina, thereby isolating the Albanians in Kosovo, whose leaders could then be more easily removed or intimidated by a show of Serbian national unity.

That is exactly what happened. Under pressure of mass rallies, the leaders of Vojvodina resigned and were replaced by people who supported the Serbian cause. The Albanians in Kosovo were then indeed vulnerable.[39] The Serbian politician who carried out this cunning tactic was to become increasingly famous in the months ahead. He was Slobodan Milošević.

Milošević had appeared to be a colorless communist bureaucrat, but he had one asset that he was to use astutely: a long friendship with Ivan Stambolić. Whenever Stambolić moved up the career ladder, he always found an important role nearby for Milošević. In 1986 Stambolić became president of Serbia, and Milošević took over his previous job as the president of the republic's League of Communists. Since tensions were high between Serbs and Albanians in

Kosovo, Stambolić sent Milošević there to cool the citizens' tempers and resolve their disputes. But by then, Milošević had established his own position in the government, taken control of the media, and prepared to challenge his mentor. The Kosovo trip became the occasion for grabbing power.

Despite being only a small minority in Kosovo, many Serbs felt that their historical ties to the place entitled them to control it. The Albanians, for their part, had frequently demonstrated in public, attempting to publicize the deplorable extent of their own poverty. Since 1981, when some 1,600 Albanians (mostly youths) had been jailed for protesting, the federal authorities had taken the Serbian side in an ethnic dispute, breaking Tito's taboo only a year after his death by declaring martial law and closing Prishtina University. By labeling the unrest as "counterrevolution," the party had allowed Serb nationalists to intervene in the autonomous province. At the time of Milošević's visit, the Serbs were claiming to be oppressed by the Albanians.[40]

There, at a rally of thousands of Serbians and Montenegrins, the mainly Albanian police used force, giving Milošević an opening to make the nationalistic promise that henceforth "nobody is going to beat these people." Instantly he became the leader of the Serbian "patriots."

During 1988, Milošević organized large numbers of mass "rallies for truth" throughout Serbia to publicize the supposedly grave plight of the Serbs in Kosovo as a matter of top national priority. Every town tried to outdo the previous rallies in showing patriotism and decorating public spaces with photos of Milošević; hundreds of thousands of Serbs turned out to attend these skillfully stage-managed "meetings," turning the baby-faced leader into a beloved populist hero.

In Kosovo on the other hand, recognition of Milošević's growing popularity elsewhere prompted extremist Albanian separatists to stage demonstrations of their own, calling for Kosovo to become a republic. This enabled Milošević to intervene with the police and the army, claiming that he was defending the integrity of Yugoslavia from secession. In March 1989, ostensibly with the approval of the Kosovan provincial assembly, a new Serbian constitution was promulgated that limited the autonomy of the provinces, thereby giving Serbia control of three votes in the federal presidency and three delegations in parliament, all of which voted in unison. Counting Montenegro, a reliable ally due to the strong links between the two republics (Milošević himself is Montenegrin), the balance in federal institutions was now four against four. This gave Belgrade an edge in the first multiparty elections that would take place within that republic. And Milošević, riding high in popularity, decided to hold early presidential elections in Serbia in December 1989 — and to run as a communist facing no opposition parties. He won a landslide victory.

Now Serbian nationalism could no longer be contained. Serbs living in other republics were stirred up by the patriotic fervor and the ideological contents of the highly publicized Academy of Arts and Sciences Memorandum. Far from trying to cool ethnic passions, Milošević spoke of the enemies that surrounded Serbia. If he believed that he could use nationalism in a controlled way, he was mistaken. He had opened Pandora's box.[41] Inflamed by his oratory, by the hate propaganda of the state-controlled press, and by Croatian President Tudjman's responsively hateful anti-Serb speeches, the Serbs would become militant, calling for the right of all Serbs to live in one state — though of course they already did so, as citizens of Yugoslavia.

Stalemate, Secession, and War

The first multiparty free elections were held in Slovenia in April 1990 and Croatia a month later. There were dozens of new parties, but the big winners were nationalists promoting separatism. Ex-communist Milan Kučan became president of Slovenia and Franjo Tudjman became the first elected president of Croatia. Slovenia had few inhabitants who were not Slovenian, but there were some 600,000 Serbs in Croatia — mostly in a high state of national consciousness — but nevertheless, Tudjman immediately proceeded to make sure that Croatia would become constitutionally a state of Croats and openly promoted anti-Serbianism.

Throughout 1990, then, three nationalisms were raging. Both Bosnia-Herzegovina and Macedonia held free elections in the autumn of 1990, bringing moderate new leaders to the fore who tried unsuccessfully to restrain the mounting antipathies that were leading to a confrontation among Serbs, Croats, and Slovenes.[42]

In May 1991 it was Croatia's turn to appoint the president of the federal presidency. Stjepan Mesić was supposed to take the helm, though as a Croatian he already openly favored the dissolution of Yugoslavia. Slobodan Milošević, now controlling the votes not only of Serbia but also of Kosovo, Vojvodina, and Montenegro, was able to block his appointment. No internal mechanism existed for resolving this stalemate. However, the "troika" of foreign ministers for the European Community (later to become the European Union) came to Belgrade the following month and insisted that Mesić be seated as president. On this occasion Milošević complied. Actually, Serbia, Slovenia, and Croatia were simply buying time in preparing the breakup of their country, which was already inexorable.[43] Milošević had no objection to the secession of Slovenia (in fact, he may have been trying to drive them out so he could deal with a Croatia without allies),[44] and the Slovenes gave no thought to the effect of their departure on the rest of the country.

The leaders of Bosnia-Herzegovina and Macedonia retained hope until the end that the country would hold together, for they did not believe their own republics could survive without Yugoslavia. In the case of Bosnia-Herzegovina this was because of its very disparate, and now volatile, ethnic mix. On June 6, 1991, Kiro Gligorov, president of Macedonia, and Alija Izetbegović, president of Bosnia-Herzegovina, addressed a meeting of all the presidents of the constituent republics of Yugoslavia. The two of them had developed a proposal for redefining Yugoslavia as a loose confederation and preventing its dissolution. Slobodan Milošević, Franjo Tudjman, and Milan Kučan rejected the proposal, saying that it was contrary to the interests of their republics.[45] The die was cast.

International Intervention

Only then — far too late — did the international community seriously attempt to intervene. Prime Minister Marković had appealed for economic assistance to the European Community in the summer of 1990, but despite his outstanding success with economic reforms they had deferred his request until he had solved the nationalist conflicts then raging. Money was to be his reward for containing nationalism; actually, Marković had required the support of the EC *in order* to continue his reforms despite the divisiveness of separatist leaders. Without it, his economic program collapsed, and every opportunity became open for the dissolution of Yugoslavia.[46] Later, Europe realized its earlier mistake and offered the government of Yugoslavia $4 billion if it would stay together. By then the offer was not even seriously considered.[47] As prime minister of Yugoslavia, Marković no longer had any stature and was not included in further negotiations.

However, as Croatia and Slovenia prepared to declare their independence, both Europe and the United States began a flurry of diplomacy. On June 22 and 23, 1991, the Conference on Security and Cooperation in Europe stated their support for the territorial integrity of Yugoslavia and the EC foreign ministers (including Germany) voted unanimously not to recognize Slovenia and Croatia if they seceded unilaterally.

U.S. Secretary of State James Baker visited Belgrade on June 21, for one day, listened to all sides, then declared that the United States opposed the breakup of the country and also opposed the use of force to hold the country together. All the participants heard what they wanted to hear. Serbians heard only that the country should stay united; the Slovenians and Croatians heard only that force should not be used against them, should they decide to secede.[48] Baker warned Tudjman and Kučan that the United States would not recognize unilateral secession and would hold those who fail to negotiate responsible for the bloodshed. He was amazed to witness Tudjman assert with blithe confidence that the Yugoslav army would not attack him if he declared independence.[49] In the Croatian leader's mind, such a declaration would not mean his republic and Slovenia were seceding from *all* forms of union, but only from Milošević's version of Yugoslavia.[50]

And on June 25, 1991, four days after Baker's visit and over the objections of many of their own citizens, Slovenia and Croatia did declare independence. Two days later war started in Slovenia. It has been called an "operetta war," for the Slovenes lost only 9 men and the JNA only 37. In fact, according to the U.S.

Ambassador Warren Zimmerman, the Slovenes succeeded only because Kučan made a deal with Milošević that the JNA would withdraw from Slovenia.[51] Croatia, on the other hand, would not win its independence so easily.

On June 30 the "troika" of European Community foreign ministers attended the session of the Yugoslav presidency in Belgrade and urged their hosts to exercise goodwill. A week later EC representatives attended another presidency meeting and extracted pledges of a three-month moratorium on implementation of Slovenian and Croatian declarations of independence. The Brioni Accord did end the war in Slovenia. The three-month moratorium agreement, however, did not prevent the war in Croatia, where Serb irregulars and the JNA launched heavy fighting by the end of June.[52]

The war in Croatia was largely a contest of public relations waged through the international media. The Croatians claimed to be exercising their right, as a nation, to self-determination. The Serbs said they had no objection to that, so long as the Serb regions of Croatia were not also dragged out of Yugoslavia; they plausibly justified their fears on the basis of the Ustasha's atrocities of 1941. Initially the press was openminded. However, unlike the Serbs, the Croat fighters allowed journalists to go wherever they wanted, even into battles, at their own risk. Those foreigners who did roam around witnessed a disproportionate number of atrocities perpetrated by Serbs. It is conceivable that, had the Serbians been equally open to visits, the journalists might have attributed a different ratio of atrocities to the two sides. In any case, the press soon came to blame the worst violence on Serbs, especially those trained in Chetnik organizations. As Slovenes and Croats deserted from the army and went over to join the Croatian National Guard or other alternative units, the JNA became predominantly Serb and was also accused of atrocities in a confidential report compiled by EC observers.[53] During that period JNA shelling destroyed two Croatian cities, Vukovar and Dubrovnik.

On September 7, 1991, the EC convened a Peace Conference on Yugoslavia in The Hague, with Lord Carrington as its chairman. Though the fighting was continuing in Croatia, Carrington continued to defend the territorial integrity of that country, without however finding any basis for compromise. Still the war continued. Germany's foreign minister Hans Dietrich Genscher now reversed his position, arguing in favor of recognizing Croatia and Slovenia.

Others, including the United States, regarded this as a grave error of judgment. The U.S. negotiator Cyrus Vance and Lord Carrington both insisted there should be no Western recognition of any Yugoslav republic until they had all agreed on their relationships. Vance told Warren Zimmerman, "My friend Genscher is out of control on this. What he's doing is madness."[54] Alija Izetbegović went to visit Genscher in Bonn, hoping to convince him that EC recognition would bring war to Bosnia. Oddly, when they met, Izetbegović failed to raise the issue, probably leading Genscher to conclude that he had no objections.[55] On December 16 and 17, Genscher succeeded in persuading the reluctant British to accept his position in exchange for some German concessions regarding the Maastricht Treaty. The EC decided to recognize the independence of any Yugoslav republic only after its claim had been investigated by its judicial commission, to be headed by a French lawyer, Robert Badinter.

Macedonia, Bosnia-Herzegovina, and Kosovo joined Slovenia and Croatia in applying. Badinter recommended recognition of all except Bosnia-Herzegovina and Kosovo (which was not a republic) but asked Croatia to institute better protection for minorities. Bosnia-Herzegovina was asked to hold a referendum before proceeding further with its plans.

But the Serbs held a referendum of their own referendum first, and 99 percent of them voted for this position: If the republic tried to break away from Yugoslavia, they would insist on forming a Serb republic within Bosnia-Herzegovina. Accordingly, their leaders proclaimed their own new republic, with its own government and currency. The EC ignored their referendum, as they had also ignored the referendum held by the autonomist Serbs in Croatia to remain within Yugoslavia. The Serbs, in turn, boycotted the referendum organized for the Badinter Commission, which took place at the end of February 1992. Of those who did vote in that Bosnian referendum, some 99 percent supported independence. The polarization within Bosnia could not be sharper. Bosnia received diplomatic recognition and a seat at the United Nations that same month. And as predicted, war was about to begin.

Oddly, the same logic underlay the Bosniac-led government and their Serbian opponents. Izetbegović had been willing to accept almost any compromise that would have held Yugoslavia together, but if, despite everything, Slovenia and Croatia seceded, he could not tolerate becoming a minority within a Serbian-dominated Yugoslavia. He would have to secede in turn. For their part, the Bosnian Serbs had also wanted to hold Yugoslavia together at all costs but if, despite everything, Bosnia seceded, they could not bear to become a minority within a Bosniac- and Croatian-dominated Bosnia. They would have to secede in turn.

This argument was identical to the one expressed a short time before by the Serbs of Croatia, who had also objected being dragged out of Yugoslavia against their will. According to Tito's system of governance in which every constituent nationality had veto power, nothing could have been imposed on them. Any referendum using Tito's consensual approach would have required *a majority of voters of each nation and each significant national minority* to accept the proposal before it could be adopted. This might have produced a stalemate, to be sure, but it certainly would have prevented two wars. Now, however, the usual European version of democracy was imposed; the majority would win and the minority would lose.

But every true democracy protects minorities (e.g., by a Bill of Rights and a legal system) from the "tyranny of the majority." Recalling the history of ethnic violence and the weakness of the rule of law in Yugoslavia, some groups had well-founded fears of a simple system of majority rule, yet their concerns were dismissed. Warren Zimmerman tried throughout that period to persuade Serbs to participate in, and accept the outcome of, the referendum Badinter required, which would have made them into a minority within an independent Bosnia.[56] As Susan Woodward notes,

> It was a matter of unresolved constitutional interpretation whether republics had the right to secede and, if so, whether individuals who identified with another constituent nation within these republics had to give their consent. In choosing [to define sovereignty in terms of] the republican borders and the claims of the majority nation for an independent state, the EC politicians made no accommodation to this second, constitutionally equal category of rights to self-determination. . . .

> [Yet the EC] had no leverage with which to persuade the Serbs in Croatia and Albanians in Serbia to be satisfied with minority rights when their rebellions were motivated, in part, by real discrimination by the governments that would be expected to guarantee them protections.[57]

Zimmerman and the EC advised the minority Serbs just to lose and to accept their defeat. Instead, they chose to fight.

The War in Bosnia-Herzegovina

The war in Bosnia came as no surprise. As soon as the cease-fire took hold in Croatia on January 2, 1992, the Serb troops began moving south in their tanks and armored personnel carriers. Later, the Bosnian soldiers in the JNA were removed from their former positions to become the 80,000-man Bosnian Serb Army and, still on the Belgrade payroll, to take up positions all around the country.

There were some efforts to prevent the war. For example, the French had proposed to the Bush administration that preventive peacekeepers be imported to support the elected government of Bosnia. This idea was rejected as containing no "exit strategy."[58] Despite its victory in the Gulf War, the U.S. officials still feared getting into another Vietnam, from which they could not extricate themselves. For this reason, they made a great point of *not threatening to use force.* As Wayne Bert notes,

> Eagleburger seemingly had no misgivings about the value of American credibility unless some overt threat was made for which there was no follow-through. Complete inaction, in his view, did not compromise U.S. credibility.[59]

Only much later, in 1995, did this U.S. policy change, after the news of massacre in Srebrenica reached President Clinton — a tale of horror in which hundreds or thousands of innocent victims were slaughtered while under the protection of Western peacekeepers.[60] Clinton blew up, claiming that the Bosnia policy was "doing enormous damage to the United States and to our standing in the world. We look weak."

But this was 1995. In 1992 there had been no willingness to intervene to prevent fighting in Bosnia. There had been an arms embargo against all belligerents, but while the Bosniacs had little access to weaponry, the Serbs had all the old JNA weapons they could use.

During the first year of the war, the Bosniac government was fighting against both the Serbs and the Croats, a fact that speaks volumes about the intentions of the Croatian leadership. Both Serbia and Croatia evidently hoped to divide Bosnia in two, sharing the two pieces, and eliminate the Bosniacs. The United Nations did send peacekeepers — the United Nations Protection Force, or UNPROFOR — but gave them no permission to protect anyone. Both sides resented or even hated them for their impotence.

The war in Bosnia was remarkably nasty, marked by atrocities, sieges, concentration camps, and organized rapes designed to complete the "ethnic cleansing" of whole regions. This is not the place to record those stories, many of which cannot even be verified. The lies and organized disinformation made truth the "first casualty" of this war, even more than some others. For one thing, the Sarajevo Bosniac government had no possibility of defeating the Serbs who surrounded their city and kept it isolated for three years. Their only hope depended on enlisting the sympathy of Western citizens to an extent that the U.S. troops would come to fight beside them. Sometimes sympathy did influence Western public opinion, as, for example, after photos reminiscent of the Holocaust were shown of a concentration camp at Omarska and later after the massacre at Srebrenica was publicized.

But how much manipulation was going on? It has been alleged that the Sarajevo leaders actually shelled their own citizens to win foreign pity.[61] Mark Danner claims that the Bosniacs tried to "make use of the misery of the enclaves to force action by the United Nations and Western countries. . . . [They] were simply trying to make use of the only weapon the peculiar and hypocritical international involvement in their country seemed to offer them."[62] I do not know that this is true, and it would be unwise to accept it uncritically, but it is possible to distort reality in a different direction by omitting all stories that have not been verified.

Whatever the truth may be, Western observers of the war came to believe, on the basis of considerable evidence,[63] that the Serbs' side was disproportionately responsible for war crimes. However justified their political cause may have been (and their initial arguments were as reasonable as those of their opponents), the Serbs lost respect internationally as a result of these reported atrocities. The great majority of Western analysts came to support the Bosniacs and to castigate UNPROFOR for doing too little on their behalf.[64]

Eventually, Bill Clinton decided to bomb the astonished Serbs, against the wishes of countries with peacekeeping troops vulnerable on the ground. Next he pressured all the belligerents to come together at an air force base in Dayton, Ohio, and negotiate a settlement to their dispute, the "Dayton Accords," a document that was signed a month later in Europe, where it is known as the "Paris Peace Plan." It called for the transfer of peacekeeping responsibility from the United Nations to NATO and for the division of Bosnia into two sectors: the Federation of Muslims and Croats and the Republika Srpska. The Muslims and Croats are the "constituent peoples" of the Federation, while the Serbs are the constituent peoples of the Republika Srpska, and each group is respectively entitled to elect politicians of its own nation in its own republic to positions in the bicameral federal legislature and the federal presidency.

The Dayton agreement stopped the war without bringing peace. At this writing, Bosnians stray only with peril into the territory of the former enemy. A war crimes tribunal is functioning in The Hague, but few of those charged have been arrested and brought to trial. Although the NATO troops (called SFOR — "Sustaining Forces") remain in place throughout Bosnia, many people believe that war will return as soon as they leave — which they must eventually do. The task, then, is to find a new system of governance that will enable each ethnic group in Bosnia to feel secure while dealing with members of other nations.

Conclusion

Of all the lessons to be learned from the tragedy of Yugoslavia, three should be emphasized here. First, the breakup of any state should be regarded as a dangerous policy that may result in warfare — especially if there is a dispute over ownership and sovereignty in a particular territory.

Second, the international community should not recognize any unilateral secession until all the relevant groups have settled their claims and accept the terms of their new relationship.

And third, the transition to democracy is not necessarily accomplished easily. Some groups may legitimately feel threatened, especially if the mechanisms that formerly protected their interests and ensured their equality are to be replaced by simple decision making by majority rule. Every democracy requires more than majority-rule voting; it requires complicated legal and institutional protections for minorities. Majority rule should be imposed only with great caution and in conjunction with alternative methods of protecting minorities. There are numerous other democratic procedures that contrast with the majoritarian system of governance and that provide greater participation for all the diverse groups within a country. Taken together, these can go far toward holding together the groups that might otherwise be separatists.[65]

I end with this note: The situation in Kosovo, where nationalistic hatred was first exploited for the personal gain of politicians, remains unresolved. In 1998, when fighting broke out there, the international community began pressuring Belgrade to hold discussions with the separatists. This is not the end of the matter, and war actually seems imminent as we go to press this summer. If the lessons are learned that should be learned, democratic governments around the world will insist that the human rights of all citizens be protected, in the former Yugoslavia and elsewhere.

Notes

1. Since the country broke apart in the 1990s, Serbs and Croats have been trying to split their common language into two — Serbian and Croatian.

2. Mihailo Crnobrnja, *The Yugoslav Drama*, 2nd ed. (Montreal: McGill-Queen's University Press, 1996), 21.

3. Crnobrnja, *The Yugoslav Drama*, 16-20.

4. Chrisopher Bennett, *Yugoslavia's Bloody Collapse: Causes, Course and Consequences* (New York: New York University Press, 1995), 29.

5. Bennett, *Yugoslavia's Bloody Collapse*, 35.

6. Crnobrnja, *The Yugoslav Drama*, 59.

7. Bennett, *Yugoslavia's Bloody Collapse*, 40.

8. Crnobrnja, *The Yugoslav Drama*, 65.

9. Bennett, *Yugoslavia's Bloody Collapse*, 43-44. See also Michael Ignatieff, *Blood and Belonging: Journeys into the New Nationalism* (New York and Toronto: Viking, 1993), 22-24.

10. For an evaluation of the various estimates, see Bennett, *Yugoslavia's Bloody Collapse*, 45-56.

11. Bennett, *Yugoslavia's Bloody Collapse*, 47.

12. Crnobrnja, *The Yugoslav Drama*, 67.

13. According to Susan Woodward, there was some dispute as to whether republican autonomy did include the right to secede from the federation. See Susan L.Woodward, *Balkan Tragedy: Chaos and Dissolution after the Cold War* (Washington, D.C.: The Brookings Institution, 1995), 31.

14. Woodward, *Balkan Tragedy*, 25-26.

15. Woodward, *Balkan Tragedy*, 15.

16. Dušan Nečak, "Historical Elements for Understanding the 'Yugoslav Question'," in *Yugoslavia: The Former and Future,* ed. Payam Akhavan and Robert Howse (Washington, D.C.: The Brookings Institution, 1995), 21-22. Also see Woodward, *Balkan Tragedy,* 37.

17. See John Bacher, "The Breakup of the Austro-Hungarian Empire," in this volume.

18. Bennett, *Yugoslavia's Bloody Collapse*, 20.

19. Woodward, *Balkan Tragedy*, 37.

20. Vojin Dimitrijević, "The 1974 Constitution and Constitutional Process as a Factor in the Collapse of Yugoslavia," in *Yugoslavia: The Former and Future*, 45.

21. Mitja Žagar, "Yugoslavia: What Went Wrong? Constitutional Aspects of the Yugoslav Crisis from the Perspective of Ethnic Conflict," a paper presented at the Science for Peace conference, "The Lessons of Yugoslavia," University of

Toronto, March 1997. It will be published in volume 3 of the series *Research on Russia and Eastern Europe,* ed. Metta Spencer (Greenwood, Conn.: JAI Press, forthcoming).

22. Dimitrijević, "The 1974 Constitution," 55.

23. Dimitrijević, "The 1974 Constitution," 60-61. On the role of the republican politicians, see Ivo Banać, "Post-Communism as Post-Yugoslavism: The Yugoslav Non-Revolutions of 1989-1990," in *Eastern Europe in Revolution,* ed. Ivo Banać (Ithaca: Cornell University Press, 1992), 168-80.

24. Žagar, "What Went Wrong?"; Dimitrijevic, "The 1974 Constitution," 61.

25. Woodward, *Balkan Tragedy,* 63.

26. Woodward, *Balkan Tragedy,* 49, 51.

27. Robert K. Schaeffer, *Power to the People: Democratization Around the World* (Boulder: Westview, 1997) 176.

28. Bennett, *Yugoslavia's Bloody Collapse,* 69-70.

29. Woodward, *Balkan Tragedy,* 61.

30. Woodward, *Balkan Tragedy,* 62

31. Woodward, *Balkan Tragedy,* 74, 78-80.

32. Michel Chossudovsky, "Dismantling Former Yugoslavia, Recolonizing Bosnia," paper presented to the conference, "The Lessons of Yugoslavia," March 1997. Chossudovsky's opinion of Marković's reform is far less favorable than that expressed by other Yugoslavia specialists, especially Christopher Bennett.

33. Bennett, *Yugoslavia's Bloody Collapse,* 117-19.

34. Žarko Puhovski, "The Bleak Prospects for Civil Society," in *Yugoslavia: The Former and Future,* 122. See also Duško Doder, "Yugoslavia: New War, Old Hatreds," *Foreign Policy* 91 (1993), 14.

35. Bennett, *Yugoslavia's Bloody Collapse,* 81.

36. Bennett, *Yugoslavia's Bloody Collapse,* 90.

37. Bennett, *Yugoslavia's Bloody Collapse,* 86-87.

38. Crnobrnja, *The Yugoslav Drama,* 95.

39. Crnobrnja, *The Yugoslav Drama,* 103.

40. Bennett, *Yugoslavia's Bloody Collapse,* 86-91.

41. Crnobrnja, *The Yugoslav Drama,* 101-6.

42. Crnobrnja, *The Yugoslav Drama,* 143-46.

43. Darko Šilović, "The International Response to the Crisis in Yugoslavia," a paper presented to the conference, "The Lessons of Yugoslavia," March 1997.

44. This was the opinion of U.S. Ambassador Warren Zimmerman as expressed in his book *Origins of a Catastrophe* (New York: Times Books, 1996), 125.

45. Dušan Janjić, "Resurgence of Ethnic Conflict in Yugoslavia: The Demise of Communism and the Rise of the 'New Elites' of Nationalism," in *Yugoslavia: The Former and Future,* 31-32.

46. Mihailo Crnobrnja, "European Union and the Breakup of Yugoslavia," a paper presented to the conference, "The Lessons of Yugoslavia," March 1997.

47. Zimmerman, *Origins of a Catastrophe,* 138.

48. Silović, "The International Response."

49. Zimmerman, *Origins of a Catastrophe*, 132-37, describes Baker's visit, portraying it as an admirable performance.

50. Bennett, *Yugoslavia's Bloody Collapse*, 158, blames the war on the military, reminding us that in 1991 the three Baltic republics had also declared unilateral independence from the Soviet Union without Western approval, yet without leading to war, since the Soviet military had not attacked.

51. Zimmerman, *Origins of a Catastrophe*, 145. This may be a minority view, however. An alternative interpretation holds that at that point Milošević did not have control over the JNA and that, furthermore, the generals were surprised to encounter armed resistance on the part of the Slovenes.

52. Zimmerman, *Origins of a Catastrophe*, 148-49; Bennett, *Yugoslavia's Bloody Collapse*, 159.

53. Bennett, *Yugoslavia's Bloody Collapse*, 160-66.

54. Vance told me in 1998 (personal communication) that he had indeed been angry with Genscher but that considerably later Genscher had admitted that he had been wrong and had apologized.

55. Zimmerman, *Origins of a Catastrophe*, 176-77.

56. Zimmerman, *Origins of a Catastrophe*, 187.

57. Woodward, *Balkan Tragedy*, 210.

58. Mark Danner, "America and the Bosnia Genocide," *New York Review of Books*, December 4, 1997, 60-61.

59. Wayne Bert, as quoted by Danner, "America and the Bosnia Genocide," 63.

60. Danner, "America and the Bosnia Genocide," 57.

61. James R. Davis, *The Sharp End: A Canadian Soldier's Story* (Vancouver: Douglas and McIntyre, 1997), 173.

62. Mark Danner, "Clinton, the U.N. and the Bosnian Disaster," *New York Review of Books*, Dec. 18. 1997, 74.

63. Jan Willem Honig and Norbert Both, *Srebrenica: Record of a War Crime* (New York: Penguin, 1996).

64. James Gow, *Triumph of the Lack of Will: International Diplomacy and the Yugoslav War* (New York: Columbia University Press, 1996).

65. The contrast between majoritarian democracy and consensus (or "consociational") democracy has best been elaborated by Arend Lijphart. See his book *Democracies: Patterns of Majoritarian and Consensus Government in Twenty-One Countries* (New Haven, Conn.: Yale University Press, 1984).

Eight

The Partition of Czechoslovakia

Petr Pithart and Metta Spencer

The division of Czechoslovakia into two separate states is frequently taken as a rare success story, especially by separatists elsewhere who like to prove that secession can be done painlessly and without bloodshed. To most of the citizens who went through the experience, however, it was less an exemplary success than a sad story of egotism, short-sightedness, and misunderstanding. Still, to some of the citizens of Slovakia, who now have the political opportunity to stand on their own feet, it does not seem sad but a risky and challenging experiment. We shall recount that tale here from the perspective of one of the participants, a prime minister of the Czech part of that federal state as its disintegration approached.

A Short History of Czechoslovakia

Two countries came into existence on January 1, 1993 as another country ceased to be. The newly independent Czech Republic includes the lands identified as Bohemia, Moravia, and Silesia, where the Czech language is generally spoken. Its sibling state, the newly independent Slovak Republic, comprises the traditionally Slovak lands and part of Ruthenia in the east. Most of its people, who are but half as numerous as the Czechs, speak a closely related Slavic language, Slovak, though more than 600,000 of them speak Hungarian. By apparently mutual consent, these two new countries created themselves by ending the country that they had shared.

Yet that country, Czechoslovakia, was itself a relatively young state, having been created in 1918 by the victors of World War I from remnants of the defeated Austro-Hungarian Empire. The country's first leader, Tomáš Garrigue Masaryk, had not always favored the breakup of the old empire, but when the time came he in fact led the way to independence and democracy. He could support this new position by pointing to a tradition of Czech statehood (which had lasted, with some interruptions, a thousand years) and to the military achievements of the Czech legions, which fought on the victorious side in the First World War. Thus Czechoslovakia, unlike other Eastern European countries, enjoyed two decades of democracy before World War II — a background that would facilitate the restoration of a liberal republic some fifty years later.

That fifty-year interval was a somber epoch for the whole region of Eastern Europe. The downfall of the Czechoslovakian state resulted from the infamous Munich Pact, by which its allies (especially Britain and France) ceded to Hitler one-third of the country, the borderland inhabited mainly by 3.5 million Germans. Half a year later, in 1939, Germany occupied the rest of the country, calling it the Protectorate of Bohemia and Moravia. The Slovaks, lacking alternatives, escaped from a similar fate by only declaring a separate state in 1939, for the first time in their history. The conservative Catholic traditionalism of the region expressed itself as support for the Hlinka Slovak People's Party, led by an old priest, Josef Tiso, who was attracted to fascism. He administered the state with Hitler's blessings throughout the war years and collaborated by sending Jews to the death camps.

When World War II ended, Czechoslovakia was reconstituted as a unitary state with some elements of asymmetric autonomy added as a concession to the Slovaks; for example, Slovakia had a Communist Party and so did Czechoslovakia, but Czechia did not. The recent war criminals were executed, including — much to the disapproval of most Slovaks — Father Tiso. To complete the vengeance of the period, nearly three million Sudeten German citizens, mainly from the Bohemian and Moravian borderlands, were expelled from the country.

In some respects the first postwar regime was pluralistic, though there were important limitations. For example, some political parties were forbidden, and any new party could be established only with the approval of the four existing ones. Then in 1947-48 the Communists took advantage of the weakness and blindness of their political rivals and organized a coup, using a combination of constitutional mechanisms, including overt threat of violence. They established a police state, and repressed their political enemies. Under this regime the Slovaks experienced a limited, asymmetric self-governance. (Only much later, after 1989, would the counter-productiveness of that asymmetry become apparent. Indeed, one can see it in retrospect as a predisposing factor in the breakup of the country. Having some limited executive decision-making capacity of its own — while Czechia did not — did not mean that Slovakia was the stronger region but instead showed its weakness. Rather than being a *counterpart* to Czechia, it appeared to be only a subsidiary component of a federal state that was almost indistinguishable from its Czech center.[1] Asymmetrical structures fostered the Czechs' tendency to consider the common state as their own, while the Slovaks resented being less than their full partner. This resentment would intensify after 1989.)

However, as early as 1968 an effort was made to overcome the asymmetry. On becoming Czechoslovakia's Communist Party leader in that year, Alexander Dubček prepared a federal constitution establishing formal equality between Czech and Slovak National Councils (parliaments) as part of the Prague Spring,[2] a remarkable liberalization that would survive only briefly. Aided by nearby satellite states, the Soviet Union launched a military invasion on August 20, 1968 to impose its heavy-handed version of socialism. The reformers were removed from power, isolated, and allowed to work thereafter only in menial jobs. A fellow Slovak, Gustáv Husák, replaced Dubček as the country's leader and abolished all the reform plans except one: the federalization of the state, which was proclaimed two months after the invasion.

The plan was to make each of the constituent republics, Czech and Slovak, sovereign. They would have their own constitutions and national councils and, in turn, would devolve a limited amount of power and sovereignty to a federation that they would create, with certain joint organs, including a constitutional court and supreme court.

Though most Slovaks accepted this federalism as a victory, the dispirited Czechs hardly bothered to oppose the weakening of the federal government, dismissing it as unimportant in comparison to the devastating effect of the recent invasion. The Czechs had, through the Prague Spring, won and again lost democracy. For their part, the Slovaks had wanted federalism more than democracy, but the Czechs knew that *without* democracy, federalism would be hollow and useless.

This proved to be the case. Article Four of the Constitution, which assigned the Communist Party the "leading role" in the society, negated the other provisions of the constitution by allowing all important decisions to be made by the Party. The National Assemblies of the Slovaks and Czechs would meet, as prescribed by the constitution, but their deliberations would count as nothing. Actually, by late 1970 the federation was strengthened, and it was decided that the economy should be unified. Work was never even begun by the Communists to write the promised separate constitutions. The Czechs, who anticipated this, were disgusted with the Slovaks' folly and selfishness, which reminded them of the time under Hitler when Slovaks, facing a terrible dilemma, had won statehood at the expense of their Czech countrymen.

The disparity of attitudes concerning federalization and democracy presaged the widening distance between Slovaks and Czechs during the period of so-called normalization — from 1968 to 1989. Only afterward would the spiritual chasm become apparent; polls would show that the normalization period had been considered by the Slovaks the most successful time in their history but by the Czechs their most miserable period.

If before the Prague Spring, asymmetry had been designed to disadvantage the Slovaks, after 1968 it worked to their advantage. To stifle reformism, the highest party organs were not created in Czechia. New jobs and educational opportunities opened for conformist Slovaks, while more than one million others — predominantly Czechs — were dismissed or blocked.

The regime was cruel. To criticize the state was to incur imprisonment, the loss of one's profession, or the denial of higher education for one's children. Yet many Slovaks adapted, taking the new federal system seriously. Some of them moved to Prague to participate in governing structures. There was a widespread feeling among the Czechs that during normalization the Slovaks governed the Czechs, who loathed the existing totalitarian state.

In fact, some independent Czech intellectuals willingly incurred the heavy penalties of criticizing the government. In 1976 a group of dissidents protested against the repression of a rock music group and formed Charter 77 the next year. They signed a document calling for the respect of human rights, and some members began meeting in each other's homes to monitor breaches of law, edit periodicals, translate books, organize "home universities," and the like. Charter 77 was a tool for the self-reflection of the society, and its members worked hard at their self-appointed tasks. There were only 1,250 signatories, for the penalties for signing were severe. Police harassment and pressure even resulted in death occasionally,[3] as in the case of the philosopher Jan Patočka. Hundreds of opponents of the regime were forced to emigrate. The most prominent chartist was playwright Václav Havel, who spent years in prison for his audacity.

In the fall of 1989, Central and Eastern Europeans finally began to take Mikhail Gorbachev at his word when he pledged that Soviet force would no longer be used to control the socialist bloc. A nonviolent revolution spread quickly from one country to the next. Czechoslovakia's turn came on November 17, when riot police attacked a student demonstration in Prague. This brutality prompted citizens to join even larger demonstrations, which grew day by day as student organizers traveled around the country, inviting workers into their movement. By the third day, Václav Havel called together dissident intellectuals and student leaders in the "Činoherni Klub," and then to the famous Magic Lantern theater, where they launched a movement: Civic Forum (CF). In Slovakia a parallel organization, Public Against Violence (PAV) was formed and its members too included intellectuals who had already expressed their dissent against the communist regime.

That regime was led by old men who were fully aware of their unpopularity. Gustáv Husák, who had led the Czechoslovak Communist Party since 1969, had already been replaced two years before by another uninspiring hard-liner, Miloš Jakeš, and a new prime minister, Ladislav Adamec. The duty fell on Adamec to negotiate with the demonstrators' new movement, Civic Forum, which had called for a general strike. Civic Forum and Public Against Violence were represented at the negotiating table by Václav Havel and Ján Čarnogurský, respectively, both of them famous dissidents who had been released only recently from prison.

By December 8, the negotiators were able to name a new government. Its president was Havel and its prime minister was Marián Čalfa, a former member of the preceding Communist government. Most of the members of the new government were not dissidents but recent members of the Communist Party or related organizations. The Civic Forum members found, to their astonishment, that the old regime put up almost no resistance to their demands. However, few of the anticommunist dissidents were prepared to fill political leadership roles yet, so they accepted others whose experience would provide the continuity that they regarded as necessary and stabilizing until a democratic parliamentary election could be held — as soon as possible. As revolutions go, it was a marvel of good humor and mutual accommodation: No one was killed, and the protesters were cautious, proceeding slowly so as to prevent bloodshed. The old regime accepted their downfall civilly, and the new leaders did not immediately take as much power as they could have claimed. Everyone called it a "velvet revolution." Only the students who had launched the revolution were disappointed because their demands had brought about few changes in the political composition of the government.

But changes did take place. The Party lost its official "leading role in society." Political prisoners were set free. The opposition replaced 120 members of the 300-member bicameral Federal Assembly. And in June 1990, only six months after the demonstrations began, free elections where held, with Civic Forum and Public Against Violence winning a great victory. Havel remained president, Marián Čalfa was prime minister, Alexander Dubček was Chairman of the Federal Assembly, and Jiří Dienstbier was foreign minister. The first moves were made toward adopting a market economy under the leadership of Václav Klaus, finance minister.

The structure of the state did not immediately change. As before, there was a bicameral legislature at the federal level — the Federal Assembly (of whose members ninety-nine were elected by proportional representation from the Czech Republic and fifty-one from Slovakia) and the House of Nations with seventy-five members from each republic. The Assembly chose the president, who chose the prime minister, who in turn put together a government that served as long as it could retain the Assembly's confidence.

The system was much the same within the two republics, except that each legislature was a unicameral national council that elected a presidium to carry out the presidential duties. In Slovakia the new prime minister was Vladimir Mečiar of Public Against Violence, while in Czechia that post was held by Petr Pithart of Civic Forum. A new phase of Czechoslovakia's history was beginning.

Antipathies and Interests after 1989

Democracy allowed new conflicts to emerge — as well as old ones that had been suppressed under communism. Civic Forum members, suddenly becoming politicians, did not necessarily agree on many issues but found their views distributed from right to left across the whole political spectrum, though the majority probably could be considered liberals or centrists. These new politicians began to form new factions that increasingly functioned as real parties, each one representing certain interests, as political parties normally do in democracies.

It is, however, debatable whether the "interests" that became politically significant were primarily realistic or symbolic in nature. The economic decisions were material and realistic in nature, but the most troublesome issue that quickly re-emerged was the old tension between Czechs and Slovaks, and one can ask whether it was based more on actual, substantive interests or on sensitivities about relative status and other symbolic considerations.

Despite the close similarity of their languages, the histories of the Czechs and the Slovaks were quite different. The Czechs had their own state starting from the beginning of the ninth century, and Prague had sometimes been the center of the Holy Roman Empire. After the Thirty Years' War the Habsburgs had ruled Czechia. The Slovaks, on the other hand, were less happy, for they had never had their own state. From 1867 Czechia had belonged to the Austrian half of the Austro-Hungarian Empire, with its constitutional liberties, while Slovakia had been under harsh Hungarian domination and cultural repression. To this day, the Slovaks' relationship with Hungary remains fraught with antagonism. There were also many cultural differences between the two republics of Czechoslovakia. The Czech republic has long been an industrial center, whereas Slovakia is more agricultural. The Bohemian city Prague is proud of its accomplishments in art, literature, scholarship, and music, whereas the Slovakian city Bratislava is less often recognized abroad for such cultural accomplishments. The Czechs have often been insensitive and blunt in making invidious comparisons between themselves and their Slovak neighbors — an attitude for which President Havel has apologized, referring to it as the "arrogance of an elder brother." In objective terms — demography, economic prosperity, and the like — the two nationalities became similar during the period of normalization.[4] But the tensions between them were not based on objective comparisons, but rather upon subjective aspirations for collective recognition.

When after the downfall of the communist regime it became permissible to discuss nationality questions, some Slovaks broached the subject of their "humiliation" — a subjective, symbolic sense that one's community ought to be accorded a higher rank in the ethnic stratification hierarchy. Those who had founded the country had hoped that the two main groups would become a single "nation" — neither Czechs nor Slovaks but "Czechoslovaks." Many Czechs claimed this identity for themselves, but the Slovaks rarely did so. The preferred solution of Slovak nationalists — the independence of a separate Slovakian state — remained unacceptable to the Czechs because the sizable population of Germans would also have wanted to secede from Czechoslovakia if the Slovaks had been able to do so.

At the same time, there were also economic issues at stake that differentiated the two republics. With the initial moves toward capitalism came unemployment, but levels of joblessness immediately became much higher in Slovakia than in Czechia: At the end of June 1992, Czech unemployment was less than 3 percent, whereas it was over 11 percent in Slovakia. The reason for this disparity was the industrial structure of the two regions. Huge factories had been built in Slovakia to foster the development of that region, and these were especially difficult to privatize. Also, under pressure from the Soviet Union, the Communist regime had put 80 percent of the arms factories in Slovakia. Now there was no market for these weapons, and anyway the new federal government planned to end all involvement in the arms trade.

Because of their different experience, the Slovaks looked back more warmly than did their neighbors on communism, which a generation or two before they had been more reluctant to embrace. In response to this reality, the Slovaks' new prime minister, Vladimir Mečiar, wanted to slow the transition to capitalism. He favored a continuation of state subsidies to failing industries, a slower privatization of ownership, and permanent state ownership in the cases of certain firms.[5]

In these policies Mečiar was at odds with the first finance minister of the Czechoslovakian federal government, Václav Klaus. In fact, Klaus was at odds with many members of his own political movement, Civic Forum, whose convictions leaned toward the center. He presented himself as an unqualified right-winger, though in fact his policies were not as radical as he claimed. The main difference between his approach and that of the majority of others in Civic Forum was that he underestimated the legal aspects of the transformation and focused on economic factors alone. He had adopted Milton Friedman's "monetarist" views. Intending to lead Czechoslovakia painlessly and quickly into a market economy, he promised that capitalism would bring prosperity almost immediately. Soon Klaus and Mečiar had developed a polarized relationship in regard to economic policies, and the growing antipathy between them would become an important factor in the partition of Czechoslovakia into two countries, as Slovak nationalists backed up their intransigent prime minister on economic matters.

One may call it irrational to break up a country over the minor disparity of economic interests between the Czech and Slovak republics, since with regard to the whole economic picture, the two regions had many more interests in common. Indeed, no one would be hurt by secession more than the Slovaks, who initiated the idea. (In the end the Czech side would share the responsibility for the breakup of the country, but this was not so at first.)

The two sides came to separatism from quite different motives; for the Czechs the rationale was economic. Throughout the country's existence, the richer Czech republic had been subsidizing Slovakia[6] — in the later years by about $300 million annually.[7] The Czech contribution to the federal budget was supposedly ten times that of Slovakia. Moreover, the amount of foreign investment in Czechoslovakia had begun to diminish[8] as the prospect of secession increased, and the Slovak side would suffer more than the Czech side from lack of capital.

From the Slovak perspective, these facts would seem to argue unmistakably against secession. Unfortunately, however, for them the economic argument cut in both directions. Though it was true that Slovakia was the net beneficiary in an unequal partnership with the Czech Republic, this was only a *material* basis for continuing the relationship. In *symbolic* terms, that inferior status was yet one more humiliation to the already wounded Slovak national pride. (Who wants be an economic burden in addition to being a cultural backwater?) Both material and symbolic issues counted. As the prospective break between the two republics became more imminent, the material considerations increased in salience, and polls showed Slovak public opinion worrying more and more about their economic future after independence. However, the humiliation factor always loomed large, perhaps most so in the unspoken debate.

Economic issues, then, which inevitably were paramount concerns for the whole country as it began a transition toward private ownership, also became intertwined with the other major conflict that divided Czechoslovakia: the renewed misunderstanding between the two main nationalities of the society. Despite much intermarriage and frequent visits to the other republic, neither group really understood the other, and the Czechs were especially unaware of offending the Slovaks by underestimating them in their stereotypes and treating them as a "third world country."[9] The problematic relationship between the two republics exacerbated another political problem — the rewriting of the country's constitution.

Constitutional Revisions

Early in 1990, the new Civic Forum government recognized the necessity of revising the federal constitution and developing constitutions for both republics, neither of which had one. The 1968 federal constitution clearly had to be adapted, at least to redefine the power of the republics and the federal organs. The political leaders of both republics asked for more powers, but there were major differences between them, the Slovak demands generally being more radical. Each of the three entities — both of the republics plus the federal government — set about developing its own constitution, though no coordination procedure existed for integrating them at each step of the way, nor did a supreme constitutional court exist. Hypothetically, all three constitutions could have been changed in incompatible ways, so that a new innovation would have been required to fit them together again.

Differences of approach soon became apparent, with Slovakia preferring a confederal structure, in which it would be linked only loosely with the Czechs. The revising went slowly, with the Slovaks in particular increasing their demands for autonomy. Symbolism was a prominent aspect of the process, as, for example, in the controversy over the name of the federation. Should it be Czechoslovak or Czecho-Slovak or Czech and Slovak Federal Republic? Initially the Federal Assembly chose the unhyphenated name, but there were public demonstrations of outrage in Bratislava, so a new decision was reached: to call the country the Czech and Slovak Federative Republic.

Another factor increasing the polarization was the Slovak National Council's decision to make Slovak the only official language of the Slovak Republic, despite the fact that more than half a million Hungarians live in the southern part of Slovakia.

As the constitutional revision dragged on through the second year, the Czechs realized that the process was creating uncertainty and costing the whole country money as investors withheld much-needed capital. Losing confidence in the federation, the Czechs began paying more attention to the constitution of their own republic. There was even a brief discussion of a tripartite federation in which Moravia and Silesia would constitute a third republic. The idea was somewhat unacceptable for the Slovaks, for it would mean that the Slovak nation was determined in the same way as that of the Moravian and Silesians — only on an ethnic basis — and it was threatening to the Czechs because, if it were implemented and then the Slovaks seceded anyway, the Czech Republic would be a "two-member" federation again, which is the most unstable kind of federation.[10] Any federation comprising only two parts is nearly impossible, since if the republics take opposing sides in a dispute, the impasse cannot be resolved by voting; with two subjects there can be no majority.

The constitutional process became a frustrating experience in which Slovak nationalists kept increasing their demands and rendering every agreement ambiguous as soon as it was reached. For example, in early 1991, they proposed a new notion: a "state treaty" to be adopted by the two national assemblies to structure the drafting of the three constitutions. The proponents of this idea argued that the 1968 constitution had been imposed on the society from above and was therefore illegitimate. Their solution was to renew the union from below, beginning by reestablishing the legitimacy of the two republics, who would then "re-marry," creating a new and fully voluntary federation. Critics of this proposal believed that it would cast doubt on the authority of the existing federal constitution. Havel opposed this "state treaty."

Another Slovak demand was that the National Councils should ratify the federal constitution. By autumn, while these proposals were being discussed, they were superseded by a new Slovak demand — for a Declaration of Sovereignty and a complete constitution of the republic's own.

Frustrated by these Slovak maneuvers, the Czechs gradually began to accept separation for their own, quite different, motives. For a time they left the constitutional matters in the hands of Havel and the other federal leaders. Havel accepted numerous compromises in the constitutional struggle, including a clause guaranteeing national self-determination in the Bill of Fundamental Rights and Liberties, but he warned that the resort to unconstitutional solutions would bring legal chaos. He pointed out the urgency of creating a constitutional court and insisted that laws were needed to provide for a referendum by which to resolve constitutional questions. Most Czechs liked the idea of a referendum, for they knew that, according to public opinion polls, neither they nor a majority of Slovaks actually wanted independence.

On the other hand, the very proposal for a referendum made people take the possibility of secession more seriously. No imaginable constitution seemed to be acceptable to all sides, and by May 1991, the Czech National Council too was examining possible scenarios for dividing the federation.[11]

Party Politics

Partition did not take place only through formal negotiations and the work on revising constitutions. Electoral politics also came to focus on the issue of nationalism versus federalism, as we can see from the record of political parties in post-communist Czechoslovakia. That story begins with the fragmentation of Civic Forum soon after its moment of triumph.

Four months after the 1990 elections, the finance minister Václav Klaus became chairman of Civic Forum with the express intention of moving it toward right-wing politics and an economy in the style of Milton Friedman. He and other like-minded deputies formed the Inter-parliamentary Club of the Democratic Right. Predictably, this move stimulated the centrists to form a club of their own: the Liberal Club of the Civic Forum. Next Klaus's group proposed that the movement become a party, which any member of a group affiliated with the Civic Forum would have to join individually. This motion passed, and the affiliated groups that could not properly belong to the same party responded by quitting Civic Forum. At first the Liberal Club did not quit and did not give up its loose organizational form, but it did change its identity, becoming the Civic Movement, led by the foreign minister, Jiří Dienstbier. In March 1991 Klaus's club became the Civic Democratic Party (CDP), which was indeed a right-wing party. A month later Civic Forum disintegrated.

The Civic Movement was organizationally weak from the outset. Indeed, the word "movement" in the organization's title was aptly chosen, in that some Chartists (especially Havel) had a reserved attitude toward standard political parties. This skepticism was not a negation of politics but rather the emphasizing of civil society, with elements of direct democracy, over partisan politics. Accordingly, the Civic Movement, which largely constituted the rump Civic Forum after Klaus had left, preferred to function as a loose movement rather than as a party. This decision would soon limit its effectiveness in organizing electoral campaigns.

A comparable fragmentation of parties also occurred in Slovakia. As early as February 1990 (before the elections) Jan Čarnogurský broke away from PAV to form the Christian Democratic Movement (CDM).

Next, in February 1991, the premier, Vladimir Mečiar, also did his part to split PAV. As in the case of Civic Forum, this disintegration resulted from an effort to make the movement into a formal party with an authoritative leader. Mečiar wanted to become chairman of a party with a nationalistic orientation, but he encountered vociferous opposition from other members of PAV. By March 5 he walked out, leading fourteen other deputies with him. In May he formed his own new party, the Movement for a Democratic Slovakia (MDS). The centrist rump group remaining from PAV merged with a smaller party and soon became known as Civic Democratic Union (CDU).

So quickly had the umbrella groups Civic Forum and Public Against Violence fragmented that by the middle of 1991 there were twelve parties represented in the Federal Assembly instead of the six parties that had been elected a year before.

Until the elections of June 1992, Mečiar faced a rival group: the Christian Democratic Movement, which Jan Čarnogurský had formed before the 1990 elections. The CDM had been the first political group in Slovakia to elevate autonomy to a serious issue by taking a favorable position toward "confederation" — a loosened relationship between the two republics, with actual separation to be postponed until the moment when the Czechs and Slovaks would enter into the European Union as two distinct states. Public opinion polls showed that this movement gave Čarnogurský a boost in popularity. Still, he did not actually carry the banner for separatism but gradually withdrew even his call for autonomy.

When later Mečiar split PAV, this action reduced his parliamentary majority so significantly that he lost his position as premier of Slovakia. Čarnogurský replaced him in that role in April 1991. Out of office, Mečiar had ample opportunity to reflect on the advantages that even moderate nationalism had conferred upon his rival. Thereafter, whereas Čarnogurský failed to press any demand for greater autonomy, Mečiar picked up the theme and used it himself with increasing political success.

The 1992 Elections

By 1992, opinions had become polarized throughout Czechoslovakia. Those moderates who had been elected as Civic Forum and Public Against Violence candidates now were affiliated to new parties, but both at the federal and the republic level, the voters rejected them. In the Czech Republic, rightists won, whereas in Slovakia, leftists and nationalists won. The composition of the Federal Assembly was so polarized that it was hard to see how the members could reach any working compromises.

According to all three constitutions, a party must receive a minimum of 5 percent of the votes if it is to be represented in parliament at all. The centrist Civic Movement did not even receive that minimum in the federal government. Whereas CF and PAV had captured 170 of the 300 seats only two years before, in 1992 only 17 percent of the Federal Assembly's deputies were reelected. The Civic Movement's leader, Foreign Minister Jiří Dienstbier, and all the other federal ministers were replaced. Only Klaus was reelected, and he declined to take over as prime minister of the federal government, which he expected would be dissolved during the following term of office. The new prime minister of the now-dysfunctional federation was Jan Strasky of the CDP. For his part, Klaus opted to stand for election to the Czech National Assembly, where henceforth most major decisions would be made, and soon he replaced Petr Pithart as Czech prime minister. His CDP had won 30 percent of the vote in Czechia, and controlled the next coalition government.

In Slovakia, Mečiar's Movement for a Democratic Slovakia won even more handily, gathering more than 37 percent of the votes. They were followed by the former communists (now renamed the Party of the Democratic Left) and the CDM. This victory gave Mečiar the satisfaction of ousting his rival, Čarnogurský, and reclaiming his position as premier.

There are many interpretations of the centrists' rout. Perhaps the Civic Movement leaders, having held office for two years, had failed to campaign effectively because of losing their "will to power." Clearly Klaus must have run a more convincing campaign, for, despite the hardships they were experiencing from the economic reforms he had launched as finance minister, the voters accepted his program for further price liberalization, budget cuts, and privatization.

On the Slovak side, however, Mečiar won without offering an economic program, but by exploiting nationalism. This outcome is hard to explain, for in mid-1992, polls showed that only 20 percent of Slovaks wanted separation, yet most Slovaks voted for separatists in the elections at about that time. Perhaps they did not realize where Mečiar intended to lead Slovakia. At first he presented the separatist idea only as a moderate call for "confederation" — a less radical proposal than the Slovak National Party's demand for full independence. In the first phases of his move toward separatism, Mečiar was calling for two separate, sovereign states that would be linked by treaty so as to coordinate their economies and well as their foreign and defense policies. He supposed that such a bond would be close enough to ensure the Czechs' continuation of their financial assistance to the Slovaks. In any case, with the centrists out of power, the right and left nationalists faced each other, and serious fighting could be expected to begin.

That expectation was not entirely fulfilled, for shortly after the election more Czechs began to see advantages for themselves in the partition of the two republics. Klaus's impressive victory demonstrated their political will to undertake rapid economic reforms. Czech nationalists began coalescing around the idea of ridding themselves of their "economic burden" — Slovakia. Klaus never took such a position openly, but his actions suggest that he willingly allowed Mečiar to trap himself in his own separatist rhetoric so that he could not easily back away from his political commitments, even when they became manifestly disadvantageous.

The only political leader who struggled at the federal level to hold the country together was President Havel, whose position became increasingly difficult, especially in Slovakia, where he was hated by the extreme nationalists. He continued making public appearances there, though sometimes he was jostled and whistled off the stage. (Czech speakers, including the senior author, learned to expect abuse — including being pelted with eggs — as the price of approaching a podium in Slovakia.) Through all this Havel sought compromise, and before the June 1992 elections he had moved far in accommodating those Slovaks who wanted a confederation in which both sides would be represented equally in all federal bodies. When his concessions were rejected and Mečiar and Klaus were elected, Havel came to regard secession as inevitable. Though he stood for election as federal president, he was defeated by the Slovak deputies and promptly resigned. No other credible political leader could be found who was suitable for the office, and it was therefore left vacant. Soon, however, Havel would serve as president of the Czech Republic, having failed to prevent its becoming independent.

Although the Federal Assembly had not authorized Klaus and Mečiar to negotiate between themselves, and although neither of them had won a majority of the popular vote in his own region, they nevertheless decided the fate of the nation in their own discussions.[12] Klaus rejected any new relationship other than that of a "functional" (which meant strong) federation; Mečiar claimed to be bound by his electoral promise to accept nothing less than increased independence for Slovakia. Knowing that the voters might not accept secession in a referendum, both Klaus and Mečiar decided against holding one, pretending that a referendum was unnecessary and possibly even dangerously provocative. Actually, polls showed that only 37 percent of the Slovaks thought secession was necessary. By then, however, 56 percent of the people of Bohemia and 43 percent in Moravia believed that secession had become necessary. Had a referendum been held, the outcome might have showed so much opposition to partition that it would have been politically impossible to carry it out.

There were some final efforts to avert the separation. In August 1992, the MDS in Slovakia developed a paper that proposed coordinating foreign and defense matters through a joint Council of Ministers of Foreign Affairs. Further, it suggested that citizens of each republic would also be citizens of the Czech-

Slovak Union and that both languages would be official throughout that union. The Czech leaders rejected this confederative compromise, and Prime Minister Strasky also expressed doubt that it would work well.[13]

The Federal Assembly never even discussed the issue until September 11, and by November 25, 1992, it ratified the proposal to dissolve the country. The decision was moot anyway; by August 26 matters had proceeded to the point of no return. Negotiators had agreed to dissolve the federation on January 1, 1993, and had established a schedule for the transition. The republics were supposed to develop laws on interstate cooperation during October. For a period, there would continue to exist a common currency and a common military.

On September 1, the Slovak National Council had adopted a constitution by a vote of 114 to 16, with 4 abstentions. This decision was the final declaration of intent to secede.[14] On January 1, 1993, Czechoslovakia ceased to exist.

The Aftermath

The world did not come to an end in January 1993, but it would be hard to argue that life improved in the former Czechoslovakia. The estrangement between the two new states immediately became official and even colder than is normal between neighboring European countries. They fell to quarreling over the division of common assets and, although they had agreed by treaty to maintain the Czechoslovak koruna as their common currency, the Slovakian economic situation deteriorated so much during the first month of independence that the two republics canceled the treaty and introduced their own national currencies. By February the Czech Republic began to set up border checkpoints, creating a new conflict between the two states that was resolved in April by their agreement to cooperate in introducing customs checks at their common border.[15] Fortunately, there was nearly no ambiguity about the location of that border, so no serious disputes arose between them over territorial claims.

Cross-border trade plummeted, causing alarm on both sides. (More than 25 percent of Czech foreign trade is with Slovakia, and more than 40 percent of Slovak foreign trade is with the Czech Republic.) Because this trade involved hard currency, of which the Slovak government lacked sufficient reserves, many Czech companies stopped exporting to Slovakia after the currency split.[16] Within months, a majority of Slovakia's major companies were threatened with bankruptcy.[17] Slovakia's trade deficit with the rest of the world also increased, and it attracted very little foreign investment in comparison to the Czech Republic, Hungary, or Poland.[18]

The Slovaks had elected parties promising a gentler path of economic reform than Klaus's way, but when their new state became free to pursue such a course, they suffered a deeper recession than the Czechs. Slovak industrial production declined by about 15 percent during the first three quarters of 1993, and unemployment increased from 10.4 percent at the time of the split to 13.8 percent by

October 31.[19] (In January 1997 it was still 12.3 percent.) The country remains dependent on raw material and energy from Russia.

In economic terms the Czechs fared considerably better than the Slovaks during the first three years of independence, though their economy also suffered from the separation. During the first few months of 1993, the Czech economy contracted and foreign investment fell short of expectations.

Václav Klaus now could pursue privatization and price liberalization along the lines he preferred. Though described in the early days as "shock therapy," his austerity program was actually not austere enough, for the foreign debt of the Czech Republic increased from $8.5 billion at the time of independence to $19.6 billion in August 1997. Formerly one of the East European countries with the lowest level of foreign indebtedness, it became one of those with the highest.[20] The currency underwent a crisis of confidence in May 1997, and six months later Klaus's government fell amid accusations of financial impropriety.[21]

Both of the new countries experienced crises involving minorities and citizenship rules. There had been high rates of intermarriage and social contact between Czechs and Slovaks during their union, but afterward dual citizenship was not allowed. The main reason for this was the approximately 500,000 Roma people in Slovakia, many of whom would have migrated to the Czech Republic if they had been free to do so. Some 200,000 Roma live in Czechia, and in both countries they became victims of increased violence from skinheads and other nationalist groups. In September 1993 Prime Minister Mečiar explicitly referred to them in a speech calling for a reduction of welfare payments so that "the extensive reproduction of socially unadaptable and mentally retarded people drops."[22]

Several other minorities found their status insecure in the new Slovakia. There is a Czech population of 50,000, a Ruthenian-Ukrainian population of 40,000 (which began calling themselves a nation and demanding new bilingual signs and other rights), and a community of 600,000 Hungarians concentrated along the border with Hungary. Even before, and especially after, independence the Hungarians found their linguistic rights attacked. They had preferred to remain within the common Czechoslovak state, since they worried about a republic-level language law that already in 1990 limited the use of non-Slovak languages. After independence their rights were further reduced by legislation prohibiting Hungarian place names and bilingual signs, exacerbating Slovakia's old conflict with the Hungarian state.[23] From time to time, particular complaints of the Hungarian minority are labeled as "irredentist" by Slovak officials as a way of offering the public some visible enemies. Czechs and Hungarians are used interchangeably to satisfy this need.

Since independence the Czechs have, for the first time in history, become a monocultural society. Czech Jews were killed in World War II; Ruthenians on the eastern side of the state were lost after Stalin demanded that President Beneš cede this part of "Ukraine"; most Czech Germans were expelled after that same war, and the remainder have assimilated; and with the elimination of the Slovak and Hungarian population by secession, an upsurge of chauvinism emerged against remaining non-Czechs, especially the Vietnamese and Roma, many of whom attempted to emigrate to Canada and Britain.

In their foreign relations, both states found themselves facing new tensions after independence, in part owing to their diminished size. The claims of the Sudeten Germans for compensation again became current. The Czechs immediately became more fearful of Germany; by accepting partition they had made it possible to argue, for the first time since World War II, that the Munich Pact was understandable. This explanation could be given: "You see — not just we Germans wanted to leave the illiberal "Czech state," but so too did the Slovaks! And they did leave at the first opportunity."

Slovakia's international tensions are primarily with Hungary, which threatened to block Slovakia's entry into the Council of Europe in June 1993. In order to forestall this, Slovakia promised to modify certain of its regulations (such as by allowing Hungarian women to omit the Slavic ending "-ova" from their last names) as recommended by the Council. Once admitted to the organization, however, Hungary did not keep its promises, leading to new complaints by legal experts from the Conference on Security and Cooperation in Europe.[24] The main source of conflict with Hungary concerned the Gabčikovo-Nagymaros dams and hydroelectric power stations on the Danube River, which had been undertaken jointly by a 1977 agreement. After the fall of their Communist regime, environmentalists in Hungary were able to block their government's participation by showing that the dam would create grave ecological damage. Slovakia did not refer the case to the International Court of Justice until it had diverted the water. The court ruled in 1997 that both countries must complete the project as agreed, but relations between them remain unfriendly.

The Czechs progressed more smoothly in developing democratic institutions than the Slovaks and were accordingly welcomed more readily into the international community. They were among the first group of formerly socialist countries invited to join NATO and the European Union. The Slovaks, on the other hand, made very little progress toward liberal democracy — and indeed lost ground under Mečiar's leadership. They were rejected for membership in the European Union and NATO because of their flawed human rights record, their violations of the rules of parliamentary democracy, their misuse of the secret police against critics of the government, their pressure on the mass media, and their intertwining of political and economic power.

Instead of restoring old brotherly ties, both of the new states have maintained exceptionally frosty relations with each other since the split. Klaus and Mečiar did not even meet again until 1997, though they had promised to do so several times a year. The intention behind this unfriendliness is deliberately to eliminate any remaining doubts that the partition was necessary. Accordingly, many people have come to say, "I see now that the breakup was inevitable. What they have been doing proves that we could not have gone on living with such people as that." Czechoslovakia is truly dead and will never live again.

Lessons

It would be a mistake to conclude that, because Slovak nationalists began the maneuvers toward separatism, their side was solely responsible for the eventual partition of the Czechoslovakia. Clearly the outcome resulted from a convergence of interests on both sides. If the Slovak separatists' interests were mostly symbolic — a desire for a more equal status with their Czech partners — the Czech separatists' interests were mostly material — a desire to end the economic burden of subsidizing a less developed region of the country and to be "liberated" to pursue more aggressive right-wing policies. The leaders of the Czech side did not openly express these preferences but allowed the Slovak leaders to "paint themselves into a corner" by claiming to want independence when they probably were issuing that demand only as a bargaining ploy. Only a minority of Slovaks evidently ever wanted independence, and as its likely financial implications became more obvious, many of those people changed their minds — or would have done so if a face-saving alternative had been available. But Václav Klaus took Mečiar at his word and declined every opportunity to save the country. The outcome is not only negative in terms of its objective consequences but shows the ineffectiveness of those new democratic institutions that were supposed to allow the citizens of Czechoslovakia to choose their own fate.

There are at least five lessons for the rest of the world to learn from the demise of Czechoslovakia. They are as follows:

First, the fact that a secession takes place does not prove that most of the citizens wanted it. Even though nationalism is almost always at a high pitch during the conflict over partition, there are always some people who are not nationalists and who cannot control the situation. The Czechoslovak instance is not the only case of a secession that was unwanted by most of the citizens. The breakup of the Soviet Union was another such case, and there are many others. This suggests that if the leaders of the country cannot themselves preserve the rights of the people, the international community has some responsibility to do so. It is customary for other countries to keep hands off, on the grounds that the issue is a domestic affair into which outsiders should not interfere. Probably not much direct intervention was appropriate in this case, since most Czechs and Slovaks came to the end with a sense of fatal resignation rather than bloodshed. However, this was not a chosen outcome — either by the majority of citizens or by the minorities whose interests were also at stake. In the absence of a referendum, the decision was legal but not fully legitimate and therefore deserves no praise. Democratic institutions need to be invented and established that can prevent such unwanted consequences in the future.

Second, there are many stakeholders whose interests and rights are involved in any case of separatism. Political decisions ought to be made with a full recognition that some minorities may suffer greatly and unfairly from a decision that may benefit one sector of the population—including sometimes (but not in this case) the majority of the voters. Even if a referendum were held, and even if a clear majority voted for secession, this outcome would not necessarily be fair to a minority of citizens, whose fundamental rights might be trampled upon. Democracy does not mean only that the majority wins; it also means that the rights of minorities are protected from the dominant majority. Yet this consideration is often ignored. In this case, the Slovaks, who started the move toward secession, have suffered more from it than the Czechs. With goodwill, far better solutions to the Slovaks' grievances could have been developed, while protecting the rights of other minorities, most notably the Roma and Hungarians of Slovakia.

Third, this case offers yet another disproof of economic determinism. Certain short-term Czech economic interests did play a part in bringing this conflict to the point of partition. However, the outcome was clearly detrimental to the Slovaks' economic interests. Nevertheless, the Slovaks bear a large part of the responsibility for the outcome, partly because for a long time they refused to acknowledge that they were being subsidized by the Czechs but even more because their national pride was aroused. The sense of ethnic humiliation may have little basis in objective circumstances but may be powerful nevertheless. Because very different interests of separatists on both sides happened to coincide, the political leaders used their power to bring about partition.

Fourth, we should address the question whether decentralization helps to prevent secessions or, on the contrary, encourages them. Since separatists generally begin their demands by calling for more autonomy, and since the federalists tend to resist that demand, it is often suggested after a partition takes place that it might have been avoided if the federal government had acquiesced to the initial demands.

In fact, it is impossible to reach any definite conclusion on the basis of evidence from particular cases. If Gorbachev had given limited autonomy to Lithuania in 1989, would the Lithuanians still be satisfied with that concession? If Yeltsin had given the same degree of autonomy to Chechnya that Tatarstan received, would Chechens still be contented members of the Russian Federation? We cannot be sure. Yugoslavia was an extremely decentralized state, yet it came apart. Switzerland is an equally decentralized state that seems unlikely to come apart. In Czechoslovakia, the relative autonomy of the two parts may have made it all the easier for the federal government's power to decrease and even dissolve completely. Arguably, no demand for independence would have arisen if there had not already been two states with separate identities and partial independence. We cannot say, however, whether the policy of fully integrating two regions politically would have been more satisfactory than the limited autonomy that, in this case, gave rise to a call for total autonomy.

Fifth and finally, we turn to the question that is most commonly posed with respect to the Czechoslovakian case: Why did it happen that this country, almost alone, broke up without violence? Is there a lesson here for separatists in other countries?

Robert Young has offered a plausible answer to this question. He notes that Czechoslovakia was unusual in that it already comprised only two republics. Initially, the Slovak leaders presented their grievances to the political bodies at the federal level. However, their real counterpart within the federation was the Czech Republic, and it seemed more appropriate for them to negotiate directly with the Czechs. To the extent that power was devolved to the level of the republics' national councils and they took over management of their dispute, the federal government correspondingly relinquished power. So quickly did its importance diminish that the federal government ceased being an attractive venue for serious politicians who wanted to participate in the big issues of the day. Young reports that in late 1992, there was "virtually no leading representative of any major party in the federal government."[25] Indeed, when President Havel himself resigned, he too indicated his readiness to stand for election to the presidency of the soon-to-be-independent Czech Republic. In Marx's language, the federal state simply "withered away"; no traumatic blow was necessary to destroy it.

Very few other separatist movements face a similar situation. In Canada, for example, the Quebec government's interlocutor in the question of separatism is the federal government of Canada, which comprises ten provinces and two territories. The federal government could not wither away while devolving its powers. There are, in fact, few countries in the world that are in this sense structurally conducive to "velvet divorce."

Notes

1. This situation was comparable to that existing at the same time in the Soviet Union, where only Russia, among all the Union Republics, lacked a government or Communist Party of its own — a fact that revealed its dominant status in the Union.

2. Alexander Dubček, *Hope Dies Last: The Autobiography of Alexander Dubček*, ed. and trans. Jiří Hochman (New York: Kodansha, 1993) 149, 154, and appendix, "The Action Program," 287-339.

3. Janusz Bugajski, *Czechoslovakia: Charter 77's Decade of Dissent* (New York: Praeger, 1987), 24, 88.

4. Milan Kucera and Zdenek Pavlik, "Czech and Slovak Demography," in *The End of Czechoslovakia*, ed. Jiří Musil (Budapest: Central European University Press, 1995), 15-39.

5. Theodore Draper, "The End of Czechoslovakia," *New York Review of Books* January 28, 1993, 23.

6. Václav Prucha, "Economic Development and Relations, 1918-89," in Musil, *The End of Czechoslovakia*, 69.

7. Draper, "The End of Czechoslovakia," 25.

8. Robert A. Young, *The Breakup of Czechoslovakia* (Kingston, Ontario: Queens University Institute of Inter-Governmental Relations, 1994), 31.

9. Sharon L. Wolchik, "The Politics of Transition and the Break-Up of Czechoslovakia," in Musil, *The End of Czechoslovakia*, 231.

10. Young, *The Breakup of Czechoslovakia*, 30-31.

11. Young, *The Breakup of Czechoslovakia*, 32.

12. Wolchik, "The Politics of Transition," 240.

13. Young, *The Breakup of Czechoslovakia*, 28.

14. Young, *The Breakup of Czechoslovakia*, 28-29.

15. Jiří Pehe, "Czech-Slovak Relations Deteriorate," RFE/RL, April 30, 1993, 1.

16. Pehe, "Czech-Slovak Relations Deteriorate."

17. "Polls Reveal Gloomy Mood Among Slovaks," *RFE/RL Research Bulletin,* May 7, 1993, 1.

18. Sharon Fisher, "Slovakia Heads Towards International Isolation," *Transition*, January 10, 1997.

19. Sharon Fisher, "Slovakia: The First Year of Independence," *Radio Free Europe Research Bulletin on Eastern Europe*, Vol. 3, No. 1, January 1994, 88-89.

20. *Mlada Fronta Dnes*, September 1, 1997.

21. Breffni O'Rourke, "The Fall of Václav Klaus," *RFE/RL* December 2, 1997.

22. Sharon Fisher, "Romanies in Slovakia," *RFE/RL Research Report* October 22, 1993.

23. Matthew Rhodes, "National Identity and Minority Rights in the Constitutions of the Czech Republic and Slovakia," *East European Quarterly* XXIX, No. 3, September 1995, 358-59.

24. Rhodes, "National Identity and Minority Rights," 362.

25. Young, *The Breakup of Czechoslovakia*, 35.

Nine

Chechen Separatism

Victor Kogan Iasnyi and Diana Zisserman-Brodsky[1]

Is Chechnya a sovereign state or a republic within Russia? This question cannot be answered definitively yet, but, according to the terms of a peace accord, the republic's status must be decided before December 31, 2001. Meanwhile the Russian government treats Chechnya in most respects as an autonomous country while insisting that it is far from independent. In practical terms, Chechnya's degree of independence is far greater than might have been anticipated when the Soviet Union was dissolved at the end of 1991. Paradoxically, its transformation evidently resulted to a great degree from unintended consequences of actions by both Chechen and Russian political and military leaders, who waged a war of secession from November 1994 until August 1996. Though the entire story of this struggle may never be known, this chapter constitutes an attempt to piece together as much of it as possible.

Chechnya and Its People

Chechnya is a small region in a crossroads between mountain ranges in the North Caucasus. Somewhat more than half the inhabitants belong to the Chechen ethnic group, while the remainder are Ingushes, Russians, Ukrainians, Jews, Armenians, and others. The Ingush people are closely related to the Chechens; they intermarry, and at times their lands, Ingushetia and Chechnya, have been united as a single Soviet republic. Both groups speak mutually intelligible Caucasian languages that are distinct from all the nearby Slavic, Turkic, and Persian languages.[2]

Between the seventeenth and the mid-nineteenth century the Chechens became converted to a Sunni branch of Islam, and the Sufi mystic tradition became prominent. By Sufi custom each disciple should be submissive to the sect's leader and there is a glorification of holy wars against the "infidels." However, though the Islam of Chechnya remains a culture of warriors, it is not a fundamentalist faith.

Chechnya has long been a geopolitical crossroads of importance to Russia. In the 1830s the tsar sought to impose complete political and military dominance over the area. For more than twenty-five years, his army fought against the fiercely independent Chechen mountaineers, many of whom then emigrated or were deported, especially to the Ottoman Empire. Nevertheless, even as recently as the early twentieth century, Chechens were still carrying out occasional acts of armed resistance against the Russians.

After the Bolsheviks took over in the North Caucasus, the area populated by the Chechens and Ingushes passed through a number of administrative transformations before being reorganized into an autonomous republic in 1936.[3] It was allocated an area of 15,700 square kilometers for its population of 700,000.

In 1940 (long before the war) and 1942 (as the Germans were approaching the North Caucasus) a number of uprisings broke out over the Chechen territory. These uprisings were anti-Russian and anti-Soviet.[4] Stalin ordered the Chechens' deportation; both they and the Ingushes were shipped off in 1944 to the east (mainly Kazakhstan) in freight trains and their republic was liquidated. An estimated 80 percent of the two groups were deported, of whom about one-third died during the first year of this ordeal.[5] Many survivors began returning home without permission after Stalin's death, and eventually the USSR Supreme Soviet rescinded their deportation orders, without however preparing their return. The Chechen-Ingush Autonomous Republic was restored, but the people did not forget that tragic period.

In the late 1990s the republic (which Chechens now officially call *Ichkeria*) occupies about 17,000 square kilometers in the eastern Caucasus. In the west it borders on Ingushetia (once again separate); the border with Dagestan lies to the east and north; the North Ossetian Republic and Stavropol Krai lie to the northwest; and independent Georgia lies to the south over the mountains.

The Soviet Union was a complicated quasi-federation with multiple levels. On the first level were fifteen so-called union republics, such as the Baltic republics, Georgia, Armenia, Azerbaijan, Moldova, Belorussia, Ukraine, the Central Asian republics, and of course the largest, Russia. Inside some of them, particularly inside the Russian Federation (RSFSR), were several levels of autonomous units with rights that were more restricted than the union republics. Chechnya was one of four "autonomous soviet republics" (ASSRs) of the

Russian Federation in which the titular nationality (Chechens) constituted an absolute majority of the population — 58 percent.[6]

The districts that now constitute part of Chechnya listed 1,084,000 inhabitants in the 1989 census, of whom 715,000 were Chechens.[7] The total population of Chechnya had declined to 850,000 by 1996, because of war deaths and the mass emigration of Russians.[8]

The proportion of Chechens among the total population of the Chechen-Ingush Autonomous Republic had been growing since its reestablishment in 1957. The Ingush and Chechens have one of the highest population growth rates of all North Caucasian peoples. By 2000 there are expected to be about 920,000 of them within the Chechen republic.

The Chechen Economy

Traditionally, the Chechens were farmers and herdsmen, and they still are predominantly rural people, though industries also exist in the cities. The production of consumer goods was given low priority, even by Soviet standards. For example, the food processing industry and agriculture were not as well developed as in neighboring Russian areas.[9] However, the capital city, Grozny, is a hub of transportation: railways, roads, and especially oil and gas pipelines.

Oil has been the most important factor in the region's economy for a long time; as early as 1893 the oil fields surrounding Grozny were exploited, and the city became a center of refining and petrochemical production. Jobs in these fields attracted many Russians; Grozny's population grew from 97,000 (68,000 Russians) in 1926 to 397,000 (210,000 Russians) in 1989.[10] (Most victims of the 1994 bombings of Grozny were Russians, not Chechens.)

Moreover, numerous countries and transnational companies have been vying for control of huge oil and gas reserves in the Caspian Sea and in the Central Asian republics. These resources are of global significance, for they will constitute a large part of the world's fuel sources in the next century. The oil reserves are estimated at over 25 billion barrels — similar to those in Kuwait and larger than the amount in Alaska's Northern Slope and the North Sea combined.[11] The known oil reserves in Chechnya itself are of very high quality, and Chechen oil-refining and processing capacity is assessed as 12 million tonnes.[12]

It is difficult to establish empirically the extent to which the wars in the post-Soviet Transcaucasus have been influenced by the rivalry of governments for control of these deposits, the existing oil pipelines, and the next pipelines that are to be built. Oil pipelines will be of great geopolitical significance well into the next century. If pipelines are built outside Russia, the newly independent states will become more self-sufficient (acquiring large incomes from transit fees or royalties on production), whereas Russia will lose a major part of its influence in the Caucasus and Central Asia. The existing Baku-Novorossiisk oil supply line has strategic importance to southern Russia, Ukraine, Azerbaijan, Georgia, and Armenia. It runs from Baku, Azerbaijan, under Grozny, past the

Russian city of Tikhoretsk, and ends at the Russian Black Sea port of Novorossiisk, where Russia intends to situate a terminal for additional pipelines from Kazakhstan and Azerbaijan.[13] (One alternative plan, supported by Western states and oil companies, but of course not by Russia, would have Azerbaijan's Caspian oil flow through Georgia to the Black Sea, whence it would be exported by tanker to Turkey and Europe, bypassing Russia altogether.)[14] These and other complex pipeline proposals will have to be sorted out in the aftermath of the war between the Russian Federation and the separatist Chechen republic. Perhaps oil interests played a big part in causing that war; if so, however, no one seems able to document the nature of the rivalry or name the interests that were involved.

Myths about Chechens

Popular prejudices about the Chechens have influenced scholarly studies of their collective identity. Analysts of Chechen society have tended to describe it as a community isolated from the process of development, with traditional, underdeveloped social organization based on clan structure and *shari'at* law.[15] Russian authors, especially, depicted Chechen assertiveness as resistance against the modernization of traditional tribal society. According to their accounts, tribal consciousness and clan interests took precedence over a nationwide political identity, so that social mobilization by nationalist ideas should hardly be possible. Russian experts tend to hold that the preservation of clan structure was the main impetus for separatist demands.[16]

Another misperception relates to the "religiosity" of the Chechens. Many Soviet scholars overestimated this factor[17] while underestimating the *national* identity of the Chechens and other North Caucasian Muslim people. In fact, ethno-linguistic bonds were a more important aspect of identity than the shared Muslim religion. Religion failed to keep ethnic political divisions from arising between different Muslim communities in Dagestan and elsewhere. Muslim solidarity expressed by political leaders was not translated into political actions in either the Georgian-Abkhazian or the Russian-Chechen conflicts.[18] The decorated Soviet general Dzhokhar Dudaev, who became the nation's leader, hardly resembled a pan-Islamic chief but rather a modern nationalist leader. His idea of independence was inspired not by holy books but rather by his Estonian friends from the Popular Front in the early years of perestroika. The more recent candidates for the presidency of the Chechen Republic also have typically secular Soviet backgrounds.

Reference to Islam is an important rhetorical device of modern Chechen political leaders. However, the idea of merging religious and state authorities was rejected by all the candidates for the presidency, including the pro-Islamic candidates[19] and even by the Muslim clergy. As a mullah from a Chechen village explained, "It's the business of politicians — not us — to run the country."[20]

The Chechens' Islamic tradition is moderate. Chechen women do not have to wear veils over their faces or flowing robes (although since the war, some of them do so) and may even be accepted as Sufi leaders (*sheikhs*). The Chechens also demonstrate rather liberal attitudes toward the use of alcohol. Sufism had merged with the struggle against Russian domination. Sufi activities are often centered around various holy places, the tombs of saints (often Sufi leaders who died fighting the Russians).[21] To a degree Sufism served in the North Caucasus as a counterpart of political dissent.[22] Moreover, dissident nationalist movements in the former USSR described their ethnic groups as practicing a kind of "national religion."[23] Religion nevertheless served as a subordinate factor in the ideologies and politics of nationalism. As elsewhere throughout the Soviet Union, the majority of people in Chechnya did not receive any religious education but were taught atheism and Marxist internationalism. Insofar as religion was practiced at all, it was an underground Islam during those years and only in the 1990s did it become a newly accepted outlook for the majority of Chechens.

Self-Determination

Although the Bolsheviks declared their policy as favoring "self-determination of peoples" in 1917, the Chechens were incorporated into the Russian Soviet Socialist Republic, and then into the Soviet Union with very little autonomy, even in the formal sense. However, the *principle* of self-determination — the right to secede — was never seriously questioned in the Soviet Union, either by the Communists or in the later years by their democratic critics. Indeed, the right was guaranteed by law, though there was no genuine possibility of achieving secession until the Soviet Union itself was on the verge of disintegrating. No liberal critique of the principle of self-determination was articulated.

The Soviet concept of self-determination maintained as an unwritten law that the titular nationality should constitute an absolute majority in the total population of a union republic, since only union republics enjoyed, hypothetically, the right to secede.

Though no official document specified the number of inhabitants required as basis for demanding secession, the population of the Chechen-Ingush ASSR was fairly comparable with the percentages in some other union republics, such as Estonia, that won their demand to become independent states.

By 1990, as in many other regions of the former Soviet Union, demands for self-determination were increasing in Chechnya. However, not only internally but internationally, there were no accepted norms governing this right. The concepts of a "people" and of "self-determination" are not clearly defined. When it came to Chechnya, foreign leaders were able to maintain an ambiguous position: "We are for peace, but the situation is an internal affair of Russia's" — a formulation that gratified the "party of war," as the Russians came to be called who sought to suppress separatism by military action. The post-Soviet Russian government had not immediately specified any rules governing the autonomy of its subunits, or any principles regarding the use of its army in domestic conflicts. This prolonged ambiguity was to result in warfare.

After the breakup of the USSR, Chechnya gained, by Soviet normative standards, an important legitimizing argument for its demand of secession: a shared border with a foreign state, the newly independent Georgia. This aspect of the Soviet concept of the right to self-determination was respected by the nationalist movements. For example, the Tatar-Bashkir movement, which was oriented to secession, did not consider it a realistic option until a corridor could be created between Tatarstan and Kazakhstan with their numerically dominant Muslim or Turkic populace. This would provide that territory with a compact Muslim population and borders with foreign states, so that it would then have a legitimate right to make separatist demands.[24]

During his competition with Gorbachev, who represented the authority of the union, Yeltsin did not institute any new normative standards but exploited nationalism. After nationalism had served him, he decided to change the standards, but they had become deeply rooted in collective perception and could not be reshaped by the mere adoption of new laws. This fact was not realized by Yeltsin's administration when it decided to ban secession by ethnic units. The rebellious faction refused to accept the new rules.

The Chechen nationalist movement had emerged before the breakup of the USSR, albeit without radical demands. It probably would have remained too weak to achieve statehood had the Russian army not intervened. However, it can be explained by neither social backwardness nor "religiosity." Instead, as an ordinary secular political movement of national identity, it can be explained adequately in terms of three well-known theories of modern nationalism, which are worth reviewing here.

Theories of Nationalism

One explanation of nationalism was offered by Karl Deutsch in his *mobilization-assimilation* theory. According to Deutsch, if the rate of social mobilization is greater than that of assimilation to the dominant culture, the balance in a state system is disturbed and nationalism is likely to emerge.[25]

Because the Soviet Union was committed to preserving ethno-cultural differences, one cannot expect to find high rates of assimilation among the former Soviet nationalities. The rates of retaining the native language among the Chechens are high, despite their fifteen to twenty years of deportation to Siberia or Kazakhstan, where they lacked national schools and a press.[26] In 1959, fully 99 percent of the total Chechens claimed their vernacular as the native language and the same percentage was reported in 1979. In 1989 only 2 percent of all Chechens used Russian as their native language. A comparison of these data to the rates of linguistic assimilation of another deported nationality, the Soviet Germans, would show a striking difference: in 1959, 75 percent of all Germans claimed German as their mother tongue. This dropped to 67 percent in 1970 and 49 percent in 1989.

Still, in 1989 some 74 percent of the total Chechens claimed proficiency in the Russian language. For comparison, only 56 percent of the Ukrainians and 36 percent of the Estonians said they had a good command of Russian.

On the one hand, the Chechens refuse to be assimilated into the "higher culture" (their linguistic nonassimilation is highlighted by extremely low rates of mixed marriages). On the other hand, their mass fluency in Russian attests on the high level of accommodation to the "higher culture." The level of fluency in a language of the host society seems almost irrelevant to the emergence of nationalism. The combination of nonassimilation and accommodation may equally encourage ethnopolitical assertiveness and integration into the wider society on the basis of multiculturalism.

A second theory — the theory of *internal colonialism* — also helps explain Chechen nationalism.[27] This model sees socioeconomic stratification, in which class and ethnicity coincide, as a result of a premeditated state policy dividing labor along cultural lines. The relationship between Chechen ethnicity and socio-economic opportunity can be seen in the nature of the region's economy.

The socioeconomic organization in the Chechen-Ingush Autonomous Republic during the Soviet period retained its typically colonial structure. There were practically no Chechens among the industrial management, professionals, scientific workers, civil administration, and high-ranked party functionaries. Russian sources admitted that "specific conditions of Chechen national development made many of them unprepared for work in modern industries."[28]

As an explanation for egregious inequality, this is disingenuous. The truth is that the extermination of the tiny stratum of the Chechen intelligentsia during the 1930s purges, the genocide of the 1940s, and subsequent restrictions on their enrollment into institutes of the higher education were premeditated political decisions that *suppressed* the integration of the exiled people into the modern society. The results for the Chechen people proved devastating. In 1963 there were 106 males and 13 females per 1,000 urban dwellers of Chechen origin with more than elementary school education. The next lowest Soviet rates are found among the Kabardinian males — 220 per thousand — and Tajik females — 165 per thousand — which cannot even be compared to those of the Chechens. In 1975 the Chechens demonstrated the lowest rates of higher education as well; there were 9 specialists with higher education per 1,000 Chechens (or 0.9 percent). There were counted only 13 scientific workers per 100,000 Chechens. Next in rank order were the Bashkirs with 68.[29]

These facts are consistent with a theory of "internal colonialism." The suppression of Chechens' socioeconomic status was not accidental but surely arose from official policies of overt discrimination and, in the earlier periods, even persecution. One cannot be surprised, therefore, that nationalism emerged in

Chechnya; what is surprising is that initially it generated only limited aspirations for independence.

A third theory that partially explains the Chechen case is that of *relative deprivation*. Like the theory of internal colonialism, it holds that nationalist behavior is stimulated by the resentment over being positioned unfavorably in comparison to one or more other ethnic communities. Any difference between the two models is only a matter of emphasis, for these are compatible approaches. While internal colonialism theory stresses the *actual facts of deprivation*, relative deprivation theory focuses on the *collective perception* of ethnic communities as to their statuses.

Studying the issue of relative deprivation, some scholars have concluded that what was important in provoking nationalist militant behavior is not so much personally experienced deprivation as a general concern over the fate of the nation, an attitude that might be called "fraternal deprivation."

In his speech at the second convention of the National Chechen Congress in June 1991, Dudaev described the USSR as a colonial empire, pointing out that the Chechen nation had been robbed of its "religion, language, education, science, culture, natural resources, ideology, mass media, leadership cadres, and rights to freedom and life."[30] Unfortunately, nothing in Dudaev's speech was a rhetorical exaggeration. After the deportation all mosques in the territory of the disbanded autonomous republic had been closed, and the first one was reopened only in 1978. During the exile there was not a single school where the Chechen language was taught. In 1970 the circulation of the republican newspapers in Russian totaled 90,000 copies, while the circulation in Chechen did not exceed 16,000 copies.

Scholars studying relative deprivation have found that symbolic images play a more important role than actual grievances.[31] The perception of deprivation reflects not so much an immediate state of affairs as a symbolic image of "accumulated" national grievances. Past and present, real and insinuated, may be compressed into one symbolic image. In his speeches, Dudaev pointed to "three centuries of the uninterrupted warfare" (to wit: the Russian war of conquest of the eighteenth and nineteenth centuries, the 1920-21 war, the elimination of the Mountain Republic, the deportation under Stalin, and the subsequent annihilation of one third of the Chechen population).[32]

From the very beginning, Russian rule in the Caucasus was based on force. In the nineteenth century the Russian administration in Chechnya and Dagestan used such methods as blowing up the house of a suspect, killing the family inside, and allocating Chechen women to Russian officers.[33]

The deportation of the Chechens in February 1944 was accompanied by unprecedented cruelty. In some remote mountain areas where an order to clear the territory of Chechens within twenty-four hours could not be accomplished on time, those who could not move quickly enough — pregnant women, children, and the elderly — were gathered together and massacred.[34]

The 1956 rehabilitation of the deported peoples and then the restoration of the Chechen-Ingush Autonomous Republic in 1957 did not bring reconciliation. The homecoming had been poorly prepared, heightening tensions between the returning Chechens and Ingush and those who had settled on their land and homes.[35] In 1957 anti-Chechen riots took place in Grozny. The rebels displayed such slogans as "Down with Checheno-Ingush autonomy" and "Kill the Chechens." Participants of the anti-Chechen pogroms received lenient sentences.[36]

Stereotypes of ethnic minority groups, as portrayed by the ethnic majority, are an important factor in the symbolic deprivation felt by these minorities.[37] No other negative ethnic image in the USSR could be compared with that of the people of the Caucasian origin in general and the Chechens in particular. The "Chechen Mafia" became a cliché long before the outbreak of Chechen separatism.

Regardless of how much factual support could be adduced regarding this cliché, it was unquestionably embellished by Russian prejudice — and it must have injured Chechen dignity. The Russian leaders seem to have believed that the Chechen separatism was only an epiphenomenon of a struggle between criminalized clans and that, as Vice-President Aleksandr Rutskoi stated, Dudaev's supporters did not exceed 250 bandits.[38]

A sense of relative deprivation involves the minority's social comparison[39] of itself to the dominant ethnic group or to "all others."[40] Another comparison also seems essential for nationalist movements: a comparison against the society's *own normative standards.*[41] In the USSR paramount significance was given to the right to self-determination — especially the right of secession. This normative principle was questioned by neither the opponents nor the champions of the Soviet regime. When social comparison was made between candidates for secession, Chechnya actually shared most of basic geographic and demographic characteristics with the former Soviet socialist republics that secured their right to secession.

Let us sum up this discussion of nationalism by noting that the Chechen movement for independence is far from unique. Indeed, it is an ordinary phenomenon in today's world, and it can be explained within the same framework as hundreds of other modern, secular nationalistic movements. The Chechens did not assimilate into Soviet society but retained their own culture and language while accommodating to the dominant Russian culture. They were therefore readily positioned for nationalism, especially since they had long been conspicuously subjected to discrimination and to symbolic affronts to their collective status. The emergence of nationalism should not surprise anyone familiar with their history. Nevertheless, Chechen nationalism initially was not sufficient to win independence; ironically, it was the Russian political and military leaders who strengthened the sentiment by attacking the republic.

The Emergence of Chechen Separatism

At first the growth of Chechen nationalism was regarded as a political anomaly. The nationalist demands of the Baltic peoples, Crimean Tatars, and Georgians had been formulated long before and were widely known, but the sudden development of radical demands by the Chechen movement was initially perceived as only a tribute to fashionable nationalistic rhetoric. These demands appeared in November 1990 at the inaugural meeting of the Pan-national Congress of the Chechen People (hereafter the Chechen Congress). The delegates represented a spectrum of political orientations ranging from moderate Communists (including the chairman of the republic's Supreme Soviet, Doku Zavgaev) to liberal democrats to advocates of the Islamic path. The Congress, which had elected the retired Soviet general Dzhokhar Dudaev as chair of its executive committee, proved to be politically influential. After the convention the Supreme Soviet of the Chechen-Ingush Autonomous Republic declared the republic's sovereignty on November 27, 1990. (Earlier, in August 1990, sovereignty had been proclaimed by Tatarstan. Both of these autonomous republics were imitating the Russian Federation, which had proclaimed its sovereignty on June 12, 1990.)

Originally the nationalists' objectives were rather modest — to escape from the Russian federation and to elevate their country from the status of an *autonomous* to a *union* republic. This would enable them to sign a union treaty with the USSR on the equal basis with the other fifteen former union republics.[42]

The second convention of the Chechen Congress (June 8-9, 1991), enunciated more radical demands and rhetoric.[43] Calling for early elections of the Chechen president and parliament, for adoption of a new constitution and a law on citizenship, and for a referendum on the status of the republic, the Chechen Congress set conditions for signing a treaty with the USSR or the RSFSR. These conditions included a demand for the trial of those guilty of the crimes of genocide against the Chechen nation, payment of compensation for these crimes, establishment of a government structure based on democratic principles, and "unconditional recognition of the right of the Chechen nation to sovereign independence."[44] This last demand was made in correspondence with the RSFSR's own "Declaration of State Sovereignty," which declared that its sovereignty had been proclaimed to secure the right of "every people to self-determination in their chosen national-state and national-cultural form." All such declarations are regarded by some specialists as contrary to the Soviet constitution, but Yeltsin — then campaigning for election to the Russian presidency — was appealing to the non-Russian voters by promising to maximize the autonomy of all the republics inside Russia, including Chechnya. The new Union Treaty that was then being negotiated had already proposed to treat these internal republics as equal to the

Soviet republics. There is a controversy over the matter, with some arguing that, had it been adopted, it would have undermined the territorial integrity of Russia. Thus the status of autonomous republics such as Chechnya was a pawn in the struggle between the centralizing Soviet leader, Gorbachev, and the Russian Federation leader, Yeltsin.

During the August 19-21 attempted coup in Moscow, the Chechen National Congress and in particular its chair, Dzhokhar Dudaev, spoke decisively against the junta, fully supporting the actions of the Russian president. A big rally, launched as a protest against the putsch on August 19, turned out to be a ten-week-long demonstration by the forces of opposition against the pro-Communist leaders of the republic, most of whom had failed to take any stand during the putsch.

Though barely meeting the standards of contemporary democracy, the energetic actions of the Chechen Congress resulted in the disbanding of the Supreme Soviet of the republic. A Provisional Council was appointed, composed of representatives from the major political factions, and it called parliamentary and presidential elections.

Unexpectedly, the RSFSR leadership not only failed to reciprocate the support that the Chechen Congress had given them during the recent putsch but demonstrated increasing animosity toward them and Dudaev.[45] In fact, this policy contributed to building the new Chechen political identity by helping to unite the Chechen people against a common enemy.

On November 27, 1991, Chechnya's presidential elections were held, and 72 percent of the eligible voters participated. Of those voting, about 90 percent supported Dudaev; three other candidates received the remaining 10 percent of the votes. Nevertheless, the Russian authorities declared the elections illegitimate — an assertion that remains debatable.[46] As critics Emil' Pain and Arkady Popov point out, the population of some regions of the republic that disagreed with Dudaev's proposals were excluded from the election; the campaign lasted only two weeks and took place under a state of emergency; and there were numerous violations of the elections procedures.[47] The famous human rights activist Sergei Kovalev agrees that "Dudaev's legitimacy was far from indisputable."[48] On the other hand, some international observers did not consider that the norms of democracy had been violated,[49] and the editor of *Nezavisimaia gazeta*, V. Tretiakov, predicted in an editorial that the failure of the Russian authorities to accept Dudaev as a legitimate president and to negotiate with him would have catastrophic effects.

Soon after the presidential election the Russian authorities offered encouragement to Dudaev's opponents. President Yeltsin proclaimed a state of emergency throughout Checheno-Ingushetia. This immediately augmented the anti-Russian feelings of the population and their support for Dudaev.

Whether his election was legitimate or not, Dudaev made full use of his presidential powers. He declared martial law and mobilized the National Guard. His forces blocked the landing of jet planes with the Russian troops at the airport. Russian and Chechen forces were kept from clashing only because the Russian parliament refused to authorize the prolongation of the state of emergency and evacuated the Russian troops from the airport.

Throughout the next three years Dudaev continued to use his power successfully against the Russians. With the support of the local population he successfully demanded the withdrawal of all Russian military units from Chechen territory, and they left the great bulk of their arms for his army. He also took over the local police and KGB, so that Russia soon had little leverage in Chechnya. Any military intervention in Chechnya thereafter would surely result in heavy casualties. By mid-1993, Dudaev had driven his opponents out of Chechnya.

Nevertheless, during those three years Dudaev's government proved to be ineffective and marked by criminal behavior. He did not know how to resolve conflicts among the elite or solve economic problems. The next presidential election in Chechnya was supposed to be held in 1995, and as the time drew nearer, Dudaev's popularity was plummeting. According to many observers, if the Russian government had waited for those elections to take place, he would almost certainly have been defeated and probably replaced by someone more cooperative.[50] However, instead of waiting or negotiating with him, the Russian leaders dealt with his rivals.[51] By April 1994, they were supporting Umar Avturkhanov, who was organizing Dudaev's opponents.

Still, while he remained in office, Dudaev was extremely combative. During that summer hundreds of deaths resulted from the increasingly bloody fights between his forces and the armed opposition. Abandoning the passive approach, Yeltsin's government turned to providing Dudaev's opponents with arms, tanks, and combat personnel. Some advisers to the Russian government strongly opposed this type of support, feeling sure that such military intervention would only strengthen popular support for Dudaev.[52] Their predictions would be fulfilled. The war did not unfold according to a predetermined political plan, but rather because leaders bungled the pursuit of their real objectives.

The Approaching War

During 1993 several developments had taken place that can be seen, in hindsight, as exacerbating factors leading to war. There was, above all, the growing antagonism between Dudaev and Yeltsin, who in fact needed to support each other against internal enemies. Both presidents resorted to violence in 1993 to dissolve their parliaments and strengthen their personal power. Moreover, a third political figure played an important part in shaping public opinion: Ruslan Khasbulatov, the chairman of the Russian Parliament and an ethnic Chechen. He supported the territorial integrity of Russia against Dudaev and opposed the strengthening of presidential power in Russia. Khasbulatov was at least as popular as Dudaev in Chechnya, and when he returned there to offer himself as a of the opposition, he might have been useful to Russia if he had not been Yeltsin's bitter enemy.

Two other changes need to be noted as well that took place in the closing weeks of 1993: the adoption of Russia's new constitution and military doctrine. The constitution, which was influenced by nationalism specialist Sergei Shakhrai's views of territorial integrity, ruled out any further recognition of independence of units of the Federation such as Chechnya.

The military doctrine defined "illegal military formations inside Russia" as one of the most important potential enemies for the legitimate Russian military. The Russians were then in the process of withdrawing from Germany, Central Europe, and the Baltic countries. Many hundreds of tanks were therefore sent to the northern Caucasus — a number in excess of the 700 tank units per flank permitted by the agreements of Vienna and Tashkent. It became necessary to justify these excesses on the international level by demonstrating that Russia was experiencing some form of armed threat. According to some analysts, this was a significant consideration in the thinking of some military leaders who were involved in the events leading up to war. This interpretation is not universally accepted, however; the more common view holds that the Russian military leaders by no means wanted to fight a war in Chechnya.

Even more difficult to appraise are the economic factors. It is impossible to determine the truth of the many rumors concerning criminal economic interests that supposedly were to be hidden in the numbers showing war losses and destruction.

Some economic facts are known. In December 1992, President Yeltsin ordered the founding of an all-Russian state oil company, Rosneft, which was meant to include Chechen representatives. However, Dudaev rejected that option and launched his own Chechen company instead, while retaining considerable control over the existing pipeline near Grozny. Some have speculated that Chechen control was so threatening to Russian interests that they considered it as warranting military action.

Dozens of other analysts have offered other speculative theories about factors that may have contributed to Russian decision to fight a war in Chechnya. Some say, for example, that President Yeltsin believed it possible to win a small war quickly and cover himself in political glory. Others say that the ultra-nationalist politician Vladimir Zhirinovsky had demonstrated to Yeltsin the electoral profitability of "showing the Russian flag." Some say that the Russian government was alarmed about the criminality of Dudaev's regime and felt it necessary to restore a rule of law in his republic. Still others suppose that some Russian military officers, in search of a new enemy, identified it as "illegal military formations" such as Dudaev's army. Others claim that arms dealers saw the war losses as an excellent way of covering up their illegal traffic and reducing surplus tanks and other weaponry, thereby justifying a new round of weapons manufacture.

There may be some truth to some or all of these theories, but none of them can be established.

What does seem clear is that the popularity of Ruslan Khasbulatov in Chechnya probably influenced the complex dynamics of that situation. Khasbulatov had been one of the parliamentary leaders whose opposition to Yeltsin had culminated in Yeltsin's ordering the army to shell the Russian parliament, killing hundreds of the people who were inside. Khasbulatov had been imprisoned after that event, but upon his release he found himself immensely popular in Chechnya. He was an enemy of both Dudaev and Yeltsin (along with Yeltsin's puppet opposition leader, Zavgaev). Khasbulatov did not favor the separation of Chechnya from Russia, and his popularity in fact drew Chechens' support away from the separatist leader Dudaev. If matters had continued along these lines without being interrupted, Khasbulatov might well have resolved the situation so that separatism would dwindle away. However, Yeltsin considered it intolerable for Khasbulatov to be the one to save the situation. Indeed, he would even prefer a military solution, if it seemed likely to succeed quickly, rather than a peaceful solution led by his arch-rival, who would then become an even more prominent leader of the entire Russian Caucasus.

Whatever Yeltsin's motives may have been, in November 1994 Russians were involved in a direct attack on Grozny and destroyed the Chechen airport with unmarked planes. The attack was a fiasco, but Dudaev captured some of the men and put them on television to prove that the attack was not carried out only by fighters from the Chechen opposition. Within hours, Khasbulatov's popularity had plummeted, never to revive; hardly any Chechen was willing anymore to remain part of Russia. Moreover, the disastrous military event was sufficient to commit the Russian government to even more direct actions. The war was on. It would result in between 50,000 and 100,000 deaths.

The War, Step by Step

On December 11 Russian troops began a large-scale invasion of Chechnya, coming from Northern Ossetian bases. They surrounded Grozny but did not fight seriously until the night of December 31, when tanks moved straight to the city center and were surrounded by Chechen defenders. Almost all the tank crews died. The heavy street fighting kept civilians from leaving Grozny, making them de facto hostages.

After a second assault in February and March 1995 the Russian forces finally seized Grozny, but the Chechen fighters withdrew to the mountainous regions of the republic, where they could mount their defense.

Many residents of Chechnya (not only ethnic Chechens) were imprisoned in "filtration points" without being charged of any legal offense. They were tortured, and many disappeared. One list, published officially only in July 1995, included hundreds of names. The village of Samashki supported Dudaev; the

Russian troops destroyed it on April 7. Hundreds of Russian soldiers were imprisoned by the resistance, and some were ill-treated and subjected to atrocities.

Under OSCE auspices, the Russian government began negotiations with Dudaev, but without result. A land battle was going on in the mountains, supported by air raids on many villages. After one Chechen unit, headed by Commander Shamil Basaev, had received no orders from its superiors and understood the situation as a call for action on Russian territory, it moved to the town of Budennovsk in Stavropol Krai with a plan to attack an air base. Unable to finish the operation, they captured a hospital instead, taking thousands of hostages. Russian commandos tried to storm the hospital and killed many hostages who were used as living shields. Russian Prime Minister Viktor Chernomyrdin spoke with the terrorists by phone, arranged a cease-fire, and permitted Basaev and his men to return to Chechnya, accompanied by 150 volunteer Russian hostages, of whom eleven were from the corps of journalists.

Thereafter military activities were stopped until October 23, when guerrillas attempted to kill a Russian general, Anatolii Romanov, who had become one of the leaders in the peace process. After that, the peace-building activities were not officially discontinued, but there was not much serious intention behind them.

Meanwhile the date of elections in Chechnya was set by Moscow, which then recognized the former Communist leader of the Chechen-Ingush ASSR, Doku Zavgaev, as the winner. He supported the military intervention by the federalist forces, so the Russian government stopped negotiating with the separatists. Numerous villages were destroyed in early 1996. In March, Dudaev's forces captured Grozny for a few days and then lost it again.

Presidential elections were scheduled in Russia for June 1996. As part of his campaign for reelection, Boris Yeltsin agreed to negotiate with Dudaev with the mediation of the president of the Republic of Tatarstan in the Russian Federation, Mintimir Shaimiev. When Dudaev did not agree immediately, he was killed under unclear circumstances on April 21. His successor, Zelimkhan Iandarbiev, met with Chernomyrdin in Yeltsin's presence in the Kremlin and signed a new cease-fire agreement. The political future of Chechnya was not discussed in the documents, leaving that aspect open to interpretation.

As soon as Boris Yeltsin won a victory in two rounds of voting in June-July, the war resumed. The new secretary general of the Russian Security Council, Alexander Lebed, was the politician with the third highest rating of all candidates, after Yeltsin and Ziuganov, the Communist candidate. Lebed announced that it would be impossible to negotiate with the Chechens. However, when the Chechens then recaptured Grozny in August, Lebed decided to visit Chechnya himself; there he reversed his position and negotiated a new cease-fire with the chief of the Chechen military staff, Aslan Maskhadov.

On August 31, the two men signed a political agreement that would allow any decision on Chechnya's independence to be deferred — if necessary, until 2001. Many in the Russian leadership did not approve the agreement, but the withdrawal of troops from Chechnya had already begun, and that process went forward. Yeltsin dismissed Lebed in October and substituted a bureaucrat, Ivan Rybkin, and a "new Russian" millionaire, Boris Berezovsky, but they continued making pragmatic agreements to end the war.

Support and Opposition to the War

Throughout the war, there were numerous organizations and individuals who tried to influence political and military decisions, with varying degrees of success. Protests were slow in getting started because many Russians had difficulty believing that their government would organize large-scale violence anywhere, especially inside Russia. However, some independent peace organizations, such as Memorial, the Committee of Soldiers' Mothers, Nonviolence International, the Quaker Peace Service, and Omega, showed enormous dedication in witnessing and resolving the crisis. The majority of Russian TV and newspaper reporters were actively opposed to the war; some of them cooperated with peacemaking organizations.

Some politicians also searched for nonviolent answers; for example, Grigorii Iavlinsky, the leader of the Iabloko party, offered Dudaev a promise to stay in Chechnya as long as necessary. Boris Nemtsov, governor of Nizhni Novgorod, collected more than a million signatures from residents of his region calling for peace in Chechnya. The famous human rights campaigner Sergei Kovalev came to Chechnya in December 1994 with a delegation of three parliamentary parties (Russia's Choice, Iabloko, and Communist) and stayed there for several weeks. The mission was important from the standpoint of establishing the authority of those critics, for at that time no one could suspect Kovalev of being opposed to Yeltsin, and the other Russian groups were by no means angry toward the government. However, Kovalev's criticism became so strong that he was dismissed from his parliamentary role as a human rights commissioner.

Iabloko and Russia's Choice, with the assistance of the Russian nongovernmental organizations (NGOs) Memorial and Right to Life and Human Dignity, prepared political propositions for the step-by-step solution of the crisis.[53] Those proposals were then adopted as features of the agreements between Lebed and Maskhadov.

There were a few international organizations that criticized Russia's attack on Chechnya; Amnesty International and Human Rights Watch/Helsinki protested against human rights violations witnessed by them and by Russian NGOs, and prepared reports that were accepted by the United Nations and the Council of Europe. The Organization on Security and Cooperation in Europe (OSCE) established a mission in Chechnya in May 1995, which became a real mediator during the most difficult negotiations.

Otherwise, the international community adopted a tolerant attitude toward the war. Despite the death of dozens of foreign journalists and humanitarian workers, their own states remained indifferent to the fighting. President Bill Clinton consistently stressed his "understanding" of Russian measures. Initially the European Union urged Russia to negotiate directly with the separatists as one of the conditions for a large loan that had been planned since 1995. However, as soon as the negotiations began formally in May 1995, the restrictions were withdrawn without waiting for any result. The EU Council of Foreign Ministers discouraged member countries from expressing diplomatic protests. For its part, the United Nations limited its interventions to supporting the mission of the High Commission of Refugees. The Council of Europe issued a declarative recommendation in favor of a peace solution and resistance against human rights violations, but here again the organization made no attempt to use real influence toward these ends. The Council admitted Russia in January 1996, in spite of the war, presumably for the sake of helping Yeltsin's presidential campaign.

After the War

The war caused an immense amount of damage and cost vast sums of money and possibly as many as 100,000 deaths. Only in May 1997 did it end officially, when President Yeltsin and Aslan Maskhadov, the newly elected president of Chechnya, finally signed an agreement in Moscow.

Who won? It is easier to say who lost: Russia. Most Russian soldiers were young, ill-equipped, and sometimes even unfed conscripts who usually did not know why they were fighting the Chechens. Demoralized, they were regularly defeated. In military terms, the Chechen fighters proved to be far more effective.

But Russia lost in more ways than militarily. The war was launched by orders of the Security Council, an organization whose deliberations are never disclosed to the public. Some astute political observers believe that President Yeltsin may have taken the decision against the counsel of his wiser advisers, but the truth may never be revealed. In any case, it became clear that President Yeltsin can wield far more power than the heads of most other democratic governments. Just as Russians were beginning to grasp democracy, the bitter war experience turned many into cynics, as they observed how little political accountability existed in their new democracy.

Certainly Russia lost the war: One year later it was clear that the Russian government no longer exercised effective control over Chechen territory. But it can hardly be said that Chechnya "won" the war — for years after the war, the Chechen government also did not exercise effective control over its own territory. Armed warlords (some perhaps connected to the elected government, others probably functioning as independent freelance criminals) were engaged in assassinating foreign Red Cross workers and taking numerous visitors and journalists hostage, including those whose orientation during the war had been actively anti-militarist and pro-Chechen. The Chechen counter-intelligence "fought against spies" using all the methods of the Stalinist tradition. President Maskhadov offered rewards to put a halt to the kidnappings and terrorism, but without result. No government was in control of Chechnya.

Yet there were influential persons who sought to impose new rules. Conspicuously, a new enthusiasm for religious fundamentalism could be seen in politicians who previously had been moderate Sunnis or secular Communists. In September 1997, for example, an Islamic court in Grozny found a married couple guilty of murder; their public execution was televised. Such a practice, which violates Russian laws, was called "medieval" by the Russian prime minister,[54] but was defended by Chechen officials. Religious extremism was not a *cause,* but rather an *effect,* of the war.

By the summer of 1998 there was evidence that Chechens were attempting to foment inter-ethnic conflict in adjacent republics of Russia, especially Dagestan. This would require the intervention of Russian troops to quell the unrest, but the actual result would more likely be to instigate a new local war against Russia. The Chechen objective would be to sever Dagstan from the Russian Federation, giving Chechnya access to much-needed transportation routes for trade purposes.

The future remains unpredictable. Almost certainly some type of independence must be established, but it is not clear how substantial that will be. Shortly after the war, only a minority of Chechens would not accept anything less than an entirely autonomous, sovereign state. The majority, including President Maskhadov, were more pragmatic, they probably would have settled for some symbolic declaration of independence, which might then be almost ignored. However, by the fall of 1997, Russia had not offered anything at all — not even a symbolic form of independence — and anger was rising again in Chechnya.

Conclusions

Chechen nationalism is far from exceptional in the late twentieth century. It is a phenomenon that can be seen in numerous countries around the globe. No unique explanation is required to account for its emergence. To understand it we have only to recall the actual persecution and the symbolically significant relative deprivation to which the Chechen population was exposed.

Nevertheless, the rise of Chechen nationalism did not mean that there was anything inevitable about the tragedies that have taken place in the Caucasus. Separatism might have been limited or even reversed if at certain points history had taken a different course. Those who believe that secession was a mistaken aspiration for Chechens may attribute the blame to the following list of factors.

First, there was the ideology of self-determination, which had hardly been criticized during Soviet days. Virtually everyone, including democrats, took for granted the notion that every "people" is entitled to "self-determination," which includes the right to secede. Had this doctrine been discussed and analyzed in public discourse over a longer period of time, its inherent practical and moral difficulties would have become apparent. On the other hand, the inadequacy of public discourse on this topic is widespread, not only of the formerly socialist countries but elsewhere as well.

Second, several obvious circumstances created great difficulty for those seeking to bring orderly change to Chechnya during the 1990s. For example, Dzhokhar Dudaev was able to force the Russian troops to withdraw and leave their weapons behind. Moreover, there were numerous new opportunities to use illegitimate electoral procedures to gain extraordinary political powers, both in Chechnya and Russia.

Third, eventually a new constitution was offered that reversed the nationalistic principles on which President Yeltsin's policies themselves had recently been grounded. This change did not meet with full public approval.

Faced with a new separatist leader of Chechnya whose election was dubious, the Russian government floundered, unable effectively and consistently to (a) recognize Dudaev and negotiate with him, or (b) ignore him while continuing to function in the normal way as the federal government, or (c) replace his government in a legitimate, recognized way. Instead of pursuing any of these options, the Russian officials initially tried and failed to block Dudaev, then ignored him for two years while he demonstrated his inability to govern, then tried again to replace him in ways that antagonized the citizens of Chechnya and rekindled their support for him.

According to Sergei Kovalev, if Yeltsin had been willing to negotiate, most members of Dudaev's own cabinet had been willing, well after the war began, to accept a version of "independence" that included a common currency with Russia, a common military, a common citizenship, a joint foreign policy, and an integrated economy.[55] Edward Walker's article in this volume argues, as does Kovalev, that the Chechens would have accepted a degree of sovereignty comparable to that won by Tatarstan. It was only by blundering, counterproductive bullying, and finally warfare that the Russian government brought about a situation in which this outcome no longer seems acceptable.

Notes

1. Victor Kogan Iasnyi gratefully acknowledges the assistance of Guillaume Legros for assistance in preparing the English version of this paper.

2. Most newspapers, television, and documents are written in Russian. After the war President Maskhadov issued a degree that documents henceforth be prepared in Chechen, but this cannot be carried out because the Chechen lexicon has not been developed to cover technical and legal concepts.

3. In 1921 the territory populated by Chechens and Ingushes became a part of the Soviet Mountain Republic which included Chechnya, Ingushetia, Ossetia, Kabarda, Balkaria, and Karachai. In 1922 the Soviet government established the Chechen Autonomous Region; in 1924 the status of an autonomous region was given to Ingushetia (in 1924, when six autonomous regions had been created on

its territory, the Soviet Mountain Republic ceased to exist). In 1934 the two autonomous regions were merged and the Chechen-Ingush Autonomous Oblast (Region) was established.

4. The true distribution of Chechen preferences on this matter is debatable. Aleksandr Nekrich (*The Punished Peoples*, trans. G. Saunders [New York: W.W. Norton, 1978], 56) estimates that more than 18,500 Chechens and Ingushes were drafted into the army and that several hundreds were part of the garrison of the Brest Fortress. On the other hand, the "Unofficial Chechnya Home Page" states, "During World War II, the Chechens and other peoples in neighboring territories collaborated with the invading German Army against the Russians. They did this not because they favored the Germans, so much as they hated the Russians and wanted to be free of Russian domination." Many scholars believe that this statement reflects current opinions in the region and not necessarily the views that prevailed in the 1940s. In any case, this attitude is general and openly expressed in the late 1990s.

5. Edward Kline, "The Conflict in Chechnya," a briefing paper available on the Internet from the Andrei Sakharov Foundation, of which he is president, at http://www.wdn.com/asf/index.html.

6. Tuva, North Ossetia, and Chuvashia are the others.

7. Calculated from data presented by Kline, "The Conflict in Chechnya."

8. Yury Nikolaev, ed., *The Chechen Tragedy: Who is to Blame?* (New York: Nova Science Publishers, 1996), 5-6.

9. Nikolaev, *The Chechen Tragedy*, 7.

10. Kline, "The Conflict in Chechnya."

11. Ariel Cohen, "The New 'Great Game': Oil and Politics in the Caucasus and Central Asia," *The Heritage Foundation Backgrounder No. 1065*, January 25, 1996.

12. Nikolaev, *The Chechen Tragedy*, 6- 7.

13. Cohen, "The New 'Great Game'." He cites testimony of Ambassador John Maresca, U.S. State Department, in a hearing on ethnic violence in Transcaucasia, Commission on Security and Cooperation in Europe, 103rd Congress, First Session, March 8, 1993, 8.

14. Liz Fuller, "New Geo-Political Alliances on Russia's Southern Rim," *Radio Free Europe (RFE) Report*, April 25, 1997.

15. Alexandre Bennigsen and S. Enders Wimbush, *Muslims of the Soviet Empire* (London: C. Hurst and Co., 1985), 184.

16. V.S. Drozdov, "Chechnya: Exit From the Labyrinth of Conflict?" *Russian Social Science Review* November-December 1996, 40

17. Bennigsen and Wimbush, *Muslims of the Soviet Empire*, 186. See also F. Bryan, "Internationalism, Nationalism and Islam," in *The North Caucasus Barrier*, ed. Marie Bennigsen Broxrup (London: Hurst & Company, 1992), 195-215.

18. An idea of pan-Caucasian solidarity, which was expressed in Dudaev's appeals to the reestablishment of the Mountain Republic, found the same weak response among the peoples of the North Caucasus. A similar proposal has been raised again since his death, however, evidently with the approval of the president of Georgia, Eduard Shevardnadze.

19. See Maskhadov's interview in *Nezavisimaia gazeta,* January 18, 1997; and I. Rotar', "V ponedel'nik v Chechne proidut vybory prezidenta i parlamenta," *Nezavisimaia gazeta* , January 25, 1997.

20. Olivia Ward, "Religion rules for Chechen voters," *Toronto Star,* January 27, 1997.

21. Bennigsen and Wimbush, *Muslims of the Soviet Empire,* 23.

22. F. Bryan pointed out that "before the end of the Communist rule" religious *samizdat* became popular in Chechnya and some other Muslim autonomous republics of the North Caucasus. (F. Bryan, "Internationalism, Nationalism, and Islam," in *The North Caucasus Barrier,* 203-04.)

23. For details see Diana Zisserman-Brodsky, *Ethnic Samizdat and Ethnic Politics in the USSR,* Ph.D. dissertation, Jerusalem, 1994, 57-58, 214-15.

24. See Kukshar, "Short article on the suppression of the Tatar Bashkir," *Archiv Samizdata* (AS) 3085 (April 1977).

25. See Karl Deutsch, "Social Mobilization and Political Development," in *American Political Science Review* 55, 1961: 493-514.

26. Bennigsen and Wimbush, *Muslims of the Soviet Empire*, 185.

27. See, for example, Michael Hechter, *Internal Colonialism: The Celtic Fringe in British National Development, 1536-1966* (London: Routledge and Kegan Paul, 1975).

28. Nikolaev, *The Chechen Tragedy*, 10.

29. Calculated from V. I. Kozlov, *Natsional'nosti SSSR,* Moscow 1982.

30. Published in the Chechen independent newspaper, *Bart,* no. 6 in June 1991. Cited from M. Broxrup, "After the Putsch, 1991" in *The North Caucasus Barrier,* 232.

31. See Reeve Vanneman and Thomas Pettigrew, "Race and Relative Deprivation in the Urban United States," *Race,* 1972, 13; D. Kinder and D. Sears, "Prejudice and Politics: Symbolic Racism versus Racial Threats to the Good Life," *Journal of Personality and Social Psychology,* 1981, 40.

32. As cited by M. Broxrup, "After the Putsch," 233.

33. On Russia's methods of "pacifying" the Chechens, see I. Badley, *The Russian Conquest of Caucasus* (London, 1908); M. Gammer, "Russia's strategies in Conquest of Chechnya and Daghestan," in *The North Caucasus Barrier,* 45-49.

34. In 1990 a special commission investigated the massacre in Khaibakh. The document of August 20, 1990, issued by the commission, concluded, "The Commission finds the fact of mass extermination of people in Khaibakh to have been proven, and regards it as genocide." The document was published in *Tak eto bylo,* eds. V. Sldobnikova and S. Alieva (Moskva: Insan 1993), Vol. 2, 185.

35. For qualified account see A. Kosterin, Letter to the First Secretary of the Central Committee of the CPSU, N. S. Khrushchev, in *Tak eto bylo,* 230-34.

36. See M. Masiutko, "A Letter to the Supreme Soviet of the Ukrainian SSR," 1967, *Arkhiv samizdata,* no. 950.

37. On this issue see Zisserman-Brodsky, "Ethnic Samizdat," 38-41.

38. Cited in M. Broxrup, "After the Putsch," 229.

39. See Leon Festinger, "A Theory of Social Comparison," *Human Relations*, 1954, 7.

40. Zisserman-Brodsky, "Ethnic Samizdat," 67-68.

41. See A. de Carufel, "Factors Affecting the Evaluation of Improvement: The Role of Normative Standards and Allocator Resources," *Journal of Personality and Social Psychology*, 1979, 37, 856.

42. M. Broxrup, "After the Putsch," 231-32.

43. See translation of the Chechen Congress's documents in M. Broxrup, "After the Putsch," 232-34. The Russian authors, almost four years after the second convention, described the events: "In summer 1991 the world was informed that a certain, not completely defined part of the Checheno-Ingushetia, seceded from the RSFSR and USSR and proclaimed itself an independent state called the Chechen Republic." (Emil' Pain and Arkadii Popov, "Da zdravstvuet revol'utsiia!" *Izvestiia*, February 7, 1995); T. Muzayev, "Chechenskaya Respublika. Organy Vlasty I Politicheskye Sily." (The Chechen Republic: Power Structure and Political Bodies.) Moscow, Panorama, 1995, pp. 166-69.

44. As translated by M. Broxrup, "After the Putsch," 233.

45. Russian policy toward the Chechen Congress was influenced by the views of then-Vice-President Aleksandr Rutskoi and by Sergei Shakhrai, the "leading expert" on nationality policy, who attempted to formulate the policy of "new Russian federalism."

46. See, for example, E. Pain and A. Popov, "Da zdravstvuiet revoliutsiia!," *Izvestiia* , February 7, 1995.

47. Emil' A. Pain and Arkady A. Popov, "Chechnya," Chapter 2 in *U.S. and Russian Policymaking with Respect to the Use of Force*, eds. Arkady A. Popov, Jeremy R. Azrael, and Emil' A. Pain (RAND, 1996). Available on the Internet at http://www.rand.org/publications/CF/CF129/CF-129.chapter2.html.

48. Sergei Kovalev, "Russia After Chechnya," *New York Review of Books*, July 17, 1997, 27.

49. See M. Broxrup, "After the Putsch," 236.

50. Kovalev, "Russia After Chechnya."

51. Payin and Popov, "Chechnya."

52. Payin and Popov, "Chechnya."

53. *Izvestiia*, February 20, 1996.

54. "Moscow Condemns Grozny Executions," *RFE Report*, September 5, 1997.

55. Kovalev, "Russia after Chechnya," 27.

Ten

Negotiating Autonomy: Tatarstan, Asymmetrical Federalism, and State Consolidation in Russia

Edward W. Walker

As the Soviet Union approached its final collapse in 1991, Russia found it-self under many of the same centrifugal pressures that were tearing apart the USSR. Like the USSR, the Russian Soviet Federated Socialist Republic (RSFSR) was a multinational "federation," the only such self-defined federation among the USSR's 15 union republics. Host to 130 officially recognized ethnic minorities (or "nationalities" in Soviet parlance) that made up 18.5 percent of its population, the federation consisted of 88 constituent units, 31 of which were ethnically defined "*avtonomii*" (autonomous formations).[1] These avtonomii were ranked in a three-tier hierarchy with varying rights and privileges — 16 autonomous republics, five autonomous *oblasts*, and ten autonomous *okrugs* — all but one of which has its own eponymous ethnic group, or "titular nationality."[2] Russian officials feared that these avtonomii would follow the lead of the USSR's union republics and demand autonomy, "sovereignty," and finally full independence.

Hoping to preserve Russia's territorial integrity, officials in Moscow began considering various schemes for redesigning Russia's federation structure. In particular, plans were drawn up for returning Russia to the system of regional *gubernii''* that had existed in the Tsarist period. Under this scheme, Russia's new federation would consist of ten to fifteen large gubernii'' (e.g., the Russian Far

East, Eastern Siberia, Western Siberia, the Middle Volga, the Black Earth zone), each of which supposedly shared broad cultural similarities and integrated economies. The principal intent of the plan was not, however, to spur economic growth. Rather, it was to eliminate Russia's ethnically defined subnational governments in the hopes of making secession less likely.

Following these discussions at the time, I was initially somewhat sympathetic. Ethnically defined subnational governments would, I suspected, entrench and politicize ethnic identities, making conflict inevitable and permanent in a country that was, after all, ethnically quite homogeneous (81.5 percent Russian). Reflecting on the American experience, it struck me that the United States might well have fractured had its federation included an "Anglo-American State of Connecticut," a "Dutch-American State of Pennsylvania," an "African-American State of Virginia," or a "Native-American State of Oklahoma." At the least, ethnicity would have been even more politicized as the stakes of interethnic conflict were raised, particularly if the "titular" peoples in each case had a sense of territorial proprietorship and institutionalized privileges (e.g., guaranteed access to government jobs). Nor was the experience of existing federations with ethnically defined constituent units reassuring; even prosperous and orderly Canada was threatened with secession by French-speaking Quebec. Finally, there was the record of the other "ethnic federations" in Eastern Europe and the USSR: Czechoslovakia, Yugoslavia, and the USSR had already fragmented or were on the verge of fragmenting along the lines of often arbitrary ethnic borders.

After reflection, however, I concluded that any attempt to redraw Russia's internal borders substantially would be a political disaster. Massive re-districting would have been resisted by many national minorities, and this resistance would likely have been violent in many cases. Likewise, the substantial and powerful elite in Russia's nonethnic regions, most of whom would lose their jobs, would have vehemently resisted the plan. The result would have been a further weakening of an already feeble administrative apparatus and possibly a descent into anarchy. While reasonable people might disagree over whether Russia would be better off in the long run with different internal borders, abandoning its inherited federal structure in the short run would have risked catastrophe.

Fortunately, Boris Yeltsin and his advisors came to this same conclusion (although many Russian public officials and "nationality experts" continue to express support for a purely territorial federal system). Instead, Yeltsin attempted to solve Russia's federation crisis by adopting a "Federation Treaty" to be signed by the federal government and each member of the federation that would institutionalize a coherent and stable division of powers between Moscow and the *sub''ekty*. His hopes, however, were not to be realized. A Federation Treaty (actually, three separate treaties) was indeed signed in March 1992, but two republics, Tatarstan and Chechnya, refused to initial it. Chechnya, in fact, continued to insist that it was a fully independent state. Moreover, Russia's intensifying economic crisis and the deepening tensions between the president and his opponents in Moscow was weakening the federal center even as it encouraged individual sub''ekty to escalate demands for greater autonomy and privileges.

As a result, federal authorities found themselves under growing pressure to afford individual sub''ekty particular deals and rights not afforded others. As this process of bilateral bargaining gathered momentum, Moscow officials began to consider the possibility of committing formally to a system of "asymmetrical federation" for Russia. Such an arrangement, its defenders reasoned, would allow federal authorities to negotiate a devolution of powers with individual sub''ekty on a case-by-case basis, thereby accommodating their particular conditions, needs, and capacities.

Like many observers at the time, I was initially skeptical of this scheme. Asymmetrical federalism, I suspected, would prove both unjust and unstable. Individual sub''ekty would win preferential treatment on the basis of political influence, not genuine need. Poor and politically weak republics (e.g., Tuva) would suffer, while economically advantaged and politically influential republics (e.g., Tatarstan) would benefit. This would contradict the widely-accepted principle that federal governments should redistribute wealth from rich to poor regions. Moreover, special deals afforded individual sub''ekty would likely promote a competitive game of one-upmanship in which each member of the federation would outbid others in demanding concessions from the center. This outbidding might well lead to the fragmentation of Russia. Alternatively, it might provoke the federal government to crack down on the sub''ekty, effectively destroying Russian federalism and risking widespread violence.

Nevertheless, Russia began to move, both de facto and de jure, toward a system of asymmetrical federalism. The most dramatic moment in this process occurred on February 15, 1994, when the federal government, after two years of negotiation, signed a bilateral "power-sharing treaty" with the Republic of Tatarstan that afforded the latter extensive autonomy. This was followed by similar treaties with other ethnic republics and eventually by treaties with many of Russia's nonethnic regions as well.

Seven years after the collapse of the Soviet Union, and five years after the signing of the power-sharing treaty with Tatarstan, the Russian Federation survives. And not only has it survived, it has managed to preserve the entirety of its territory; not even Chechnya (although it may yet prove an exception) has received international recognition as an independent state, the mark of a successful secessionist campaign. Rather than leading to the collapse of the Russian state, asymmetrical federalism appears to have contributed to its territorial consolidation. Only in the case of Chechnya, which Moscow tried to suppress by force rather than political means, is there a significant possibility that Russia's external borders will be changed in the foreseeable future.

How has Russia managed to preserve its territorial integrity? And why did asymmetrical federalism not bring about Russia's fragmentation? To answer these questions, I focus below on the case of Tatarstan, the republic that, along with Chechnya, seemed the most likely to secede in late 1991. While Chechnya has been the most radical of Russia's republics, Tatarstan has been the most influential — indeed, many in Moscow, including Yeltsin and his allies, argue that the "Tatarstan model" was the savior of Russian territorial integrity.

The Roots of Tatarstan's Political Identity

The Republic of Tatarstan is located some 450 miles east of Moscow to the west of the Ural mountains at the confluence of the Volga and Kama rivers and along European Russia's lines of communication with Siberia and the Russian Far East. The landlocked republic is surrounded by other constituent units of the Russian Federation. Unlike Chechnya, it consequently has no border with a foreign state. The titular nationality of the republic, the "Volga Tatars," are Russia's largest national minority, numbering 5.5 million in 1989 out of a total RSFSR population of 147.0 million (3.8 percent). An additional 1.1 million Tatars lived outside the RSFSR in other Soviet union republics, bringing the total number of Tatars in the USSR to 6.6 million.[3] However, of the RSFSR's 5.5 million Tatars, only 1.7 million (32 percent) actually lived in the Tatar ASSR itself, with large concentrations in Bashkiria (1.12 million), other areas of the Volga-Urals region, Central Asia, and Azerbaijan.[4] Of Tatarstan's 3.6 million residents, only 48.5 percent were Tatars, with 43.3 percent being Russians.[5] In total, Tatarstan's population of 3.6 million was larger than that of five of the union republics — Estonia, Latvia, Lithuania, Turkmenistan, and Armenia — while territorially it is larger than the three Baltic states combined.[6]

Tatarstan is relatively developed socioeconomically. In 1989, 73 percent of the population lived in cities, although it was significantly less urbanized than Russia as a whole: 63 versus 86 percent.[7] It is also highly industrialized, with significant defense, petrochemical, and timber/pulp/paper industries. Officials in Kazan frequently note that in the late 1980s the total industrial output of the Baltic republics did not match that of Tatarstan. The republic has the former Soviet Union's largest truck manufacturer — the massive Kama Automobile Plant (KamAZ) in Naberezhnye Chelny — as well as a major producer of helicopters, the Kazan Helicopter Works. Importantly, it is also home to significant oil reserves; proven reserves total some 700 to 800 million tons, with production at around 12 million tons per year (approximately 7 percent of Russia's annual output in 1994). The republic's oil is, however, of poor quality and is expensive to produce. Tatarstan also has significant reserves of natural gas, coal, and other natural resources and it is home to one the largest oil and gas pipeline systems in Eastern Europe.

The Volga Tatars are a Turkic-speaking, Sunni Muslim people of the Hanafi School. Linguistically, they are descendants of Turkic-speaking Kypchak tribes who migrated across the Urals in the ninth and tenth centuries and mixed with Finno-Ugric and Slavic peoples already present in the region. By the end of the ninth century, a distinct Bulgar civilization had emerged in the Middle Volga region, which adopted Islam in 922, some seven decades before the conversion of Russia to Orthodoxy.[8] The Bulgar civilization was, however, destroyed by the Mongol Golden Horde, and it was not until after the collapse of Mongol rule that a distinct "Tatar" culture began to emerge in the region in the era of the Kazan Khanate (circa 1445-1552).[9] However, in 1552 Kazan was stormed by Russian troops under Ivan the Terrible. Many of the inhabitants of the city were put to death, the lands of the local nobility were expropriated, and the Khanate's economy and social system were effectively destroyed. Moreover, the territory was occupied by the Russians, marking Russia's passage to an imperial power.[10]

Despite political and demographic pressures over the following centuries of Tsarist rule, the Tatars demonstrated a remarkable cultural resiliency.[11] By the end of the nineteenth century, the Volga region had become a center of intellectual learning and enlightened Islamic thought even as the Tatar national intelligentsia was engaged in a project of cultural and religious revival. They seized the opportunity presented by the chaos of the Russian Revolution to form an independent "Idel'-Ural Republic" on November 29, 1917. The Republic was short-lived, however, and on May 27, 1920, the Tatar Autonomous Soviet Socialist Republic was incorporated into the RSFSR. The Bolsheviks promptly purged the republic of its "bourgeois nationalists" and went on to repress Tatar "national Bolsheviks" led by Mirsaid Sultangaliev. Finally, Stalin's assault on Islam devastated the republic's political, cultural, and religious elite along with much of the Tatars cultural heritage, included most of the region's mosques.

Tatar nationalist sentiments nevertheless survived, surfacing most notably in 1936 with the adoption of the Stalin constitution for the USSR. Representatives of the republic requested that, in view of the size of its population and territory, as well as the distinctiveness and vitality of Tatar culture, Tatarstan's status be raised to that of a full union republic. The petition was denied, however, Stalin's position being that all union republics had to have an external border. Tatarstan would raise these same demands, and again be denied, during public discussions of the Brezhnev constitution of 1977.

Tatarstan experienced a period of rapid urbanization and industrialization in the wake of World War II, thanks in part to the discovery of significant oil reserves in 1946.[12] Russian in-migration increased as Russians arrived in search of jobs, particularly in the cities, and assimilation pressures on Tatars intensified accordingly. By the end of 1980s, only 12 percent of Tatar children in the republic were being educated in their native language. And although Tatars had a high rate of native language retention — 96.6 percent of Tatars in Tatarstan and 83.2 percent for all Tatars in the USSR — the use of Tatar was declining, particularly for the younger generation.[13] Russian was the language of government and the workplace, while Tatar was becoming essentially a "home language." Very few Russians in the republic bothered to learn Tatar (1.1 percent in 1989), although 77 percent of Tatars could speak Russian.[14] The rate of intermarriage between

Tatars and Russians was high (roughly one-third of all marriages in the republic), while the use of Tatar in mixed marriages was extremely low. Finally, the percentage of Tatars who considered themselves believers in Islam was low and declining — 17.9 percent in 1967 and 15.7 percent in 1980.

For all these reasons, Tatar nationalists could credibly argue that Tatar culture was under serious threat by the late 1980s.[15] Indeed, Tatarstan appeared to have all the ingredients for a potent nationalist movement. Tatars had a strong sense of ethnic distinctiveness rooted in their traditional Islamic beliefs, distinct language, and record of intellectual and cultural achievement. Tatar nationalists could plausibly argue that Tatar language and culture were in crisis, while "ethnic entrepreneurs" could employ a centuries-old history of resistance to Russian domination and "colonialism," the Russian disdain for Tatar culture as manifested in Russian representations of the "Mongol-Tatar yoke" and "Asiatic backwardness," and a record of resistance and episodic rebellion against Russian occupation. And Tatarstan's political elite faced the same incentives as elites in the union republics and avtonomii in the disintegrating Soviet Union to "play the ethnic card" to mobilize popular support and preserve their position.

To be sure, other factors seemed to militate against radical nationalism in Tatarstan. Its location made it particularly vulnerable to pressure by the Russian government. Russians made up almost as large a percentage of the republic's population as did Tatars, while there were more Tatars living outside the republic than inside. And relations between Tatars and Russians had traditionally been good. Yet these same factors did not prevent secession or interethnic violence elsewhere in the former Soviet Union and Eastern Europe. Nagorno-Karabakh, like Tatarstan, was an enclave surrounded by the state (Azerbaijan) from which it fought to secede. Strategic vulnerability and a seemingly hopeless military balance did not prevent the Chechens or Abkhazians from declaring independence and waging wars of secession. Abkhazians made up a far smaller percentage of Abkhazia (17.8 percent) than Tatars did in Tatarstan, as well as a much smaller minority of the total population in Georgia than Tatars were in Russia. High rates of intermarriage and seemingly harmonious relations did not keep the Croats, Serbs, and Muslims from fighting a brutal interethnic war in Bosnia. And a large diaspora did not keep Russia from pressing for independence from the USSR.

Tatarstan's Sovereignty Campaign

It is hardly surprising, then, that Tatarstan, like most of the USSR's union republics and avtonomii, witnessed significant nationalist mobilization in 1988. Under the leadership of the Tatar Public Center (*Tatarskii obshchestvennyi tsentr*, or TOTs), which held its founding Congress early in the year, Tatar nationalists began demanding greater autonomy for the republic, recognition as a full union republic within the USSR, greater protections for Tatar culture, and a gradual approach to independence.[16] A more radical nationalist group, the Ittifak (Alliance) National Party, was established in early 1990 and began demanding that Tatar be made the republic's sole state language, that Russians be denied citizenship, and that the republic declare immediate independence. The most prominent leader of the group, Fauzia Bairamova, was particularly blunt in her hostility to Russians, demanding, for example, an end to mixed marriages. Other groups in the republic began to articulate various pan-Turkic, pan-Tatar, and pan-Islamic political agendas. By late 1990, Tatar nationalist demonstrations were displaying Islamic flags along with banners reading, "Tataria Is Not Russia — Down with Russian-Soviet Slavery" and "Tatars, Throw Off the Russian Yoke." Predictably, Russians in the republic, concerned about their security and future in the republic, began to organize in their own defense.

The key figure in the political course taken by Tatarstan in the coming years was Mintimir Shaimiev, an ethnic Tatar who had been appointed CPSU first secretary in Tatarstan in October 1989.[17] Whether for reasons of expediency or out of conviction, Shaimiev immediately made clear that he was committed to a multinational understanding (*mnogonatsional'nost'*) of Tatar statehood. His strategy, to which he would adhere with great consistency in the coming years, was to defend the rights of Russians within the republic, oppose radical Tatar nationalism while supporting Tatar cultural revival, and press Moscow vigorously for greater autonomy while adopting an equivocal stance on independence.

Importantly, Yeltsin and his allies in Moscow also adopted a multinational understanding of Russian statehood. On June 12, 1990, the RSFSR issued a "Declaration of State Sovereignty" that confirmed that the new Russian state would not adopt an ethnic understanding of citizenship by referring repeatedly to "the peoples" (*narody*) of Russia, not to Russians (*russkie*) or a single people (*narod*).[18] The declaration said nothing, however, about a special status for Tatarstan, which Tatarstan's leaders were already demanding. Disappointed, Shaimiev announced that Tatarstan would soon issue its own sovereignty declaration. In need of the avtonomii as allies in his intensifying struggle with Gorbachev, Yeltsin responded by supporting Tatarstan's sovereignty claims. Most dramatically, he arrived in Kazan on August 5, 1990, and made his famous statement urging the avtonomii to take "all the sovereignty you can swallow."[19]

The Tatar Supreme Soviet responded by issuing its own sovereignty declaration on August 30, 1990.[20] The declaration made no mention of Tatarstan being a constituent unit of the RSFSR. Instead, it was to serve as the basis for a new Tatarstan constitution, the conclusion of a USSR "Union Treaty," and "treaties with the RSFSR and other republics." It also asserted that Tatarstan's constitution and laws had "supremacy" (*verkhovenstvo*) on the territory of the republic. Despite Yeltsin's erstwhile support, RSFSR officials quickly articulated their opposition to these claims and similar demands being advanced by Russia's other avtonomii.

Over the course of late 1990 and early 1991, Tatarstan became caught up in Gorbachev's struggle to preserve the Soviet Union and the political battle between an increasingly assertive RSFSR government under Yeltsin and an increasingly defensive Gorbachev and USSR government. As this struggle progressed, Shaimiev and his advisors came to the conclusion that the RSFSR government was the principal obstacle to greater autonomy for the republic. Tatarstan therefore refused to include a question on the Russian presidency on ballots in the republic during the March 1991 referendum on the preservation of the Union. Moreover, its electorate voted overwhelmingly (87.5 percent) in favor of preserving the Union. When elections for an RSFSR president took place on June 12, 1991, turnout in Tatarstan was only 36.6 percent, and of those who participated, only 45 percent voted for Yeltsin (compared with 57 percent across the RSFSR). The same day, Tatarstan held its own inaugural presidential elections. Over two-thirds of voters participated, with Shaimiev, who had picked an ethnic Russian to be his vice-presidential running mate, winning an overwhelming majority.[21]

As the struggle over a new "Union Treaty" for the USSR continued, Tatarstan made clear that it would insist on being a full signatory to any treaty and that a separate bilateral treaty would be required to define Kazan's relationship with the RSFSR. When it appeared that an agreement had finally been reached, it was announced that Tatarstan would participate in the signing ceremony scheduled for August 20, 1991, in Moscow.[22] However, the day before the scheduled signing Moscow conservatives launched an ultimately abortive coup. Shaimiev, either because he was convinced that Yeltsin and his democratic allies represented the greater obstacle to Tatarstan's autonomy or because he was convinced the coup would succeed, made the mistake of siding with the putschists.

Yeltsin and the RSFSR government emerged greatly strengthened after the failure of the coup. Displeased by Shaimiev's support for the putschists, they concluded that Shaimiev was at heart a communist conservative and an opportunist who was using Tatarstan's sovereignty campaign to save his political career. Ruslan Khasbulatov, then a Yeltsin ally who had replaced the latter as chairman of Russia's Supreme Soviet, threatened to disband the Tatar parliament. Although Khasbulatov's threat was not carried out, it reinforced the belief in Kazan that Moscow "democrats" were the republic's principal political enemies. Relations between Tatarstan and the RSFSR deteriorated further when Yeltsin declared a state of emergency and dispatched federal troops to Checheno-Ingushetia to suppress radical nationalists in the republic. In the face of armed resistance by the Chechens and opposition from the RSFSR Supreme Soviet, Yeltsin lifted the state of emergency and withdrew Russia's troops from the republic. However, Kazan interpreted the incident as further evidence of Yeltsin's hostility to the political demands of the ethnic republics.

Relations between Tatars and Russians inside the republic also deteriorated in the wake of the failed coup. Reports surfaced that paramilitary groups of both nationalist Tatars and Russians were forming. On October 12, Ittifak's Bairamova published a particularly intemperate anti-Russian article.[23] Equally inflammatory statements were made by Russians.[24] Khasbulatov, who had replaced Yeltsin as the Chairman of the RSFSR Supreme Soviet and was becoming notorious among Tatar nationalists for his aggressive anti-Tatar rhetoric, reportedly stated that Shaimiev "should be brought to Moscow in an iron cage" and threatened a "second taking" of Kazan.[25]

Matters came to a head on October 15, 1991, the anniversary of Ivan the Terrible's storming of Kazan, an event that had been officially celebrated as a "day of liberation" in the Soviet period. As deputies to Tatarstan's Supreme Soviet met to discuss a referendum on the republic's status, a nationalist crowd numbering some 2,000 gathered outside in Kazan's Freedom Square. When the protesters learned that the Supreme Soviet had voted against a declaration of independence, they attempted to storm the parliament building. They were turned back by a police cordon, but the clash left six demonstrators and five militiamen in the hospital, two with serious injuries.[26]

Shaimiev nevertheless continued his efforts to ameliorate interethnic tensions. He condemned the violence and issued a decree banning paramilitary groups. He also indicated that the concerns of the demonstrators, if not their methods, were justified, and he asked that Tatarstan's Supreme Soviet decree that October 15 no longer be an official holiday. He also made clear that Tatarstan would not be a party to the "Federation Treaty" that Yeltsin was then advocating if the treaty did not recognize Tatarstan as a sovereign state associated with Russia on the basis of a separate bilateral treaty.

Radical Tatar nationalists nevertheless continued to press their agenda. In early February 1991, an all-Tatar Kuraltai (Congress) convened in Kazan.[27] Organized by Ittifak and attended by Tatars from around the former Soviet Union, the Kuraltai declared Tatarstan's independence, proclaimed Tatar to be the republic's only state language, adopted a state flag and elected a seventy-five-member Milli Medzhlis (National Assembly). When the Milli Medzhlis convened in late March, it declared itself the supreme legislative body of all Tatars and asserted the right to veto any laws or decrees that violated the spirit of Tatarstan's sovereignty declaration or the interests of ethnic Tatars living inside or outside the republic. Shaimiev responded that the Kuraltai and Milli Medzhlis had no legal authority within Tatarstan, and he reiterated that Tatarstan would pursue its autonomy demands "exclusively in a civilized and constitutional way."[28]

In the face of mounting pressure from Moscow to sign the Federation Treaty, Tatarstan decided that the time had come to hold a referendum on the republic's status. The language of the referendum, however, was the subject of heated debate. Radicals demanded a straightforward vote on independence while federalists were opposed to any referendum. Eventually a compromise formulation was agreed upon: "Do you agree that Tatarstan is a sovereign state and a subject of international law that is building relations with Russia and other republics and states on the basis of equal treaties?"

Despite its ambiguity, the question tersely captured Tatarstan's position at the time. As a sovereign state and a subject of international law, the republic had the right to enter into a bilateral, state-to-state treaty with the Russian government, or any other government, in which it would voluntarily delegate some of its sovereign powers. The most provocative clause in the referendum, and the one that Moscow would consistently reject, was that the republic was a "subject of international law," which Moscow felt would imply that Tatarstan was an independent state. Claims to "statehood" and "sovereignty," in contrast, were more acceptable — each had an ambiguous meaning inherited from the Soviet period, and ambiguity provided room for compromise. At the same time, the referendum's wording allayed the fears of Russians and Tatar moderates. It did not assert that Tatars were demanding "self-determination" (which would have implied that ethnic Russians were not part of the "self"), nor did it indicate that the republic would press for full independence and international recognition. Indeed, the ambiguous wording of the referendum doubtless enhanced its popularity; polls indicated that a significant majority of Tatarstan's electorate favored autonomy and "sovereignty" but that an even greater majority was opposed to secession.[29]

Tatarstan's referendum plans provoked the most serious crisis in Moscow-Kazan relations in the post-Soviet period. Immediately, the Russian government began to step up pressure. Russia's vice-president, Aleksandr Rutskoi, called on Yeltsin to declare a state of emergency and to blockade the republic, while Vice-Premier Sergei Shakhrai described the referendum as a *coup d'état*.[30] Russia's Constitutional Court ruled that the referendum and the 1990 sovereignty declaration violated the Russian constitution because both assumed that Tatarstan was not a part of the Russian Federation.[31] Radio Rossii reported that the legislature in one of Tatarstan's Russian-dominated cities, Bugul'ma, had announced its own referendum on secession from Tatarstan.[32] Rumors began to circulate of Russian troop maneuvers near the republic's borders, while the Russian Interior Ministry informed Tatarstan's officials that all heavy weapons in the possession of the local militia were being removed, a decision that Kazan interpreted as preparation for armed intervention. In addition, the RSFSR Procurator General announced criminal charges against Ittifak's Bairamova for inciting interethnic hatred, and he sent a delegation to the republic to inform local election officials that they would be criminally liable if they helped carry out the referendum. Finally, the head of the procuracy in the republic, who was a Russian, approached the head of the republic's election commission, a Tatar, and ordered him to close the polling stations.[33]

Nevertheless, Tatarstan's parliament refused to cave in. It reaffirmed its intention to proceed with the referendum on March 16, 1992, rejecting suggestions that the referendum's wording be changed. It reiterated, however, that the referendum did not ask the electorate to approve secession. This was not enough to satisfy Moscow. On March 18, the chairman of Russia's Constitutional Court addressed the Russian parliament and urged it to enforce the Court's ruling.[34] Yeltsin, too, condemned the referendum, and while he asserted that "the main thing is to act carefully, gradually, and in a friendly manner," he also appealed to Tatarstan's Supreme Soviet to comply with the Constitutional Court's ruling. And in a separate appeal to the people of Tatarstan broadcast on national radio, he made clear his belief that, despite Shaimiev's reassurances, the main goal of Tatarstan's leadership was full independence.[35] Shaimiev responded with his own television appearance in which he reiterated that the republic was not asking for an endorsement of secession, and he asked the citizens of Tatarstan to vote "yes." Tatarstan television then ran clips of Yeltsin's summer 1990 visit to Kazan and his appeal to the republics to "take all the sovereignty you can swallow."[36]

On the eve of the vote, officials in the republic feared that the local procuracy and militia would comply with Moscow's orders and close down the polling station. They likewise feared that election officials would refuse to implement the referendum or that "spontaneous" street violence would break out. To their relief, and to the surprise of many in Moscow, the referendum proceeded without incident on March 20, 1992. Indeed, Moscow's pressure seemed to backfire. The referendum was approved by 61.4 percent of those voting, and turnout was an impressive 81.6 percent, which meant that just over 50 percent of eligible voters had approved the initiative.[37] And the extent of support for the initiative suggested that many Russians had apparently voted "yes," albeit in fewer numbers than Tatars.[38]

The referendum was a decisive moment in Tatarstan's post-Soviet political history. In effect, a condition of multiple sovereignty had been resolved in favor of the republic's authorities. Previously, it had not been clear to whom local officials, including the local procuracy and militia, were answerable. The fact that local officials had ignored Moscow's demands that they not allow the referendum to the proceed, that the referendum had proceeded without incident, and that over 50 percent of the electorate had supported the ballot initiative meant that from that moment on Moscow had no one to turn to inside the republic who would carry out its orders.

For good reason, then, the results of the referendum cheered Tatar nationalists. The chairman of TOTs, Marat Muliukov, asserted that Tatarstan was now an independent state that warranted UN recognition, and he insisted that parliamentary deputies who had opposed the referendum be removed.[39] Shaimiev, on the other hand, was typically more circumspect. Seeking to reassure both local Russians and Moscow, he asserted that Tatarstan would "always be with Russia," and he argued that "we must not break centuries-old economic and cultural links." The republic's goal was not secession — rather, it was a bilateral treaty with Moscow in which powers assigned to the national government in areas such as defense and foreign policy would be delegated from below.[40] Yeltsin, too, made clear after the referendum that he preferred compromise by stating that he was not opposed in principle to a treaty with Kazan. And he reiterated that force should never be used to resolve Moscow's disagreements with the republic.

With the endorsement of the two presidents, negotiations over a bilateral treaty began almost immediately. Delegations from Moscow and Kazan met in Moscow on March 30-April 2, 1992, even as the Federation Treaty was being signed by the federal government and the sub''ekty excepting Tatarstan and Chechnya. The negotiations concluded with a protocol that merely confirmed that the two sides would soon reconvene.

Over the next two years, periodic negotiations between Kazan and Moscow would result in a series of intergovernmental agreements (*soglasheniia*) that resolved, at least temporarily, many of the most pressing conflicts between Moscow and Kazan. Agreement on a treaty (*dogovor*), however, would not come until February 1994. Shaimiev's political challenge in this period was to maintain the support of both Tatarstan's electorate and its political and economic elite, which required a firm hand in negotiations with the Russian government; avoid provoking Moscow's hardliners, many of whom continued to advocate the use of force to "restore constitutional order" in Tatarstan; and to preserve peace between Tatars and Russians within the republic.

Key to his success in meeting this challenge was his ongoing commitment to *mnogonatsional'nost'*: shortly after the referendum, he announced that Kazan would host a "Congress of Peoples of Tatarstan" that would stress the importance of ethnic peace and the republic's traditions of cultural tolerance, in contrast to the nationalist agenda of the all-Tatar Kuraltai held in February. In his opening speech to the Congress, which convened on May 23-24, 1992, and was attended by some 700 delegates from Tatarstan and elsewhere, Shaimiev noted that despite its many problems, the republic had managed to avoid significant inter-ethnic violence. Extolling the multinational character of the republic, he went on:

> By virtue of its geopolitical location, Tatarstan and its capital, Kazan, have played the role of a connecting link between West and East. They have been a meeting place of different civilizations, cultures, and confessions. Having lived together for centuries, people have worked out their own form of multinational discourse that has facilitated, and still facilitates, the mutual enrichment of languages and cultures and deep traditions of understanding and cooperation.[41]

In the following months, Shaimiev reached out to moderate Tatar nationalists through his support for a modest program of Tatar cultural revival. New Tatar-speaking primary and secondary schools and gymnasiums were established, state support increased for Tatar language training in Russian-speaking schools, a Tatarstan Academy of Sciences was set up, Tatar cultural centers were established in Tatarstan and elsewhere, and Tatar-language newspapers and other publications proliferated. Kazan also funded schools where the languages of instruction were Russian, Chuvash, Udmurt, Mordovan, and Marii. It also moved carefully on symbolic issues. Tatarstan's tricolor flag has a green stripe at the top to represent the Tatars, a red stripe at the bottom to represent the Russians, and a white stripe in the middle representing the other minorities of the republic. Communist-era names of streets, towns, factories, squares, and so on were changed only slowly because new names for public spaces confronted Tatarstan's authorities with a choice between contradictory mythologies of the past, one of which portrayed Russians as conquerors while the other portrayed them as liberators and modernizers. The government therefore tried to be even-handed as possible as it gradually abandoned the symbols and mythologies of communism.

Tatarstan also proceeded cautiously on economic reform. Shaimiev's "soft approach to the market" (*miakoe vkhozhdenie v rynok*), as it was called, entailed a gradual liberalization of prices and a slower approach to privatization than Moscow's. The fact that Shaimiev was from the communist nomenklatura may have influenced the program. So, too, did Tatarstan's political experience during the Gorbachev era, which made its leaders suspicious of "marketization from above" by Moscow's "democrats." But Tatarstan's leaders were also concerned that "shock therapy" would contribute to Russian-Tatar polarization. Instead, measures were taken to preserve welfare protections for the population, and a major, and apparently quite successful, anticrime campaign was launched in March 1993. Polls indicated that Tatarstan's electorate viewed these measures as prudent attempts to counter the negative consequences of marketization.

At the same time, the republic distanced itself economically from Moscow. On May 21, 1992, the Tatarstan Supreme Soviet adopted a law that effectively secured its "fiscal sovereignty" by implementing a single-channel tax system. Moscow responded by cutting off all federal disbursements to Kazan's budget. Kazan then stopped virtually all payments to the federal treasury even as it began to cooperate with other republics attempting to assert their fiscal autonomy.[42]

Nevertheless, Kazan went to considerable lengths to reassure Moscow that its political agenda was moderate. For example, it indicated a willingness to reach an agreement on fiscal matters before the republic's legal status was resolved. And it frequently reminded Moscow that, unlike Chechnya, Tatarstan was not pushing for complete independence. Accordingly, Kazan did not attempt to establish border controls, create a separate customs regime, create a separate currency, or establish its own national guard.[43] And neither did it press for international recognition, despite the language in the March 21 referendum characterizing the republic as "a subject of international law."[44]

By the end of 1992, however, talks were at a standstill, in part because the federal government was increasingly preoccupied by the executive-legislative crisis in Moscow. Tatarstan's Supreme Soviet reacted by ratifying a new constitution for the republic on November 6, 1992. The new constitution reaffirmed many of the principles expressed in the 1990 sovereignty declaration. It reconfirmed the nonethnic basis of the republic's statehood, with Article 1 asserting that Tatarstan was "a sovereign democratic state that expresses the will and interests of the entire multinational people (*vsego mnogonatsional'nogo naroda*) of the republic." Predictably, Tatarstan's constitution was criticized by both hard-liners and moderates in Moscow as a threat to Russia's territorial integrity.

By the end of 1993, the evidence suggested that Shaimiev's strategy was pay-ing dividends. Not only had relations with Moscow stabilized but tensions be-tween Russians and Tatars in the republic were abating. Polls indicated that radi-cal nationalist parties like Ittifak were supported by less than 2 percent of the electorate.[45] Support for Shaimiev and the Tatarstan government, on the other hand, was growing despite popular disappointment with the economy.[46] When Yeltsin managed to convince his opponents in Moscow to conduct on all-Russia referendum on Russia's future on April 25, 1993, the Tatarstan government indi-cated that, while it would not prevent the referendum from being held in Tatarstan, it would urge Tatarstan's voters to boycott it. As a result, only 20 percent of eligible voters turned out in the republic, again suggesting that not only a majority of Tatars but also many Russians in the republic supported Shaimiev's political course.[47]

By early September 1993, it had become clear that Yeltsin's plans for adopt-ing a new constitution that would resolve the executive-legislative impasse in Moscow was faltering. He therefore abandoned efforts to find a legal solution to Russia's deepening crisis of power and launched his "democratic coup" of September 21 by decreeing that the Supreme Soviet be disbanded. After many deputies refused to comply with the decree and incited supporters to launch an armed uprising in Moscow, Yeltsin ordered the Russian army to storm the Supreme Soviet on October 4, 1993. Having learned his lesson from the August 1991 coup, Shaimiev was careful not to take sides during the crisis.

With his victory in the October crisis, Yeltsin moved quickly to adopt a new constitution for Russia. The final version of Russia's new constitution, how-ever, did not please the republics, above all Tatarstan; it neither recognized the republics as "sovereign states" nor included language on Tatarstan's special sta-tus. In addition, the verbatim text of the Federation Treaty had been removed. Nevertheless, the constitution provided generally for a reasonable and flexible di-vision of powers between national and subnational governments.

When the new constitution was put to a popular referendum on December 12, 1993, Tatarstan again announced that while it would not prevent the referendum from taking place on its territory, neither would it facilitate it. Nor would Shaimiev or the republic's other major political figures run for election to the new Russian legislature. With television and radio stations in the republic urging residents of the republic not to turn out for either the referendum or the parliamentary elections, Tatarstan's electorate once more supported the republic's leadership — only 13.8 percent of eligible voters turned out. In addition, elections for representatives to the new Federation Council, the upper body of Russia's new legislature, did not take place in the republic because three candidates could not be found to run. One of five district elections for the State

Duma did not proceed for the same reason, and in the districts where elections were held, the validation threshold of 25 percent was not reached.[48] As a result, Tatarstan did not send a single representative to Russia's new legislature.

With the executive-legislative impasse finally resolved in Moscow, Yeltsin began to press ahead with efforts to reach an agreement with Kazan. At the time, Yeltsin was anxious to present himself as the consolidator of Russian statehood, and he needed an agreement with Kazan to show the Russian people that his administration had genuine achievements to its credit. Shaimiev, on the other, had apparently been chastened by Yeltsin's willingness to use force against his opponentsin this and had decided that it was time to institutionalize Tatarstan's autonomous status by coming to terms over a treaty. Accordingly, it was finally announced on February 14, 1994, that an agreement had been reached. The treaty, "On the Delimitation of Jurisdictional Authority and the Mutual Delegation of Powers between the State Bodies of the Russian Federation and State Bodies of the Republic of Tatarstan," was signed by Presidents Yeltsin and Shaimiev and Prime Ministers Chernomyrdin and Sabirov the following day.[49]

The treaty entailed concessions by both sides. The key passage stated that "that the Republic of Tatarstan, as a state (*gosudarstvo*), is united with (*ob'edinena s*) the Russian Federation on the basis of the Constitution of the Russian Federation, the Constitution of the Republic of Tatarstan, and the Treaty on the Delimitation of Jurisdictional Authority and the Mutual Delegation of Powers between State Bodies of the Russian Federation and State Bodies of the Republic of Tatarstan, and participates in (*uchastvuet v*) international political and economic relations." Thus, while Tatarstan accepted that it was "united with" (*ob''edinena s*), not merely "associated with" (*assotsirovana s*), Russia, as stated in its constitution, Moscow did not insist that the republic be described as a constituent unit (*v sostave*) of the Russian Federation. Rather, the treaty implied that Tatarstan was united with Russia on the basis of the treaty and, in this sense, the two parties were formally equal. Indeed, Tatarstan considers the Russian constitution binding on its territory only to the extent that it regulates the Russian state in carrying out powers specifically assigned to it by the treaty. And although its officials are reluctant to state this publicly, Kazan insists that the treaty takes precedence over *both* the republic's constitution and the Russian constitution. At the same time, Moscow accepted language stating that the treaty is "guided by" (*rukovodstvuias'*) *both* the Russian Federation constitution and the constitution of Tatarstan, which indicates recognition of the latter despite its contradictions with the Russian constitution. And it also agreed to language affirming the "universally recognized rights of peoples to self-determination."

An Unstable Relationship

Because it was not an "international" agreement between independent states, the treaty did not require legislative ratification in either capital but came into force automatically seven days after the signing ceremony. Shakhrai, by then Russia's Minister for Nationalities and Regional Policy, hailed it as "a great breakthrough in the promotion of federal relations" and "the sole means to preserve the nation's territorial integrity." And he expressed the hope that the treaty would serve as a model for the resolution of Moscow's disagreements with Chechnya.[50] Shaimiev agreed, arguing that the treaty "affirms a new model of relations founded on the principles of law and justice."[51] Predictably, however, there were vigorous critics of the treaty in both capitals.[52]

Having come to an understanding with Tatarstan, Yeltsin and his advisers turned their attention to Chechnya. Unlike Tatarstan, Chechnya continued to insist on full independence and had been far more intransigent in its dealings with Moscow. Yeltsin's government nevertheless launched another initiative in late 1993 to early 1994 to reach an agreement with the Chechen president, Dzhokhar Dudaev, but to no avail. By the summer of 1994, Moscow was stepping up pressure on Dudaev by increasing its military and financial support to the Chechen opposition. Despite his support, the anti-Dudaev Chechen opposition was defeated in a battle in Grozny in November, and the Chechen government proceeded to parade captured Russian soldiers before national television cameras. Yeltsin and his Security Council responded to this humiliation by ordering the Russian military to invade.

Over the next two and a half years, the Russian military would find itself engaged in a brutal and debilitating war that would lead to some 40,000 deaths, destroy much of the infrastructure of the republic, drain untold resources from the federal budget, and totally demoralize the Russian armed forces. The war would virtually guarantee that the Chechens, who had been internally divided before the war, would remain united in their hostility to Moscow and would never become a "normal" member of the Russian Federation. Contrary to Moscow's hopes, then, the war only increased the likelihood that Chechnya will eventually secede from Russia.

In contrast, relations between Moscow and Kazan improved significantly over this same period. Elections in Tatarstan for the federal legislature took place as scheduled on March 13, 1994. Despite calls by Tatar nationalists for another boycott, turnout in the republic was high (68 percent), a remarkable endorsement of the republic's leadership when contrasted with the 14 percent turnout in December. Shaimiev was elected to the Council of the Federation with 91.2 percent of the vote, as was the chairman of the Tatarstan legislature, also an ethnic Tatar. Of the five deputies elected to the Duma, three were Russian, one was Tatar, and one was Jewish.[53] Yeltsin made a two-day visit to the republic in late

May in which he reiterated his position that the treaty was a model for the further decentralization of the Russian Federation. By the end of the year, relations between Kazan and Moscow had improved to the point that Russia's Foreign Ministry was arranging foreign trips for Tatarstan's officials, inviting them to Russia's embassies and consulates and helping them contact foreign investors.

Nevertheless, there are numerous unresolved disagreements between Kazan and Moscow that require constant management and goodwill in both capitals. Above all, there are still unresolved legal ambiguities regarding Tatarstan's status and contradictions between the Russian and Tatarstan constitutions, which requires that both sides accept a considerable measure of legal ambiguity and deliberate vagueness to avoid further conflict.[54] For example, as noted earlier, Tatarstan's constitution asserts that it is "supreme" on its territory and that republic laws preempt those of the federal government, while the Russian constitution asserts that it is binding throughout the territory of the Federation and that federal laws have priority unless they violate the federal constitution. Likewise, Tatarstan's constitution asserts that the republic is "associated with" (*assotsirovana s*) Russia, while the treaty uses the term "united with" (*ob''edinena s*), and the Russian constitution describes the republic as "part of" (*v sostave*) the federation and identifies Tatarstan as one of Russia's 21 republics. It is also not yet clear whether the staffing of the judiciary, police forces, procuracy, arbitrage courts, and notary services falls within the jurisdiction of Kazan or Moscow, or whether staffing issues somehow are to be resolved jointly.

There are also tensions on economic matters. While a de facto single-channel tax system has been accepted by Moscow, tax collection is technically subject to joint jurisdiction, and Kazan determines its own budget and the rates of taxation in the republic. While its contributions to the federal budget are specified by agreement, there are still serious disagreements on fiscal matters. In particular, the Russian Defense Ministry has repeatedly fallen into arrears on payments for purchases from enterprises in the republic; by the summer of the 1995, it reportedly owed some 96 billion rubles (approximately $19 million). Kazan finally announced on July 11, 1995, that it would stop all payments to the federal budget until the debt was paid, which took approximately six weeks.[55]

Political conflicts are also complicating the relationship. Kazan's efforts to establish direct political and economic ties with foreign governments are objected to by many in Moscow. Of particular concern are the republic's ties with Abkhazia, an autonomous republic in Georgia before the Soviet collapse that has been engaged in a bloody secessionist conflict with Georgia since 1992. In search of allies to support its autonomy campaign, Tatarstan signed an interstate Treaty of Friendship and Cooperation with Abkhazia on August 17, 1994. The Georgian Foreign Ministry condemned the treaty as an illegal interference in the internal affairs of Georgia, while the Russian Foreign Ministry described it as a violation of the Russian-Georgian Friendship Treaty of February 1994.[56]

Tatarstan was also a consistent and vigorous opponent of the war in Chechnya. As relations between Grozny and Moscow deteriorated over the course of 1994, Shaimiev offered his services as a mediator, indicating that he would try to convince Dudaev of the benefits of a treaty-based relationship with Moscow. Shaimiev also urged Yeltsin, both publicly and privately, to meet with Dudaev as a gesture of goodwill. However, neither Moscow nor Grozny responded to his offers or advice. When Moscow finally launched its invasion, Kazan viewed it as a political disaster not only for Chechnya and for Russia but for Tatarstan as well. Accordingly, Shaimiev continued to call for a ceasefire and a negotiated solution to the conflict and to offer to help negotiate a settlement.

Relatedly, there are disagreements between Moscow and Kazan over military service obligations for the republic's citizens. The February 1994 treaty seems to grant the federal government a right of conscription. However, Article 8 of an intergovernmental agreement on military issues of March 5, 1994, states that Tatarstan's conscription quota is to be determined by agreement with the republic and that only volunteers from the republic can serve abroad.[57] Tatarstan interpreted this to mean that citizens of Tatarstan could not be forced to serve in Chechnya, and it vigorously objected when some were.

All these conflicts must be managed carefully if relations between Moscow and Kazan are not to deteriorate. Confrontational politics in either Moscow or Kazan, by current or future governments, would likely bring an end to the ongoing negotiations that are required to manage their complicated relationship. Likewise an outbreak of Tatar-Russian violence within the republic would almost certainly precipitate a crisis in relations between Moscow and Kazan, particularly if it were perceived as having been provoked by either government.

For now, Shaimiev appears to be firmly in control in Tatarstan. Although he is frequently criticized by the Tatar intelligentsia for authoritarian tendencies, he claims to be supported by a substantial majority of the republic's electorate. At the same time, he has the support of the bulk of the republic's political and economic elite. Maintaining this support in the long run will likely depend on Shaimiev's ability to manage relations with Moscow and on the republic's economic performance. Fortunately for Shaimiev, there are signs that the republic's economy is starting to turn around.[58] And equally important, polls indicate that relations between Tatars and Russians in the republic have improved dramatically since their nadir at the end of 1991.[59]

Asymmetrical Federalism and Russia's Territorial Integrity

Thus, rather than leading to a collapse of the Russian state, negotiated and asymmetrical federalism appears to have helped defend Russia's territorial integrity. Yeltsin's only alternative, given Russia's circumstance in 1992-94, would have been to use force to impose Moscow's writ on the recalcitrant republics and regions. Such a course, which had proved so ineffectual during Gorbachev's campaign to preserve the USSR, had also failed in late 1991 when Yeltsin tried to restore federal authority in Checheno-Ingushetia. And it would later prove a disaster with the invasion of Chechnya. While accepting negotiated asymmetries was risky, so too did a resort to force risk provoking widespread violence and a weakening of the Russian state.

This is not to say that asymmetrical federalism or negotiated autonomy is a panacea or a model for other countries regardless of circumstances. On the contrary, they may simply be the least worst option. It could be, for example, that peaceful divorce is preferable. Rather, the claim is that, if the goal is the preservation of a state's territorial integrity, then asymmetrical federalism *may* be an effective means for attaining that goal and indeed may be the only option available. Conversely, legal dogmatism, or the assumption that a transparent, symmetrical, and constitutionally entrenched system of federalism can be established in all circumstances, may be unrealistic.

It is also true, however, that ethnically defined subnational governments with asymmetrical relations with the national government will entrench ethnic identities, thereby ensuring that ethnic tensions and conflicts over preferential policies, language policy, and so on persist. The U.S. case shows that they also persist without asymmetical ethnic federalism. The particular arrangements that are negotiated for autonomous areas are therefore likely to prove unstable and require continuous management at both the national and the subnational level. If they are mismanaged, tensions could spiral into violence or secession. Of course, for those who value the preservation of traditional cultures and languages, the entrenchment of separate identities may well be worth the price of persistent conflict, risks of violence, and political divorce.

The critical point, however, is that asymmetrical federalism does not lead inexorably to state disintegration. In each case, the costs and benefits of secession will vary, but in most cases, the costs of moving from autonomy to secession will be considerable. So far, the Russian national government has had sufficient leverage to ensure that, with the exception of Chechnya, subnational governments have not moved from autonomy to secession.

What was Moscow's leverage that prevented Kazan from pressing too far? First, Moscow's position was greatly strengthened by the refusal of the international community to recognize Tatarstan's independence without Moscow's approval, a position that was well understood by both Moscow and Kazan at the time. Aware that formal recognition, with all its implications of finality under international law, was not imminent, Moscow could afford to be patient. Kazan, on the other hand, knew that a unilateral declaration of independence would be ignored abroad and thus would only provoke Moscow without bringing the largely symbolic benefits of international recognition. In addition, Tatarstan's inability to obtain international recognition provided Moscow with considerable economic leverage. Tatarstan needed international investment for its economic recovery. But because Moscow was the internationally recognized sovereign power in the republic, it could insist that foreign investors abide by Russian laws. It could also discourage foreign investors by warning them of the risks of conflict and by portraying the republic's leadership as a cabal of old guard communists, as Moscow in fact did on a number of occasions.

Second, the direct costs of independence — including the costs of creating a foreign ministry and a diplomatic corps, of establishing some sort of representation in foreign capitals and international organization, of membership fees in international organizations, of setting up border controls and collecting customs duties (assuming no customs union), and of creating some kind of military that would raise the costs of invasion to Moscow — would have been considerable. Indirect costs, however, would probably have been even greater. A different legal regime or tariff schedule, for example, would likely have increased transactions costs within the republic significantly.

Third, Tatarstan was highly vulnerable to direct political and economic pressure by Moscow. Had Kazan pushed too far, Moscow could have established border controls, levied duties on cross-border trade, and even imposed a full-scale trade embargo. Despite its oil extracting facilities, an embargo would have led to an acute energy crisis because of Tatarstan's lack of oil refining capacity. Russia could also have denied the republic's citizens dual citizenship, insisted that its citizens obtain visas before entering Russian territory, rerouted pipelines around the republic to eliminate transit fees, and charged fees for the use of Russia's airspace and the transshipment of exports across Russian territory. Finally, Moscow could have poisoned interethnic relations in the republic by playing up threats to Russians even as it discriminated against the 3.8 million Tatars in Russia.

Fourth, Tatarstan's ability to find reliable allies among the other sub''ekty was hampered because the sub''ekty are divided along numerous lines of cleavage (regions versus republics, agrarian economies versus industrial economies, conservative-oriented elites versus reformist-elites, etc.). Moreover, the very fact that there are eighty-nine sub''ekty makes it difficult for them to overcome collective action problems and coordinate challenges to the federal government.

Finally, authorities in Kazan were always concerned that pushing too far would lead to Moscow to introduce troops into the republic. However irrational and counterproductive such a course might have been, there could be no guarantee that moderation would prevail at the federal level. And it was widely believed, both in Kazan and in Moscow, that invading Tatarstan would be a far less challenging military task than was invading Chechnya.

On the other hand, Tatarstan had its own very considerable leverage. After Moscow's failure to prevent the March 21, 1992 referendum, federal authorities could not rely on the republic's police or procuracy to carry out its orders. In addition, the absence of a significant Russian military presence made it impossible for Moscow to use locally based troops to intimidate Tatarstan's government or to enforce a state of emergency. To impose its writ by force, Moscow would have had to send federal troops into the republic, a move that would likely have been met by some (unpredictable) degree of armed resistance by the Tatars. And while the extent of this resistance might have been limited, Moscow would have been forced to govern a hostile population under the critical eye of the international community. Finally, Russia's other republics and regions would have vigorously resisted the use of force against a republic that, unlike Chechnya, had consistently indicated a willingness to negotiate and had never expressed an intention to secede.

Moscow's economic leverage was also limited. Tatarstan's defense industries produced hardware that was essential to Russia's military, which meant that the Defense Ministry opposed an economic embargo. Tatarstan could also have reacted to an embargo by cutting off the flow of oil and gas through the republic's vital pipeline system. Moreover, creating an economic crisis in the republic might have radicalized the Tatars, just as it had the peoples of the Baltics when similar tactics had been tried by Gorbachev. It might also have made Shaimiev's political position precarious, and any replacement here might have proven more, not less, hostile to the national government. Finally, with its significant industrial capacity, natural resources, and economic infrastructure, Tatarstan was less dependent on budgetary subventions from Moscow than most of Russia's other ethnic republics, which meant that the suspension of intergovernmental budgetary transfers had a limited impact on the republic.

Perhaps most important, however, was Tatarstan's occupation of the moral high ground. Kazan constantly reminded Yeltsin of his statement in August 1991 urging the republics to take "all the sovereignty you can swallow." Indeed, the republic used the very same arguments in defense of its autonomy and "sovereignty" that Yeltsin had used during his campaign for autonomy and sovereignty for Russia in 1989-91. To have used force against a republic that had managed to contain interethnic conflict, that had consistently advocated negotiations to resolve differences with Moscow, that posed no security threat to Russia, and that was not pressing for secession would have been an act of naked hypocrisy.

This leverage has allowed Tatarstan to carve out a very considerable degree of autonomy for itself; indeed, by 1995 the republic was essentially self-governing. Tatarstan officials proudly note that the Russian flag does not fly over government buildings in the republic. The republic defines its own structure of government, elects its own president and legislature, adopts its own laws, collects all taxes on its territory, determines taxation rates in the republic, and has trade and political links with other republics and regions and with foreign governments. Moreover, it will be difficult for Moscow to limit this autonomy significantly in the future. The treaty is entrenched by Article IX, which specifies that neither the treaty itself nor its individual provisions "may be unilaterally repealed, altered, or supplemented," as well as by the fact that no termination date is set. Should hard-liners come to power in Moscow and try to impose their will unilaterally, Tatarstan will simply ignore anything that it considers a violation of the treaty or the associated intergovernmental agreements. The only recourse for Moscow would then be resort to force, an option already so discredited by the debacle in Chechnya.

Notes

1. *Natsional'nyi sostav naseleniia RSFSR* (Moscow: Goskomstat, 1990).

2. The exception was Dagestan, which was home to ten officially recognized national minorities. The RSFSR consisted of 57 nonethnically defined constituent units (45 *oblasts,* 10 *krais,* and the "federal cities" of Moscow and Leningrad). In 1991, the autonomous oblasts, with the exception of the Jewish Autonomous Oblast in the Russian Far East, were given the status of autonomous republics, and together they were renamed "republics" (*respubliki*). In 1992, the Chechen-Ingush ASSR formally split into separate Chechen and Ingush Republics. As a result, the Russian Federation today is comprised of a total of 89 *sub''ekty* (including Chechnya): 21 republics, one autonomous *oblast,* ten autonomous *okrugs,* 55 *oblasts,* and six *krais.* While consideration was given to changing the name of the constituent units of the federation from "subjects" (sub''ekty) to "members" (*chleny*) on the grounds that the former connoted greater subordination than the latter, the term *"sub''ekty federatsii"* was retained in the 1993 constitution. The conventional distinction in Russian political discourse is between respubliki (the 21 "republics") and the regions (the 66 oblasts and krais, or "regions"), a practice I follow below. I also adopt the Russian term *sub''ekt* for the constitutuent units of the federation as whole, much as länder is used in English to refer to the constituent units of the Federal Republic of Germany.

3. Throughout this paper, we use the terms "Russians" and "Tatars" to designate ethnic Russians and ethnic Tatars, respectively, notwithstanding the fact that almost all Tatars are Russian citizens and many Russians are citizens of Tatarstan.

4. D. M. Iskhakov, *Tatary: Populiarnyi ocherk etnicheskoi istorii i demografii* (Nabereznhye Chelny: Gazetno-knizhnoe izdatel'stvo KAMAZ, 1993), 18-21. The 1989 census listed 157,376 Tatars in Moscow alone.

5. Appendix 1, R.I. Musina, "K voprosu o meste i roli religii v zhizni sovremennykh Tatar," in *Sovremennye natsional'nye protsessy v respublike Tatarstana* ed. D. I. Iskhakov and R. I. Musina (Kazan: Kazanskii nauchnyi tsentr, 1992), 128. In neighboring Bashkiria, there were almost as many Tatars (1.12 million) as in Tatarstan (1.77 million) and more Tatars than ethnic Bashkirs (28.4 percent to 21.9 percent of the total population, with Russians at 39.3 percent).

6. *Natsional'nyi sostav,* 110.

7. *Natsional'nyi sostav,* 123.

8. Azade-Ayse Rorlich, *The Volga Tatars: A Profile in National Resistance* (Stanford: The Hoover Institute, 1986).

9. Ron Wixman, "The Middle Volga: Ethnic Archipelago in a Russian Sea," in *Nations and Politics in the Soviet Sucessor States,* eds. Ian Bremmer and Ray Taras (New York: Cambridge University Press, 1993), 187.
10. Marie Bennigsen Broxrup, "Tatarstan and the Tatars," in *The Nationalities Question in the Post-Soviet States,* 2nd ed., ed. Graham Smith (New York: Longman, 1996), 76.
11. Some Tatars were converted, however, and there is therefore a significant community of Tatar *starokreshchenye* (Old Christians) as well as *novokreshchenye* (New Christians), the difference being when they converted.
12. Iskakhov, *Tatary,* 15.
13. See Jerry F. Hough, "Sociology, the State and Language Politics," *Post-Soviet Affairs,* forthcoming.
14. D. M. Iskhakov and R. Musina, *Sovremennye mezhnatsional'nye protsessy v Tatarskoi SSR* (Kazan: Kazanskii nauchnyi tsentr, 1991).
15. R. I. Musina, "K voprosu o meste i roli religii v zhizni sovremennykh Tatar," in *Sovremennye natsional'nye protsessy v respublike Tatarstana,* 52-64.
16. For a description of political groups and parties in Tatarstan in this early period, see D. M. Iskhakov, "Neformal'nye ob''edineniia v sovremennom Tatarskom obshchestve," in *Sovremmennye natsional'nye protsessy,* 5-52.
17. *Pravda,* October 2, 1989, 2. Shaimiev had been the chairman of the republic's Council of Ministers, having made his way up the party ladder as an apparatchik with a background in agriculture.
18. The declaration's preamble asserted that it expressed the will of the "peoples" of the RSFSR, not of "the Russian people"; Article 1 reiterated that the RSFSR was "a sovereign state created by the peoples united within it"; Article 3 asserted that the "RSFSR's multiethnic people are the repository of sovereignty and are the source of state power"; and Article 4 stated that the RSFSR's sovereignty was being proclaimed in order to guarantee, inter alia, the right of "every people to self-determination in their chosen national-state and national cultural form." From "Declaration of the State Sovereignty of the RSFSR," in *Perestroika in the Soviet Republics: Documents on the National Question,* eds. Charles F. Furtado, Jr. and Andrea Chandler (Boulder: Westview, 1992), 325-26.
19. *Argumenty i fakty* 35, September 1-7, 1990, translated in FBIS-SOV-90-172, September 5, 1990, 113.
20. Reprinted in *Belaia kniga Tatarstana: Put' k suverenitetu,1990-1993,* ed. Rafael Khakimov (Kazan, 1993), 4 (henceforth BK).
21. *Izvestiia,* June 13, 1991, 2.
22. BK, 18-19. The protocol's first point stated that the delegations had agreed "to establish relations on the basis of treaty-forms of regulation, taking into consideration their key interests but without infringing on the interests of other republics and the Union as a whole." It also recognized "the desire of the Russian Soviet Federated Socialist Republic and the Republic of Tatarstan, as participants in the Treaty on the Union of Sovereign States, to renew and raise their status."
23. She wrote, "Just how can we hold a discussion about independence, make demands on Russia, and protect ourselves by forming an army? Just how can we shut up the local Russians who are raising a howl against independence? The

leaders of Tatarstan are still pretending to be good fellows, while both the Russians and the Jews are laughing at us in a mocking way. They eat our bread, but they don't even consider us human beings. . . ." As translated from Tatar into Russian in *Kazanskie vedomosti* and republished in *Izvestiia,* November 25, 1991, 4, and translated into English in *CDSP,* vol. 43, no. 47, 1991, 3.

24. For example, the newspaper of the Tatar nationalist faction, *"Suverenitet"* (Sovereignty), published an article entitled "The Birth of Fascism?" that consisted of letters to the editor from angry Russians with passages such as "Kill all the stinking ethnics." The article pointed out that a Russian-language newspaper had printed a campaign promise by the extreme Russian nationalist Vladimir Zhirinovsky: "And I'll resettle the Bashkirs and the Tatars in Mongolia. There's filth and syphilis there, so let them live there." *Nezavismaiia gazeta,* November 26, 1991, 3, as translated in *CDSP,* vol. 43, no. 47, 1.

25. Khasbulatov reportedly made these remarks during an interview with reporters from *Izvestia Tatarstana.* According to *Nezavisimaia gazeta,* in an issue in which it reprinted excerpts of the published version of the interview, a decision was made not to publish his more incendiary remarks in *Izvestia Tatarstana* because of fears that they would promote tensions in the republic. However, as the *Nezavisimaia gazeta* article put it, "Remarks about the 'iron cage' in which those who disagree with the Russian Republic lawmakers will supposedly be taken to Moscow and about a possible 'second taking' of Kazan have already become part of the folklore of Tatarstan's politicians." *Nezavisimaia gazeta,* November 27, 1991, 3, as translated in *CDSP,* vol. 43, no. 47, 4. The published part of the interview quoted Khasbulatov as asserting that "Russia is getting nothing [from Tatarstan]. Tataria's foul chemical industry isn't giving anyone anything," and he went on to insult the republic's leadership: "You have no real leader today. . . . You have people who want to hold on to their official positions." The Tatars, he went on, "are building a feudal principality. You like medieval obscurantism, is that it?"

26. *Pravda,* October 17, 1991, as translated in *CDSP,* vol. 43, no. 42, 29.

27. *Izvestiia,* February 3, 1992, 2.

28. RFE/RL Daily Report, February 4, 1992.

29. *Konstitutsionnyi vestnik,* no. 14, (Moscow 1992), 66. The deliberate ambiguity of the referendum anticipated by several years the similarly ambiguous referendum on Quebec's sovereignty in 1995. Tatarstan's leaders were, however, more explicit in their denials that they were pursuing independence than were Quebec's leaders.

30. *Izvestiia,* March 17, 1992, 2.

31. *Rossiiskaia gazeta,* March 16, 1992, 1-2.

32. *RFE/RL Daily Report,* March 4, 1992.

33. Author's interview with Rafael Khakimov, Kazan, July 22, 1995.

34. *Moscow News,* March 25, 1992.

35. *Rossiiskaia gazeta,* March 20, 1992, 1, and TASS, March 21, 1992.

36. *Rossiiskaia gazeta,* March 21, 1992, 1.

37. Author's interviews with Rafael Khakimov, Kazan, July 16, 24, 25, 1995.

38. *Izvestiia,* March 23, 1992.

39. Support for the referendum was higher in predominantly rural areas (75.3 percent), while in urban areas, where there were higher concentrations of Russians, only 58.7 percent voted "yes." In particular, 51.2 percent of those voting in Kazan voted "no." Reportedly, a division of paratroopers in Ul'ianovsk was put on maneuvers to intimidate the republic. (Author's interviews with Rafael Khakimov, July 21, 22, 23, 1995, Kazan). Khakimov also recalled that on March 22, 1992, all stockpiles of weapons were withdrawn from the republic. He argued that international obervers in Tatarstan at the time were a major a deterrent to intervention by Moscow because "at the time Russia was afraid of America."

40. *Rossiiskaia gazeta*, March 24, 1992, 1.

41. BK, 23.

42. *Materialy s''ezda narodov Tatarstana,* (Kazan: Tatarskoe knizhnoe izdatel'stvo, 1993), 8.

43. For example, Tatarstan, Yakutia, and Bashkortostan issued a joint statement condemning the language of a July 13, 1992 Russian Federation law on the budget system that gave the Russian government and the Central Bank the authority to punish sub''ekty that did not meet their obligations to the federal budget. *Nezavisimaia gazeta,* August 15, 1992, 1.

44. For background, see *Kontseptsiia natsional'noi bezopasnosti Respubliki Tatarstana: osnovnye polozheniia politicko-voennogo kharaktera,* Kazan: Vsetatarskii obshchestvennyi tsentr, 1994.

45. See Ann Sheehy, "Russia's Republics: A Threat to Its Territorial Integrity?," *RFE/RL Reports*, vol. 2, no. 20, May 14, 1993, 34-40.

46. *Mnogonatsional'nyi Tatarstan*, 48 and Musina, "K voprosu o meste. . .", 7.

47. A poll of Russians taken in certain Soviet successor states and Russia's republics in the summer of 1992 showed that the desire of ethnic Russian to emigrate from Tatarstan was, along with the Baltic states, Ukraine, and Kazakhstan, quite low, at only 6 to 11 percent, compared to 37 percent who wished to leave Checheno-Ingushetia. *Nezavisimaia gazeta,* July 31, 1992, 5.

48. For a discussion of Yeltsin's efforts to win the support of the republics in his struggle with the Supreme Soviet in 1992-93, see Gail W. Lapidus and Edward W. Walker, "Nationalism, Regionalism, and Federalism: Center-Periphery Relations in Post-Communist Russia," in *The New Russia: Troubled Transformation,* ed. Gail W. Lapidus (Boulder: Westview, 1995), 79-113.

49. I have analyzed the constitution's federation provisions in "Federalism Russian Style: The Federation Provisions in Russia's new Constitution," *Problems of Post-Communism,* July-August, 1995, 3-12.

50. ITAR-TASS World Service, February 15, 1994, and Interfax, in FBIS-SOV-94-032, 37.

51. *Krasnaia zvesda*, Feruary 17, 1994, in FBIS-SOV-94, February 18, 1994, 15.

52. For example, Gennadii Ziuganov, leader of the Communist Party of the Russian Federation (CPRF), characterized it as "unacceptable" (Federal Information Systems Corporation, Official Kremlin International News Broadcast, February 16, 1994). In contrast, the Tatar writer, Zulfat Hakim, condemned the treaty as a betrayal in a letter to Shaimiev: "According to the Russia custom you have exchanged three kisses with Yeltsin. For your long-suffering

people, living in particularly difficult days, it is as if you had spat three times in their faces from the height of a Russian Golden Dome. . . This treaty. . . will bring no blessings to the people of Tatarstan. On the contrary, tragically, it has confirmed the subjugation of Kazan to Moscow. It is the first time in our history that a document, legalizing the rule of Russia over Tatarstan, has been signed. It is a crime against our ancestors, a crime against the nation. To accept this yoke is a betrayal of our forefathers who fought to defend Kazan in 1552." Quoted in Broxup, "Tatarstan and the Tatars," 87. Broxup is herself highly critical of the treaty.

53. Rashit Akhmetov, "Tatarstan: The Post Electoral Ethno-Political Situation," in *Bulletin: Network on Ethnological Monitoring and Early Warning of Conflict* (Cambridge, Mass.: Conflict Management Group, June 1995), 53-54.

54. For an analysis, see Irina A. Umnova, "Konstitutsiia Rossiiskoi Federatsii, Konstitutsiia Respubliki Tatarstana, Dogovor Mezhdu Rossiiskoi Federatsiei i Respublikoi Tatarstana" (June 1994, unpublished paper.)

55. In May 1994, Soskovets and Panskov had signed a document committing Moscow to paying the debt, but Moscow had failed to abide by the agreement.

56. Most notably, in July 1995, as the Russian government was beginning to distance itself from Abkhazia and other secessionists movements in the wake of the debacle in Chechnya, the speaker of the Federation Council, Vladimir Shumeiko, accused the Abkhazians of genocide and compared Ardzimba to Dudaev. Shaimiev condemned the remarks and called for a debate in the Federation Council on Shumeiko's statement, but his proposal was rejected. Since the strong communist performance in the December 1995 elections, the Duma has become even more pro-Abkhaz.

57. Article II.9 of the treaty states that the republic has the right to establish the terms of alternative military service within Tatarstan but only "for citizens who have a right to have their military service commuted under federal law". Article 1 of the March 1994 agreement states that the federal government determines the procedures for military service for citizens of the republic, and Article 8 states that Tatarstan's conscription quota is determined by agreement with the republic and that only volunteers from the republic can serve abroad.

58. Over the first six months of 1995, Tatarstan's economy outperformed Russia's as a whole (97 percent) as well as that of neighboring Nizhegorodsk aia oblast (99.8 percent) and Bashkortostan (98.7 percent).

59. For example, only 4 percent of the republic's Russians indicate that they intend to leave, a significantly lower figure than in many of Russia's other republics. Instead, many Tatars and Russians plan to immigrate to the republic from Central Asia (a possible source of increased tension, however, given the limited housing stock). Leokadia Drobizheva, "Nationalism and Democracy in the Post-Soviet Russian Federation," in *Nationalism, Ethnic Identity and Conflict Management in Russia Today*, eds. Gail W. Lapidus and Renee de Nevers (Stanford: Center for International Security and Arms Control, Stanford University, 1995), 17. See also Drobizheva, 23, and Airat Aklaev, "Ethno-political Conflicts and Crises in the Russian Federation and the Problems of Legitimacy: Four Cases with the Russian Federation," in *Nationalism, Ethnic Identity and Conflict Management*, 31-45.

Eleven

The Tamil Secessionist Movement in Sri Lanka (Ceylon):[1] A Case of Secession by Default?

M. R. R. Hoole

In July 1983 the worst bout of communal violence against the Tamils took place. President Jayawardene of Sri Lanka and his United National Party (UNP) government were implicated. Thereafter, India covertly armed and trained the militant Tamils. The almost exclusively Sinhalese government forces perpetrated thousands of massacres and disappearances of Tamil civilians.[2] The government also took military steps to impose settlements of marginalized Sinhalese in predominantly Tamil areas. The regime in Colombo enjoyed very little sympathy abroad and many Sinhalese watched with alarm as democratic freedoms were trodden under. By 1985 the legitimacy of the Tamil separatist cause stood at its peak.

India's sponsorship had built small disparate bands of Tamil guerrillas into an army of several battalions commanded by rival warlords, whom Indian state agencies hoped to play against one another. Accountability of these forces to the Tamil people largely disappeared. By early 1985, stories began to circulate of widespread torture and the elimination of dissenters within militant groups. Dissidents within the Peoples' Liberation Organization of Tamil Eelam (PLOTE) went public by issuing a book, but the problem was endemic to other Tamil groups as well, notably Tamil Eelam Liberation Organization (TELO) and the Liberation Tigers of Tamil Eelam (LTTE, or "Tigers"). In May 1985, following the Sri Lankan Army's massacre of about seventy Tamil civilians in a northern coastal town, the LTTE carried out a massacre of over 150 mainly Buddhist pilgrims.[3]

Although many Tamils rationalized this murder of Sinhalese civilians as an act of self-defense, an important threshold had been crossed. A year later, the LTTE took advantage of a split in the leadership of the fellow Tamil militant group TELO to launch an all-out brutal attack on it. By the end of 1986, through terror, cunning, and murder, the LTTE had made itself the sole militant group in the struggle. It then banned all other groups.

The LTTE had appealed to the authoritarian nationalism of the Tamil middle class and represented itself as the only force that stood between the Tamils and an oppressive Sri Lankan state. But its own history carried some liabilities. Having lost the moral high ground, many Tamils became disillusioned, questioning a liberation struggle that had modeled its actions on its chief oppressor, the Sri Lankan armed forces.

Internal repression and attacks on free expression in matters of conscience became more fundamental to the LTTE's struggle than its armed confrontations with the Indian and Sri Lankan forces. In 1998, the Tamil community is disillusioned, seeing little prospect that the conflict will end. The more privileged sections drift toward the West as immigrants or refugees. With a casualty rate of about one to one, the LTTE must recruit from the most vulnerable sections of the populace.[4] Many of the recruits are children and young women from the poorer strata.

By developing support in the Tamil emigrant diaspora and links with the global underworld of narcotics and arms, the LTTE acquired a staying power to which the consent of the people was marginal. It carried out massacres of Muslim and Sinhalese civilians in the North-East.

Unable to stabilize itself in the existing regional order, the LTTE rejected attempts at political resolution in 1987, 1990, and 1994. It used suicide assassins to kill Prime Minister Rajiv Gandhi of India in 1991 and several leading political figures in Sri Lanka. The Tamils became virtual prisoners in their home territory. The LTTE easily mobilized Tamil youths to perform suicidal acts of sacrifice for the "Leader."[5]

The Sri Lankan state, brutalized by its own chauvinism and violence, could not deal with the phenomenon it had spawned. Its own paranoia and violence further alienated the Tamils, giving substance to the LTTE's image as their savior. For the people of Ceylon, only uncertainty lies ahead.

A Brief History of the People of Ceylon

Sri Lanka's present ethnic or linguistic distributions do not correspond to those of ancient times. Iron Age urban centers emerged around the tip of the Indian peninsula from about 900 B.C. Anuradhapura became a center in Ceylon, and Madhurai became the seat of rulers in South India. Iron Age people, called the "Nagas," lived in small kingdoms in South India and Ceylon.[6] From about 600 B.C., dynasties with North Indian antecedents were becoming influential in the South.[7] Hinduism, Buddhism, and Jainism came to Southern India and Ceylon, along with their sacred languages Sanskrit and Pali.[8] The Nagas, according to the chronicles, were among the early converts to Buddhism. The other important population were the aboriginal peoples of Ceylon and India.[9]

For two millennia a constant flow of people crossed the Palk Straits between South India and Ceylon. Along with Buddhism and Brahmanical rites, there were also thriving cults of prehistoric territorial gods. The ancient linguistic map is uncertain. Sinhalese inscriptions appeared in the last quarter of the first millennium A.D. Some Sangam Tamil poets of the first or second century A.D. were probably from the Nagas in Ceylon.[10] The polity was largely decentralized, with Anuradhapura enjoying "ritual sovereignty" over the regional kingdoms.[11] From the sixth century A.D. exchanges with South India flourished. The capitals of Ceylon became cosmopolitan centers.

The Middle Ages saw Ceylon enmeshed in dynastic alliances encompassing both sides of the Palk Straits. Parakramabahu I (A.D. 1153-86) tried to centralize power repressively, causing the collapse of Ceylon's famed "hydraulic civilization."[12] The country gradually separated into largely Tamil- and Sinhalese-speaking regions. The former comprised the kingdom of Jaffna and a series of kingdoms or chieftaincies.[13]

When the Dutch ruled the maritime regions (A.D. 1656–1796), they created three regions for the administration of justice. Two regions comprised the Midwest and South-East, where the chief vernacular was Sinhalese, and the other comprised the North and East, where the chief vernacular was Tamil.

The British Administration

The British replaced the Dutch as the colonial power in 1796 and brought the whole island under their control. The boundaries of the provinces were largely administrative conveniences, but as grievances took shape after independence in 1948, boundaries in both the North and the Sinhalese South also delimited emerging identities. History, however tenuous, was brought into support these distinctions. With the ethnic polarization of post-independence politics, the Tamils experienced discrimination, communal violence, and alienation from the state. The Northern and Eastern provinces assumed political significance.[14]

The Politics of Division: Crossing the Threshold

There was no significant ethnic consciousness until the late nineteenth century. The British administration's census of 1827 categorized people primarily under caste labels without referring to language. This continued the Dutch practice and was largely in keeping with the prevailing sense of identity. Kingship in Kandy, for example, had a caste qualification, so the last few kings of Kandy had to be brought from South India. Following their enthronement, these Hindus readily became protectors of the Buddhist religion. The term "Sinhalese kings" is a misnomer; only from 1871 onward did the census reports designate the "nationality of inhabitants" in part by language. Caste ceased to be an official category.

"Nationality": The New Categories of Identity

The case of the Muslims who spoke Tamil remained a contentious issue. The Moor commercial class in Colombo had no links with the large Muslim community in the Eastern Province who were socially integrated among the Tamils.[15]

The census reports of 1901 and 1911 divided the Tamils into Ceylon and Indian Tamils, the latter being mainly plantation labor of recent Indian origin. The Sinhalese were divided into Kandyan and Low-Country. The Kandyans felt more affinity to the Tamils of the North-East than to the commercially ascendant Low-Country Sinhalese elite, by whom they felt threatened.

Until the second half of the nineteenth century language was not a significant source of identity and the distinction between Hinduism and Buddhism was blurred. Today's ethnic divisions would have been alien to people of that time.

Nationalist politics of the twentieth century destroyed the older spirit of pluralism. Official categorization also forced many to adopt new identities. For instance, the Roman Catholic Karawe caste community were mainly Tamil speaking; those who were literate were generally literate in Tamil. But from the nineteenth century they have appeared as Sinhalese in census reports.

The Kandyan Kingdom, which had held out against colonial rule, was conquered in 1815 by the British, who opened up large tracts of hill country to coffee and tea plantations. South Indian laborers were imported, many of whom died of disease during transportation. After clearing the forest they lived on the plantations, separated from the native Kandyan Sinhalese.

Westernized by 300 years of colonial rule under the Portuguese, Dutch, and British, the growing Low-Country Sinhalese entrepreneur class took advantage of opportunities that the plantation economy opened up to local capitalists. The Kandyan land-owning class, who lacked previous experience of colonial rule, were no match for them. Some Kandyans spent beyond their means, became indebted to the new Low-Country Sinhalese capitalists, and started losing their mortgaged property to them. At the end of the nineteenth century the Kandyan elite resented the Low-Country Sinhalese rather than the plantation Tamils, toward whom they formed an easy rapport. Linguistic identity was weaker than caste identity.

The Low-Country Sinhalese entrepreneur class promoted the Buddhist revival and was a major voice in politics, but it was excluded by the Moor merchant class from the import-export trade in Colombo. The Sinhalese expressed their rivalry by invoking the supposed historical mission of Sinhalese members of the

"Aryan race": to preserve this land sacred to Buddhism. These claims were based on the selective reading of colonial scholars, such as linguists who identified Sinhalese as an Aryan language, distinct from Tamil.[16]

The Status of Minorities

This nationalism turned against the minorities, who were considered impure interlopers. Anagarika Dharmapala, an early twentieth century "Buddhist reformer," objected to the Indian laborer as representing the lowest stratum of Indian society.[17] Rather than criticize the British colonial order, he directed his suppressed resentment against its victims, who became scapegoats. Dharmapala's prejudices reflected the vested interests of his class. Unable to create a broadly national spirit, his politics became antiminority rather than anticolonial. The concerns of the Sinhalese elite were concentrated around a few urban centers. They accumulated property in rural areas and retained political power but did little to uplift the Sinhalese masses.

When reforms in 1931 allowed Ceylon a large measure of self-government under universal adult franchise, the populist appeal of Sinhalese ideology gathered momentum. The emerging Left remained the only alternative to communal politics.

Important in the history of the Tamils was the arrival in Jaffna of American missionaries in 1812, who had originally hoped to work in Galle in the South. The security considerations of the British, then at war with France, would only countenance their presence in out-of-the-way Jaffna, where they found conditions favorable for missionary work. They created Jaffna College, supported by a network of schools.[18]

Unlike the South, Jaffna society did not produce a comparable entrepreneurial class. Instead, education was pursued assiduously and advancement sought in teaching, the professions, and government service. The importance given to education by American missionaries bore fruit far away, as teachers from Jaffna spread to all parts of the country.

The Tamils and Muslims in the rural North and East looked to Tamils in Jaffna for leadership, but their economic interests depended on agriculture, not government jobs. An educated Jaffna man's skills were sought after in all parts of the country. However, in Jaffna itself farming and related trades continued to be the main economic activity. Except for urban Batticaloa and Trincomalee, the whole of the East and the rural North continue to make few modern advances.

In the 1920s and 1930s educated youths, as represented by the Jaffna Youth Congress, who had been inspired by the Indian freedom struggle began to demand independence from Britain for a united Ceylon.

As communalism gained in the South, the populist Tamil Congress was formed in the early 1930s. Until then the Tamils had not seen themselves as a minority but as one of the two main communities in the island. This perception explains why the pre-independence Tamil Congress did not consider its demand of 50 percent representation for the minorities as unreasonable.

Independence, Citizenship, and Political Parties

After independence in 1948, the anglophile United National Party (UNP) government deprived the plantation (Hill Country or Indian) Tamils of their citizenship and the vote. Although the Left opposed it and many Sinhalese parliamentarians were uneasy, the Tamil Congress leadership supported the plan. The minorities then constituted about 30 percent of the population. Depriving more than a third of them of the vote opened the door to the worst forms of majoritarian populism.[19]

Alarmed by the ease with which a government could legally deprive a section of the minority of the vote, dissenters in the Tamil Congress opposed those bills and formed the Federal Party. The Federal Party saw the protection of the people of the North-East as lying in the creation of an autonomous Tamil-speaking region in the Northern and Eastern provinces. Among the issues it raised was the colonization of Sinhalese in those regions.

There had been a consensus that Tamil and Sinhalese should jointly replace English as official languages. However, in 1956 Solomon W. R. D. Bandaranayake's Sri Lanka Freedom Party (SLFP) captured power on the populist slogan of making Sinhalese the sole official language within twenty-four hours. The Federal Party's original fears seemed well founded.

The Road to Secessionism

The first attempt at political resolution was a pact negotiated between Prime Minister S. W. R. D. Bandaranayake and the Federal Party. It envisaged regional councils where people of the North-East would enjoy considerable autonomy, particularly regarding land settlement (colonization). A pledge was also given to look anew at the question of Hill Country Tamils rendered stateless by act of parliament in 1949.

The pact was abrogated when J. R. Jayawardene of the defeated UNP mounted an agitation by arousing Sinhalese fears. This was followed in 1958 by communal violence and the government appeared unwilling to strongly protect the Tamils.

The Federal Party and the UNP government of 1965-70 again agreed to offer much autonomy to the North-East, though they dropped the plan after Sirimavo Bandaranayake's SLFP opposition and its Left allies, turning communal, campaigned against it. The new 1972 republican constitution introduced by the Left-alliance government made no gesture toward the Tamils.

This rejection followed the "standardization" of university entrance marks introduced the previous year. Sections of the Sinhalese elite had persuaded the government to unilaterally raise the entrance thresholds for applicants examined in Tamil, particularly to the science-based courses.[20] This was a psychological blow to Tamils in Jaffna, who were not more privileged than the Sinhalese elite in Colombo, the principal beneficiaries of language-based preference. It also proved that the state was antiminority and could wield arbitrary power against them with impunity — a message confirmed by state complicity in communal violence.

Secession: The Example of Bangladesh

Until the birth of Bangladesh with the aid of Indian arms in 1971, Tamil secessionism had been a fringe movement. Bangladesh breached a consensus when a former colony was split and the UN accepted the fait accompli. The Federal Party held a rousing commemoration of the birth of Bangladesh in the Jaffna town hall. People began to dream that India might carve out a new Tamil nation in Ceylon. The militant nationalist youth thought of starting a rebellion to set the scene for Indian intervention; this remained part of their thinking into the mid-'80s. Other Left groups argued that inviting India into this would be disastrous and advocated instead alliances with like-minded political groups in the South.

During the mid-'70s the Federal Party merged with smaller nationalist parties to form the Tamil United Liberation Front (TULF). In 1976 the TULF passed a resolution to separate and establish the state of Eelam comprising the Northern and Eastern provinces, which were regarded as the Tamil "Homeland." The TULF regarded this mainly as a vote-catching slogan among Tamils and a bargaining position with the government.

The Politics of Self-Pity

Although the Sinhalese were a majority in Ceylon, nationalist ideology gave them the self-perception of a beleaguered minority — an Aryan people with a historic obligation to preserve this land sacred to Buddhism, threatened by hordes of Dravidian and Hindu Tamils in South India. The saw the state machinery as a means to outmaneuver the minorities. Elite politics on both sides were characterized by self-pity.

The UNP, led by J. R. Jayawardene, won a landslide victory at the 1977 elections. Communal violence followed, often instigated by UNP figures. Movements sprang up encouraging Tamil victims to settle in the North-East and secure the "Tamil Homeland" against state attempts to break it up through establishing colonies of Sinhalese poor. The small militant movement began to undertake bank robberies, the bombing of a local passenger aircraft, and selective assassinations, including those of politicians opposed to the TULF.

The UNP further centralized power in 1978, proscribed the Liberation Tigers, and enacted the Prevention of Terrorism Act and, later, the new Emergency Regulations of June 1983, permitting the secret disposal of bodies.[21] Tim Moore of the International Commission of Jurists (ICJ) reported that from July 1979 until June 1983, twenty-three Tamils had died in army or police custody. This mere rivulet was soon to become a flood. Repressive laws were drawn up, ostensibly for use in Tamil areas, but later used in the restive South.[22]

Under Jayawardene a powerful cabinet member was Cyril Mathew, notorious for his anti-Tamil rhetoric. Mathew brashly championed the Sinhalization of the Eastern Province through encroachments sponsored by his ministry, ostensibly to protect historic Buddhist sites. He used other means as well, such as the introduction of state corporations into Trincomalee in the East, where around 80 percent of those employed were Sinhalese.[23] JSS, the UNP trade union he built up, had been identified with anti-Tamil violence and goon squad activity against other trade unions. Mathew came from a caste of fairly recent South Indian origin, as did S. W. R. D. Bandaranayake and J. R. Jayawardene, a fact illustrating the tensions that contribute to violent identity claims.

Nationalism in State and Church

The communal violence of July 1983 was unprecedented in its severity and in the involvement of the state. After fifty-three Tamil detainees were murdered in prison, the Tamils came to see separation as necessary and inevitable. India, which had been looking askance at the pro-Western Jayawardene government, began training recruits to militant groups. The Jayawardene government proscribed secessionism, threw the TULF out of parliament, and created military units specializing in terror.

Civil war with the Tamils of the North-East brought unforeseen relief to the Hill Country (Indian) Tamils — plantation workers whose experiences of violence and starvation in the 1970s had forced many of them to move to the Tamil-dominated North-East. Hill Country Tamils were also among the worst victims of the July 1983 violence. Two pacts concluded between the governments of India and Ceylon in 1964 and 1974 had agreed that of the 975,000 stateless Hill Country Tamils present in 1964, 375,000 would be granted Ceylon citizenship (Sri Lankan after 1972) while 600,000 would receive Indian citizenship. The demand for Indian citizenship was spurred on by the violence and deprivation of the 1970s, but tapered off by 1983 because of disillusionment among those repatriated in India. The granting of Sri Lankan citizenship to those remaining had also been extremely slow.

But with the civil war and the influx of refugees, India stopped repatriating Hill Country Tamils for Indian citizenship in 1983. Parliament therefore accelerated the granting of Sri Lankan citizenship to those who applied. However, their percentage had declined from 11.16 percent of the population in 1971 to 5.6 percent in 1981.

Under the British, Protestant Christians had been privileged, and the churches were influential. In 1959, over 60 percent of the university admissions were from Christian mission schools. Under pressure from the Buddhist establishment, the government took over most of these schools in 1961, stopping government funding and making the charging of fees illegal.

The Roman Catholic Church, which has the largest number of Christians, had fought a rearguard action. The churches lost some prestige but remained influential. When a coup attempt against the government of Sirimavo Bandaranayake failed, most of the implicated armed forces officers turned out to be Christians.

Christians began identifying with Sinhalese and Tamil nationalism. Polarization within the church increased as Tamil secessionism gained momentum. Influential elements of the Tamil Church in the North came to ignore the moral questions and publicly support the LTTE, diminishing the Church's potential for healing.

Colonization, the Tamil Homeland Controversy, and the Neglect of the South

The North-East is subject to extensive demographic change through government policy. In political discourse, such notions as "Tamil Nation" and "Tamil Homeland" reflect a reaction against state oppression. Following every bout of violence from 1958, Tamil refugees fled to the Northern and Eastern provinces for safety. This made state-sponsored settlements of Sinhalese an even more contentious issue.

The island of Ceylon, which covers about 25,000 square miles, divides broadly into wet and dry zones. The wet zone — the South-West quadrant of the country and the central hills — receives 90 to 200 inches of rainfall annually. Most of the rest of the country is the dry zone, receiving 50 to 60 inches of rainfall annually, nearly all in the monsoon season. The ancient hydraulic civilization, situated in the dry zone, irrigated with river water flowing from the central hills.

The hydraulic civilization collapsed by the fourteenth century A.D. and the central dry zone (today's North-Central Province) became almost deserted. This region formed a natural barrier between what came to be a largely Tamil-speaking region in the North-East and the largely Sinhalese-speaking population in the South-Western wet zone.

Restoration of breached tanks in the dry zone was begun by the Dutch in the eighteenth century and continued by the British from the 1850s. This encouraged migration into the central dry zone, which retained its plural character until recently.

Major demographic shifts came with self-government in the 1930s and the launching of huge "Colonization Schemes" from the late 1940s. These schemes to restore or construct reservoirs in the dry zone brought mainly Sinhalese populations from poorer parts of the wet zone into new "colonies." This transformed the plural central dry zone into an almost exclusively Sinhalese area. Tamils were concerned by the transformation of large parts of the Eastern Province into almost exclusively Sinhalese areas, where the ideological overtones of government policy were barely hidden.

It had been difficult to sustain a population in the dry North-East because social organization had broken down. The higher orders became exploitive, while life became unbearable for those at the bottom. Colonial armies, passing through on military expeditions, also had a destabilizing effect.

In the 1827 census the Tamils in the North-East had formed 17 to 20 percent of the total Ceylon population. This had declined to 8.6 percent by 1981. Under a unitary system of government elected by "one person, one vote" universal franchise, the Tamils lacked a voice in the development of the North-East.

From the 1940s the government built irrigation works in the wet zone and planned the migration of principally Sinhalese poor from the populous wet zone into the dry zone. This was ostensibly meant to relieve landlessness among peasantry in the former area. Enormous subsidies were given at state expense. The Gal Oya, Kanthalai, and Allai schemes increased the Sinhalese population in the Eastern Province from about 5 percent in 1901 to 25 percent in 1981, the balance being 42 percent Tamil and 34 percent Muslim. During communal violence the Tamils in colony areas were among the most vulnerable and were progressively pushed out from 1956. During the 1980s, particularly in Trincomalee District in the East, the almost totally Sinhalese armed forces brazenly destroyed property and depopulated Tamil villages.[24]

By 1984 colonization had little to do with economic development or social uplift. The Weli Oya scheme was begun on the border of the Northern and Eastern provinces after the state, in an undisguised act of terror, drove out the Tamil inhabitants. This course was marked by the government's massacres of Tamils and countermassacres of Sinhalese, principally by the LTTE.[25]

The Sinhalese population in the Trincomalee District had increased from 4 percent in 1901 to 34 percent in 1981, while the Tamil population over this period dropped from 60 percent to 36 percent. The densely populated Tamil-speaking area was less irrigated than the neighboring Sinhalese districts.

If the state were nonsectarian and there were adequate political representation of regional interests, the mobility of populations would have been unobjectionable. However, colonization as it was practiced obliterated Tamil cultural and religious associations overnight. The stark contrast between the long-held belief in the Tamil character of the East, and the actual position of the Tamils following colonization and violent demographic manipulation by the state, was the driving force behind Tamil secessionism in the East. It was a reaction of despair. Dry zone land settlement was inspired by the class interest of policy makers as an "alternative land reform" to avoid radical land reform in wet-zone areas.

As for the structures perpetuating underdevelopment, we can compare the number of schools by region in 1959 preparing candidates for science-based courses at the University of Ceylon.[26] Only a handful of students were prepared at Galle, the deep South center of Sinhalese cultural revival where huge resources had been spent in turning people into colonists. This became the heartland of the People's Liberation Front (JVP)-led Sinhalese youth rebellions of 1971 and

1987-89. The leaders of the JVP had become disillusioned with the traditional Left during the '60s. They mobilized mainly among rural Sinhalese youth. Their ideology appealed to Marxist rhetoric, the Cuban revolution, and Sinhalese nationalism. Their first uprising of April 1971 was crushed within weeks. A key event leading to the second JVP uprising of July 1987 was the banning of the party in August 1983. President Jayawardene's UNP regime cynically blamed the JVP and two other Left parties for the anti-Tamil violence of the previous month in which the UNP was the main executor.

The JVP used the occasion of the signing of the Indo-Lanka Accord (July 1987) and the arrival of the Indian Peacekeeping Force in the North-East to launch its second uprising. Its campaign was overtly nationalist and anti-Indian. The ground had been prepared by the UNP's previous anti-Indian rhetoric, which was now shown to be empty. The new uprising resulted in fear, confusion, and paralysis for more than two years. In suppressing it the state forces used methods of terror that had been practiced in the war against the Tamils. About 20 000 Sinhalese youth were killed during the uprising.

There are important differences between the JVP and the LTTE. The ideology of the LTTE was overtly Tamil middle-class anti-Sinhalese. The JVP's ideology was clearly anti-middle class and anti-ruling class. Unlike the LTTE, it thus had few promoters among expatriates abroad. Also, it could modulate its anti-Tamil character in appealing to different audiences. Unlike the LTTE, which conducted several massacres against Sinhalese, the JVP's numerous killings were mostly politically motivated and the victims were seldom Tamils. Its main social and caste base was that from which colonists were recruited for colonization schemes.

The JVP opposes any devolution of power to the North-East. It maintains that the problem will disappear with the coming of socialism after its (JVP's) accession to power. The JVP recruited heavily in the colony areas and, ironically, so does the Sri Lankan Army, when meeting the needs of fighting the Tamil insurgency.

Although the Sinhalese elite had led a religious and cultural revival activity, its values were those of an idyllic, agrarian community, managed benignly by their elite. There was little interest in motivating the Sinhalese toward modern education. Postindependence developments are in part a crisis in this vision for Sinhalese society that was stubbornly translated into colonization schemes.

Predictably, candidates from Colombo and Jaffna secured a disproportionate share of university places for science-based courses according to merit. When "standardization" was introduced in 1971 to curb Tamil entrants by raising their entry mark, the ruling elite did not admit that their distorted vision of development had been to blame. They instead vilified the Tamils as having acquired a privileged position from the supposed British policy of "divide et impera." It did not matter that the American missionaries who came to Jaffna in 1812 could hardly be regarded as advocates of *Pax Britannica*. The vaunted colonization schemes were another grand gesture of populist nationalism that exacerbated conflict.[27]

The Quagmire of Tamil Nationalism

The weakness of Tamil nationalism was that it was based on the narrow interests of the educated middle class and geared toward preserving its influence in the professions and the public sector. Only when these were threatened were federalism and secession advocated. Election politics, lacking an active party organization to campaign on issues and mobilize people at the grassroots level, was literally conducted out of lawyers' chambers. The Federal Party, for instance, could at best reach gentlemen's agreements with governments in power through its Tamil elite representatives in Colombo. It did not mobilize the people to hold governments to their promises. Tamil Congress, the pioneer nationalist party, hardly had a base in the rural East. When the British prepared the constitution for independent Ceylon in 1945, the Congress did not ask for federalism but unreasonably demanded 50 percent representation for the minorities — then comprising the Tamils (about 23 percent), Ceylon and Indian Moors (6 to 7 percent), Malays, and Burghers (people of European extraction) — forming in all about 30 percent of the population. By 1949 the Congress went along with disenfranchising Tamil labor of Indian origin.

The Rise of the Federal Party

At first the Federal Party, which replaced the Congress as the leading Tamil party, projected a greater sense of purpose, but its structural weaknesses was the same. Its "Satyagraha" protest of 1961 was a flash-in-the pan of only a few months. It underrated the masses as an intelligent force that, if mobilized, could sustain a long struggle on such issues as colonization. It also regarded the Sinhalese masses with contempt and arrogance, failing even to talk to them and thus giving the Sinhalese ruling class a free hand to manipulate Sinhalese fears.

By July 1983 the Federal Party/TULF stood largely discredited as capitulatory. Having done handsomely in the North-East at the 1977 elections on a separatist platform, the TULF in 1981 agreed with President Jayawardene on District Development Councils (DDCs) as a "viable alternative to separation." In the DDC elections in June 1981 the government brazenly attempted vote rigging, and its armed forces burned the Jaffna Public Library. The DDCs were allowed no more than municipal council powers; the weak TULF had misplaced its trust in Jayawardene.

This weakness was evident from the 1960s but was countered by Tamil nationalist symbolism portraying their supposedly ancient martial glories and going for such stunts as signatures in blood. It was maintained that the Tamils were weak because they were divided. By 1972, Federal Party politicians castigated their parliamentary rivals (that is, other Tamil politicians) as traitors requiring dire punishment. Instead of examining its failures rationally, the party vilified the Sinhalese masses and leaders. Nationalist politics had thus imbued the Tamil people with a fatalistic sense that nonviolent protest could not succeed against the "Sinhalese State."

The Federal Party introduced concepts of a "Tamil Homeland" and the "Nation of Tamil Speaking Peoples." Its intention was positive: to bring the Muslims, who were also Tamil speaking, under the same umbrella. The move received significant support from the Muslims, who shared Tamil concerns regarding the use of the Tamil language and state-sponsored colonization in the Eastern Province. However, the Federal Party failed to motivate people to accept differences, reduce communal friction, and bring a sense of common identity. Once the party started using Tamil nationalist symbolism, the Muslims no longer wanted to be a part of this movement.

From the early 1970s the course was set for the rise of a Tamil militant movement. Several left-leaning political groups were drawing inspiration from liberation struggles elsewhere. A number of them disavowed communalism and tried to link up with like-minded groups in the South.

The Tamil Militants and Muslims in the East

The Tamils in the East and the Muslims share linguistic and clan ties. Like the Tamils, most Eastern Muslims are farmers, but Muslim traders are prominent in the economy of Tamil speaking parts of the East. This powerful trader class was envied and stereotyped by the Tamils. Although most Muslims are concentrated in the East, these traders form a diaspora throughout the country. Commercial and religious ties therefore influence the relationship of Muslims in the East to the central government. The ties of Muslim politics with Tamil nationalism and secessionism have therefore been uneasy. Until 1984, however, because of common grievances against the state (e.g., language and colonization) significant numbers of Muslim youth joined the Tamil militant groups. From ·1984, the government tried to inflame the differences between the two communities to the point of irreconcilable hatred (e.g., by using Muslim hoodlums to attack Tamil villages). The government did not get far with this strategy because the Muslims did not want trouble with the Tamils. Yet the Tamil militant groups promoting "Tamil speaking peoples" failed to handle relations with Muslims sensitively but took an aggressive, militaristic approach.

Tamil groups opposed to the LTTE, who enjoyed a favored position during the Indian Army's presence (1987-89), used it on occasions to punish and humiliate Muslims, who gave valuable logistic support and some recruits to the LTTE without, however, respecting them. An LTTE attack in December 1987 left over eighty Muslims dead. After the withdrawal of the Indian peacekeeping force in December 1989, with the consent of President Premadasa's UNP government, the LTTE became the effective power in the East. It went beyond collecting taxes to controlling religious and political activity among Muslims, as it did among Tamils. This soured relations, even while Muslim leaders tried to work out a compromise. The LTTE's totalitarian leader-centered ideology rejected pluralism of any sort. The LTTE broke off talks in June 1990 and went to war with the Premadasa government, treating Muslims as a fifth column and murdering surrendered Muslim policemen. The Government used Muslims' resulting anger to have agents point out Tamils allegedly close to the LTTE, who were then killed.

The LTTE responded by targeting Muslims as a community, whereupon the government recruited and armed Muslim home-guards, who were ineffective except in reprisals against unarmed Tamils. Although government forces were responsible for massacres and disappearances of several thousand Tamils, they led the Tamils to believe that the Muslims were the killers. Thus anti-Muslim feeling was a main factor motivating Eastern Tamil youth to join the LTTE in the months following June 1990.

The Liberation Tigers

The extremist group, the Liberation Tigers of Tamil Eelam, began by assassinating parliamentary politicians opposed to the TULF, whose ideological baggage it inherited. Castigating its opponents as traitors, it imposed itself as the sole group. It too lacked a vision of the potential of the people, whom it required only as servants or blind recruits. Every one of its actions decreased the power of the people. Its repression of the Tamil people isolated them and forced them repeatedly into new bouts of war.

From 1983 to 1987 the LTTE accepted Indian patronage and training and even boasted that it had become the means for exercising Indian dominance over Sri Lanka. It tried to sell itself to the Indian authorities as the most reliable partner in comparison with other Tamil groups under Indian patronage.[28]

In June 1987 the Sri Lankan forces were about to overcome the LTTE's last bastion in Jaffna. Instead of supplying the LTTE with the sophisticated weapons it had wanted, India imposed the Indo-Lanka Accord on both the government of Jayawardene and the LTTE. India then sent its troops into the North-East as a peacekeeping force, to the relief of the people. Committed to the territorial integrity of Ceylon, India would not countenance Tamil secession but stood for powersharing by all Tamil parties under elections. India did not favor a totalitarian LTTE regime. The LTTE formally accepted all this and was granted overwhelming influence in the Interim Council that was to be formed.

In the meantime, however, it attacked other militant groups and engineered a war with the Indian Army, whose wrath brought great suffering on the people. The LTTE also created suffering in other situations, such as in the Jaffna hospital, where it provoked attacks on the people and ran away, leaving them to suffer.[29]

In 1989 the LTTE commenced formal talks with President Premadasa, who had succeeded Jayawardene, with a view to bringing about the withdrawal of the

Indian Army. Premadasa, who also was fighting the JVP insurrection in the Sinhalese South, offered a populist anti-India platform. The LTTE, as newly converted Sri Lankan patriots wanting the foreign army out, found common cause with Premadasa. The Sri Lankan forces even supplied the LTTE with weapons and logistics to attack the Indian Army and the Tamil groups aligned to them. In early 1990 the LTTE promised to lay down its arms once the last Indian soldier had quit, as happened in March 1990. Premadasa too spoke about resolving Tamil grievances such as colonization.

However, in June 1990 the LTTE resumed the war. In the Eastern Province they surrounded the police stations. In the hope of talking matters out, the government ordered the policemen to surrender without resistance. The LTTE massacred hundreds of the Sinhalese and Muslims among the surrendered policemen and took to the jungles as the Sri Lankan Army moved in and massacred or disappeared thousands of Eastern Tamils.[30]

Thus did the LTTE get out of every cul-de-sac through provoking a new round of violence, gaining recruits through the anger of the Tamil people. The inclusion of Muslims among the policemen massacred pushed Tamil-Muslim relations to new depths. The government too had recruited Muslim home guards, armed them, and equipped them for reprisal violence against Tamils.

The LTTE saw no contradiction in boasting of being India's favorite agents one day and then Sri Lankan patriots some months later. It has annihilated all other shades of Tamil opinion as traitors. While its statements to international audiences in English have talked of federalism and democracy, these have not been repeated in Tamil at home. Tamil nationalists pay no attention to the embitterment of Muslims, who shared the "Tamil Homeland." Among the casualties of this politics are the Tamil people and the conceptual viability of the Tamil Homeland and Tamil Nation.

Tamils and the Right to Self-Determination: Theory and Reality

With numerous secessionist movements springing up in the postcolonial world, there is an urgent need to develop theoretical and legal criteria to examine secession in the light of international law, which recognizes the "right to self-determination of peoples." The principle of self-determination of peoples first appeared in Articles 1 and 55 of the UN Charter. This was generally interpreted as applying to people in colonial situations. In 1966 the UN General Assembly adopted two human rights covenants that were circulated for ratification among member states. Part I of Article I, which was common to both covenants — the International Covenant on Civil and Political Rights (ICCPR) and the International Covenant on Economic and Social Rights (ICESR) — stated: "All peoples have the right to self-determination. By virtue of the right they freely determine their political status and freely pursue their economic, social and cultural development."

Martin Ennals[31] has noted, "Nowhere is there a process for arbitration, no definition of terms, no UN body which will entertain the complaints about self-determination as such. It is a right which creates expectation without fulfillment. People are dying for a right which is known to exist but nowhere is defined."

Lord Avebury (Eric Avebury)[32] points to cases such as Eritrea and East Pakistan that had cried out for international intervention on the basis of the right to self-determination, but where much blood was spilt for the lack of such a process. One might add East Timor and the Kurdish territories among those needing relief through international processes that do not exist.

Avebury suggests that the UN appoint a High Commissioner for Self-Determination "charged with the duty of examining all claims [in the first instance], rejecting only those which in his or her opinion were manifestly ill-founded. The claims would then be analyzed according to criteria specified by the General Assembly, including:

1. Previous history of statehood or existence as a separate territorial entity
2. Geographical unity
3. Ethnicity
4. Language
5. Religion
6. Culture
7. Existence of separate institutions
8. Evidence of will to separation.

I must clarify my use of the term "self-determination," whose practical application to an individual cases poses so much ambiguity. In cases of "peoples," such as tribal people or a diaspora without a territorial identity, "self-determination" could hardly imply the right to secede. Even for communities having in some sense a territorial identity such as the Québécois of Canada and the Tamils of Ceylon, secession poses such painful problems as are ably described by Spencer in chapter 1. I personally believe as a general rule that secession should be discouraged and every effort should be made to give substance to the "right to self-determination" without invoking secession. For the Québécois as for the Tamils, territorial association (as distinct from possession) is crucial to their sense of identity. Minimally, the Northern and Eastern Provinces (the present North-Eastern Province) of Ceylon have been the destinations of Tamil refugees during bouts of communal violence. The territorial association of the Tamils with the North-East has been threatened actively by government policy. Lawless conduct of government forces impaired the security of Tamils within this area, caused massive displacement, and increased the virulence of the Tamil militancy to self-destructive heights.

In such cases the "right to self-determination" cannot be meaningful unless this territorial association is guaranteed and the legacy of state oppression is come to terms with through political arrangements and healing processes as would give confidence to the minority concerned. Attempts at political resolution could fail because of faults on both sides — and the Tamil side has been much to blame in this case — but it would be dangerous to rule out secession as a possibility for international legal processes to resolve and leave it to default. By ruling out secession, repressive "sovereign" governments could take it as a license to indulge in territorial and demographic surgery to obliterate a minority's identity and security. Leaving secession to default is also likely to encourage adventurist groups totally at variance with the aspirations of ordinary people that observe no restraint in their quest for power.

I shall therefore take "self-determination" as regards the Tamils of Ceylon to include secession as an extreme possibility when all healthier means of resolution fail. I believe this is how Ennals and Avebury have read the current trend in international law.

We shall now examine the Tamil case in respect of these criteria above. It may satisfy points 1 and 2 in the sense of separate territorial entity and geographical unity, although claims to a previous history of statehood in the modern sense are weak, as seen from the earlier historical sketch. Also, points 4 and 6 may be largely true, considering Tamils and Muslims as one group in the North-East. In the case of point 8, the TULF argued that the election results of 1977 gave a mandate for separation, considering the total percentage of votes polled in the North-East. The TULF polled over 70 percent of the votes in the Northern Province. However, in the East the results reflected the effects of state-sponsored colonization of Sinhalese and the rejection of the Tamil nationalist program among the majority of the Muslims and some of the Tamils.

We encounter then significant difficulty in appraising criteria. With a view to formulating a workable doctrine on the right to self-determination, Martin Ennals poses some questions that are relevant in the Tamil case:[33]

1. How does self-determination relate to democracy when the demographic composition of an area has been changed?
2. Are there indications which could provide early warnings of the need for preventive measures?
3. How can self-determination enhance the implementation of Article 25 of the ICCPR that provides that "every citizen shall have the right and opportunity to take part in the conduct of public affairs, directly or indirectly through freely chosen representatives?

The concept of self-determination for the Tamils had long guided the thinking of the Federal Party as well as the government of Ceylon (Sri Lanka). In 1949, when the Federal Party was formed, it spoke of the unsuitability of the unitary constitution, adding:

We believe that the only means of ensuring that the Tamils are guaranteed their freedom and self-respect by law, and of solving their problems in a just and democratic manner is to permit them to have their own autonomous state, guaranteeing self-government and self-determination for the Tamil nation in the country; and to work indefatigably to the attainment of this objective.[34]

The immediate context of this resolution and call for federalism was the disenfranchisement of Tamil plantation labor of recent Indian origin.

The threat to the integrity of the "Tamil Homeland" posed by state-sponsored colonization of Sinhalese was raised in a Federal Party statement of April 1951 in relation to the Gal Oya scheme in the Eastern Province. It spoke of the "inalienable right of the Tamil speaking people to the territories which they had been traditionally occupying." This reference to "Tamil speaking people" was an attempt to include the Muslims as part of the "Tamil Nation," who together with the Tamils then comprised 95 percent of the Eastern Province population. Later statements vacillated between "Tamil people" and "Tamil speaking people."

The 1956 general elections which brought Bandaranayake's SLFP to power on the slogan of "Sinhala only" also established the Federal Party as the leading Tamil Party. This was followed by communal violence in the Gal Oya and Padaviya schemes on the borders of the Eastern Province. The violence by Sinhalese employees led to the loss of Tamil lives and the expulsion of Tamils and Muslims from both schemes.

The abrogated pact of 1957 had envisaged the establishment of regional councils enjoying far-reaching powers over colonization. Then came the 1958 communal violence and the deterioration continued.

The TULF, the successor to the Federal Party, in its 1976 resolution for separation mentioned the serious inroads made into the "Tamil kingdom" by a "state-aided colonization . . . calculated to make the Tamils a minority in their own homeland." It was then resolved that the (separate) state of "Tamil Eelam shall consist of the Northern and Eastern Provinces."

The tone of the TULF documents of 1976 and 1977 contrasted sharply with the moderation of the early Federal Party documents. New frustration had led to the beginnings of the militant movement, and the strong new resolution was essentially a bargaining position made in response to the militant mood of the youth. Also, the TULF believed it had a strong case in the emerging interpretation of international law.[35]

However, the UNP government of J. R. Jayawardene resorted to a chauvinist course. The communal riots of 1977, 1981, and 1983 led to the civil war and an effort to obliterate the geographical contiguity of the largely Tamil speaking Northern and Eastern provinces. Security forces were sent to the East to foment violence between Muslims and Tamils.[36] Sinhalese villagers were armed, ostensibly for defense against Tamil militant attacks. But the usual pattern was for home guards to stay out of sight during such an attack, and then take reprisals against the nearest Tamil village. To both sides, the people, whether Sinhalese, Muslim, or Tamil, became pawns.

The Indo-Lanka Accord of 1987 imposed on the government of Sri Lanka the merger of the Northern and Eastern Provinces into the North-East Province, although, formally at least, the merger was subject to a referendum in the East. This was a major concession to the Tamil homeland idea.

In the late 1990s, the civil war continues and the LTTE claims secession on the basis of its control over large sections of Tamils in the North-East. Where the LTTE is concerned, however, the linkages between self-determination, human rights, and democracy are nonexistent.

The Importance of Self-Determination as a Process

The Tamils' experience shows the limitations of framing formal criteria for self-determination and conducting the debate mainly in a legal framework. Both the Tamil leaders and the governments that opposed Tamil self-determination were guided by emerging interpretations of international law.

To use legalistic criteria is to pose artificial questions. For example: "Do the peoples of Ceylon have separate histories or a common history?" and "Do all Tamil speakers (who are the majority in the North-East) form one people, or are they separate peoples? Do in particular Tamils and Muslims constitute one people?"

The answer to the first depends on what parts of history one emphasizes and how one interprets them. As to whether Tamils and Muslims constitute one people, Tamil nationalists would argue by the linguistic criteria used to define Indian states — according to which they would be one people. In the light of Tamil militant violence against Muslims, this would be questionable. Take also the suggestion that a UN Committee on Self-Determination should have the power to conduct a referendum in the territory concerned. Given the prevailing atmosphere of terror and the history of colonization, a referendum would be a poor guide for making far-reaching decisions.

Whether Ceylon is one nation or separate nations is determined not by ancient history but rather by the politics of the last few decades. If the Tamils and the Muslims in the North-East had developed an identity as the "Tamil speaking people(s)" that would have aided the Tamil cause. However, that process was destroyed by the intolerance of Tamil nationalist ideology.

From mid-1994 there were healthy developments among the ordinary Sinhalese people, leading to a massive electoral mandate for peace and human rights. There was a new willingness to understand the problems of the Tamils. The press too became more open, along with a large international presence in the country that included aid agencies and nongovernmental organizations. Unfortunately, no comparable flexibility can be seen on the Tamil side.

Missed Opportunities for Intervention and Prevention

The postindependence history of Ceylon includes several instances where constructive international interventions should have taken place:

• 1948-49: *Declaring Tamil labor of Indian origin noncitizens (i.e., stateless) and depriving them of the vote.* Aside from Idi Amin's Uganda, Ceylon was the only former British colony to take such a harsh measure against people who had arrived during the recent colonial period. The Federal Party in the early 1950s took the matter to the Privy Council in Britain, arguing that the parliament was in violation of Section 29 of the constitution, which forbade legislation discriminatory to a community. The Privy Council upheld the government's action on the grounds that the parliament of Ceylon had the right to define citizenship, which the British framers of the constitution of 1948 had left undefined.[37] Had there been available an appeal to an international body on the basis of the UN Charter of Human Rights, as distinct from an interested party, Ceylon's tragedy might have been averted.

• 1951: *Colonization schemes affecting the demography of the Eastern Province.* Concern was first raised in the 1940s, again in 1951, and continuously thereafter. It was not a simple question of development but affected communities' rights to land, water,[38] and the quality of their representation.[39] In 1979 the World Bank-supported Accelerated Mahaveli Program went ahead, leaving important questions unanswered. Some means of applying to an international body should have been available, perhaps without ruling out such projects altogether (though white elephants they turned out to be).

Intervention was called for on other occasions, including the Sinhala Only Act of 1956, standardization of university admissions by purely linguistic criteria in 1971, and the several bouts of communal violence since 1956.

Interventions should not be confined to governments alone. Attention should be paid to aggrieved parties. The Federal Party's public display of intolerance in 1972, as evidenced by its spokesmen branding Tamil opponents as traitors, should have been nipped in the bud.

The Right of Secession

We come now to a suggestion made in the Martin Ennals Memorial Symposium on Self-Determination:[40]

> It is the knowledge that the option of secession is not available to the peoples who constitute a minority that gives the dominant group the strength and ability to continue with impunity, if it chooses to, its policies and programs of oppression. But if international law were to subordinate territorial integrity to the right of "all peoples" to self-determination by recognizing a principle that the members of a cohesive social entity within a sovereign state are entitled to freely determine their political status, the impact would be quite remarkable. . . The recognition of such a principle will shift the focus from the rancorous assertion of

rights to the far more productive exercise of formulating the terms and conditions of co-existence. A numerically small ethnic, religious or linguistic group, conscious that it has the right to secede, will begin to examine the viability of secession in political, social and, above all, economic terms. These considerations will probably compel such a group to remain within the existing state, but on terms negotiated by it with the dominant group.

This suggestion is predicated on the prospect that it would usher in a "fair and just rule of law." While I would not exclude the right to secession for the reason stated at the beginning of the quotation, how and when that right is to be exercised under the "right to self-determination" has no simple answer. The suggestion may be appropriate for highly developed democracies where supranational institutions have already made inroads into national sovereignty, as in Western Europe and perhaps North America. In this case secession may bring irritation and later disillusionment without affecting life significantly. The experience of "humiliation" which Spencer (chapter 1) cites as a motive for secession among Québécois would be novel in a Third World context.

What is important, whether in advanced democracies or in the Third World, is the active cultivation of a culture of accommodation and a readiness to understand the grievances of others. Without this, legal processes would be limited or even destructive.

In a Third World context, the secessionist crisis reflects the inaccessibility of institutional remedies in matters of basic human rights. But once a Tamil separatist movement such as the LTTE held the initiative and could paralyze Tamil society, it became difficult for even a well-meaning government to institute remedial measures. Separatists must portray the Sinhalese majority and the government in Colombo as evil and unchanging, thus giving remedial measures no chance. Yet laws have been passed to give Tamil equal status with Sinhalese as an official language; all remaining Hill-Country Tamils have been given citizenship; and bodies have been instituted to monitor human rights.

But to make these measures work requires organized pressure groups of Tamils, whose success would run counter to Tamil nationalist interests. The same could be said of foreign-aided projects and rehabilitation of war-torn areas. Left to itself, the accumulated inertia of the government machinery, its corruption, and its propensity to discriminate against Tamils would surely enhance the Tamil secessionist cause. The tendency to default exists on both sides, while the enormous potential for the peoples to live together remains largely untapped.

In such cases the right to secession as an easy option would be destructive. International intervention should in the first instance go through a systematic process of making governments accountable.

On the one hand we have the Sri Lankan state driven by the inertia of a powerful sectarian ideology. Its armed forces are almost entirely Sinhalese. The Tamils are grossly underrepresented in the public services and invisible in the higher rungs. These conditions have stimulated demand for an alternative Tamil state structure.

On the other hand, since July 1983 hundreds of thousands of alienated Tamils have settled down in the West. There the LTTE has won an audience unconcerned about the harm of this politics for the people at home. There has also been an exodus of Tamils from the North-East to the South, where they are harassed by the authorities and shunned by employers. Even when there are new openings in the politics of the South, the Tamil elite cannot come out of the shadow of the LTTE, make a gesture of goodwill, and understand the anxieties of the Sinhalese.

Several factors are interacting: the globalization resulting from modern technology, communication, and commerce; the vested interests of a migrant diaspora that differ from those of the group remaining in their troubled home; and the power of a militant force driving toward — and driven by — sociopolitical fragmentation.

The first phase of Tamil nationalism was a feeling of powerlessness, a loss of people's sense of responsibility to exert themselves in nonviolent protest. In a later stage, people watch LTTE videos from living rooms in the West, applauding tricked and brainwashed twelve-year-olds performing suicidal feats of "martyrdom" for the LTTE leadership.

In turn the Sinhalese have acquired legitimate fears of the global spread of Tamils. Developments in neighboring Tamil Nadu have favored fascist and anti-Sinhalese support groups for the LTTE. Amidst these fears the Sinhalese have to be persuaded to agree to a previously unthinkable federal status for the Tamil speaking region, not with any certainty of halting the fragmentation but only as a means of offering space for good sense to prevail. Making the Sri Lankan government accountable would also help multiethnic pressure groups working for a just solution to the crisis become more effective.

The right to self-determination stands or falls with human rights. To many outside observers, violations of human rights remained violations by the Sri Lankan forces against the Tamils, who were fighting for self-determination. What the Tamil people were doing to themselves was mostly lost sight of. Today this Tamil society lacks the capacity to express its wishes on such basic matters as the welfare of its children or to influence its so-called representatives.

What might be an eventual resolution to this crisis? We have encountered two strands of thought. One that comes through in the references I have cited (Ennals, Avebury, and Jayawickrema) tends to see the right to secession positively. The other, advocated by Spencer and Schaeffer in this volume, sees the problem of overlapping sovereignties. Both cite examples where these have arisen out of the historical experience of communities. Spencer speaks of nonterritorial constituencies and a nonterritorial future. Both these theoretical frameworks seem not to come to terms with a typical Third World situation.

In Ceylon, one could win acceptance at mass level on ideas with some historical legitimacy. The idea of a federal Ceylon with units for the Tamils of the

North-East, the Kandyan Sinhalese, and the Low-Country Sinhalese was first put forward by S. W. R. D. Bandaranayake in the 1920s.[41] In 1957, he as prime-minister signed the B-C Pact with the Tamil leadership, which envisaged regional councils with considerable autonomy. Although abrogated later, it remains the basis for all subsequent attempts at a political solution.

Many Sinhalese see the Tamil insistence on continuing the North-East as one unit (merged in 1987) to be laying the foundation for a future separate state. Against federalism there is a myth that Ceylon has from ancient times been a "unitary" Sinhalese state. Only when some relative stability has been attained could one experiment with nonterritorial constituencies. Such an idea has not gone beyond seminars attended by select groups.

What are the other possibilities? Federation with India was mooted in the 1930s. The idea died and Sinhalese nationalism has generally been anti-Indian. But from Jaffna the Indian coast is barely 20 miles of easy navigation, while Colombo is 250 miles. Both India and Ceylon have adopted open economies. The course of economic integration too is likely to transform political ideas.

Notes

1. In this chapter, the name Ceylon refers to the geographical entity, wbile Sri Lanka refers to the post-1972 republic and its institutions. [Editor's note.]

2. See the Amnesty International Reports *Disappearances in Sri Lanka* of September 10, 1986, and *Recent Reports of Disappearance & Torture* of May 1987. The UN Working Group on disappearances in December 1986 listed Sri Lanka among 7 countries where more than 200 cases needed clarification. Tamils dead or missing from July 1983 to July 1987 totaled about 8,000. See the *Saturday Review*, Jaffna, 1984-87.

3. Most Sinhalese are Buddhists.

4. See University Teachers for Human Rights (Jaffna) Briefing No. 2, *Children in the North-East War* (UTHR: n.d.).

5. D. J. Somasundaram and S. Rajadurai,"War and Suicide in Northern Sri Lanka," *Acta Psychiatrica Scandinavica*, January 1995; D.J. Somasundaram & S. Sivayokam, "War Trauma in a Civilian Population," *British Journal of Psychiatry*, 1994, 165: 524-27; D. J. Somasundaram, "Mental Health in North Sri Lanka in 1994" (paper delivered at the Conference on Victims of War in Sri Lanka, London, September 1994).
From 1963 to 1975 Jaffna society had a very high suicide rate. With the onset of the war this dropped sharply. The authors suggest that in place of cohesiveness that war often brings to groups in the face of an external threat, this war has brought about "signs of despair and resignation to fate."

6. See, for example, S. U. Deraniyagala, *Prehistoric Archaeology of Sri Lanka* (Colombo: Department of Archaeological Survey, 1992); K. V. Raman, "Brahmi inscriptions in Tamil Nadu: An Historic Assessment," *The Sri Lanka Journal of South Asian Studies* I (1, 1976). See also Sastri, below. Any attempt to confine the ancient peoples of Ceylon to two or three well-defined categories

should have been questioned earlier. Sudharshan Seneviratne, an archaeologist, has uncovered remains of communities older than those such as at Sigiriya that are pre-Aryan (before 600 B.C.). Some of these unclassified communities used metals and urn burials. Sinhalese ideology claims exclusiveness and original possession of the Island. The supposed Aryan origin of the Sinhalese is now recognized as failing to fulfill the claim of original possession. The "Naga" origin of Tamils was found useful by Tamils in the battle for antiquity over the then supposedly Aryan Sinhalese. We must treat "Nagas" as a collection of diverse groups, some of whom were Naga (or Serpent) worshippers — a cult once common to much of India and Ceylon.

7. This is exemplified by the Vijaya myth and by the journey to South India of Pandava Arjuna in the Mahabharatha legend. See Mudaliyar C. Rasanayagam, *Ancient Jaffna* (1926; reprinted by Asian Educational Services, New Delhi, 1984), 33-36; and R. A. L. H. Gunawardana, "The People of the Lion," in *Sri Lanka: History and Roots of Conflict*, ed. Jonathan Spencer (London: Routledge, 1990).

8. K. A. Nilakanta Sastri, *A History of South India*, 4th ed. (Madras: Oxford University Press, 1975).

9. *The Mahavamsa or The Great Chronicle of Ceylon*, trans. from Pali by Wilhelm Geiger (Government of Ceylon, 1960).

10. Rasanayagam in *Ancient Jaffna*, 178. For excavations in Jaffna, see Ragupathy, "Early Settlements in Jaffna: An Archaeological Survey" (Madras: Cre-A, 1987).

11. C. R. A. Hoole, *Modern Sannyasins, Parallel Society and Hindu Replications: A Study of Protestant Contribution to Tamil Culture in 19th century Sri Lanka, Against a Historical Background* (Berne: Peter Lang, 1995), chapters 5 and 6. Ritual sovereignty is also evident in the distribution of Bo saplings brought to Anuradhapura during the third century B.C. The Mahavamsa account suggests that the recipients are regional kingdoms.

12. The term "hydraulic civilization" was introduced by Karl A. Wittfogel to refer to the social organization of those societies capable of building huge irrigation systems and stupendous monuments. See his *Oriental Despotism: A Comparative Study of Total Power* (New Haven, Conn.: Yale University Press, 1957); also *The Collapse of The Rajarata Civilization in Ceylon and The Drift to the South-West*, ed. K. Indrapala (Ceylon Studies Seminar, University of Ceylon, Peradeniya, 1971).

13. Some were small; others rich and influential. See J. P. Lewis, *A Manual of the Vanni Districts of Ceylon* (1895; reprint, New Delhi: Navrang, 1993). S. Arasaratnam, *Ceylon Journal of Humanities and Social Sciences*, Vol. 9, No. 2, 1966.
The one-time prosperity of Thampalakamam and Kanthalai is referred to by Fr. Fernao de Queyroz in his *The Temporal and Spiritual Conquest of Ceylon* (1656, trans. Fr. S. G. Perera 1930), 66*ff.*

14. The 1981 census recorded a total Ceylon population of 14.85 million, of whom 2.088 million lived in the North-East. The breakdown of Ceylon's population is as follows: Sinhalese 74 percent (about three-eighths of whom are Kandyan); Tamils 18.2 percent (Ceylon Tamils 12.6 percent, Hill Country [Indian] Tamil 5.6 percent); Muslims 7.4 percent; others 0.4 percent. The Indian Tamils formed about 12 percent of the population at independence in 1948. The

citizenship laws passed over the next year made nearly all of them noncitizens. They are now a significant electoral force in the Hill Country. See "Sullen Hills," UTHR (Jaffna), *Special Report No. 4*, 1992. On the fate of those repatriated to India, see T. N. Gopalan, *Repatriates in Nilgris — A Saga of Struggle* (Kotagiri, S. India: Dalit Action Research & Extension Services Centre). In 1981, Buddhists formed 69.1 percent of the population, Hindus 15.5 percent and Muslims 7.4 percent. Christians represented 6.6 percent of the ethnic Sinhalese population and 14.8 percent of ethnic Tamils (18 percent among Ceylon Tamils). The proportion of Christians in Sri Lanka as a whole has declined from 9 percent in 1945 to 7.6 percent in 1981. In 1981 about 72 percent of the Ceylon Tamil population lived in the Northern and Eastern Provinces.

15. See Maruan Macan-Markar's "Nation Building: A Muslim Perspective," in *Nation Building in Sri Lanka*, ed. Gnana Munasinghe (Shramaya, Colombo, 1993). Both authors trace the dilemma faced by the Tamil-speaking Muslim community in fashioning a national identity. Macan-Markar argues in favor of Ceylon as a cosmopolitan nation based on individual rights rather than group rights.

16. Gunawardana, "The People of the Lion," 7-10. Mudaliyar W. F. Guna–wardena in the 1920s declared that Sinhalese, like Tamil, was a Dravidian language. A recent advocate of the theory of the common origins of Sinhalese and Tamil people and their languages was Dr. C. de S. Wijesundara. Such Buddhists seek to trace their roots to the earlier conversion of the Nagas of Ceylon rather than to the Asokan emissary Mahinda. (See, for example, D. A. T. Perera, "Who brought Buddhism to Sri Lanka: Gautama Buddha or Mahinda Thera?" *Sunday Island*, May 22, 1994.)

17. Kumari Jayawardana, *Ethnic Consciousness in Sri Lanka: Continuity and Change in Sri Lanka* (Navrang, New Delhi: Committee for Rational Development, 1984). Jayawardana says: "Competition in trade is a key element in understanding ethnic and communal rivalry in Sri Lanka." The animosity of Sinhalese traders to the foreign domination of trade was expressed by Dharmapala by referring to "merchants from Bombay and peddlers from South India," the latter being largely Indian Moors. The Europeans were left out in those colonial times. What should have been an anticolonial struggle expended itself in anti-minority rhetoric.

18. C. R. A. Hoole, *Modern Sannyasins*, Chapter 12.

19. Rajan Hoole et al, *The Broken Palmyra, The Tamil Crisis in Sri Lanka: An Inside Account* (Claremont, Calif.: Sri Lanka Studies Institute) chapter 1, and Jayawardana, *Ethnic Consciousness in Sri Lanka*. Jayawardana suggests that the disenfranchisement of Tamil Hill Country labor was aimed to weaken the Left. The vote of the Hill Country Tamils had been decisive in returning fourteen Left candidates.

20. C. R. de Silva, "The Impact of Nationalism on Education," in *Collective Identities, Nationalism and Protest in Modern Sri Lanka*, ed. Michael Roberts. The proportion of Tamil admissions to science based courses dropped from 40 percent in 1970 to 19 percent in 1975, as the criteria changed from merit to language-based preference to district quotas. See de Silva, *Sinhala-Tamil Relations and Education In Sri Lanka: The University Admissions Issue — The First Phase, 1971-7*. Under the UNP government in 1977 the admission criteria settled

down to 30 per cent on merit, 55 percent on district quotas and 15 percent for backward areas. The last was criticized by Virginia Leary as being in part ethnic preference in a disguised form. She advocated a movement toward merit. International Commission of Jurists, "Ethnic Conflict and Violence in Sri Lanka" (report on mission to Sri Lanka in July-August 1981 on behalf of ICJ by Professor Virginia A. Leary, Faculty of Law and Jurisprudence, State University of New York at Buffalo).

21. The "Liberation Tigers" law enabled the president to ban any political party which in his opinion "advocates violence and is engaged in unlawful activities." Also in force in late 1979 was Emergency Rule in the Northern Province. The Civil Rights Movement of Sri Lanka observed in 1979 that these laws "contain provisions that go far beyond any reasonable or permissible requirement of national security. They provide for arrest without warrant and without obligation to inform relatives of the fact of such an arrest. . . . Characteristic of the measures introduced in 1979 has been the idea of protecting the state against the people, while the concept of protecting the people against the state has been sadly absent."

22. Leary, "Ethnic Conflict and Violence."

23. UTHR (Jaffna) *Report No 11* , chapter 2 and appendices II-IV.

24. In Trincomalee District, state-aided colonization pushed up the Sinhalese population from 4.5 percent in 1901 to 33.6 per cent in 1981, just second to the Tamil population making up 36.4 percent. Out of this Tamil population of 93,510, 6,767 were Tamils of Indian origin, several of whom came after the 1977 communal violence. See chapter 2 of UTHR (Jaffna) *Report No. 11* of February 1993, chapters 4 and 5 of *Report No. 12* of November 1993 and 1.7 and 1.8 of *Report No. 13* of June 1994. Section 2.3 of *Report No. 11* describes the deportation of Indian Tamils. Chapter 4 of *Report No. 12* describes some of the depopulated villages and the experiences of the inhabitants. Chapter 2 and appendices II-IV of *Report No. 11* and 5 of *Report No. 12* show how administrative and military means were used in demographic manipulation. 1.7 and 1.8 of *Report No. 13* give estimates of the distribution of Tamil refugees.

25. UTHR (Jaffna), *Special Report* of September 1993. See also *Information Bulletin* "Padaviya-Weli Oya: Bearing the Burden of Ideology," February 1995.

26. Colombo has fifty-four such schools; Jaffna twenty-nine; Kandy fifteen; Galle four. See K. Nesiah, "From School to University," in *Education and Human Rights in Sri Lanka*, The Christian Institute for the Study of Religion and Society, Jaffna, 1983.

27. See Patrick Peebles, "Colonization and Ethnic Conflict in the Dry Zone of Sri Lanka," *Journal of South Asian Studies*, February 1990 and Sunil Bastian, *Control of State Land: The Devolution Debate* (Colombo: International Centre for Ethnic Studies, 1995).

28. *The Broken Palmyra*, 352.

29. *The Broken Palmyra* discusses LTTE provocations at Kokkuvil refugee camp, Jaffna Hospital.

30. UTHR (Jaffna) *Reports 4-8*, "Someone Else's War," 27-51.

31. Martin Ennals, "Democracy and Self-Determination," International Alert, September 1991.

32. Lord (Eric) Avebury, "Self-Determination: The Way Forward," International Alert, July 1992.

33. Avebury, "Self-Determination: The Way Forward."

34. A. Amirthalingam, *The Path to Our Destiny*, in The Silver Jubilee Souvenir of the Federal Party, Jaffna, 1974.

35. See the ICJ report of 1981/83; Leary, "Ethnic Conflict and Violence."

36. See UTHR (Jaffna), *Reports 6, 7* and *11*. Shortly after the Special Task Force was deployed in the East, one of their early actions in May 1985 was to get Muslim hoodlums to attack Tamils and burn Tamil houses. See also documents of the Civil Rights Movement and Amnesty International of that period.

37. Kumari Jayawardana, *Ethnic Consciousness in Sri Lanka.*

38. In the Kanthalai scheme, colonies were planted upstream while the existing Tamil and Muslim farmers were downstream. The latter now have little influence in managing the water. In time encroachers and the government sugar factory upstream began to take precedence over the downstream native farmers in the supply of water. Pledges given in the 1950s had become a dead letter by 1990. New Sinhalese AGA divisions have been carved out in Trincomalee district, effectively keeping land from Tamils and Muslims, who lacked influence with the Great Land-Owner in Colombo. See also Peebles, "Colonization and Ethnic Conflict," and Bastian, *Control of State Land.*

39. Ampari District is an example of how colonization affects a minority. Prior to the Gal Oya scheme in the late 1940s, about 30 percent of its population was Tamil. After colonization about 20 percent are Tamil. Owing to a division of the Tamil vote between different parties, not one of the six MPs elected from the district in 1994 is Tamil. The same could now also happen in the Trincomalee District.
Of the 196 MPs elected in 1994, seventeen are Tamils from the North-East and six are Tamils from the Hill Country, a group which recovered the right to citizenship from the late 1970s onward. Thus the elected Tamil representation has declined from 20 percent of the elected MPs in 1947 (when they were 23 percent of the population) to 12 percent in 1994 when they were about 18 percent of the population. Disenfranchisement of Hill Country Tamils and colonization had both worked to depress the representation of minorities to the benefit of the majority.

40. Nihal Jayawickrema, "Self-Determination," Report of the Martin Ennals Memorial Symposium on Self-Determination (Saskatoon, Canada: International Alert and University of Saskatchewan, March 1993), 7, 8.

41. Michael Roberts, "Ethnic Conflict in Sri Lanka and Sinhalese Perspectives: Barriers to Accommodation," *Modern Asian Studies* 1978, Vol. 12: 353-76.

Twelve

Quebec: A Unique Case Of Secessionism

Reg Whitaker

Secessions seem to happen away from the so-called developed liberal capitalist democracies of Western Europe and North America. Secessions and attempted secessions have been relatively widespread phenomena in the Third World. The collapse of the Soviet Union and its empire have led to a proliferation of secessions from the decomposing state structures of the former Communist bloc.

But secessions in the West are another matter. The last example of a peaceful secession in Western Europe is the separation of Sweden and Norway as long ago as 1905. Ireland broke away from the United Kingdom mainly as the result of a campaign of guerrilla warfare in the early 1920s; the residual conflict over Ulster has continued at a violent level. There are of course secessionist movements that have emerged with varying degrees of strength and effectiveness in various Western European states among national minorities: Scots, Welsh, Catalans, Basques, Corsicans, Bretons, to name some of the more visible examples. In some cases, these movements have assumed violent, clandestine forms of action; in others, legitimate parliamentary channels have been used. In a few cases, both routes have been pursued simultaneously. None have been able to assert the degree of political effectiveness achieved by Sinn Féin in Ireland seventy or so years ago. Typically, bursts of apparent growth and enthusiasm are followed by rapid declines. In some instances, short-term revivals provide some continuity; in others, decline appears terminal. In the late 1990s, even the most respectable and successful such movement, Scottish nationalism, seems mired in an electoral rut with few reasonable prospects for an upward turn in fortunes. The inconsequential nature of these Western European movements stands in contrast to the burst of secessionist and attempted secessionist movements in other parts of the world. Yet before any generalizations are drawn about Western state stability versus post-Communist and Third World volatility, one exception demands close examination.

The Quebec sovereignty movement has nothing in common with secessionists in post-Communist and Third World states, and very much in common with secessionists in Western Europe. Yet, unlike the latter, it has shown strength and persistence. It has been able to mobilize support at both the elite and mass levels and create powerful political instruments to advance the cause. It has transformed the party system first in Quebec and then at the national level to make secession one of the established, "centrist" options available to Quebec voters. It has attracted influential interest in business and commercial milieus, wide support among labor and social movements, and has come close to establishing a cultural and ideological hegemony over large sections of Quebec society. Although a referendum on sovereignty in 1980 failed by a large margin, a second referendum fifteen years later failed by less than 1 percent to achieve a Yes that would have precipitated a profound crisis in the Canadian federal state. Thus by any measure the secessionist movement in Quebec has been resoundingly successful, even if not yet at the final stage of attaining the goal.

Why does the Quebec movement stand alone among Western secessionists in its relative success? The obverse of this question is equally intriguing: Why does Canada stand out among Western states in the relative weakness of its national state structures and the magnitude of its national legitimacy crisis? Other states have been discovering significant legitimacy problems around their political institutions. Italy, like Canada, has seen its national political party system collapse and move into new and uncharted waters. The British have witnessed a gathering storm around the venerable institution of the monarchy and the rapid disintegration of the ruling party of almost two decades. Apparently there is generally declining legitimacy for institutions that have endured for generations. Yet nowhere else than in Canada does this crisis as yet threaten the very survival of the national state itself.

Quebec's Presence in National Political Institutions

The power of the secessionist movement is manifested indirectly as well as directly. For three decades now, national politics has been dominated by the "national unity" crisis. In the 1960s, in response to the so-called "Quiet Revolution" — Quebec's compressed modernization drive — proposals were launched for reconfiguring the Confederation agreement that had been in place for a century. None of these schemes actually came into being, but the decade was in many ways dominated by the "Quebec question." In 1963 the Royal Commission on Bilingualism and Biculturalism was created with great fanfare and controversy and held public hearings across the country. Eventually the Official Languages Act, enshrining bilingualism in institutions of the national government and requiring a degree of bilingualism in the private sector as well (i.e., mandatory bilingual labeling on all products sold in Canada), came into force in 1969 and has remained the law of the land.

Another, later federal commission recommended decentralization of powers to the provinces. In 1971 a special federal-provincial constitutional conference actually developed unanimity around a draft revision of the Constitution, which failed when the Quebec government withdrew its support in the face of hostile public opinion in that province. In the aftermath of the failed 1980 referendum on sovereignty, a bruising federal-provincial and intraprovincial battle eventuated in the revised Constitution Act of 1982 which, despite being motivated above all by the desire to retain Quebec, was rejected by that province, which alone refused to sign the binding new agreement. In 1987, unanimity was briefly achieved by the federal and provincial first ministers in a draft of a further constitutional revision (the Meech Lake Accord) designed to reconcile Quebec to what it perceived as deficiencies in the 1981 revision by adding provisions recognizing Quebec as a distinct society, providing it with a constitutional veto, and further devolving powers to the provinces. Yet the Meech Lake Accord failed to achieve ratification after a three-year-long bitter conflict that pitted English Canadian mass opinion against the "elitist" control of the process by the politicians.

Then another round of constitutional discussions was launched in the aftermath of Meech's failure and under the renewed threat of separation emanating from Quebec. The Charlottetown Accord of 1992 again achieved unanimity among federal and provincial political elites, but was rejected by the public in a national referendum in 1992. The national political agenda in Canada has been Quebec driven for more than three decades. This does not mean that Quebec always, or even often, gets what it wants. It does mean that the national agenda is to a large degree set and defined by Quebec's demands and by Ottawa's perception (very often wrongheaded) of how best to respond to these demands.

From 1947 through 1998, Canada has normally been governed by prime ministers from Quebec (three francophones and one fluently bilingual anglophone); prime ministers from outside Quebec have presided for only twelve years, the last three for a total of only twelve months since 1968. The national party system was until 1993 firmly premised upon the principle that whichever party gained ascendancy among Quebec voters would rule the country. This has most often been the Liberals, but the Conservatives dominated Quebec and Canada from 1984 to 1993. A national social democratic party, the NDP, was stalled as a perpetual third party in the federal Parliament due mainly to its failure to attract Quebec support. Because of party dependency on Quebec support for electoral success, Quebec almost invariably held a crucial place within the caucus of the governing party. The promotion of Quebec preoccupations in the councils of government was institutionalized in the senior levels of the bureaucracy where Quebec/francophone representation became a leading consideration.

Decentralization of Federalism

The Canadian Confederation began in the 1860s as a highly centralized affair, but has evolved into one of the more decentralized federations in the world. Canadian federalism has always experienced tension between two distinct axes: first, the division of powers between the federal and ten provincial governments typical of all federations; and second, the binational axis between francophone and anglophone Canada. The latter has itself been a cause of ambiguity, whether the one axis was a pan-Canadian "French Canada" including francophone minorities in other provinces,[1] or Quebec, as the one jurisdiction with a francophone majority. The former was the preferred strategy of Pierre Trudeau as an explicit counterweight to the nationalist aggrandizement of the provincial state in Quebec, but the long-term trend has been sharply away from "French Canada" toward "Quebec." "French Canada" has little unity and no common political representation; Quebec is a dynamic political jurisdiction with its own state apparatus and a relatively purposive sense of direction.

But the "binational or dualist" axis often collides with the federal axis, especially when it is Quebec, one province among ten as well as the effective embodiment of the "French fact," playing a double role. Thus persistent demands from Quebec for "special status" (that is, a special devolution of powers to that province alone), or for constitutional recognition of the Quebec government's special role in promoting Quebec's "distinct society," or for a veto over constitutional amendments for Quebec have tended to generate resistance from other provinces and from public opinion outside Quebec. This resistance is premised upon the notion that all provinces should be on an equal footing, without special treatment: an understandable concept were the federalist dimension the only axis, but one that rather flies in the face of the binational reality. It is as if Canada were a hybrid in which Belgium or Switzerland had been grafted onto Australia or the United States. The result is a body politic that is constantly working at cross purposes with itself.

In recent years, attempts have been made to float the concept of "asymmetrical federalism" as a way of formally reconciling the two axes. In this scheme, Quebec would gather more provincial powers than other provinces, an imbalance that might be countered by reducing Quebec's presence in national political institutions. Asymmetrical federalism has proved an impractical proposition in a Canada where a Cartesian thirst for symmetry on both sides of the national divide seems bent on bringing matters to a confrontational head rather than seeking workable, if messy, compromises. Yet if formal or constitutionalized asymmetry has been eschewed, elements of asymmetry nevertheless have been woven into the practical fabric of federal-provincial policy making, as the direct result of pressures from the province of Quebec. Since Quebec built the first modern, efficient bureaucratic provincial state apparatus in Canada in the 1960s, the government of Quebec has proved a powerful antagonist of Ottawa, winning a number of concessions over the years, including the right to opt out of certain programs promoted by Ottawa (e.g., the national pension scheme does not include Quebec, which administers its own plan). Similarly, Quebec's agreement with Ottawa on immigration recognizes that province's special requirements with regard to promoting francophone immigration. Quebec therefore receives federal financial assistance for receiving immigrants that is not offered other provinces.

Much of Ottawa's preeminence in federalism derived from its historically superior fiscal capacity, and its willingness in the past to use this, through the device of shared-cost programs, to intrude into areas of policy that constitutionally had always belonged to the provinces. While Quebec had often been able to opt out of such ventures, thus intensifying the practical degree of asymmetry in the system, economic trends have turned against centralization and toward promoting a more generalized decentralization. By the late 1990s, under the impact of the debt crisis and the imposition of neo-liberal market models upon public policy, Quebec — even with a sovereignist government — has natural allies in the other wealthy provinces and in the right-wing opposition in the federal parliament for across-the-board devolution of powers and greater decentralization of federalism. On this issue, Quebec's long term strategy as a provincial government dovetails with a fiscally constrained federal government's desire to reduce its transfers to the provinces and get out of areas that it feels it can no longer afford.

As a province, Quebec, under both federalist and sovereignist governments, has accomplished much of the nationalist agenda that first emerged in the early 1960s. One significant achievement has been the enactment of language legislation protecting the French language in the one North American jurisdiction in which French is the language of the majority.[2] An economic imbalance that had existed between francophone and anglophone Quebecers has now been righted; Francophones successfully pursue careers in the public and private sectors in Quebec, with no evidence remaining of the historic injustices that drove the nationalist impulse a couple of generations ago. An economic space has been opened up for an emergent Québécois business class and a web of public supports for small and medium Quebec enterprise, known collectively as "Quebec, Inc.," has been constructed. Quebec continues to suffer from the structural problems of a declining rust-belt industrial base, and perhaps from some reluctance on the part of outside capital to commit to the uncertain and volatile political atmosphere in the province. Quebec as a province has been able to carve out a substantial degree of political and economic space within the constraints of the existing federal system.

Contradictions of the "National Unity" Discourse

All this suggests that Quebec and Quebec concerns have been central to Canadian national political life. This preoccupation has deeply influenced the dominant discourse of Canadian politics, to the extent that a "national unity" doctrine has been hegemonic in Ottawa for decades. According to this doctrine, the leading imperative of national government is holding the country together. National bilingualism has always been a central tenet of this faith, as has symbolic representation of "French Canada." One of the curiosities of the national unity doctrine has been its decidedly asymmetrical consequences for the representation of the cultural identities of the two national pillars, English and French Canada. The latter, which for most practical purposes tends to coincide with the province of Quebec and which regards itself as "Québécois" rather than "Canadien français," is sharply defined by contrast with the weakly constructed identity of "English Canada" — especially since the precipitous postwar decline of the influence of Britain and English symbols and culture in a Canadian society deeply penetrated by non-British immigration and shaped by multiculturalism and multiethnicity.

Yet while a Québécois identity has been more and more self-confidently articulated, an English (or "rest-of") Canadian identity has been actively discouraged by the champions of national unity. "Canada" is seen as a "binational marriage" between Quebec and the rest. Quebec, meanwhile, has a distinct cultural identity that she brings as a partner to the marriage: this is officially welcomed and even celebrated. But the other partner is not supposed to have a separate identity; this might be seen as threatening, as something that might be imposed by the non-francophone majority upon the francophone minority. That the "other" Canada includes Quebec is a central dogma of the national unity faith. Thus the "marriage" (to use this overworked metaphor) is a peculiar one indeed: Quebec is "married" not to another partner but to the relationship itself.

The national unity discourse has given rise to increasing resentment among Canadians outside Quebec, first against the demands and costs of national bilingualism, and then against the very notion of the priority of national unity as against economic and social issues. Successive governments have deepened the feelings of alienation among anglophone voters by responding to criticism in the usual counterproductive manner of elites accustomed to setting agendas without interference. "National unity" has been protected in the same manner that other orthodoxies accepted by all the "right thinking" people have been protected in the past. Thus criticism of bilingualism was excoriated from the pulpits of power and, for many years, virtually excluded from public debate — except as falling within the category of "extremism" or the "lunatic fringe." This of course only fed populist paranoia against the ubiquitous "they" who ruled the society and were conspiring to deny voice to the people (a great many of whom were indeed deeply suspicious of bilingualism and national unity orthodoxy).

The Failure of Elite Accommodation

To understand both the fury of this populist reaction, it is necessary to understand the historic reliance placed upon elites and elite accommodation in the business of yoking together Canada's "two solitudes." The concept of "consociationalism," developed to explain the peculiarities of "pillarized" European societies like Belgium, the Netherlands, Switzerland, and Austria, was applied in the 1960s and 1970s to the functioning of national political institutions in Canada.[3] The basic thrust of this approach — that there was minimal contact between the main sub-national groups or "pillars" at the mass level (that indeed too much contact at this level would actually be counterproductive, increasing friction), while the burden of "nation saving" was borne by the elites who found it in their own self-interest to find ways to negotiate power-sharing bargains at the center — did have a good deal to commend it as historical description. Until recently, national political institutions were infused with the spirit of something like the consociational model. Indeed, the very degree of apparent symbolic accommodation with Quebec's rising aspirations over the past few decades, as reflected in the strong Quebec representation in Ottawa outlined above, is itself proof of the seriousness with which the elite accommodationist version of national unity has been pursued. As a descriptive model, consociationalism had some power. But ironically, it was being applied just as its empirical foundations were being undermined. A crucial assumption — the will and capacity of the elites to fulfill their ascribed nation-saving role — came under assault with the adherence to the goal of secession on the part of significant sectors of the Quebec elites.

By 1970, with the founding of the Parti Québécois (PQ) and its rapid emergence as the chief opposition party in Quebec politics, followed by its quick ascent to provincial office in 1976, the Quebec elites had divided into supporters of federalism and advocates of independence. Every election in Quebec from 1970 on has been in effect a kind of informal plebiscite on the question of separation, not to speak of the two formal referenda on the subject called as a result of PQ victories at the polls. The consociational model cannot be stretched to include a situation in which some elites struggle to hold the federal state together, while others struggle to rip it apart. Thus all the attempts to boost symbolic representation of Quebec at the center have failed to impede the growth of secessionist sentiment. Given that years of publicly visible deference to Quebec representation culminated in 1995 with 60 percent of francophone Quebecers voting for sovereignty, it is hardly surprising that widespread cynicism pervades English Canadian attitudes towards any further accommodation.

Consociationalism was never merely a descriptive model. It also has a clearly prescriptive thrust. Consociational democracy seems to work best when the elites of the national cultures or pillars are given the greatest possible autonomy by the constituents of their own groups. The greater the constraints upon the various elites imposed by their own constituents, the less free they will be to make the kind of accommodations with the other elites that the system of elite bargaining requires. The masses should be deferential in leaving the business of nation saving to their elites; the latter should preferably be armed with a weak programmatic mandate from their own constituents, but a carte blanche to deal as they see fit with other elites on the national ground where the pillars alone intersect. This is all very well, and may indeed indicate behaviors that are functional to any system resembling the pillarized model. But there is no ducking one controversial implication of such thinking: as prescription, consociationalism is forthrightly elitist and distinctly hostile to mass democracy. This has been its Achilles heel in relation to the model's putative applicability to Canada.

For the past few decades, Canada has struggled to contain the Quebec challenge as if it were a functioning consociational system. Yet at the same historical moment, the elite-driven political system has been radically undermined by the democratization of both Quebec and English Canadian societies. Political sociologists examining Canadian public opinion once declared that Canadians were deferential to authority, relative to the more egalitarian and populist attitudes prevalent in the United States.[4] This is hardly the case anymore. As deference to elites has declined, so too has the viability of a political system that historically placed great stress on relatively autonomous elite bargaining and minimal levels of accountability to mass constituencies.

A society that was historically divided along cultural and linguistic lines into two distinct national groups became clamorous and disputatious as these two nations grew more self-conscious of their identities and democratic aspirations, and more aware of their distinctiveness, one from the other. Paradoxically, however, the stress these developments placed upon national political institutions, which was very great indeed, tended to promote frantic attempts to cope in a familiar but now increasingly anachronistic manner. The response to the democratic erosion of elite-driven politics was to readjust the mechanisms of elite accommodation. These attempts have clearly failed, as the dismal history of constitutional reform demonstrates decisively from Meech Lake through Charlottetown to the 1995 referendum. Worse, attempts at resuscitating elitism have been like red flags to the democratic bull. The net result of elite-driven nation saving: Quebec is closer than ever to secession, while Canadian democracy has been infused with an unhealthy air of populist paranoia and distrust of any national public purpose.

Democracy and Destabilization

The Quebec sovereignty movement has from its beginnings in the early 1960s sought to mobilize public support as its primary tactic. This mobilization of support can also be seen as a democratic surge striking against established institutions and the constitutional order. In a country with an inherited British parliamentary tradition and a traditional aversion to extraparliamentary democracy, the historic significance of the two Quebec referenda on sovereignty should not be underestimated. Although there were some Canadian precedents for plebiscites, they had been rare occurrences.

In 1980 the Quebec government asked its citizens to give it a direct mandate to negotiate a form of "sovereignty-association" with the rest of Canada. Any agreement negotiated would be further subject to popular ratification in a subsequent referendum. The challenge to the rest of Canada posed in this proposal was not merely to the survival of the existing constitutional arrangement; at another level, it was a pointed challenge to the legitimacy of the existing understanding of parliamentary and constitutional democracy. A democratic majority in support of radical alteration to the constitutional fabric would be a brute fact transcending "normal" constitutional and political practice. There was little open discussion in English Canada of how to respond if a majority did in fact favor the sovereignist project, but the mere possibility raised alarm. The marked reluctance to raise hypothetical scenarios, for fear of making them likely to happen, indicated a deep anxiety in the rest of the country that such a majority would be, in effect, unanswerable. In the event, Quebecers themselves chose not to press the issue, but in doing so they established that they indeed did have a "right" to self determination, one based firmly in the power of a democratic majority. This was strengthened yet further in 1995 when Quebecers came close to showing the concrete will, as well as the hypothetical right, to separate.

There are a number of unresolved questions around the definition of a "people," the relationship of "majorities" (and how they are properly constituted) to the effective expression of the collective will, the place and voice of minorities and especially national minorities like the aboriginal peoples, and so on, which will be examined in more detail later. Suffice to say that the emergence of a mass sovereignist movement in Quebec has had the effect of a democratic bomb that has reverberated powerfully against the foundations of the old constitutional/parliamentary order in Canada. The fallout, by no means confined to Quebec, has had some perverse repercussions, but it has certainly debilitated the traditional political elites.

One of the most perverse effects of the rise of the sovereignty movement has been on democratic practice in the rest of Canada, although this was an unintended consequence never sought by the sovereignists. The threat of separation threw the federalist elites both outside and inside Quebec into a permanent crisis since the 1960s. The only way they understood nation-saving was to try repeatedly to rejig the rules of elite accommodation, to cut deals behind closed doors, and to insist that the fate of the nation was too important to be left in the unstable and untrustworthy hands of the people. The net effect of their efforts was to further highlight the gulf between the people and the elites and to confirm in the populist mind of English Canada that the "constitution," "federalism," and "national unity" were smokescreens deployed by the nefarious "them," out to do "us" wrong. A democratic thrust from Quebec thus emphasized precisely those areas of policy concern traditionally most removed from popular participation, and this in turn fed a popular reaction of distrust and paranoia in the rest of Canada: a perverse result indeed.

Constitutionalism versus Populism

Just how powerful the populist reaction was could be seen in the Meech Lake and Charlottetown fiascoes. In the case of Meech Lake, a delicate and intricate deal for reform of the Constitution that for once gained widespread support in Quebec, was negotiated by the prime minister and the ten premiers in secret sessions and presented to the country as, in effect, a fait accompli in 1987. It was the finest hour for the political elites. The deal had, however, to be ratified by Parliament and the provincial legislatures before taking effect. Unaccountably, the first ministers set a timetable of three years for the ratification process, which had to be unanimous. Outside Quebec, a powerful populist backlash against the deal emerged, part of which might be attributed to resentment against enshrining Quebec's "distinct society" status, and part to democratic dislike of deals concluded by "eleven white men behind closed doors," as the popular pejorative phrase put it. Public hearings in various provinces provided the worst of all possible worlds: Democratic discontent was vented, while the politicians rather smugly lectured the people about their alleged irresponsibility and insisted that not a single semicolon in the intricate and complex deal could be altered. Provincial elections produced two new premiers with no personal stake in the accord, one of whom became a kind of populist tribune on behalf of anti-Meech sentiment. Despite frantic last minute attempts by the first ministers to patch together a compromise before the time limit for ratification ran out, the entire process ended in total failure in 1990. Symbolically, the death blow was administered by a lone aboriginal member of a provincial legislature who refused to give the necessary unanimous consent on the grounds that the aboriginal peoples had been ignored in the accord. In this he really was standing in for very many Canadians, aboriginal and non-aboriginal, who rejected the very notion, inherent in Meech, of a "Quebec round" of constitutional revision designed exclusively to meet the Quebec challenge.

Increasingly, English Canadian constitutional discourse was premised upon a newfound principle, that of the "equality of the provinces," a concept that has neither historical nor legal substance, but which apparently articulates powerful feelings about egalitarianism now prevalent in English Canada as it condenses around the constitutional issue. The negative implication of this principle is obvious: No constitutional distinction nor any form of special status would be tolerated for Quebec that could not be similarly extended to all the other provinces. In effect, English Canadian opinion was increasingly assertive about denying the binational axis of the Canadian political community, while insisting upon the supremacy of the federal dimension (ten provinces, of which Quebec is merely one, with no privileged status as the homeland of French Canada). There was widespread consensus that any further constitutional discussion would have to be a "Canada round" that would speak to the needs and demands of all Canadians, not just Quebecers.

For their part, Quebecers, both sovereignists and federalists, expressed outrage and humiliation that a deal signed unanimously by the first ministers that had embodied a kind of minimum acceptable position for Quebec, had been dumped in the dustbin. English Canada, they argued, had "given its word" — and then reneged. English Canadians found it difficult to get across to Quebecers that a handful of politicians could not "deliver" millions of Canadians without gaining their express consent.

The "Canada round" soon opened with a federalist government in Quebec threatening to hold a referendum on sovereignty. This time greater efforts were made to engage larger numbers of people in the process, including a commission that acted somewhat like a radio open-line show in attracting free-floating expressions of the opinions of "ordinary Canadians," and a handful of ad hoc consultative conferences where representatives from different elements of civil society exchanged views. However, calls for a constituent assembly or some other formal mechanism for nonpolitical participation went unheeded. In the end, the negotiating table was widened to include representatives from Canada's leading aboriginal organizations, as well as the first ministers (excluding the premier of Quebec, who boycotted the process). The Charlottetown Accord reflected this different mix, including much of Meech, with a watered-down recognition of Quebec's distinctiveness, along with an elaborate plan for aboriginal self-government and some features designed to respond to particular regional demands from English Canada (such as the long-standing Western demand for an upper chamber of Parliament that would be elected on an equal regional basis rather than appointed). This time it was apparent that popular ratification would be a requirement and a national referendum was held in late 1992.

Although all the premiers and all the established political parties in parliament were in support, as well as the national aboriginal leadership, Charlottetown quickly fell victim to populist distrust. Almost every group that had not been directly represented at the negotiating table (such as the national umbrella feminist committee, for example) turned up in opposition during the referendum campaign. Anti-elitism was so strong that even those representatives who did get to the table were attacked by others in their group as having sold out: thus the support of the aboriginal leadership for the accord's provisions on native self-government failed to convince a majority of aboriginal people, close to two thirds of whom living on reserves where the votes were counted separately voted No. The Yes campaign seemed driven by an elitist conception that the politicians knew best what was good for the people and that the latter should follow the lead of their betters. This was symbolized by the prime minister publicly tearing up a copy of the Constitution to demonstrate the result of a No vote. The No campaign tended toward dire predictions of what was allegedly encoded within the agreement.

In the event, Charlottetown failed the test of popular referral. A national majority voted No, as did Quebecers, although apparently for quite different reasons. Quebecers thought Charlottetown did not give enough to Quebec, denying legitimate aspirations for the recognition of Quebec's distinctiveness and for a high degree of autonomy. Canadians outside Quebec thought it gave Quebec too much, violating the principle of the equality of the provinces. That was an alarming enough result from the point of view of national unity. But equally alarming to the political elites was a further message from English Canada: provision for popular ratification of constitutional changes did not rectify the democratic deficit revealed in Meech Lake. If the process that produced the document submitted for ratification was judged insufficiently democratic, then popular ratification simply provided a more efficient mechanism for rejection.

After the 1992 Charlottetown referendum, observers began to talk about constitutional "gridlock" in Canada. The aptness of this metaphor became apparent following the 1994 electoral victory of the sovereignists in Quebec and the subsequent 1995 referendum on sovereignty. Neither the federal government nor the other provinces felt able to seriously offer the prospect of future constitutional change as a counter to the vigorous renewed sovereignist thrust in Quebec.

But if the constitutional obsession has failed to produce results, another, equally alarming, trend emerged out of the Charlottetown experience, which we might call the "constitutionalization" of ordinary politics. Instead of competing for resources within the constitutional rules in the manner of other liberal pluralist states, Canadians had been turned toward an idea of politics as a contest over the rules themselves.[5] This raises the stakes immensely and infects political discourse with the zero-sum-game rhetoric of "rights as trumps." This subtext of Charlottetown became starkly evident in the subsequent general election.

Transformation of National Political Institutions

The Charlottetown referendum was the first wave in a two-wave convulsion that has transformed the structure of national politics in Canada. The second wave, one year later almost to the day, was the general election of 1993. Together these events have redrawn the political map, not merely in a partisan sense but in a deeper sense of political community and the nature of politics. During Charlottetown, the three established parties — the governing Conservatives, the Liberal official opposition, and the perennial third party, the social democratic NDP — were all part of the pro-Charlottetown consensus (just as they had been solidly behind Meech Lake). In the eyes of opponents, the party leaderships looked like co-conspirators against the public interest. Opponents were found in abundance within each of these parties, as well as outside; none of the parties proved able to mobilize their memberships or their organizations to deliver the Yes vote. One new grouping, the Reform Party, with only a single MP and one member of the Senate, actively sought to challenge the all-party consensus by leading the anti-Charlottetown opposition in English Canada. In Quebec, the sovereignists were in the lead in opposition, while the federalist Liberal government in Quebec offered ineffectual support.

In the general election of 1993, the ruling Conservative Party, in office for nine years and winner of two consecutive national majorities, was all but destroyed, retaining only a derisory two seats in the 285 seat House of Commons. The Liberals, once the dominant force in national politics, returned to their traditional status as the "government party" with a majority based on representation from every province. But if the Liberal return seemed to confirm traditional patterns, everything else about the election suggested radical discontinuity with the past. A governing party — one with roots that went back to the very beginning of Canadian history — had been effectively swept off the map. So had the social democratic party. In place of the two wounded parties were two new parties. The secessionist Bloc Québécois, with the second largest number of seats, assumed the mantle of Her Majesty's Loyal Opposition. The Reform Party finished close behind the BQ by virtue of replacing the Tories and the NDP as the real opposition in English Canada. In the 1997 election, Reform replaced the BQ as official opposition, with the latter slipping to third position in the party standings.

This means more than a mere replacement of party names. It represents the introduction of new political discourses and a new political geography with potentially profound implications for the future of the Canadian federation. The sharp regional and national divisions of the election were widely noted. The BQ, not surprisingly, runs candidates only in Quebec but dominate in that province. Reform was, and remains, a party of English Canada alone, with no presence in Quebec.

But more significant than the mere fact of regionalism was the manner in which these regional bases had been constructed. Both parties mobilized support through overtly ideological, programmatic appeals. This ideologizing of political discourse was unprecedented, but, more unsettling, the process was mutually exclusionary — that is, the mobilizing appeals were such as to harden the divisions between Quebec and the rest of Canada, and had the effect of reinforcing sharply contradictory perceptions of Canada and Quebec on the two sides of the national divide.

The emergence and rapid success of the BQ was an innovation in federal politics. When the first PQ government came to office in 1976 and prepared for the initial sovereignty referendum of 1980, it entered the fray without any sovereignist allies among the Quebec members of the federal parliament. Even more devastating to their position, the prime minister, Pierre Trudeau, was the acknowledged leader of the federalist forces in Quebec who could boast not only of a virtually unanimous bloc of Liberal MPs from Quebec but of very high personal approval ratings in Quebec public opinion. The Quebec federalists could claim the dominant Quebec presence in the federal government level as an effective antisovereignist counterpoint to the sovereignists' capture of the provincial government. Asked by the PQ to make a definitive choice between the two governments in the 1980 referendum, the people of Quebec, including at least a narrow majority of francophones, refused and opted instead to retain both levels. Four years later, Quebec voters showed they were not wedded to the federal Liberal party as such when they shifted their electoral allegiance massively to the Conservatives, now led by yet another federalist Quebec prime minister, Brian Mulroney.

These electoral decisions were evidence not merely of continued federalist allegiance, but also of participation in national political choices between the established party options in terms of the policy and leadership discourses that characterized partisan debates across the country. For instance, in 1988 Quebec voters chose to strongly support the Conservatives' initiative of the Canada-U.S. Free Trade Agreement in an election where every other province save one gave majority support to the other two parties who were opposed to the agreement. In this case, strategic voting intervention proved quite effective in resolving a major policy dispute in favor of the preferences of Quebecers.

The BQ was formed in the first instance in parliament out of defecting Quebec nationalist MPs, mainly Tory, disillusioned by the Meech Lake fiasco. The leadership came from the most prominent defectee of all, the charismatic Lucien Bouchard, who had been Prime Minister Mulroney's key Quebec lieutenant. The Bloc's capture of close to three quarters of Quebec seats in the 1993 election signaled a sharp discontinuity with the past electoral behavior of Quebec voters. Unlike the Liberals and Tories who had previously vied for Quebec votes, the BQ was not merely anti-federalist, but in a deeper sense offered an ideological alternative to the pragmatic brokerage politics of the past. The BQ represents above all the politics of identity, in which Quebecers were asked to respond to an appeal for national solidarity that transcended all social and economic cleavages other than the national cleavage between Quebecers and Canadians outside Quebec.

At the heart of this politics was the demand for recognition as a distinct people that could only be satisfied by sovereignty. But its raison d'être as a party is to put itself out of business by helping to bring about independence for Quebec and thus the end of any place for Quebec MPs in the federal parliament, and all its particular policy positions are deeply colored by that all consuming ideological commitment. With the BQ-dominated Quebec caucus in Ottawa, Quebec has already seceded, at least in part, from the federal governing institutions.

These developments would have been impressive enough were it not for equally dramatic developments transforming the party system outside Quebec. The rise of the Reform party also signals a great deal more than meets the eye.[6] Brokerage politics, with its National Unity consensus and its pragmatic redistribution of resources through the agency of the state along liberal pluralist criteria, had become debilitated by the fiscal crisis of the capitalist state (a condition common throughout the Western world) and by the legitimacy crisis of elites (also common in general to other democracies, but quite specifically embodied in Canada's ongoing constitutional impasse). The smug "we know best" consensus around acceptable and unacceptable ideas had stifled debate for some time on certain key issues. Bilingualism and multiculturalism (the latter paradoxically seen by Quebec nationalists as a cynical federal counterweight to "cultural dualism" that would recognize Quebec as an equal partner, but seen in Ottawa rather as a centerpiece of National Unity incorporating the "other ethnics" into the consensus) had attained the status of sacred cows that must be protected from public criticism. Yet these policies were deeply unpopular with many English Canadians. The economic costs associated with these programs were not great, but they were highly charged with symbolism. To middle class and many working class taxpayers restive about paying for welfare state programs which they could see offering little benefit to themselves, the symbolism was that of "special treatment for special interests." There was widespread alienation from policies seemingly designed to promote minority identifications above the symbols of the majority. Reform gave voice to those who felt themselves disenfranchised by the liberal orthodoxies prevalent in Ottawa and excluded from participation in public debates.

Despite liberal fears about uncorking genies, this is probably a healthy development for Canadian democracy: Exclusion breeds paranoia and potentially more extreme forms of protest (as witness some malignant right-wing movements in Europe). By giving voice to these concerns and by their remarkable electoral success, Reform has transformed political discourse in English Canada by expanding the boundaries of what is permissible. Moreover, by advocating a series of concrete reforms to make political institutions more representative and more accountable (introduction of referenda on important policy issues, recall of MPs by their constituents, free votes in the House of Commons), Reform has infused a new democratic thrust into Canadian politics. It has challenged not only traditional elite domination, but it has also threatened the old pragmatic brokerage model of party politics with its emphasis on programmatic, ideologically driven political action.

The rise of Reform is pregnant with significance for the future place of Quebec. For the first time the House of Commons has a major party, in fact the real official opposition from Canada outside Quebec, that does not share in the National Unity consensus that had formerly united all "legitimate" parties. This has had very specific consequences for federal strategy in the face of the sovereignist challenge. One of the most strongly held elements of the National Unity consensus — accepted by all parties in Ottawa and by premiers in the provinces outside Quebec — had been that it was impolitic and unacceptable to discuss how or whether Quebec secession might be negotiated in the event of a Yes vote. Such discussions did take place among academics and privately funded think tanks, but official references to hypothetical responses were considered inappropriate, with the potential to legitimize the possibility and thus become a self-fulfilling prophecy. Reform pioneered the idea of a "two-track" strategy: one set of responses if Quebec remained, and another set if Quebec chose to leave. Prior to the 1995 vote, Reform was insistent upon enunciating the clear principle that a Yes vote of whatever magnitude, even 50 percent plus one vote, should automatically trigger negotiations to bring about separation. Following the referendum, Reform has led opposition to the Liberal government's attempt to respond to the Quebec challenge through federal initiatives toward recognizing some attenuated "special status" for Quebec within Canada. The notion of the equality of the provinces has now been raised in Reform discourse to a veritable cornerstone of the Canadian constitutional edifice, and in this the party is echoed by a number of premiers, of every party stripe, and by an apparently substantial body of public opinion. The obverse of this proposition is that if Quebec is unwilling to live with this "equal" status, then serious consideration should be given to the second track, that is, to define the rest of Canada's terms of separation — and to do so in advance of an actual demand from Quebec following a successful referendum result.

Two significant strands of the political elite, first the sovereignists in Quebec, and now the populists in the rest of Canada, have broken free of the obligations of elite accommodation inherent in the National Unity discourse — and they each face the beleaguered Liberal government across the floor of the national parliament.[7]

Sovereignty and Recognition

It is now time to turn attention to the sovereignty movement itself, its nature and direction. If the sovereignty movement represents a unique case of a flourishing secessionist movement in an Western liberal democratic state, it is also the case that the evolution of contemporary Quebec nationalism has followed a trajectory unlike that of any other minority nationalism in the West.

Quebec nationalism is predominantly a liberal project, in both senses that liberalism is generally understood: politically liberal in its acceptance of pluralism and its emphasis on procedural justice as the basis of the state, rather than some overarching public good; and economically liberal in its acceptance of markets and competitiveness as the fundamental basis for the allocation of resources. Although it has been depicted by unfriendly observers as an atavistic reaction to modernity, that characterization should rather be stood on its head: Quebec nationalism is a product of modernity, and is incomprehensible except in the frame of the familiar anxieties and dilemmas of modernity.[8] One of the great paradoxes of the Quebec-Canada imbroglio is that the quarrel is essentially one within liberalism.

The essential similarity of Quebec and English Canadian values has tempted many observers into a mistakenly optimistic view of the prospects for integration. There is a common fallacy that suggests that convergent values will push a divided society toward a shared identity. Quebec offers a case study of why this proposition is mistaken.[9] Values have little to do with identity, other than to provide some of the content of an identity already formed. Convergent values have not, after all, led English-speaking Canadians to join the United States, nor have they reconciled Quebec nationalists to a status as one among ten provinces. Shared values may actually spur resistance to integration, so long as the attributes of a distinct identity are present.

When Quebec was still a society dominated by a rural Catholic traditionalist ethos, it was not only the French language that acted as a natural barrier to English Canadian and American penetration, there was also a cultural barrier. Today, in the era of globalized mass culture, Québecois identity may be more threatened. If identity politics are really, as Charles Taylor argues, about recognition, then shared values may very well increase the insecurity of those seeking recognition of difference from others who are so very much like them. It is characteristic of arguments for sovereignty that they are generally not couched overtly in the language of identity and recognition. This too is a product of a liberalism that finds its most facile and acceptable voice in the technocratic language of economics and public policy making. Sovereignists tend to argue in terms of the distribution of powers between Ottawa and Quebec City, and of Quebec's alleged inability to regulate and promote its economic development satisfactorily within the "straitjacket" of an "overly centralized" federalism.

Another variant is the claim that Quebec is a net loser in the overall balance sheet of federal-provincial transfers of resources. These dollars and cents arguments are eminently contestable (indeed the proposition that Quebec is a net loser in federal-provincial transfers is quite flatly untrue, even if widely believed by credulous Quebec voters[10]). There is a thinness, an artificiality, to such arguments that suggest that they are not ultimately authentic, that they are standing in, as it were, for the real arguments. Nor do they make much impact on the population at large. It was widely agreed that the turning point in the 1995 referendum, when a hitherto stagnant level of support for sovereignty suddenly erupted, came when Lucien Bouchard took over effective leadership of the Yes side from the technocratic Jacques Parizeau, and began stirring voters with his nationalist eloquence into an emotional response. The inauthenticity of the technocratic discourse is revealed in rare moments when sovereignists speak of their feelings of "humiliation" at Quebec's "rejection" by English Canada.

Ironically, the demand for identity recognition is a very modern, even post-modern, phenomenon. In a slightly different mode, with regard to race, ethnicity, gender and sexual identity, it is one of the leading elements of contemporary democratic conflict. Yet as an aspirant nation-state that wishes to take its place among other states in the global political economy, a sovereignist Quebec is uncomfortable about speaking in tones usually associated with minority complainants. Hence the vocabulary of technocratic liberalism is drawn on to express more emotive striving toward the "imagined community" of a sovereign state when a distinctive identity will be formally recognized in the eyes of others.

Nowhere is this paradox more peculiarly revealed than in the untrammeled enthusiasm shown by the sovereignists for economic globalization and the consequent decline of the nation state. Instead of fearing globalization as a threat to the viability of small states, sovereignists have embraced virtually all its manifestations, including NAFTA and continental free trade. Not only does globalization appeal to the technocratic modernity the sovereignists cultivate, but it has the concrete political advantage of focusing on the increasing irrelevance of the national government in Canada. Globalization of capital has drastically undermined the regulatory role played by national states, especially smaller ones like Canada: The fiscal and monetary policy toolboxes are depleted, and even the capacity of national states to control the outflow of capital has been severely impaired. Thus what was once a powerful argument against going it alone has been removed. In the era of NAFTA, argues the PQ, who needs Ottawa any longer? A sovereign Quebec could take its place beside Canada, Mexico, and the United States in an economic framework that makes more sense in a era of globalization than an anachronistic Canadian federation. (Similar arguments are made, to less apparent effect, by Scottish Nationalists who style themselves better Europeans than the English and speak of the nuisance of Westminster in the era of Maastricht.)

This is an argument with some force, but it also reveals how profoundly liberal the PQ's idea of sovereignty really is. If it is a fundamental characteristic of liberalism to separate the economic from the political,[11] the PQ have transformed the idea of secession from a liberal federation into an act that itself affirms liberalism. The Quebec sovereignist vision is one that abandons all pretense of national control over economic life, even as it concentrates all its attention on the achievement of the trappings of political independence. The first referendum in 1980 was to seek a mandate to negotiate "sovereignty-association" with the rest of Canada. Association was then understood (these were pre-free trade days) in terms of an elaborate set of joint institutions that would serve to replace the institutions of federalism in regulating economic matters of common interest. Although representation was generally supposed to be equal on these bodies, an exception was made for the monetary commission for joint central banking functions: Here a Canadian majority would be accepted.

By 1995, formal mechanisms of association were no longer deemed necessary (and in any event had proved unacceptable even in principle to the rest of Canada); but a putative "partnership" with Canada was posited as a likely result of negotiations arising out of a Yes vote. The PQ now suggests that a sovereign Quebec would simply adopt the Canadian dollar as its official currency, thus abnegating any independent monetary policy.[12] The PQ has thus consistently eschewed any real ambition to pursue an autonomous national economic course. This may be perfectly reasonable under current international circumstances, and may indicate a lucid realism on the part of the sovereignists quite far from the nationalist romanticism often attributed to secessionist adventures. Nonetheless, it raises a troubling question: Why the dogged insistence on narrowly constructed technocratic arguments for the allegedly fatal shortcomings of federalism, when independence will not even claim the trappings of economic sovereignty, let alone the substance? We are forced to return to the point that the sovereignists speak a language that masks their meaning. Political sovereignty is what they are really after, and political sovereignty is about the symbolism of recognition. Good liberals, they have separated the economic from the political. Prudently leaving the former field to the competitive forces of global markets, they turn their energies toward conquering the field of symbolic representation. Perhaps this is not so surprising. It is what one might expect from a politics of identity.

Sovereignty and the "Magic Doorway" to the Future

In keeping with this restrained nationalist vision, and with a clear eye on the caution and nervousness of the Quebec electorate facing a leap into the dark, the PQ has for years assiduously worked the theme that the transition to sovereignty will be risk free. In this they appear to have been remarkably successful, to judge from the results of the 1995 referendum and the apparent imperviousness of a substantial section of the population to threats of the dire economic consequences of forcing a break emanating from the federal government or from business. In the PQ vision, a Yes vote will open a magic doorway or, to shift the metaphor, it will be the equivalent of the "transporter beam" in the Star Trek television series: Quebec will be instantaneously whisked from federalism to sovereignty intact. Everything — society, economy, culture — will be magically recreated just as they were before sovereignty, except that now they will be topped by the fleur-de-lis national flag. Everything, as the sovereignists tirelessly stress with Freudian insistence, will be "normal."

There is irony here. Quebec separatism began its modern career with a strong sense of social injustice and a vision of an independent Quebec as a better world. There was a radical, national liberationist wing of the movement in the 1960s, that eventually burnt itself out with rhetorical extremism and violent terrorist tactics, but the longer term residue was a socialist element in the PQ. The hard experience of government in the late 1970s and early 1980s did much to shrivel radicalism, but as late as the 1995 referendum, the PQ was busy constructing (with considerable success) a "social coalition" of labor and social movements behind the Yes campaign.

Yet when the government in 1994-95 held a series of regional hearings around the province on the theme of sovereignty, they received an unexpected message from many witnesses: Sovereignty for what? Why go though the process of separation if the intention is to arrive back in the same place, that is, in a society in which nothing has changed, except for symbols of national status? In a sense, the means have consumed the ends. Reassurances of continuity finally overwhelm the discontinuity that was, after all, the point of the exercise in the first place. Sovereignty loses its content, but is pursued anyway as an end in itself. Perhaps this last judgment should be qualified in light of the specific political economic context of the late 1990s. The PQ's reassurances of stability and continuity, its relentless emphasis on the moderation and safety of its economic liberalism, can be read as the usual behavior of left-wing movements seeking respectability and an entree to the corridors of power by gutting their own raison d'être (namely, the well-worn pattern of European socialist and social-democratic parties purchasing a license for office by renouncing anything in their programs that challenges capitalism). Upon assuming the premiership in early 1996, Lucien Bouchard made it clear that his first priority was to get Quebec's "fiscal house in order" by sharply reducing expenditures. The same neo-liberal agenda of slashing social programs and infrastructure, and sacking public employees was adopted in Quebec as in other North American jurisdictions.

Yet the capacity of the PQ to convince its working class and economically underprivileged supporters that it is really their best advocate, should not be underestimated. Some of this appeal obviously derives from nationalism, but nationalism alone could not forge the left-wing alliance of social solidarity that came together for the referendum. This has taken place within a broader policy context in which the federal government has reduced its leading role and offloaded costs for social programs onto the provinces.

Against a federal government in apparent retreat, the sovereignty movement has juxtaposed a vision, a dream of nation that includes promises of betterment. It remains to be seen whether the end of the federal fiscal deficit, forecast for 1998, will permit a more positive face of federalism to be demonstrated in the future.

Ethnic versus Liberal Nationalism

The sovereignist project has demonstrated considerable strength and durability among francophone Quebecers. Sixty percent support for sovereignty among francophones is a powerful base upon which to build for the future. Political circumstances may of course cause this level to oscillate over the next few years, but the prospect of any dramatic deflation of the support gathered in 1995 seems very unlikely, save in the surprising circumstance of a comprehensive constitutional settlement as strong as the Meech Lake Accord being guaranteed by the rest of Canada. The fact remains, however, that 60 percent francophone support was not enough to produce an overall Yes vote. Moreover, there is a real question surrounding the legitimacy of a "50 percent plus one" vote in bringing about the dissolution of a country. If, as the federal government later hinted, some higher level should be appropriately set (60 percent, two-thirds?) before negotiations on independence would be triggered, the numbers evident in 1995 would indicate that an extraordinarily high level of support among francophones will be required to win. But this paradox points to a huge problem inherent in the sovereignist project: What is the nature and composition of an effective majority in a liberal, pluralist society to bring about a fundamental change in the political community? Despite the liberalism of the PQ, it raises the uncomfortable question of ethnicity and its relation to the composition of an effective majority.

The problem was notoriously highlighted on referendum night, October 30, 1995 when the premier of Quebec, Jacques Parizeau, addressed the party faithful after the narrow defeat. "Let's stop talking about the francophones of Quebec," he declared. "Let's talk about us (nous). Sixty percent of us voted in favor. . . It's true we have been defeated, but basically by what? By money and the ethnic vote. . . in the long run, finally, we will have our own revenge and we will have our own country." These remarks were received with almost universal opprobrium, from inside the PQ as well from outside. The next day, Mr. Parizeau announced his retirement. He was perhaps the messenger executed for bringing unwelcome news. As part of its pervasive liberalism, the PQ has distanced itself from a narrow, exclusionary nationalism based on the core ethnic group. Instead, sovereignist thinkers have formulated a concept of territorial nationalism. This is an inclusionary, nonethnic nationalism that recognizes the plurality of groups within the territory. At the abstract level of principles, this is very much to be welcomed. Yet there is an enormous problem. Neither the anglophone community, nor the so-called "allophone" communities (that is, those immigrants to Quebec whose mother tongue is neither English nor French), nor Quebec's aboriginal peoples, have shown the slightest interest in joining forces with this admittedly liberal inclusionary nationalist project of territorial sovereignty. That is why a clear majority of francophones has not been able to achieve an overall electoral majority for a Yes vote: all the nonfrancophone minorities have voted overwhelmingly against.

There is a paradox at the heart of developing Quebec nationalism. Liberal, pluralistic, civic nationalism — the very nationalism that all modern, rightthinking sovereignists prefer — is necessarily territorial rather than ethnic, inclusive rather than exclusionary. Sovereignty based upon a territorial nationalism of course assumes the protection of minority rights. More, it never admits a privileged ethnos or religion or national ideology, and thus a citizenship divided into first and second classes. A territorially sovereign Quebec will never be like Israel with its two distinct levels of citizenship based on ethnicity and religion, nor like Iran of the mullahs, nor like the Irish Republic in its earlier days with its privileged entrenchment of Catholicism, and certainly not anything even remotely resembling the racist structure of the old apartheid South Africa. But if territorial nationalism possesses solid, respectable pluralistic credentials, it too has its darker, intolerant side.

Sovereignty based on territoriality admits of no violation of territory; the territory of the nation is and must be sacrosanct. In this guise, nationalism can be at one and the same time pluralistic and imperialistic, inclusionary and intolerant. This comes out most decisively in relation to the claims and declarations of intention by Quebec's national minorities, the native peoples. The sovereignists have refused, flatly, bluntly and apparently irremediably, to contemplate the notion that national self-determination is a right of First Nations in any way comparable to Quebec's right to national self determination. PQ official spokespersons have reiterated tirelessly that Quebec's borders are nonnegotiable under any circumstances.

The clear statement of intent from the Cree of northern Quebec not to accept the jurisdiction of a self-proclaimed sovereign Quebec over their ancestral lands has been brusquely rejected by the PQ as having no legal force — as opposed to their own claim to territorial sovereignty which they insist will be recognized internationally as legally valid. Similarly, notions of local community self-determination in the form of democratically expressed opt-outs in areas contiguous to Ontario and New Brunswick borders have been angrily, even contemptuously, scorned by the PQ. "Territorial" nationalism, as opposed to ethnically based nationalism, is an idea with a certain dynamic of its own, although not without certain contradictions. Sovereignist professions of liberal intent toward minorities are sincere enough, but they do nothing to reassure those minorities, especially the native peoples as national minorities, that they are not the victims of an egregious democratic double standard. Why in the world, they ask, should anyone accept the strange assertion that the majority within a particular territorial subjurisdiction of the Canadian federation has a unilateral right to national self-determination to the point of definitively rupturing the federation's territorial and political integrity through secession, while at the same time declaring with utter self-assurance and finality that the boundaries of this new successor state will be inviolable against any further secessions?

How, in short, does this particular majority, itself after all a minority within the larger existing political community, get to obviate the capacity of minorities within the minority to express their rights as local majorities? And how does this majority, constituted as it is on a territorial basis, get away with the simultaneous assertion of its own national status along with its concomitant non-recognition of the national rights of the First Nations who cohabit the same territory? Ditto for the assertion of the democratic authority of the Quebec minority-as-majority along with the refusal to recognize the democratic force of local minorities-as-majorities. It is but a short step from questions like these to the heated identification of the sovereignist project as imperialistic and authoritarian. When this happens, the sovereignists, secure in their own liberal and democratic credentials, indignantly contest the bona fides of their opponents and hint pointedly that the latter are mere catspaws for reactionary elements outside Quebec who would deny Quebec's democratic right to national self-determination. Debate disappears, to be replaced by something debilitating and hopeless (to borrow a phrase): a dialogue of the deaf. If sovereignty is actually proclaimed in the near-future, much worse could follow.

The sovereignists do not generally understand the paradox of their own formulation of territorial nationalism, that with the best of liberal intentions, it creates a political space where further debate about nationality is forced into silence, or into the all-too-likely but calamitous consequence of enforced silence, violence. Their critics, on the other hand, do not usually recognize that it is precisely their liberal intentions that have led them to place such extreme reliance on territorial integrity.

"Sovereignty" as a concept is an exacting taskmaster. It bespeaks paramountcy, superlative strength or efficacy; it disdains all rivals, holds all challenges in contempt. The sovereignists admit the anachronism of this concept in the present age when they speak enthusiastically of Quebec as a prospective partner in NAFTA, a participant in international economic bodies and consortia like WTO, the IMF, and the World Bank and a generally good citizen of the global world economy. Yet this has not led them to downplay the domestic power of political sovereignty within a Quebec whose economic borders will bleed and blur into the greater capitalist world outside. Far from it, for the untrammeled exercise of internal political sovereignty is their bottom line, as it were, the sole rationale for the entire risky exercise, and one that must be vehemently asserted the more that the economic aspects of sovereignty mock and subvert the very concept itself. And since they have most reasonably defined sovereignty as based not on ethnicity but territory, it is the territorial integrity of the Quebec nation that is infused with the strongest charge of sovereignty in its original imperious guise.

After independence, only the Quebec government will negotiate and sign self government agreements and financial arrangements with the native peoples who reside on Quebec territory. From the point of view of the native peoples, this would represent not merely a loss of bargaining leverage, but far more significantly, a fundamental denial of their national rights to self-determination. They can hardly accept being swept out of one political jurisdiction and into another without their consent, without in effect abandoning claims to national status.

Sovereignty and Partition

The Cree and the Inuit of northern Quebec are particularly strategically placed to contest the territorial ambitions of an independent Quebec. They are the majority on the ground, they have their own instruments of self-government, and they have demonstrated, by separate referenda held on the eve of the general referendum of 1995 that they are virtually unanimous in opposition. The Cree have demonstrated considerable skill in cultivating public support for their cause in both the United States and in Europe, and can count on influential foreign opposition to unilateral Quebec assertions of sovereignty over their territory.[13] Northern Quebec was not an original part of Quebec territory upon Quebec's entrance into Confederation in 1867, with parts being added later, the largest and most northerly as recently as 1912 (thus the territory is not part of any putative original confederal bargain, but was transferred from the federal government). The Cree will resist any attempt by Quebec to enforce its jurisdiction over the north after a declaration of sovereignty, and might seek Canadian military assistance. Yet, however unenforceable Quebec's claim might be, it has a huge stake in the north, since it is the site of the vast James Bay hydroelectric complex, a crucial element in the economic viability of Quebec.

This explosive issue, and the desire of other geographically concentrated minorities to opt out of an independent Quebec, has raised the question of potential partition to accompany independence. The response of the PQ to the tentative suggestion by Ottawa that if Canada is divisible, so is Quebec, is very revealing of a profound contradiction at the heart of the sovereignty project. "Canada," Mr. Bouchard said, "is divisible because it is not a real country. There are two peoples, two nations, and two territories and this one is ours. It will never, never be partitioned." On the basis of territorial nationalism, the PQ claims that Quebec borders are sacred and indivisible; then they turn about and say Canada is divisible because Quebec is a "separate nation" or "people" that has a right to secede. Both claims cannot logically be made at the same time. If Mr. Bouchard's critique of Canada is correct, then the claim to indivisibility of Quebec fails. The aboriginal peoples are separate "nations" or "peoples" as much as Quebec, and therefore they have every right to opt of a secessionist Quebec. If his critique of Canada is incorrect, then Quebec has no right to secede itself. This muddle, of course, does not bother the sovereignists who are eager and insistent upon having it both ways, but it does point to a potentially devastating land mine lying along the road to a peaceful secession à la the Czechs and the Slovaks.[14] This is especially so in light of hardening attitudes on the part of English Canada following the trauma of the near-Yes vote in 1995, and the pressures on Ottawa to stiffen its resolve and play much tougher in advance of any future referendum.

However civilized the contest has so far been between federalists and secessionists (certainly by comparison with such conflicts in other parts of the world, it has been remarkably restrained and civilized), we may be entering a period when tensions will be rising and the potential for chaos and even violence accompanying a move toward secession increases. If partition is forced onto the negotiating table — and it will almost certainly come from the Cree in the first instance — a very unstable situation could develop with eerie echoes of the Yugoslav disaster. Partition or negotiable borders inexorably raise the question of minorities within minorities and population transfers. Who is to say where or why the process would stop before something very much like ethnic cleansing under another name might become the order of the day? Nobody wants such an appalling scenario to come about. But great social and political disasters are often the unexpected consequences of rash actions on the basis of earnest but contradictory motives.

Notes

1. These minorities vary in size, from New Brunswick, where the numbers are sufficiently large (33 percent in 1991) and concentrated geographically as to constitute something like a concurrent majority required for effective government (New Brunswick is the only province to opt for official bilingual status under the Constitution), to quite small minorities in other provinces such as British Columbia. Everywhere, although perhaps less so in New Brunswick, francophone minorities have been experiencing a steady erosion of language retention from generation to generation. The sovereignty movement in Quebec, by opting for separation, has effectively abandoned the non-Quebec francophones. It is doubtful if a post-secession Canada would maintain the apparatus of bilingual services (again, New Brunswick would be the exception).
2. The Language Law of 1976 was initiated by a PQ government and later amended and protected against constitutional challenge by a Liberal government in 1989. It provides for French as the language of work, the predominant language of commercial signs, and the language in which all Quebecers (save those whose parents' mother tongue was English) must be educated.
3. Kenneth McRae, ed., *Consociational Democracy: Political Accommodation in Segmented Societies* (Toronto: McClelland & Stewart, 1974).
4. The original advocate of "deference to authority" as a Canadian characteristic is Seymour Martin Lipset, still trying to cling to the notion in his most recent work, *Continental Divide: The Values and Institutions of the United States and Canada* (New York: Routledge, 1990). This has been effectively challenged by Neil Nevitte, *The Decline of Deference: Canadian Value Change in Cross-National Perspective* (Peterborough: Broadview Press, 1996).
5. This point has been made most eloquently by Janet Ajzenstat, "Decline of procedural liberalism: the slippery slope to secession," in Joseph H. Carens, ed., *Is Quebec Nationalism Just? Perspectives from Anglophone Canada* (Montreal: McGill-Queen's University Press, 1995) 120-36.
6. The Reform Party is a unique Canadian concoction of old-time Western Canadian populism, contemporary neoliberal fiscal policies, and strong emphasis on grassroots democratic accountability. In two federal elections it has consoli-

dated its hold in the most westerly provinces, but remains shut out of both Quebec and Atlantic Canada and is weak in Ontario.

7. In 1997 an interesting initiative came from the provincial premiers, with federal approval. The Calgary Declaration commits the premiers to a constitutional recognition of both the equality of the provinces and the "uniqueness" of Quebec. Somewhat surprisingly, the Reform Party has endorsed this declaration, but the sovereignists have rejected it.

8. Charles Taylor has written most perceptively about the modernity of Quebec nationalism. See his *Reconciling the Solitudes: Essays on Canadian Federalism and Nationalism* (Montreal: McGill-Queen's University Press, 1993). See also his *Multiculturalism and The Politics of Recognition* (Princeton: Princeton University Press, 1992).

9. For a sharply focused discussion of this point, see Wayne Norman, "The Ideology of shared values: a myopic vision of unity in a multi-nation state," in Carens, *Is Quebec Nationalism Just?*, 137-59.

10. For a report on a poll that shows that a majority of Quebecers erroneously believe themselves to be net givers rather than takers, along with corrective statistics, see Richard Mackie, Léger & Léger/Journal de Montreal/Globe and Mail Poll, *The Globe and Mail,* January 27, 1996, A1.

11. Ellen Wood, "The separation of the economic and the political," *New Left Review* 127 (1981).

12. Cynics might suggest that Canada anyway can exercise only the pretense of a monetary policy; the PQ appears willing to forego even the pretense.

13. They have also marshaled formidable legal and constitutional opinion for their cause. See the massive documentation in Grand Council of the Crees, *Sovereign Injustice: Forcible Inclusion of the James Bay Cree and Cree Territory. into a Sovereign Quebec* (Nemaska, Quebec: Eeyou Astchee, 1995).

14. For possible scenarios of separation, see the optimistic Robert Young, *The Secession of Quebec and the Future of Canada* (Montreal: McGill-Queen's University Press, 1995) and the pessimistic Patrick Monahan, *Cooler Heads Shall Prevail: Assessing the Costs and Consequences of Quebec Separation* (Toronto: C.D. Howe Institute, 1995).

Conclusion

If you have been keeping a tally of the benefits and disadvantages of secession, the minuses on your score sheet probably far exceed the pluses. The extent of this disparity enables us to sum up our own balance sheet in a pithy way.

When secession takes place, it does not reduce the antagonism between the ethnic groups as hoped but rather perpetuates and exacerbates it. The economic costs are heavy; rarely do either of the successor states benefit from the split, and usually both suffer. Waves of refugees flee or are expelled from their former homes. Families, businesses, and friendships are broken. Warfare usually precedes the partition of the state, and it may continue for generations afterward. In the successor states, minorities typically are even more disadvantaged than before the split, and the new governments are often even less democratic than the ones that preceded them, though the separatists may have argued their case in the name of democracy. One partition does not necessarily end the matter, for separatist movements may arise sooner or later in one or all of the successor states. Finally, the postsecession states often are disadvantaged in geopolitical terms by being smaller and weaker than the countries that they replaced and hence newly vulnerable to military and other pressures from countries that are now comparatively stronger. All these consequences had been observed in previous waves of secessions, and the same pattern has been repeated, with a few exceptions, in the post-Cold War wave.

Having issued these lugubrious warnings to potential separatists, we can turn to the pragmatic project of distilling the primary causes of separatism and evaluating possible ways to limit it in the future. In the introduction I offered a checklist of factors that others have identified hypothetically as causing the partitioning of states. On the basis of the preceding chapters we can conclude now that most of those factors evidently do play a part in the process. Four factors deserve special notice, for they all generally precede the rise of a separatist movement.

Origins of Ethnic Separatism

Economic factors. Separatism tends to emerge during economic crises or when there is a competition among ethnic groups over material assets — especially territory.[1] Conflicts of economic interests, including anticipated ones, such as oil reserves or a projected oil pipeline, may loom large in the calculations of separatists, though their estimates may be unrealistic. Thus Ukrainians in the Soviet Union, Quebecers in Canada, and Slovaks in Czechoslovakia have believed they were paying more than their share of the state's costs when in fact they were recipients of subsidies. Separatists typically believe that their group will profit from secession, and this belief provides an important motive, though it usually turns out to be mistaken when the actual costs of partition are counted. However, material interests are not the separatists' only motives.

Resentment and humiliation. To economic factors must be added a symbolic dimension: the sense of being humiliated. In every case of ethnic separatism at least one (and often several) of the society's cultural groups felt resentment or envy about their status, with or without justification. For example, the Serbs in Yugoslavia felt oppressed when the fears of other groups about Serbian dominance probably were more realistic.

In situations of ethnic stratification, the privileged group may reject the new demands of the lower-status group for formal equality. The outcome is determined by the sentiments of both sides: envy by the subordinate group and arrogance by the dominant one.

Propaganda. In the post-Cold War period, politicians with self-serving motives have instigated waves of nationalistic fervor by organized propaganda campaigns. These demagogues typically have been communists who, fearing the loss of their leadership roles, substituted another collectivist ideology — nationalism — for the more familiar Marxist doctrine of struggle.

A political/constitutional impasse. A separatist dispute arises when certain leaders see their minority group's fundamental rights as threatened but the existing legal or constitutional mechanisms cannot rectify the injustice. For instance, when the Sri Lankan government declared Sinhalese to be the country's only official language and moved Sinhalese populations into Tamil lands, the Tamils were outvoted and unprotected by constitution or law. Another example: The elected leaders of both republics in Czechoslovakia, as well as of the Croatian, Slovenian, and Serbian Republics in Yugoslavia, disagreed on fundamental economic policies, and all had a constitutional right to block any proposed solution. Despite the urgency, there was no legal means of breaking this impasse.

In such irreconcilable situations people may regard separatism as the only option. Regrettably, it offers no shortcut to democracy but in fact turns out to be counterproductive. From so many negative results any empirical researcher must conclude that a new approach is required for integrating a multicultural society democratically.

Democracy: Both Source and Remedy of Separatism

It should come as no surprise that waves of democratization and of secession coincide. After all, only when a country begins holding free and democratic elections does voting matter very much. Then, however, if an ethnic group constitutes a minority, its members often find themselves outvoted on issues that affect their lives. If they are compactly distributed in one region of a multiethnic country, they will surely see that by seceding they would immediately become a majority of voters in their own country instead of being an outvoted minority in "someone else's" larger country.

Mature democracies provide some protection of minority interests. In a democratizing country, on the other hand, the main criterion of progress seems to be to hold early, free, multiparty elections, and then implement the majority's decision. But to a minority group that fears for its dignity and security, elections may seem less urgent than the preservation of their human rights and culture. They may fear with good reason that the majority can vote to attack them, seize their property, or deprive them of the right to speak their language. Unless preceded by strong legal protections of their rights and freedoms, the adoption of rule-by-majority may only prompt them to take the risky option of declaring independence. Thus the transition from dictatorship can be fraught with violence and the prospect of partition.

Democratization requires revision of a country's constitution — and the sooner the better, since it is important to establish the decision-making procedures before the conflicts arise. The revising of constitutions turns out to be a serious problem for democratizing countries; in the absence of a fully accepted amending formula, a stalemate between factions may arise that soon creates the prospect of secession.

Ten Approaches to Managing Diversity

Despite the hurry, it is important to get the constitution right, and this is a complicated problem. Two different voting systems, for example, may be equally democratic, yet produce diametrically opposite results. The framers of a constitution select some of the following ten principles to employ for harmonizing incompatible groups:

1. *Overcome the diversity.* Do not take a decision until all the groups form one unified "mainstream" community. This may come about through the use of consensual decision-making methods, or perhaps over time, through assimilation into a common "melting pot." (Disadvantage: Either way, it may take too long.)

2. *Allow each group in the society to govern itself.* This is the millet system writ large. Such a system may work if each person's group membership is unmistakable, so that it is clear which rules apply. It is easier if groups live in segregated districts, harder if individuals are allowed to switch membership readily. (Disadvantages: Besides fostering inequality, this makes ethnic identity involuntary, which is no longer acceptable in modern society. Anyway, no group can make *all* its own decisions; everyone in a multicultural society must at least drive on the same side of the road. And how much autonomy should a group have? If its members vote to mutilate the genitals of young girls, must the other groups accept that? If not, what are the limits?)

3. *Separate the groups into two or more independent countries,* each with its own rules, to be determined democratically. (Disadvantages: See all the preceding chapters regarding the shortcomings of this approach.)

4. *Take a vote. The majority will win, and the minority should accept its every decision without complaint.* This principle can be applied either by electing the decision makers or by direct decision-making in referendums. (Disadvantage: It does not prevent the "tyranny of the majority.")

5. *Take a vote when necessary, but protect minority rights by constitutional safeguards.* This is the standard approach of liberal democracies. (Disadvantage: It may not satisfy groups that are always outvoted.)

6. *Adopt asymmetric federalism.* A federal state with a nationalistic province may be able to work out a special agreement giving that province a right to make its own laws. In fact, all provinces may want their own unique relationships to the center. (Disadvantage: Political opponents may see this flexibility as giving an unfair advantage to a particular province. Russia granted such special autonomy to Tatarstan, and might have agreed to a similar form of asymmetric federalism with Chechnya, had the issue been approached skillfully. Canada, on the other hand, has consistently refused an asymmetric accommodation with Quebec as a "distinct society," insisting instead on the principle of universalism.)

7. *Decentralize power.* Distribute almost all the power to a confederation or commonwealth of republics only loosely connected to the central government. We have reviewed several such proposals for devolution in Tatarstan, Chechnya, Sri Lanka, and Canada, as well as Yugoslavia and Czechoslovakia before they broke up. (Disadvantages: Not all loose confederations work well. International financial institutions demanded that Yugoslavia retain a central government strong enough to enforce the financial promises required for loans. A decentralized state also has difficulty coordinating environmental policies. Besides, decentralization may be irreversible. If devolution to the republics or provinces proves unsuccessful, there will be great difficulty in recentralizing power. It is inadvisable for any central state to give absolute veto power over constitutional revisions to its provinces, as Czechoslovakia and Yugoslavia did.)

8. *Practice "subsidiarity" in a federal or confederal system* so that each decision is made by the smallest practicable unit — perhaps even at the neighborhood level. (Disadvantages: This "local democracy" principle usually is of no help to minority groups, who are outvoted anyway under it. Besides, it may provide no means of resolving such fateful questions as: Shall future states of the United States permit slavery?)

9. *Form nonterritorial electoral constituencies.* Allow minorities or other interest groups to form constituencies in which their members' votes are aggregated, regardless of where they live. Each unit will elect a number of parliamentarians in proportion to its size. A Canadian electoral reform commission recommended this as a way of guaranteeing representation to aboriginal people, wherever they live in Canada. The same principle could be extended to other minorities living dispersed outside their group's "home" province. If all francophones, wherever they live in Canada (or all Tamils in Sri Lanka, or all Slovaks in Czechoslovakia) could vote as a single constituency, they would be fairly represented in parliament and would have less incentive to secede.[2]

However, ethnic constituencies should not be the only kind of nonterritorial constituency, and voters should always have alternative options. In a stable democracy, the salience of ethnicity dwindles and is replaced by other identities, such as gender and occupation. Every democratic constitution should encourage that trend and enable citizens to reregister in a different constituency at will.[3]

(Disadvantages: In any system of nonterritorial constituencies, some still win and others lose. And in a highly charged situation, such as Bosnia under the Dayton Accords, politicians representing ethnic constituencies sometimes refuse to deal with each other. In such a case, all ethnic constituencies will be fraught with conflict.[4])

10. *Weighted referendums.* A weighted referendum gives minorities some possibility of winning a fair vote, thereby making secession seem less attractive. Moreover, a weighted referendum has another advantage too: increasing every voter's opportunity to influence what she cares about most, at the price of leaving some decisions to be decided by the people who care more about them. In an annual referendum with, say, twenty propositions, all voters are permitted to "spend" their votes as they please on the various propositions. One voter might spend ten votes opposing proposition B, five votes supporting proposition F, and five votes opposing proposition K, skipping all the other propositions. Another voter might spend all twenty of his votes supporting proposition F, and so on.

Imagine a country in which each ethnic constituency, however small, has a right to put one proposition on the weighted referendum each year. This system will offer opportunities to minorities while also satisfying the majority. Occasionally a small group's members will spend most of their votes on an issue that is dear to their hearts (such as preserving their right to offer school courses in their own language) and win because other voters are indifferent to the matter.

The minority's victory will be acceptable to the majority, for if they had cared greatly about the matter they could have blocked it.

(Possible disadvantage: The very power of this innovation may encourage voters to take it extremely seriously, thus polarizing public opinion. It cannot, and should not, be the only form of governance in a state.)

Transitions to Democracy

It makes a difference which combinations of the aforementioned approaches to democracy are used by a democratizing state. Perhaps equally crucial are the *sequence* in which democratic processes are implemented, and the governmental system characterizing the *starting point* from which a country begins adopting democracy. The matter of sequence has already been mentioned; the Dayton Accords made a serious mistake, for example, by requiring that elections be held in Bosnia before war criminals were ousted from leadership roles. The criminals simply got themselves elected and clothed themselves in new legitimacy.

The objective is to reach democracy, but it may not come easily in countries beginning the transition as communist regimes or dictatorships. Nationalism emerged almost irrepressibly in the Soviet Union as soon as free speech was permitted. Empires in general, where by definition populations are subjected to external authoritarian rule, may not easily shift to democratic ways. However, not all empires are alike, and countries that had been part of the British Empire historically have been most successful in making the transition to democracy.[5]

Separatism in the Breakup of Empires

Moreover, with eighty years of hindsight one can even regret the dissolution of the Austro-Hungarian and Ottoman Empires, for they had features that were favorable starting points. Both might have become democracies through a smoother course of change than did their successor states. Most modern-thinking people of the day had celebrated when the victors of World War I broke up the two states. This was supposed to deliver a coup de grace to states that had long been deteriorating and liberate their "imprisoned nations" for rapid democratization.

Instead, in geopolitical terms, the breakup of both empires left attractive fragments over which the great powers would compete for hegemony. World War II, which is often depicted as the second stage of World War I, was a fight among those powers — especially Germany, Britain, and Russia — largely for Habsburg and Ottoman lands. A generation later, those territories still have not been reassembled into units of their former size or military power, but instead the fragmenting continues; the former Yugoslavia and Czechoslovakia had been broken up into seven new states by 1994, with the possibility of further splits to come. This continued fragmentation is not limited to the former Habsburg and Ottoman lands in Europe. British Palestine, itself the product of partition of the former Ottoman lands, was subsequently partitioned between Jordan and the new state of Israel. This partition failed as a result of Israeli conquest in the 1948, 1956, 1967, and 1973 wars; the subpartition of the West Bank is now under discussion. And Turkey itself, as well as other neighboring countries, faces separatist demands for the creation of a "Kurdistan."

Yet besides separatist trends there are countertendencies too toward integration. Europeans are restoring old Habsburg unity and coherence, now as the European Union, capable of inhibiting, say, a resurgent Germany. They could have democratized the Austro-Hungarian empire and created the EU two generations ago, had they seen the usefulness of what they were dismantling. It would, of course, no longer have been an empire.

Though far from egalitarian, the two old multicultural empires had managed relations among their diverse ethnic communities with greater stability and civility than their successor states. Even while fraying around the edges, the Ottoman Empire had governed the Middle East well in comparison to the endemic ethnic warfare since its breakup. No atrocities occurred in that empire on the scale of the genocide of two million Armenians in Turkey immediately after its dissolution. The millet system had enabled religious communities to live together peaceably, each enjoying virtual political autonomy without territorial sovereignty.

But during their geopolitical and economic decline, both empires had also been losing legitimacy, while newer egalitarian principles — notably universality and citizenship — gained moral weight as the basis for democracy. Whereas the old Ottoman rulers had accommodated to each ethnic community's unique needs, modern values insisted that a state's laws and rights ought to be extended universally and equally to all citizens. But to balance particularism against universalism remained problematic; both Woodrow Wilson and Lenin still considered ethnic groups entitled to secede from a multicultural state. Others innovated with new political institutions embodying modern principles, while protecting the rights of cultural groups. For example, the Austrian social democrats' system allowed individuals to affiliate voluntarily with an ethnic group, forming a constituency regardless of where members were distributed territorially.

World War I put a stop to such experiments. Henceforth a nation was to be both a sovereign territory and an ethnic community. This "solution" was a blunder, confounding incompatible principles of representation and promoting cultural uniformity within each state.

The new post-Versailles political institutions were flawed, but they represented honest attempts by statesmen to reconcile worthy, if incompatible, principles — universalistic citizenship and cultural diversity — and so these early mistakes seem forgivable today. Post-Cold War separatism seems less principled and less forgivable.

Separatism in the Breakup of the Socialist Bloc

The partitions of formerly socialist states after 1989 were accomplished by a few powerful politicians. Some of them — notably Yeltsin, Shushkevich, Kravchuk, Klaus, Meciar, Milošević, Kučan, Tudjman, and Dudaev — instigated crises as a means of expanding their power. In fact, the citizens did not usually choose separatism at all; it was thrust upon them. Often there was no referendum, and polls suggest that, given a chance, citizens might have voted against secession.

However, these politicians faced problems not entirely of their own making. Yeltsin claims that he had "no choice" but to break up the Soviet Union, since the Ukrainians had decided to leave it. In Czechoslovakia and Yugoslavia no procedures existed for amending obsolete constitutions; each component republic held veto power. To break impasses, both federal states were dissolved — in the former case by the Czech and Slovak prime ministers, who could have done otherwise, and in the latter case by Milošević, Croatian and Slovenian separatists, and foreign powers. Germany pressed for early recognition of the breakaway republics, and the United States insisted on majority rule instead of the veto that had previously protected minority rights in Yugoslavia. There existed a choice only between bad and worse options; the politicians chose the worse. Still, these demagogues witnessed around them some popular support for secession, which in some cases was the majority opinion. What was the source of nationalism's renewed appeal?

It is often interpreted as the thawing of deep-frozen World War II nationalism. According to this explanation, the communist regimes had suppressed old ethnic conflicts instead of working them out in open discussion. History had been papered over and people had been forbidden to recount their bitter experiences. With freedom of speech came renewed freedom to hate.

Yet this is only a partial explanation. The deeper truth is even darker: Separatism was even promoted by brave dissidents in the Soviet bloc who were willing to sacrifice everything for the sake of democracy. For example, Elena Bonner defends Armenians' right to secede in Nagorno-Karabakh. Oddly, the Eastern dissidents who clearly recognized Lenin's and Stalin's other mistakes completely failed to critique their separatist doctrine of self-determination. Thus the unsolved earlier mistakes reemerged to test a new generation that, in the West and especially the East, had inherited a defective theory of political integration that supported separatism. It was an error that has by now doomed millions.

Globalization and Theories of Political Integration

This flawed theory conflated two kinds of in-group solidarity: the first uniting the citizens of a state (who pay taxes into a common pool, live under the same laws, and in wartime fight side by side in the same platoons) and the second uniting people of a common nationality during periods of ethnic consciousness.

By attempting to reduce the two types of loyalty to one, the theory prescribed that people of like ethnicity live within the same boundaries as citizens of the same democratic state, and that all others live elsewhere. Separatism is a corollary of the principle.

But according to an alternative principle of political integration, which is far more familiar in liberal democracies, citizenship is supposed to trump ethnicity. Indeed, patriotism is considered legitimate, whereas ethnic politics is disreputable; all high-minded voters are expected to ignore the ethnicity of the candidates. (However, this rule is sometimes bent, so that an oppressed minority group can elect deputies of its own.)

High-mindedness notwithstanding, even in mature democracies ethnic groups often do pursue some kind of political representation. When their numbers and geographical distribution across voting districts and national boundaries frustrate this aspiration, they may turn to separatism and irredentism.

In our quest for a satisfactory compromise, there is no particular reason for privileging ethnicity. Ethnic consciousness fluctuates and, with integration into a well-functioning democracy, may largely be supplanted by other forms of political solidarity based on class, gender, or identification with particular issues such as environmental protection or animal rights. I, for one, hope that ethnic consciousness dwindles away completely, but it does not matter what you or I prefer; the point is to find a way to satisfy the (perhaps transitory) claims of ethnic politics without having to partition states. The most promising way to accomplish this is to facilitate the formation of constituencies in which votes are aggregated in voluntary units, not in geographically defined catchment areas. One might register within an ethnic constituency but, when the spirit of nationalism wanes, change to a constituency of, say, environmentalists.

But how can identity politics be accommodated when it transcends national boundaries? A solution to this problem may also contribute to solving the new problems of globalization. There is an urgent need for democratic structures through which citizens can participate in transnational decision making. The United Nations and most other proposals for global governance assume a federal model whereby territorially defined states constitute the building blocks. Such a system imports the flaw of existing states (their failure to distinguish between citizenship and ethnicity or other forms of identity) plus one more: the difficulty of preventing totalitarian rule in a global state where power is not checked by any comparable external power.

We can now consider an alternative form of world governance as a system of worldwide regimes, each one separately regulating or monitoring a specific field, such as air quality, electronic communications, scientific research, or the protection of human rights in minority populations. Groups of experts and citizens avidly interested in these fields (including ethnic group leaders) could register in worldwide "constituencies" and elect their own members to decision-making positions in the corresponding regime. In this participatory democracy the structural units of governance will not be states but networks of citizens discussing issues through electronic media and exercising political influence through their communities of discourse.

The Pragmatics of Preventing Separatism

If the preceding discussion seems too visionary to be immediately practicable, there are numerous policies that the international community could adopt sooner or even this year. Let us close with a few recommendations.

Political Interventions by the International Community

Most authors of these chapters warn against extending ready diplomatic recognition to separatists. However, there can be no objection to it if all the major stakeholders have reached an agreement on the details, including the distribution of jointly-owned property and debts. If there is no such agreement and the central government is losing its ability to function, other nations should support it as long as possible. If it fails anyway (as in the former Yugoslavia) perhaps the country should temporarily be made a protectorate (possibly under a revived UN Trusteeship Council) while the matter is negotiated. Other nations and non-governmental organizations should ensure freedom of press and of speech.

Even to prevent secession, it is often unwise for the central government to impose military control over a dissident population. During negotiations, the central government should invite international peacekeepers to tense spots. If matters deteriorate, the peacekeepers should be authorized to disarm local militias and protect victims in enclaves rather than stand by, watching acts of genocide.

The international community should warn separatists that they will not receive diplomatic recognition if they secede unilaterally. This warning should accompany increasing support to minority groups if their human rights are violated. If people may not secede, they must have recourse to other means of self-preservation.

Wealthy democratic countries should use political and economic incentives to support the rights of oppressed people elsewhere. Separatism sometimes arises where minorities feel they have no other means of self-defense. The world must provide alternatives.

International Law

Long-standing ambiguities of international law have frequently encouraged separatist movements. This must be changed. The United Nations General Assembly should be asked to request an opinion of the International Court of Justice clarifying the minimum conditions that should be met by any separatist movement before receiving diplomatic recognition. The UN could also establish a process for the review of separatists' claims. Where valid grounds exist for secession, partition should be overseen by an international committee. Anyone recalling that 40 to 50 percent of all recent wars have been wars of secession must see such legal intervention as a practical way of reducing suffering. With the diplomatic initiative of any member of the United Nations, this promising project can, and should, be completed by the early twenty-first century — not a moment too soon.

Notes

1. Czechoslovakia was an exception with respect to territory, since the border between the Czech and Slovak lands was largely incontestable.

2. Moreover, the devolution of power for direct self-governance by nonterritorially based constituencies is becoming conceivable. One such utopian idea, for example, anticipates a francophone province of Canada that is not Quebec, but comprises all francophones who wish to belong to it, pay their taxes to it, receive their health cards from it, and so on. Such a notion may become realistic, but not soon.

3. Besides, such nonterritorial constituencies might tend to replace political parties, which aggregate political power on multiple issues. Any undermining of political parties would be unfortunate. Therefore, some officials (say, the president and one of the houses of a bicameral legislature) should continue to be elected by territorial constituencies.

4. It has been proposed, for example, as a temporary solution to Bosnia's polarization that three lists of candidates, representing the nominees respectively of Croat, Bosniac, or Serbian parties, be presented to all voters. Every candidate would have to appeal to all three ethnic communities. This would prompt all candidates to moderate their positions. Under Dayton, each candidate can be elected without support from any other ethnic community — a system that encourages ethnic extremists.

5. Seymour Martin Lipset, Kyoung-Ryung Seong, and John Charles Torres, "A Comparative Analysis of the Social Requisites of Democracy," *International Social Science Journal* 46 (1993): 168.

Select Bibliography

Abeysinghe, Ariya. *The Accelerated Mahaveli Development Program.* Colombo, Sri Lanka: Quest 105, Centre for Society and Religion, 1990.

Ahmad, F. *The Making of Modern Turkey.* London: Routledge, 1993.

Ajzenstat, Janet. "Decline of Procedural Liberalism: The Slippery Slope to Secession." In *Is Quebec Nationalism Just? Perspectives from Anglophone Canada,* edited by Joseph H. Carens. Montreal: McGill-Queen's University Press, 1996.

Akbar, M. J. *India: The Siege Within.* New York: Penguin, 1985.

Akhmetov, Rashit. "Tatarstan: The Post Electoral Ethno-Political Situation." In *Bulletin: Network on Ethnological Monitoring and Early Warning of Conflict.* Cambridge, Mass: Conflict Management Group, 1995.

Aklaev, Airat. "Ethno-political Conflicts and Crises in the Russian Federation and the Problems of Legitimacy: Four Cases with the Russian Federation." In *Nationalism, Ethnic Identity and Conflict Management in Russia Today,* edited by Gail W. Lapidus and Renee de Nevers. Palo Alto: Center for International Security and Arms Control, Stanford University, 1995.

Akşin, S. *Jön Türkler ve Ittihat ve Terakki* (Young Turks and the union and progress). Istanbul: 1980.

Albayrak, S. *Turkiye'de Din Kavgasi* (The religious struggle in Turkey). Istanbul: Arastirma Yayinlari, 1991.

Ali, Rabia and Lawrence Lifschultz. "Why Bosnia?" *Monthly Review* 45 (1994): 1-28.

Ali, Tariq. *Can Pakistan Survive?* London: New Left Books, 1983.

Amnesty International. *Disappearances in Sri Lanka.* London: Amnesty International, 1986.

―――. *Recent Reports of Disappearance & Torture.* London: Amnesty International, 1987.

Anderson, Benedict. *Imagined Communities: Reflections on the Origin and Spread of Nationalism.* London: Verso, 1983; rev. ed. New York: Verso, 1991.

Arasaratnam, S. "The Vanniar of North Ceylon: A Study of Feudal Power and Central Authority, 1660-1760." *Ceylon Journal of Humanities & Social Sciences* 9 (1966).

Aslund, Anders. "Should the Soviet Union Get Western Assistance after the Coup?" Stockholm: Stockholm Institute of Soviet and East European Studies, 1991.

Atasoy, Y. "Gokalp Sosyolojisindeki Bazi Kavramlar" (Some concepts in Gokalp's sociology). Ankara: Middle East Technical University, Department of Sociology, 1985.

Bailey, F. E. *British Policy and the Turkish Reform Movement.* New York: Howard Fertig, 1970.

Banac, Ivo. "Post-Communism as Post-Yugoslavism: The Yugoslav Non-Revolutions of 1989-1990." In *Eastern Europe in Revolution,* edited by Ivo Banac. Ithaca: Cornell University Press, 1992.

Barkan, O. L. "The Price Revolution of the Sixteenth Century." *International Journal of Middle East Studies* (1975).

Bastian, Sunil. *Control of State Land: The Devolution Debate.* Colombo, Sri Lanka: International Centre for Ethnic Studies, 1995.

Bauman, Zygmunt. "Soil, Blood and Identity." *The Sociological Review* 40 (1992): 675-701.

Behar, B. E. *Iktidar ve Tarih, Türkiye'de 'Resmi Tarih' Tezinin Olusumu, 1929-1937* (Power and history, the formation of the "Official History" thesis in Turkey, 1929-1937). Istanbul: AFA Yayıncılık, 1992.

Beigbeder, Yves. *International Monitoring of Plebiscites, Referenda and National Elections.* Dordrecht, the Netherlands: Martinus Nijhoff, 1994.

Bennett, Christopher. *Yugoslavia's Bloody Collapse: Causes, Course and Consequences.* New York: New York University Press, 1995.

Bennigsen, Alexandre and S. Enders Wimbush. *Muslims of the Soviet Empire.* London: C. Hurst and Co., 1985.

Berkes, N., trans. *The Development of Secularism in Turkey.* 1964. Reprint. Montreal: McGill University Press, 1976.

———, trans. *Turkish Nationalism and Turkish Civilization, Selected Essays of Ziya Gökalp.* New York: Columbia University Press, 1959.

Birch, Anthony. *Nationalism and National Integration.* London: Unwin Hyman, 1989.

Bookman, Milica Zarkovic. *The Economics of Secession.* New York: St. Martin's Press, 1993.

Braudel, F. *The Perspectives of the World: Civilization and Capitalism (15th-18th Century).* Vol. 3. London: Fontana Press, 1979.

Breuilly, John. *Nationalism and the State.* Chicago: University of Chicago Press, 1985.

Brilmayer, Lea. "Secession and Self-Determination: A Territorial Interpretation." *Yale Journal of International Law* 16 (1991): 177-200.

Brock, Peter. "Dateline Yugoslavia: The Partisan Press." *Foreign Policy* (1993): 152-72.

Brown, Michael E. "Causes and Implications of Ethnic Conflict." In *Ethnic Conflict and International Security,* edited by Michael E. Brown. Princeton: Princeton University Press, 1993.

Broxrup, Marie Bennigsen. "After the Putsch, 1991." In *The North Caucasus Barrier,* edited by M. B. Broxrup. London: Hurst and Co., 1992.

———. "Tatarstan and the Tatars." In *The Nationalities Question in the Post-Soviet States,* edited by Graham Smith. 2d ed. New York: Longman, 1996.

Brubaker, Roger. *Citizenship and Nationhood in France and Germany.* Cambridge, Mass.: Harvard University Press, 1992.

Bryan, F. "Internationalism, Nationalism and Islam." In *The North Caucasus Barrier,* edited by M. B. Broxrup. London: Hurst and Co., 1992.

Buchanan, Allen. *Secession: The Morality of Political Divorce from Fort Sumter to Lithuania and Quebec.* Boulder: Westview Press, 1991.

Buchheit, Lee. *Secession: The Legitimacy of Self-Determination.* New Haven, Conn.: Yale University Press, 1978.

Budiša, Dražen. "Opposition in Wartime." Interview by Johanna Bjorken in *Uncaptive Minds* 6 (1993): 71–79.

Bugajski, Janusz. *Czechoslovakia: Charter 77's Decade of Dissent.* New York: Praeger, 1987.

Burlatsky, Fedor. *Russkie gosudari* (The Russian rulers). Moscow: Shark, 1996.

Buturović, Amila. "Producing and Annihilating the Ethos of Bosnian Islam." *Cultural Survival Quarterly* (Summer 1995): 29–33.

Carens, Joseph H., ed. *Is Quebec Nationalism Just? Perspectives from Anglophone Canada.* Montreal: McGill-Queen's University Press, 1996.

Cassese, Antonio. *Self-Determination of Peoples: A Legal Reappraisal.* 1993.

Chaliand, Gérard, and Jean-Pierre Rageau. *Strategic Atlas: A Comparative Geopolitics of the World's Powers.* New York: Harper and Row, 1985.

Chesnov, I. "Civilization and the Chechen," manuscript, 1995. In *Russian Social Science Review,* July-August, 1996.

Cohen, Albert. *Delinquent Boys: The Culture of the Gang.* Glencoe, Ill.: Free Press, 1955.

Connor, Walker. "Ethnonationalism in the First World." In *Ethnic Conflict in the Western World,* edited by Milton Esman. Ithaca, N.Y.: Cornell University Press, n.d.

Costa, Nicholas J. "A Balkan Danse Macabre." *East European Quarterly* 27 (1993): 479–87.

Crankshaw, Edward. *The Fall of the House of Habsburg.* London: Longmans, 1963.

Crnobrnja, Mihailo. *The Yugoslav Drama.* Montreal: McGill-Queen's University Press, 1994.

Crystal, David, ed. *The Cambridge Factfinder.* Cambridge: Cambridge University Press, 1993.

Cviic, Christopher. *Remaking the Balkans.* New York: Council on Foreign Relations Press, 1991.

Davis, Garry. "'The U.N. Can Do Nothing!' Admits Secretary-General Boutros-Ghali." *World Citizen News* 9 (August–September 1995): 1.

Davis, James R. *The Sharp End: A Canadian Soldier's Story.* Vancouver: Douglas and McIntyre, 1997.

Davison, R. H. *Reform in the Ottoman Empire, 1856–1876.* Princeton: Princeton University Press, 1963.

———. "Nationalism as an Ottoman Problem and the Ottoman Response." In *Nationalism in a Non-National State: The Dissolution of the Ottoman Empire,* edited by W. W. Haddad and W. Ochsenwald. Columbus: Ohio State University Press, 1977.

de Carufel, A. "Factors Affecting the Evaluation of Improvement: The Role of Normative Standards and Allocator Resources." *Journal of Personality and Social Psychology* (1979) 37: 856.

de Silva, C. R. "The Impact of Nationalism on Education: The Schools Takeover of 1961 and the Universities Admission Crisis 1970–1975." In *Collective*

Identities, Nationalism and Protest in Modern Sri Lanka, edited by Michael Roberts. Colombo: Marga Institute, 1979.

Denitch, Bogdan. "Toward A Democratic Foreign Policy." *Dissent* (Spring 1993): 153-56.

———. "Stop the Genocide in Bosnia." *Dissent* (Summer 1993): 283-87.

———. "Tragedy in Former Yugoslavia." *Dissent* (Winter 1993): 26-34.

Deraniyagala, S. U. *Prehistoric Archaeology of Sri Lanka.* Colombo, Sri Lanka: Department of Archaeological Survey, 1992.

Despres, Leo, ed. *Ethnicity and Resource Competition in Plural Societies.* The Hague: Mouton, 1975.

Deutsch, Karl. "Nationalism and Social Communication, Social Mobilization and Political Development." *American Political Science Review* 55 (1961): 3-4.

Deutsche Bank. *The Soviet Union at the Crossroads: Facts and Figures on the Soviet Republics.* Frankfurt: Deutsche Bank, 1991.

Dimitrijević, Vojin. "The 1974 Constitution and Constitutional Process as a Factor in the Collapse of Yugoslavia." In *Yugoslavia: The Former and Future*, edited by Payam Akhavan and Robert Howse. Washington, D.C.: The Brookings Institution, 1995.

Ding, Wei. "Yugoslavia: Costs and Benefits of Union and Interdependence of Regional Economies." *Comparative Economic Studies* 33 (1991).

Drobizheva, Leokadia. "Nationalism and Democracy in the Post-Soviet Russian Federation." In *Nationalism, Ethnic Identity and Conflict Management in Russia Today*, edited by Gail W. Lapidus and Renee de Nevers. Palo Alto: Center for International Security and Arms Control, Stanford University, 1995.

Dubček, Alexander. *Hope Dies Last: The Autobiography of Alexander Dubček,* edited and translated by Jiři Hochman. New York: Kodansha, 1993.

Eastwood, Jr., Lawrence S. "Secession: State Practice and International Law after the Dissolution of the Soviet Union and Yugoslavia." *Duke Journal of Comparative and International Law* 3 (Spring 1993): 349.

Eberhard, Wolfram. "Concerns of Historical Sociology." *Sociologus* (Berlin) 14 (1964).

Elkins, David J. *Beyond Sovereignty: Territory and Political Economy in the Twenty-First Century.* Toronto: University of Toronto Press, 1995.

Emsley, C. *British Society and the French Wars.* London: Rowman, 1969.

Epstein, Howard, ed. *Revolt in the Congo 1960–64.* New York: Facts on File, 1965.

Febvre, Lucien, and Henri-Jean Martin. *The Coming of the Book: The Impact of Printing, 1450–1800.* London: New Left Books, 1976.

Festinger, Leon. "A Theory of Social Comparison." *Human Relations* (1954): 7.

Findley, C. *Bureaucratic Reform in the Ottoman Empire: The Sublime Porte, 1789-1922.* Princeton: Princeton University Press, 1980.

———. "The Advent of Ideology in the Islamic Middle East." *Studia Islamica* (1982).

Flanagan, Tom. *Waiting for the Wave: The Reform Party and Preston Manning.* Toronto: Stoddard, 1995.

Gardels, Nathan. "Dangers of Self-Determination: Interview with Prime Minister Felipe Gonzalez." *San Francisco Chronicle,* October 28, 1991.

Garthoff, Raymond L. *The Great Transition: American–Soviet Relations and the End of the Cold War.* Washington, D.C.: The Brookings Institution, 1994.

Geiger, Wilhelm, trans. *The Mahavamsa* or *The Great Chronicle of Ceylon.* Colombo: Government of Ceylon, 1960.

Gibb, H. A. R., and H. Bowen. *Islamic Society and the West.* London: Oxford University Press, 1962.

Gilford, Henry. *The Black Hand at Sarajevo.* New York: Bobbs Merrill, 1975.

Glynn, Patrick. "The Age of Balkanization." *Commentary* 96 (1993): 21-24.

Gorbachev, Mikhail, and Boris Yeltsin. *1500 dnei politicheskogo protivostoianiia* (1500 days of political opposition). Compiled by L. Dobrokhotov. Moscow: Terra, 1992.

Gow, James. *Triumph of the Lack of Will: International Diplomacy and the Yugoslav War.* New York: Columbia University Press, 1996.

Grand Council of the Crees. *Sovereign Injustice: Forcible Inclusion of the James Bay Cree Territory into a Sovereign Quebec.* Namaska, Quebec: Eeyou Astcheee, 1995.

Greenfeld, Liah. *Nationalism: Five Roads to Modernity.* Cambridge, Mass.: Harvard University Press, 1992.

Guinier, Lani. *The Tyranny of the Majority: Fundamental Fairness in Representative Democracy.* New York: The Free Press, 1994.

Gunaratne, M. H. *For a Sovereign State.* Colombo, Sri Lanka: Sarvodaya, 1988.

Gunawardana, R. A. L. H. "The People of the Lion: The Sinhala Identity and Ideology in History and Historiography." In *Sri Lanka: History and Roots of Conflict,* edited by Jonathan Spencer. London: Routledge, 1990.

Gündüz, I. *Osmanlilarde Devlet-Tekke Munasebetleri* (State-Tekke relations in the Ottoman Empire). Ankara: Seha Yayinlari, 1983.

Gurr, Ted R. *Minorities at Risk: A Global View of Ethnopolitical Conflicts.* Washington, D.C.: United States Institute of Peace Press, 1993.

Halperin, Morton H., David J. Scheffer, and Patricia L. Small. *Self-Determination in the New World Order.* Washington, D.C.: Carnegie Endowment for International Peace, 1992.

Havrylyshyn, Oleh, and Williamson, John. *From Soviet Disunion to Eastern Economic Community.* Washington: Institute for International Economics Policy Analysis in International Economics, 1991.

Hayes, Carlton J. H. *Nationalism: A Religion.* New York: The Macmillan Company, 1960.

Heater, Derek. *National Self-Determination: Woodrow Wilson and his Legacy.* New York: St. Martin's Press, 1994.

Hechter, Michael. *Internal Colonialism: The Celtic Fringe in British National Development, 1536-1966.* London: Routledge and Kegan Paul, 1975.

Held, David. *Political Theory Today.* Cambridge, England: Polity, 1991.

Heyd, U. *Foundations of Turkish Nationalism.* London: 1950.

Higgins, Rosalyn. *Problems and Process: International Law and How We Use It.* Oxford: Clarendon Press, 1994.

Hilferding, Rudolph. *Das Finanzkapital* (Financial capital). Berlin: J.H.W. Dietz, 1947.

Hobsbawm, Eric. *Nations and Nationalism Since 1780,* Cambridge: Cambridge University Press, 1994.

Hobsbawm, Eric, and Terence Ranger. *The Invention of Tradition.* Cambridge: Cambridge University Press, 1983.

Honig, Jan Willem, and Norbert Both. *Srebrenica: Record of a War Crime.* New York: Penguin, 1996.

Hoole, C. R. A. *Modern Sannyasins, Parallel Society and Hindu Replications: A Study of Protestant Contribution to Tamil Culture in 19th Century Sri Lanka, Against a Historical Background.* Berne: Peter Lang, 1995.

Horowitz, Donald L. "Ethnic and Nationalist Conflicts." In *World Security: Trends and Challenges at Century's End,* edited by Michael T. Klare and Daniel C. Thomas. New York: St. Martin's Press, 1991.

Hough, Jerry F. "Sociology, the State and Language Politics." *Post-Soviet Affairs,* forthcoming.

Hroch, Miroslav. *Social Preconditions of National Revival in Europe: A Comparative Analysis of the Social Composition of Patriotic Groups among the Smaller European Nations.* Cambridge: Cambridge University Press, 1985.

Huntington, Samuel P. "Democracy's Third Wave." *Journal of Democracy* 2 (Spring 1991).

Ignatieff, Michael. *Blood and Belonging: Journeys into the New Nationalism.* Toronto: Penguin Books, 1993.

Inalcık, H. "The Nature of Traditional Society, Turkey." In *Political Modernization in Japan and Turkey,* edited by R. E. Ward and D. Rustow. Princeton: Princeton University Press, 1964.

———. "The Application of Tanzimat." *Archivum Ottomanicum* 3 (1973).

———. "Military and Fiscal Transformation of the Ottoman Empire, 1600–1700." *Archivum Ottomanicum* 6 (1980): 283–338.

———. "The Emergence of Big Farms, Ciftliks: State, Landlords and Tenants." In *Studies in Ottoman Social and Economic History.* London: Variorum Reprints, 1985.

———. *The Ottoman Empire: The Classical Age, 1300–1600.* New York: Praeger, 1973. Reprint. London: Phoenix, 1994.

Indrapala, K. "The Origin of the Tamil Vanni Chieftaincies of Ceylon." *The Ceylon Journal of Humanities* 1 (July 1970).

———, ed. *The Collapse of The Rajarata Civilization in Ceylon & The Drift to the South-West.* Peradeniya, Sri Lanka: Ceylon Studies Seminar, University of Ceylon, 1971.

Iskhakov, D. M. "Neformalnye ob''edinenia v sovremennom Tatarskom obshchestve" (Non-formal associations in contemporary Tatar society). In *Sovremennyi mezhnatsional'nye protsessy v Tatarskoi SSR,* edited by D. M. Iskhakov and R. Musina. Kazan, Russia: Kazanskii nauchnyi tsentr, 1991.

Iskhakov, D. M., and R. Musina, eds. *Sovremennyie mezhnatsional'nyie protsessy v Tatarskoi SSR* (Contemporary inter-ethnic processes in the Tatar SSR). Kazan, Russia: Kazanskii nauchnyi tsentr, 1991.

Islamoğlu-Inan, H. "State and Peasants in the Ottoman Empire: A Study of Peasant Economy in the North-Central Anatolia During the Sixteenth Century." In *The Ottoman Empire and the World Economy,* edited by H. Islamoglu-Inan. Cambridge: Cambridge University Press, 1987.

Ismail, Quadri. "Unmooring Identity: The Antinomies of Elite Muslim Self-Representation in Modern Sri Lanka." In *Unmaking The Nation: The Politics of Identity and History in Modern Sri Lanka,* edited by Jeganathan and Ismail. Colombo, Sri Lanka: Social Scientists Association, 1995.

Issawi, C. *The Economic History of Turkey: 1800–1914.* Chicago: University of Chicago Press, 1980.

———. "The Transformation of the Economic Position of the Millets in the Nineteenth Century." In *Christians and Jews in the Ottoman Empire,* Vol. 1, edited by B. Braude and B. Lewis. New York: Holmes and Meyer, 1982.

Janjić, Dusan. "Resurgence of Ethnic Conflict in Yugoslavia: the Demise of Communism and the Rise of the 'New Elites' of Nationalism." In *Yugoslavia: The Former and Future,* edited by Payam Akhavan and Robert Howse. Washington, D.C.: The Brookings Institution, 1995.

Jayawardana, Kumari. *Ethnic Consciousness in Sri Lanka: Continuity & Change.* In *Sri Lanka: The Ethnic Conflict: Myths, Realities & Perspectives.* Navrang, New Delhi: Committee for Rational Development, 1984.

Kaminski, Piotr. "Who Started the War?" *Uncaptive Minds* 6 (1993): 9-13.

Kaplan, Robert. *Balkan Ghosts.* New York: St. Martin's Press, 1993.

Karpat, K. "The Stages of Ottoman History." In *The Ottoman State and Its Place in the World History,* edited by K. Karpat. Leiden: E. J. Brill, 1974.

———. "The Transformation of the Ottoman State, 1789-1908." *International Journal of Middle Eastern Studies* 3 (1972).

———. "Millets and Nationality: The Roots of Incongruity of Nation and State in the Post-Ottoman Era." In *Christians and Jews in the Ottoman Empire,* Vol. 1, edited by B. Braude and B. Lewis. New York: Holmes and Meyer, 1982.

Karpinski, Jakub. "The Southern Slavs." *Uncaptive Minds* 6 (1993): 5-8.

Kasaba, R. *The Ottoman Empire and the World Economy: The Nineteenth Century.* Albany, N.Y.: State University of New York Press, 1988.

Kedourie, E. *Nationalism in Asia and Africa.* Cleveland: 1970.

Kelly, Petra, Gert Bastian, and Pat Aiello, eds. *The Anguish of Tibet.* Berkeley, Calif.: Parallax Press, 1991.

Keyder, Ç. "The Political Economy of Turkish Democracy." *New Left Review,* no. 115 (1979).

———. *The Definition of a Peripheral Economy: Turkey 1923-1929.* Cambridge: Cambridge University Press, 1981.

———. *State and Class in Turkey.* London: Verso, 1987.

Keyder, Ç., and H. Islamoğlu-Inan. "Agenda for Ottoman History." *Review* 1 (Summer 1977).

Khakimov, Rafael I., ed. *Belaia kniga Tatarstana: Put'k suverenitetu, 1990-1993* (The white book of Tatarstan: the path to sovereignty, 1990-1993). Kazan, Russia: 1993.

Kinder, D and D. Sears. "Prejudice and Politics: Symbolic Racism versus Racial Threats to the Good Life." *Journal of Personality and Social Psychology,* 1981: 40.

Knight, David B. "Geographical Perspectives on Self-Determination." In *Political Geography: Recent Advances and Future Directions,* edited by Peter Taylor and John House. London: Croom Helm, 1984.

Kohr, Hans. "Disunion Now: A Plea for a Society Based upon Small Autonomous Units." *Commonwealth* (September 26, 1941).

Kolko, Gabriel. *The Politics of War.* New York: Random House, 1968.

Kovać, Oskar. "Foreign Economic Relations." In *The Position and Strategy of Serbia in the New European Order,* edited by Tomislav Popovic. Belgrade: Institute of Economic Sciences, 1992.

Kucera, Milan and Zdenek Pavlik. "Czech and Slovak Demography." In *The End of Czechoslovakia,* edited by Jiri Musil. Budapest, London, New York: Central European University Press, 1995.

Kushner, D. *The Rise of Turkish Nationalism.* London: Frank Cass, 1977

Lapidus, Gail W., and Edward W. Walker. "Nationalism, Regionalism, and Federalism: Center-Periphery Relations in Post-Communist Russia." In *The New Russia: Troubled Transformation,* edited by Gail W. Lapidus. Boulder, Colo.: Westview, 1995.

Leary, Virginia A., and International Commission of Jurists. "Ethnic Conflict and Violence in Sri Lanka." n.p.: ICJ, 1983.

Lenin, V. I. *Imperialism, the Highest Stage of Capitalism.* New York: International Publishers, 1939.

Leslie, Peter. "Ethnonationalism in a Federal State: The Case of Canada." In *Ethnoterritorial Politics, Policy and the Western World,* edited by Joseph Rudolph and Robert Thompson. Boulder, Colo.: Lynne Rienner Publishers, 1989.

Lewis, J. P. *A Manual of the Vanni Districts of Ceylon.* 1895. Reprint. New Delhi: Navrang, 1993.

Lind, Michael. "In Defense of Liberal Nationalism." *Foreign Affairs* (May-June 1994).

Lipset, Seymour Martin. *Continental Divide: The Values and Institutions of the United States and Canada.* New York: Routledge, 1990.

Lipset, Seymour Martin, Kyoung-Ryung Seong and John Charles Torres, "A Comparative Analysis of the Social Requisites of Democracy," *International Social Science Journal* 46 (1993): 168.

Luxemburg, Rosa. *The National Question: Selected Writings by Rosa Luxemburg.* Compiled by Horace Davis. New York: Monthly Review Press, 1976.

Macan-Markar, Maruan. "Nation Building: A Muslim Perspective." In *Nation Building in Sri Lanka,* edited by Gnana Munasinghe. Colombo: Shramaya, 1993.

MacKenzie, Lewis. *Peacekeeper — The Road to Sarajevo.* Vancouver: Douglas and McIntyre, 1993.

Mardin, S. *The Genesis of Young Ottoman Thought: A Study in The Modernization of Turkey's Political Ideals.* Princeton: Princeton University Press, 1962.

———. "Center-Periphery Relations: A Key to Turkish Politics?" *Daedalus* (Winter 1973).

———. *Din ve Ideoloji* (Religion and ideology). 2d ed. Istanbul: Iletisim Yayinlari, 1983.

———. *Jön Türklerin Siyasi Fikirleri, 1895–1908* (The political thoughts of the young Turks, 1895–1908). 2d ed. Istanbul: Iletişim Yayınları, 1983.

———. "The Naqshibandi Order in Turkish History." *In Religion in Modern Turkey: Religion, Politics and Literature in a Secular State,* edited by R. Tapper. London: I. B. Tauris & Co., 1991.

Marriot, J. A. R. *The Eastern Question: An Historical Study in European Diplomacy.* Oxford: Clarendon Press, 1924.

Masaryk, Tomáš G. *The New Europe: The Slav Standpoint.* 1918. New ed., edited by W. Preston Warren and William B. Weist. Lewisburg: Bucknell University Press, 1972.

Masiutko, M. A Letter to the Supreme Soviet of the Ukrainian SSR, 1967. Arkhiv samizdata, no. 950.

Matthews, Robert O., Arthur G. Rubinoff, and Janice Gross Stein, eds. *International Conflict and Conflict Management.* 2d ed. Scarborough, Ont.: Prentice-Hall, 1989.

May, Arthur. *The Passing of the Hapsburg Monarchy.* Vol. 2. Philadelphia, Penn.: University of Pennsylvania Press, 1966.

McMichael, Philip. "Global Restructuring: Some Lines of Inquiry." In *The Global Restructuring of Agro-Food Systems,* edited by Philip McMichael. Ithaca, N.Y.: Cornell University Press, 1994.

McNeill, William H. *Polyethnicity and National Unity in World History.* Toronto: University of Toronto Press, 1985.

McRae, Kenneth, ed. *Consociational Democracy: Political Accommodation in Segmented Societies.* Toronto: McClelland and Stewart, 1974.

Medvedkov, Olga. *Soviet Urbanization.* London: Routledge, 1990.

Monahan, Patrick. *Cooler Heads Shall Prevail: Assessing the Costs and Consequences of Quebec Separation.* Toronto: C. D. Howe Institute, 1995.

Morton, Frederick. *Thunder at Twilight: Vienna 1913/1914.* New York: Macmillan, 1989.

Mouffe, Chantal, ed. *Dimensions of Radical Democracy: Pluralism, Citizenship, Community.* London: Verso, 1992.

Musina, R. I. "K voprosu o meste i roli religii v zhizni sovremennykh Tatar" (To the question of peace and role of religion in the life of a contemporary Tatar). In *Sovremennye mezhnatsional'nye protsessy v Tatarskoi SSR,* edited by D. M. Iskhakov and R. Musina. Kazan, Russia: Kazanskii nauchnyi tsentr, 1991.

Nairn, Tom. *The Breakup of Britain.* London: New Left Books, 1977.

Nekrich, Aleksandr. *The Punished Peoples,* trans. G. Saunders. New York: W.W. Norton, 1978.

Nesak, Dusan. "Historical Elements for Understanding the 'Yugoslav Question'." In *Yugoslavia: The Former and Future,* edited by Payam Akhavan and Robert Howse. Washington, D.C.: The Brookings Institution, 1995.

Nesiah, K. *From School to University, in Education and Human Rights in Sri Lanka.* Jaffna, Sri Lanka: The Christian Institute for the Study of Religion and Society, 1983.

Nesiah, K. *Devanesan.* Madras: Oxford University Press, forthcoming.

Nettl, J. P. *Rosa Luxemburg.* London: Oxford University Press, 1966.

Nevitte, Neil. *The Decline of Deference: Canadian Value Change in Cross-national Perspective.* Peterborough: Broadview Press, 1996.

Nielsson, Gunnar P. "States and 'Nation-Groups': A Global Taxonomy." In *New Nationalisms of the Developed West: Toward Explanation,* edited by Edward A. Tiryakin and Ronald Rogowski. Boston: Allen and Unwin, 1985.

Nietzsche, Friedrich. "Genealogy of Morals." In *The Philosophy of Nietzsche.* New York: The Modern Library, 1927.

Nikolaev, Yury, ed. *The Chechen Tragedy: Who is to Blame?* New York: Nova Science Publishers, 1996.

Norman, Wayne. "The Ideology of Shared Values: A Myopic Vision of Unity in a Multi-nation State". In *Is Quebec Nationalism Just Perspectives from Anglophone Canada,* edited by Joseph H. Carens. Montreal: McGill-Queen's University Press, 1996.

Owen, E. R. J. *Cotton and Egyptian Economy, 1820-1914: A Study in Trade and Development.* Oxford: Oxford University Press, 1969.

Paasche, John Hans. *The Colonial Question in Bolshevik Revolutionary Stragegy: Soviet Russia's International Congresses, 1919 to 1929.* San Francisco: Paasche, 1990.

Palmer, A. *The Decline and Fall of the Ottoman Empire.* London: John Murray, 1992.

Pamuk, S. *The Ottoman Empire and European Capitalism (1820-1913).* Cambridge: Cambridge University Press, 1987.

Park, Andrus. *Ethnicity and Post-Soviet Transition: The Case of Estonia in Comparative Perspective.* Global Forum Series. Durham, N.C.: Center for International Studies, Duke University, 1993.

Pavlowitch, Stevan K. *The Improbable Survivor: Yugoslavia and its Problems 1918-1988.* London: C. Hurst and Company, 1989.

———. "Who is 'Balkanizing' Whom? The Misunderstandings Between the Debris of Yugoslavia and the Unprepared West." *Daedalus* 123 (1994): 203-23.

Peebles, Patrick. "Colonization & Ethnic Conflict in the Dry Zone of Sri Lanka." *Journal of South Asian Studies* (February 1990).

Peiris, Paul E. *Ceylon: The Portuguese Era.* Vols. 1 and 2. 1914. 2d ed. n.p.: Tisara Prakasakayo, 1992.

Pfaff, William. *The Wrath of Nations: Civilization and the Furies of Nationalism.* New York: Simon and Schuster, 1993.

Popović, Tomislav, ed. *The Position and Strategy of Serbia in the New European Order.* Belgrade: Institute of Economic Sciences, 1992.

Project Ploughshares. *Armed Conflicts Report.* Waterloo, Ont.: Institute of Peace and Conflict Studies, 1995, 1996, 1997.

Prucha, Václav. "Economic Development and Relations, 1918-89." In *The End of Czechoslovakia,* edited by Jiří Musil. Budapest, London, New York: Central European University Press, 1995.

Puhar, Alenka. "A Letter from Yugoslavia, In the Raw." *The Journal of Psychohistory* 19 (1992): 331-42.

Puhovski, Žarko. "The Bleak Prospects for Civil Society." In *Yugoslavia: The Former and Future,* edited by Payam Akhavan and Robert Howse. Washington, D.C.: The Brookings Institution, 1995.

Ra'anan, Uri, et al., eds. *State and Nation in Multi-Ethnic Societies.* Manchester: Manchester University Press, 1991.

Raman, K. V. "Brahmi Inscriptions in Tamil Nadu: An Historic Assessment." *The Sri Lanka Journal of South Asian Studies* 1 (1976).

Rasanayagam, Mudaliyar C. *Ancient Jaffna.* 1926. Reprint. New Delhi: Asian Educational Services, 1984.

Rhodes, Matthew. "National Identity and Minority Rights in the Constitutions of the Czech Republic and Slovakia." *East European Quarterly* 29 (September 1995): 358-59.

Roberts, Michael. "Ethnic Conflict in Sri Lanka & Sinhalese Perspectives: Barriers to Accommodation." *Modern Asian Studies* 12 (1978).

Rorlich, Azade-Ayse. *The Volga Tatars: A Profile in National Resistance.* Stanford: The Hoover Institute, 1986.

Roucek, Joseph S. *The Politics of the Balkans.* New York: McGraw Hill, 1939.

Salecl, Renata. "Nationalism, Anti-Semitism, and Anti-Feminism in Eastern Europe." *New German Critique,* No. 57 (1992).

Samarasinghe, S. W. R. de A. "The Dynamics of Separatism: The Case of Sri Lanka." In *Secessionist Movements in Comparative Perspective,* edited by Ralph R. Premdas, S. W. R. de A. Samarasinghe, and Alan B. Anderson. London: Pinter, 1990.

Sastri, K. A. Nilakanta. *A History of South India.* 4th ed. Madras: Oxford University Press, 1975.

Schaeffer, Robert K. "The Entelechies of Mercantilism." *Scandinavian Economic History Review* 29 (1981).

Schaeffer, Robert K. *Warpaths: The Politics of Partition.* New York: Hill and Wang, 1990.

———. "Democratic Devolutions: East Asian Democratization in Comparative Perspective." In *Pacific-Asia and the World-Economy,* edited by Ravi Palat. Westport, Conn.: Greenwood Press, 1993.

———. *Power to the People: Democratization Around the World.* Boulder, Colo.: Westview, 1997.

———. "State and Devolution: Economic Crises and the Devolution of U.S. Superstate Power." *The International Journal of Sociology of Agriculture and Food,* forthcoming.

Scheler, Max. *Ressentiment.* Glencoe, Ill.: The Free Press, 1961.

Schwarz, Hans-Peter. "Germany's National and European Interests." *Daedalus* 123 (1994): 81-105.

Segal, Gerald. "China's Changing Shape." *Foreign Affairs* 73 (May-June 1994).

Shaw, Stanford. *History of the Ottoman Empire and Modern Turkey.* Vol. 1. Cambridge: Cambridge University Press, 1976.

Simmel, Georg. *Conflict & The Web of Group-Affiliations.* 1908. Reprint. New York: Collier-Macmillan Limited, 1923.

Smith, Anthony D. "Introduction: The Formation of Nationalist Movements." In *Nationalist Movements,* edited by A. D. Smith. New York: Macmillan, 1976.

————. *The Ethnic Revival.* Cambridge: Cambridge University Press, 1981.

Somasundaram, D. J., and S. Rajadurai. "War and Suicide in Northern Sri Lanka." *Acta Psychiatrica Scandinavica* (January 1995).

Somasundaram, D. J., and S. Sivayokam. "War Trauma in a Civilian Population." *British Journal of Psychiatry* 165 (1994): 524-27.

Staianovich, T. "Land Tenure and Related Sectors of the Balkan Economy." *The Journal of Economic History* 13 (1953).

Sully, Melanie A. *Continuity and Change in Austrian Socialism: The Eternal Quest for the Third Way.* New York: Columbia University Press, 1982.

Sunar, I. "State and Economy in the Ottoman Empire." In *The Ottoman Empire and the World Economy,* edited by H. Islamoglu-Inan. Cambridge: Cambridge University Press, 1987.

Taylor, Charles. *Multiculturalism and "The Politics of Recognition".* Princeton: Princeton University Press, 1992.

————. *Reconciling the Solitudes: Essays on Canadian Federalism and Nationalism.* Montreal: McGill-Queen's University Press, 1993.

Tilly, Charles. "National Self-Determination as a Problem for All of Us." *Daedalus* 122 (1993): 29-36.

Tokeš, Rudolf. *Bela Kun and the Hungarian Soviet Republic.* New York: Praeger, 1967.

Tomich, D. W. *Slavery in the Circuit of Sugar: Martinique and the World Economy 1830-1848.* Baltimore: Johns Hopkins University Press, 1990.

Toynbee, Arnold, and Kenneth P. Kirkwood. *Turkey.* London: Ernest Benn, 1926.

Trifunovska, Snezana, ed. *Yugoslavia Through Documents — From its Creation to its Dissolution.* Dordrecht, the Netherlands: Martinus Nijhoff, 1994.

Tunaya, T. Z. *Turkiye'de Siyasi Partiler, 1859-1962* (Political parties in Turkey, 1859–1962). Istanbul: 1952.

Türköne, M. Siyasi Ideoloji olarak Islamcılığın Doğuşu (The advent of Islamism as an ideology). Istanbul: Iletşim Yayınları, 1991.

Turnbull, C. M. *A History of Singapore 1819-1988.* 2d ed. Singapore: Oxford University Press, 1989.

Umnova, Irina A. "Konstitutsiia Rossiiskoi Federatsii, Konstitutsiia Respubliki Tatarstana, Dogovor Mezhdu Rossiiskoi Federatsiei i Respublikoi Tatarstana" (The constitution of the Russian Federation, the constitution of the Republic of Tatarstan, an agreement between the Russian Federation and the Republic of Tatarstan). Unpublished paper, June 1994.

Urquhart, D. *Turkey and Its Resources.* London: Saunders and Otley and Conduit Street, 1833.

van Bruinessen, M. "Kürtler Arasında Bir Siyasi Protesto Aracı Olarak Naksibendi Tarikati" (Naqshbandi order among the Kurds as a means of political protest). In *Kürdistan Üzerine Yazılar* (Writings on Kurdistan). Istanbul: Iletişim Yayınları, 1992.

Vanneman, Reeve and Thomas Pettigrew. "Race and Relative Deprivation in the Urban United States," *Race* (1972): 13

Viereck, Peter. *Conservatism Revisited.* New York: Collier Books, 1949.

Walker, Edward W. "The New Russian Constitution and the Future of the Russian Federation." *The Harriman Institute Forum* 5 (June 1992).

———. "Federalism Russian Style: The Federation Provisions in Russia's New Constitution." *Problems of Post-Communism* (July-August, 1995): 3-12.

Wallerstein, Immanuel. *Historical Capitalism.* London: Verso, 1983.

Wallerstein, Immanuel, H. Decdeli, and R. Kasaba. "The Incorporation of the Ottoman Empire into the World Economy." In *The Ottoman Empire and the World Economy,* edited by H. Islamoglu-Inan. Cambridge: Cambridge University Press, 1987.

Waters, Mary. *Ethnic Options.* Berkeley and Los Angeles: University of California Press, 1990.

Williams, Colin, ed. *National Separatism.* Cardiff: University of Wales Press, 1982.

Wittfogel, Karl A. *Oriental Despotism: A Comparative Study of Total Power.* New Haven, Conn.: Yale University Press, 1957.

Wixman, Ron. "The Middle Volga: Ethnic Archipelago in a Russian Sea." In *Nations and Politics in the Soviet Successor States,* edited by Ian Bremmer and Ray Taras. New York: Cambridge University Press, 1993.

Wolchik, Sharon L. "The Politics of Transition and the Break-Up of Czechoslovakia." In *The End of Czechoslovakia,* edited by Jiri Musil. Budapest, London, New York: Central European University Press, 1995.

Wolf, E. *Europe and the People Without History.* Berkeley and Los Angeles: University of California Press, 1982.

Wood, Ellen. "The Separation of the Economic and the Political." *New Left Review* 127 (1981).

Wood, John, ed. "Secession: A Comparative Analytic Framework." *Canadian Journal of Political Science* 14:1 (March 1981).

Woodward, Susan L. *Balkan Tragedy: Chaos and Dissolution After the Cold War.* Washington, D.C.: The Brookings Institution, 1995.

Yapp, M. E. *The Making of the Modern Middle East, 1792–1923.* London: Longman, 1987.

Yeltsin, Boris. *Zapiski presidenta* (The notes of the President). Moscow: Ogonek, 1994.

Yinanc, M. H. *Milli Tarihimizin Adı* (The name of our national history). Istanbul: Hareket Yayinlari, 1969.

Young, Robert A. *The Breakup of Czechoslovakia.* Kingston, Ontario: Queens University Institute of Inter-Governmental Relations, 1994.

———. *The Secession of Quebec and the Future of Canada.* Montreal: McGill-Queen's University Press, 1995.

Žagar, Mitja. "Yugoslavia: What Went Wrong? Constitutional Aspects of the Yugoslav Crisis from the Perspective of Ethnic Conflict." In *Research on Russia and Eastern Europe,* Vol. 3, edited by Metta Spencer (Greenwood, Conn.: JAI Press, forthcoming).

Zametica, John. *The Yugoslav Conflict.* Adelphi Paper 270. London: Brassey's and The International Institute for Strategic Studies, 1992.

Zimmerman, Warren. *Origins of a Catastrophe.* New York: Times Books, 1996.

Zisserman-Brodsky, Diana. "Ethnic Samizdat and Ethnic Politics in the USSR." Ph.D. dissertation, Jerusalem, 1994.

Index

About the Contributors

YILDIZ ATASOY studied and taught sociology at the Middle East Technical University in Ankara, Turkey. She completed her doctoral studies at the University of Toronto, where she is currently working in the area of transnational economy and the state system.

JOHN BACHER has a doctorate in history. He has taught peace and human rights studies at the University of Toronto and McMaster University and is currently engaged in research on environmental politics, oil, and democracy. He is author of *Keeping to the Marketplace: The Evolution of Canadian Housing Policy* (1990).

MILICA Z. BOOKMAN is professor of economics at St. Joseph's University in Philadelphia. She is the author of numerous books and articles, including, most recently, *The Democratic Struggle for Power* (1997).

FEODOR BURLATSKY was speech writer and advisor to Nikita Khrushchev. As a member of the Supreme Soviet during the Gorbachev years he was in charge of a commission to introduce human rights legislation. He also edited the newspaper *Literaturnaya Gazeta* during that period. He is author of numerous books, including *Khrushchev and the First Russian Spring*.

M. R. R. HOOLE is among the four coauthors of *The Broken Palmyra: An Inside Account of the Tamil Struggle in Sri Lanka* and a founder member of the University Teachers for Human Rights (Jaffna). He was discontinued from the University of Jaffna in May 1991 and his position has since remained a matter of dispute.

VICTOR KOGAN IASNYI has been a Russian human rights and political activist since 1988 and is chairman of the Right to Life and Human Dignity peacemaking organization. He serves on the staff of the Iabloko Party.

PETR PITHART is president of the senate of the Czech Republic. A former member of Charta 77 during the communist years and a member of Civic Forum after the "velvet revolution" of 1989, he was prime minister of the Czech Republic during the troubled period preceding the breakup of Czechoslovakia.

ROBERT K. SCHAEFFER is a professor of global sociology at San Jose State University. He is the author of *Warpaths: The Politics of Partition* (1990), *Power to the People: Democratization Around the World* (1997), and *Understanding Globalization: The Social Consequences of Political, Economic, and Environmental Change* (1997).

METTA SPENCER is emerita professor of sociology at the University of Toronto, where she coordinated an undergraduate program in peace and conflict studies. She is author of *Foundations of Modern Sociology,* editor of *Peace Magazine,* and editor of a series of books, *Research on Russia and Eastern Europe,* with JAI Press.

EDWARD W. WALKER is a political science professor at the University of California, Berkeley, where he directs a joint program in post-Soviet research based there and at Stanford University. His own current research focuses on comparative politics in the Transcaucasus.

REG WHITAKER is professor of political science at York University in Toronto. He has written extensively on Canadian and Quebec politics. His most recent book is *Surveillance in the Age of Cyberspace* (1998).

DIANA ZISSERMAN-BRODSKY received a master's degree in journalism from Moscow State University and a Ph.D. in political studies from the Hebrew University in Jerusalem. She teaches in the Department of Russian and Slavic Studies at the Hebrew University.